THE ABC's OF RELOADING

8th EDITION

Edited by Bill Chevalier

©2008 Krause Publications

Published by

Gun Digest® Books

An imprint of F+W Publications

700 East State Street • Iola, WI 54990-0001
715-445-2214 • 888-457-2873
www.gundigestbooks.com

Our toll-free number to place an order or obtain
a free catalog is (800) 258-0929.

Library of Congress Control Number: 2007942205

39516157 2/09
ISBN-13: 978-0-89689-609-3
ISBN-10: 0-89689-609-9

Designed by Kara Grundman
Edited by Ken Ramage

Printed in the United States of America

About the Editor

BILL CHEVALIER, EDITOR of The ABC's of Reloading, 8th Edition, repeats this assignment, having edited the 7th Edition which was published in 2004. He has been involved in the reloading industry for more than 30 years. His advertising agency, Chevalier Advertising, Marketing and Public Relations, Lake Oswego, Oregon, formerly handled the National Reloading Manufacturers Association (NRMA) since 1973 when he was first appointed Executive Secretary for that group. He retired in 2003. (At this writing, the NRMA is now inactive.)

Working closely with the National Rifle Association, Bill helped develop the NRA's Certified Course in Reloading, and wrote the first draft of the textbook for the course. More than 1000 NRA instructors are now certified to teach reloading.

He helped produce four of five Nosler reloading manuals, and worked with other shooting sports firms such as Nikon Sport Optics, Combined Technology, Kaltron-Pettibone (importers of Vihtavuori and Lapua products), Norma, Safari Safe, Brown Precision, Walker's Game Ear, Break Free, Marble Arms, A-Square, Babe Winkelman Productions, Hatch Gloves, Michaels of Oregon, Leupold & Stevens, Speer, Ponsness-Warren and Non-Toxic Components.

Bill helped design the NRMA's well-known reloading bench plans, which thousands of shooters have used to build these sturdy benches, and has the original bench in his Portland, Oregon home, where he loads shotshell and metallic ammo. In Chapter 18 of this book, Bill revisits that design.

About the Cover

HORNADY MANUFACTURING IS one of America's preeminent manufacturers of reloading tools, cartridge components (bullets and brass) and loaded ammunition.

The centerpiece of this loading bench is Hornady's Lock-N-Load Classic single-station metallic reloading press. This is a compound-linkage "O"-frame single-station press that is designed for the innovative "Lock-n-Load" reloading die mounting system.

Using this unique die-mounting system, the hand/loader needs to install and adjust his die set only once. When finished, the handloader simply turns out the bushing that contains the precisely-adjusted die for a given cartridge/load recipe and stows it away until needed again. Then, the handloader simply and quickly installs the bushing carrying the adjusted reloading die and processes his empty brass in noticeably less time. The special bushings fit any brand of 7/8x14 reloading dies, but only the Hornady Lock-N-Load Press.

Hornady offers this Classic press two ways: as a free-standing product, and as part of a reloading products kit.

Besides the press, the Lock-N-Load Classic Kit includes many of the items shown: powder measure; magnetic scale; *Hornady Handbook of Cartridge Reloading;* three Lock-N-Load bushings, primer catcher; priming system, hand-held priming tool' universal reloading block; chamfering & deburring tool; primer turning plate and One Shot case lube.

Hornady has a very wide line of metallic cartridge (and shotshell) reloading equipment and accessories. Other handy accessories shown on these covers include the vibratory case tumbler to clean and polish your cartridge cases prior to reloading, case prep chemicals, the auto-primer feed that

drops a new primer into position as the press is cycled, a neck-turning tool that trims cartridge neck walls to the same thickness, promoting concentric alignment and consistent bullet release, and a kinetic bullet-puller (the hammer-like device on the front cover).

See the full line of Hornady product on-line at www.hornady.com, or contact the company: Hornady Manufacturing Co., P.O. Box 1848, Grand Island, NE 68803. Telephone: 308-382-1390.

Introduction

IF THERE WERE SUCH a person who could be called the complete reloader (and there probably isn't), he or she would have to be smarter than Einstein, older than Methuselah and have a memory bigger than a main-frame computer. And while handloading your own cartridges can be a fairly simple step-by-step procedure that will yield satisfactory results, it can also be limitless in the possibilities for applying the basic principles to your own situation. And that's what makes it so fascinating.

In this book, we have tried to give you useful information, regardless of your experience (or lack of it), and make it easy to follow and understand. The more you absorb about the many facets of reloading, the more you will become fascinated by this segment of the shooting sports. In addition to information-filled instructions on getting started and perfecting your techniques, we have brought together a group of writers whose stories will stir up your brain with images of guns you have read about, hunts you wish you could have taken and reloading practices you probably have never tried.

During my years serving clients in the firearms industry, I had the privilege of knowing some of the best writers in this field, who are also some of the finest people you'll ever meet. In this volume, we have borrowed some of their expertise in reloading, shooting, guns, hunting and the outdoors. Reading their articles will broaden your understanding and appreciation of reloading, and give you a lot of enjoyment along the way.

When we are trying to get more shooters involved in reloading, we talk about the traditional benefits to reloading your own ammo. First, you'll save money. Next, you'll be a better shooter when you understand what goes into making (or remaking) a cartridge. Then, you'll be able to formulate your own load to do precisely what you want for your own (not somebody else's) kind of shooting. And reloading makes a good hobby, it's a family enterprise and it's fun. But there is more to the story. Much more.

We have not overlooked the basics about the tools and components you'll need to get into this game, and how to do it safely. There is solid instruction on how the various steps are performed, plus the hows and whys of doing them correctly. If you plan to become a serious and proficient reloader, you need to absorb and understand this information thoroughly. And you should read our discussion of interior, exterior and terminal ballistics to further deepen your understanding of our sport.

To appreciate the original articles by our authors, you should understand the basics, because you won't find much step-by-step stuff in a truly exciting story about reloading for big game. Many of these stories read like adventures, because the folks who wrote them have been there and done that. Maybe black powder shooting has piqued your interest, but how much have you read about reloading for blackpowder cartridges used in this growing sport? This book doesn't get into muzzleloading, but blackpowder cartridge guns are regaining popularity for competition and for hunting.

You'll find discussions of accuracy for hunters, some new information on handgun reloading, and you'll get some questions answered on such stuff as powder burn rates and the brass you use for reloading. And if you've ever asked yourself if women can reload, get a load of what famed woman author Sheila Link has to say on the subject.

Enjoy!
Bill Chevalier

Contents

Introduction 4

Chapter 1: Start with Safety Lead Hazards in the Shooting Sports
by Robert D. Williams, Ph.D 6

Chapter 2: The Cartridge Case 17

Chapter 3: Understanding Pressure and Headspace 30

Chapter 4: Primers 41

Chapter 5: Powders 49

Chapter 6: Bullets 60

Chapter 7: Casting Bullets 70

Chapter 8: Bullet Sizing and Lubricating 80

Chapter 9: Tooling Up for Reloading 89

Chapter 10: Rifle Cartridge Reloading 102

Chapter 11: Handgun Cartridge Reloading 116

Chapter 12: Shotgun Ammunition Reloading 129

Chapter 13: Ballistics 140

Chapter 14: Sources and Resources 144

Chapter 15: Accuracy and the Hunter by Dave Workman 148

Chapter 16: Reloading for Deer & Antelope by Chub Eastman 156

Chapter 17: Contemporary & Unique Varmint Medicine by Mike Thomas 162

Chapter 18: NRMA Bench Plans Revisited by Bill Chevalier 169

Chapter 19: Loading the Hot New Small Bore Cartridges by John Haviland ... 173

Chapter 20: Cloning Factory Ammo by Charles Petty 180

Chapter 21: New Gear for the Reloading Bench by John Haviland 188

Chapter 22: Ammo for the Big Boys by Chub Eastman 195

Chapter 23: Whose Loading Data Should You Use? By Dave Workman 201

Chapter 24: The Lowdown on Powder Burn Rates by R.H.VanDenburg Jr. 209

Chapter 25: Blackpowder Cartridge Hunting by Mike Nesbitt 215

Chapter 26: Controlling Shotshell Patterns by R.H.VanDenburg Jr. 222

Chapter 27: Non-Toxic Shot by Tom Roster 229

Chapter 28: Do You Need a Chronograph? by Mike Venturino 237

Chapter 29: Cartridge Cases by Todd Spotti 245

Chapter 30: Loading the Medium Bores for Elk by Steve Gash 252

Chapter 31: Match Loading Black Powder Cartridges by Mike Venturino 259

Chapter 32: Better Handgun Loads by Brian Pearce 268

Chapter 33: Building Light Specialty Shotgun Loads by Steve Gash 276

Before beginning
any activity, a solid
foundation is
needed to build
upon, and reloading
is no different.

Start with Safety

EVERY BOX OF cartridges, every loading manual, advises that these loadings are for "modern arms in good condition." What is a modern gun? Like any other arbitrary definition, it has fuzzy edges. Modern gun designs (such as modern-looking double-action revolvers) were developed in the late 1880s. Modern semi-automatic pistols were on the market by 1900. Bolt-action, 30-caliber rifles intended for high-pressure (40,000 to 60,000 psi) smokeless powder ammunition were in general military use by 1895. Roughly speaking, the era of modern gunmaking begins around 1886-1900.

The real issue is whether the gun for which you wish to reload can take the pressures of modern ammunition. For instance, a tightly locking Winchester Low Wall single shot or Stevens target rifle from the late 19th century can be safely used with modern, high-velocity 22 Long Rifle ammunition. To use such ammunition in a light revolver or pistol from the same era will destroy it. Even guns made as recently as the 1920s may not be safe with the high pressures generated by the high-velocity loadings. The 22 Long Rifle Reising automatic pistol of that period had a very thin breechblock, which

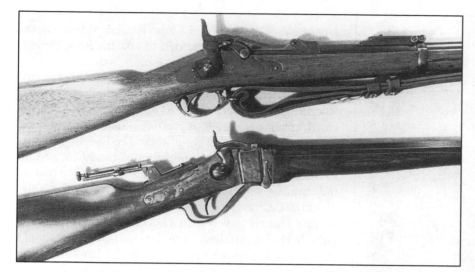

This reproduction 1874 Sharps rifle *(bottom)* is made of modern steel (4140 for the receiver and 1195 for the barrel). It is capable of handling modern high-pressure 45-70 loadings to 28,000 psi. The Allin "trapdoor" 45-70 Springfield *(top)* was made in 1888. The receiver is mild steel, casehardened. The barrel is mild "decarbonized" steel. Its maximum pressure rating, at the time of manufacture, was 25,000 psi. It is not a modern gun and must be loaded accordingly.

A 94-year-old 32 ACP Colt Model 1903 pocket pistol *(bottom)* and a Cold-War-era 9mm Makarov—both qualify as "modern guns."

regularly splits on the first firing of a high-speed round, so it is to be used with standard velocity ammunition only.

While a modern-looking revolver such as the Model 1889 Colt Navy double action looks very like the 38 Special police models that have been in use for over 60 years, it was made for the 38 Long Colt blackpowder cartridge. Some of these early guns will chamber a contemporary smokeless-powder 38 Special cartridge. However, to fire such a loading in one of these old Colts is to court disaster.

Some early smokeless-powder guns were by no means as strong as later models chambered for the same cartridge. The soft steel on U.S. Krag rifles–Models 1892/1896–was not up to the pressure of some heavy smokeless-powder loadings, and those guns began to develop cracks around the bolt locking lug after prolonged use. Krag and early 1903 Springfield rifles were inspected "by eye," the proper color indicating proper heat treatment of barrel and receiver steel. When Springfield receivers started failing with higher-pressure loadings, the heat treatment process was improved. This occurred at serial number 800,000.

The Colt Single Action Army revolver (Model 1873) is still

being made. The original was a blackpowder gun. The steel was later improved and some internal redesigning was done, making it safe for smokeless loadings. Colt has advised that guns with serial numbers below 160,000 are for blackpowder only! Except for serial numbers and a few minor details neither the '03 Springfield nor the Colt SAA has changed in external appearance since their introduction.

Early 38 Colt semi-automatic pistols (Models 1900, 1902, 1903) are chambered for the 38 Colt Automatic cartridge, no longer manufactured. The same cartridge, in terms of dimensions, is still on the market as the 38 Super Auto. This is the old 38 Auto with a much heavier charge of powder. It is poison for the older guns.

The original Model 1895 Winchester lever-action rifle was chambered for the 1903 Springfield's 30-06 cartridge. For some reason this rifle got a reputation as having an action that was stronger than the Springfield when, in fact, it was weaker.

Older guns can be fired quite safely if you are aware of their limitations and don't try for "improved" performance. Determining what is and is not a "modern" gun in

The U.S. standard 30-06 Springfield cartridge (left) and Russian 7.62x54mm Mosin rifle cartridge are not compatible. Some Russian rifles have had chambers recut to take the '06. The smaller-diameter 30-06 has plenty of room to swell and burst in the oversize Russian chamber.

The 30-06 Springfield (left) and 8mm Mauser rounds are close enough in size so the Mauser can be fired in a 30-06 chamber. This will happen ONCE! The gun will be wrecked, along with the shooter's face, by the tremendous pressures generated by an oversize bullet.

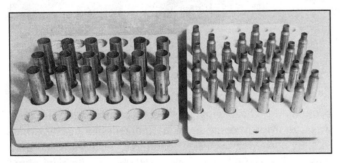

Loading blocks can be homemade from wood (left) or of moulded plastic (right). Loading blocks are not merely a convenience; they are a necessity to keep you from double-charging a cartridge case.

terms of its strength falls under the COIK limitation. COIK stands for Clear Only If Known. Therefore, defining what is a safe "modern" gun at times requires some knowledge beyond the appearance and the date it was introduced. Thus if the gun you are planning on reloading for is questionable in any way regarding the caliber, its age and/or mechanical condition, have it checked by a competent gunsmith—and if you don't like the first answer, a second opinion won't hurt.

Occasionally what might be termed "nightmare guns" turn up on the used market. These are standard rifles, often surplus military guns, which some amateur gunsmith has attempted to rework into a caliber different from the one it was originally intended to fire. The 6.5mm and 7.7mm

Japanese Arisaka and the 7.62mm Russian Mosin-Nagant rifles have been found converted to take the 30-06 Springfield cartridge.

Some were only half-converted: the chamber recut, but the barrel left untouched. In the case of the 6.5 rifle, 30-caliber bullets were squeezed down to 25-caliber in the barrel, creating tremendous pressures. Some of these rifles, amazingly, held together for a while. The Russian rifle was never intended to take the pressures of the 30-06, and no re-cutting of the chamber can replace metal at the rear of the chamber, which is considerably oversize for the 30-06 cartridge. Case swelling and eventual ruptures are a matter of time. There is no way such a butchered rifle can be made right short of rebarreling. Even then the new caliber should be one that will not give pressures greater than that of the original cartridge. If you plan to shoot and reload for a centerfire rifle, know what you have–don't guess! If, on firing some commercial ammunition, there is any sign of trouble, stop right there. What is a trouble sign? The best quick and easy means is to look at the fired cartridge case. If it looks significantly different from an unfired one, is now swollen or misshapen with a flattened or pierced primer, take the rifle and case to a good gunsmith for an analysis.

The Loading Process

The loading process is not terribly complicated, though it does involve a number of steps. Each step is there for a reason. It may not be apparent to the beginner, at the outset, why those steps are there. This often seems to be a good excuse to take a shortcut and eliminate a particular step. Here is a scenario in which the beginning reloader can find himself: You start reloading cases in what you think is a very safe manner. Each cartridge case is sized and decapped, just as this book tells you to do. Then you insert a new primer, also according to the manual. You carefully weigh the powder charge on a good scale and even weigh the bullets to make sure there's no more than 1/2-grain difference in weight. After weighing the powder charge to an accuracy level of less than 1/10-grain, you put it directly in the case and immediately seat the bullet.

Everything works fine with this system until the day you're in the process of loading and someone comes to the door. You leave a cartridge case sitting on the loading bench, charged with a small charge of fast-burning powder that has disappeared in the dark bottom of the cartridge case. After dealing with the visitor, you return to the bench to continue loading, picking up where you think you left off. You carefully measure out a charge of powder and funnel it into the case. Since you're wary of accidentally getting two charges in one case, you immediately seat a bullet and add the finished cartridge to the box you had been filling.

A double charge is exactly what resulted.

Every instruction manual will warn you not to do this. Use a loading block, a small plastic or wood tray that holds cartridge cases heads down. They cost a couple of bucks, or you can make your own by boring the proper-sized holes

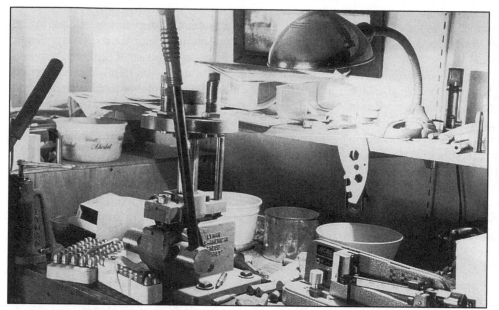

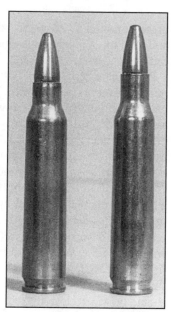

Straight from the chamber of horrors. Before your loading bench looks like this, it's time to clean up and get organized. With such a mess, it's easy to mistake and/or waste a lot of time puzzling over what's really in those various bins and boxes.

The 223 *(left)* has a shorter neck than the 222 Magnum.

All are ready to shoot, except the one in the middle is a 222 Magnum and the rest are 223. If you plan to load similar calibers, extra caution is needed to keep the cases, loaded ammunition and, in some instances, bullets separate.

through a piece of plank and gluing a flat bottom on it. A loading block is a safety device allowing the reloader a second chance to inspect charged cartridges before seating a bullet, because there might be the slight possibility that one of those cartridges got too much powder.

One new reloader recalled this exact error, much to his chagrin:

"I discovered my error while target shooting at a friend's farm. The double-charged case wrecked a nice old Springfield, the purchase price of which would have bought an amazing number of loading blocks. I was very lucky, because the people who had designed and built that Springfield had built-in some good safety features. These saved my eyesight."

Many reloaders owe a lot to those folks who designed and built their guns–people who were smarter than they are. Everybody who loads will throw double charges. The careful ones won't do it very often and they'll catch their mistakes before they are fired. Once is all it takes to ruin a gun. Once is all it takes to ruin your face, eyesight, hearing, and if you are really unlucky, kill you.

Follow the steps listed in the reloading manuals, all of them in the proper order. They are there for a good reason.

Many reloading accidents stem from simple carelessness, like avoiding steps, taking shortcuts, and not paying attention to your work. Reloading is a solitary activity. Don't try to watch television or chat with friends while you reload. Reloading is a simple task requiring concentration and paying attention to details. Close the door to the room where you reload to keep others out, especially children. If there's an interruption, stop at the completion of an operation and then deal with whatever it is. If this isn't possible, back up one step and do it over. Because it is repetitive, reloading can become routine and tedious. When it becomes boring is the time to take a break. Never reload when you are tired or ill, because this dulls your concentration.

Handling Materials Safely

Teachers constantly remind us that neatness counts. In reloading it will be your gun that will tell you, not your teacher. A cluttered, messy reloading area leads to more mistakes. Primers not put away get mixed with the next batch that may be different. Cartridge cases that are similar can be mixed and the wrong one can wind up in the loading press, jamming it, or worse—dropped in a box of loaded ammunition of a different caliber. Mismatched ammunition can wreck guns and shooters.

Primers are perhaps the most potentially dangerous component of the reloading hobby. They come packaged in little packets of 100, separated in rows or in individual pockets in a plastic holder. There is a very good reason for this. While modern primers are well sealed there is always the possibility that minute amounts of priming compound can coat an exposed surface of a primer and flake off as dust. If primers are dumped into a can or bottle this dust can accumulate and be detonated, followed by all the primers in that can or bottle, in something approaching 25/1000-second. That's faster than most people can let go of a can or bottle. Primers should never be dumped more than 100 at a time and this should be done only in a plastic primer tray. Shaking a can or bottle of primers is really tempting fate. Primer trays should be wiped clean if there is any evidence of residue on them.

The more advanced loading tools are often equipped with automatic primer-feeding devices that will occasionally jam. Dealing with such a jam is a delicate process. All primers that can be removed should be taken out before attempting to clear a jam. Problems with feeders are best dealt with via a call or e-mail to the manufacturer of the loading equipment.

Safety glasses are a must whenever you reload. When loading using an automatic primer feeder, safety glasses are absolutely vital because primers can explode. Aeronautical engineer Edward Murphy came up with a very good set of rules known as "Murphy's Laws" regarding how and why things fail, concluding that they fail at the worst possible time–airplanes when they are flying, guns when they are being fired, primer feeders when they are packed full of primers.

Modern smokeless powder is far safer to handle than gasoline or other flammable solvents, acids or caustic substances such as lye-based drain cleaners. Powder can, however, be mishandled and this leads to trouble. Powder left in a measure or unmarked container can lead to guessing about what it is, and a wrong guess can be disastrous. Powder should always be kept in the original container. Never use an old powder can or bottle because it is too easy to contaminate your powder, or mistake which label is right. Powders should never be mixed. This can happen if some is left in a measure and a different powder is poured on top. Such contaminated powder is worthless and should be discarded. Likewise, powders that are in unlabeled containers, from unknown sources, are not worth keeping. Even though they might look like another, you can't really be sure so they should be considered as "unknown" and discarded. It's not worth risking your gun–let alone your eyesight, hearing and,

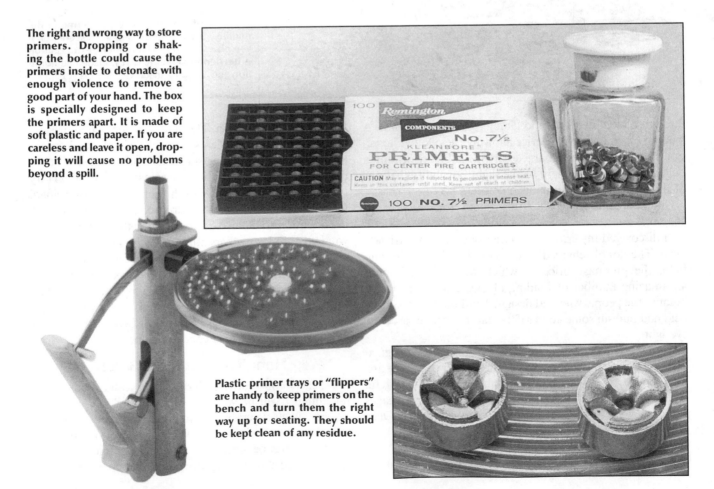

The right and wrong way to store primers. Dropping or shaking the bottle could cause the primers inside to detonate with enough violence to remove a good part of your hand. The box is specially designed to keep the primers apart. It is made of soft plastic and paper. If you are careless and leave it open, dropping it will cause no problems beyond a spill.

Plastic primer trays or "flippers" are handy to keep primers on the bench and turn them the right way up for seating. They should be kept clean of any residue.

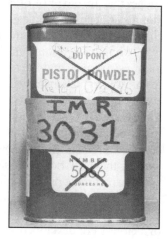

(Below) **Never store powder in an old powder can that contained a different powder, as this photo shows. Too much chance for a mistake in the future. Powder should ALWAYS be stored in the original container.**

The tall thin tube in the center rear of this progressive reloading press is filled with a stack of primers. If the feeding mechanism jams, the stack can explode if you do not clear it properly. If a jam occurs, read the manual, and if in doubt, call the manufacturer for assistance.

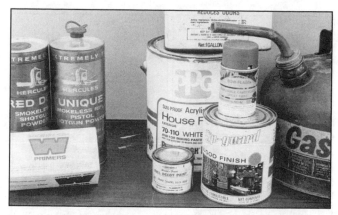

Smokeless powder is far safer to store or handle than many common household products. It is highly flammable, but less so than gasoline, petroleum-based cleaning fluids and similar household items.

yes, your life to experiment for the sake of saving a few dollars of material.

Disposing of such powder is easy, but should be done sensibly. It can be burned outside, on open ground, in small amounts of no more than a couple of tablespoons at a time. Far easier is to scatter it on your lawn or flowerbed because it adds nitrogen. It will break down in the weather rather quickly. Unexploded primers that have been damaged are best buried after soaking in a lye solution.

Failure to recognize what sort of powder you are dealing with can have disastrous consequences. Recently, a would-be blackpowder shooter bought a new-made blackpowder revolver. The dealer at the gun show didn't have any blackpowder for sale, advising the buyer to come by his shop the following week where he had plenty. The buyer really wanted to try out his new gun that weekend. A helpful neighbor allowed as how he had some old blackpowder shotgun shells. These could be broken down, he figured, the powder extracted and used.

They did that. There was powder in the shells, and it was black in color. Two heads may be better than one, so long as the cooperative effort is not simply a pooling of ignorance. When the gun fired the charge blew off the top strap, blew out the chamber being fired and the chambers on either side. Fortunately no one was seriously injured. A basic ignorance was the fault. With very few exceptions all gunpowder is colored black by a graphite coating, including the fast-burning smokeless shotgun powder that was contained in the neighbor's shells. Never guess about powder.

Related accidents have been caused by reloaders loading bullets into blank cartridges. Blanks are loaded with a very fast-burning type of powder that will produce a loud report. If a bullet is loaded on top of such powder, rather than being accelerated down the barrel, the powder burn is so rapid that the bullet has no more than begun to move before the pressure has jumped to a catastrophically high level and the bullet acts like a plug. In essence, this is a bomb.

Recognizing powder, obviously, is easiest when it is in clearly marked containers. There is, however, an additional point to be made here. Powders are identified by manufacturer, trade name and often numbers. There are powders on the market that are very similar, but not the same, which can be confused if the reloader does not have a clear understanding of what he is dealing with. The IMR Powder Co. makes a powder called IMR 4831 (formerly made by DuPont). The Hodgdon Powder Co. produces a similar powder called 4831 and is labeled H4831. The IMR powder is much faster burning than Hodgdon's and loading data for H4831 would be very dangerous to use with the IMR propellant. To confuse things a little more, both companies market a powder with the designation 4895, IMR 4895 and H4895 respectively. These are very similar in terms of their burning characteristics and are virtually interchangeable. The recent acquisition of IMR reloading powders by Hodgdon hopefully will sort out this situation.

Loading Data and Loading Manuals

The typical loading manual provides loading data for individual cartridges using a variety of powders and bullets that have been tested and found to be suitable for that particular cartridge. The powder types and charges listed for each cartridge are given as "starting loads" and "maximum loads." Often there will be an "accuracy load" listed that performed particularly well in the firearm used for the tests. This data is the result of rigorous testing over long periods of time. It involves the efforts of a number of engineers and technicians using the latest and most sophisticated test equipment available. This loading data brackets the lowest safe pressure and velocity loads up to the highest. Working

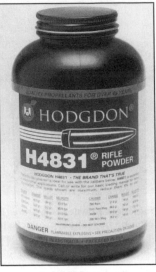

These are not the same powders, although the number is identical. Read the powder reference section for further information and never guess about the burning characteristics of a powder.

within this range, the reloader can work up a loading that performs best in his gun.

The semi-experienced reloader is occasionally tempted to go beyond the bounds of whatever loading guide he is using and try something else. This is fine if the "something else" is to avail himself of more loading books containing tried and proven data, and not simply guessing on the basis of, "What if I tried 52 grains of _____?" The dangers of exceeding the upper limits of various loadings should, by now, be clear to the reader. There is, though, an apparent danger from going in the opposite direction. A certain amount of press has been given to a phenomenon known as detonation. This involves excessively high pressures generated by reduced loads of slow-burning powders–charges below those recommended by the reloading manuals. Never guess at the burning characteristics of a powder, or exceed the recommended charges on either end of the loadings recommended in the manuals.

The weight, composition and fit of the bullet in the barrel are factors in the pressure equation. Heavier bullets boost pressures, as do those made of harder material. The size of the bullet also plays a role. The tighter the fit of the bullet in the barrel, the greater the force needed to drive it through.

When using modern components, loading problems are usually simple and straightforward, if the reloader keeps in mind that the changing of any component can affect pressure. These include the type of case (military vs. commercial), the type of primer (pistol vs. rifle vs. the magnum version of either), the make of primer or case, and the lengthening and thickening of the case mouth in bottlenecked cartridges after repeated reloadings. A final consideration is the capacity of the case. The larger it is the lower the pressure, all other things being equal.

All these factors must be carefully weighed in the loading game, particularly when working toward maximum pressure/velocity loadings. At this point, particularly with guns

of less than the best design and strongest materials, the gap between a safe maximum loading and a destroyed gun can be very close, and a slight variation in one of the above mentioned pressure factors can lead to a case rupture and disaster. The danger is greatest in what might best be termed the area of "advanced reloading." This takes in the obsolete, the foreign and the wildcat or experimental cartridge. In loading these cartridges, the reloader often finds himself on terra incognita, faced with guns whose internal dimensions may vary considerably from book descriptions, and with cartridges that are old or of otherwise doubtful quality. Often a gun may not be clearly marked as to the exact caliber. Rifles chambered for the German 8.15x46R cartridge were a popular "bring-back" following WWII. This cartridge came in many case shapes, and the rifles had bore diameters ranging from .313- to .326-inch, with .318 and .323 being the most common. Guns do turn up that have been rechambered for some cartridge other than the one listed in the books or on the barrel. When in doubt, make a chamber cast. The most common problem is that there is often little or no data on loading these cartridges. In such instances even the experienced expert must proceed with extreme caution.

On the subject of published loading data there are a couple of final caveats. Old manuals dating from the early 1950s or before were developed without the benefits of today's modern test equipment. Often the weaknesses of particular guns were not known at the time or if they were, those guns were not being used to an extent great enough to justify their inclusion in the creation of the loading data. Circumstances alter cases and those weak guns may now be in a larger supply, meeting a larger demand. There is loading data in manuals dating from the early 1950s that if used with old, low-strength rifles from the 1870s and '80s would very likely take those old rifles apart in one shot. There is now a lot of interest in shooting old cartridge rifles, and the new manuals reflect this interest with data developed especially for them.

There is also the matter of data published in magazines. This is often the work of an individual who has cooked up some handloads that he thinks are pretty good. This is sometimes an amateur working without the benefits of pressure-testing equipment. Magazines publish disclaimers to the effect that any loading data published therein is used at the shooters' own risk. It is indeed.

Firearms/ammunition expert and author Philip Sharpe received many letters during his career as a technical editor and advisor for the American Rifleman magazine. By his assessment, one of the most dangerous types of reloaders was the "instant expert." This is the person who has read one or perhaps two books on reloading. He has been doing it for a few years and has grown a towering intellect (make that ego) in the process. He has become imbued with an innate savvy of all things firearms related and wants not only to chart new courses in the reloading business, but also to share his "discoveries." This is the person who, without the aid of pressure-testing equipment or any form of metallurgical analyses, has decided to start experimenting with

The sad end of a fine old rifle–accidentally overloaded with a double charge. *(Photo courtesy of Tom Trevor)*

improved-performance loads, meaning higher velocities, heavier bullets, and more pressure. How does he know his gun can take these higher pressures? Because it's a Remington, Winchester, Mauser—whatever. More likely, he has a kind of simple faith that his guns possess hidden strength because those companies make their guns tough enough that they can't be destroyed. This is nonsense.

There has yet to be a small arm built that can't be wrecked. Firearm and reloading equipment manufacturers are constantly improving their products to make them safer and easier to use.

Of course, just plain simple mistakes can have disastrous results. One experienced reloader a few years back was reloading ammo for his Ruger No. 1. As he was adjusting his scale, he determined the load he wanted, which was within published limits, needed to be 5/10ths of a grain heavier. So he adjusted the scale, and his powder thrower, to drop 5 full grains more powder, not just 5/10ths, which put his load 4 1/2 grains over the maximum. The result was an action totally welded together. Luckily, the No. 1 has a very strong action.

Probably the best and most succinct list of safety rules you'll find is found in a little folder once offered free by the National Reloading Manufacturers Association. Even though the NRMA is currently inactive, the rules assembled by this group of manufacturers still make sense:

The Basic Rules For Reloading Safely

Introduction

Most reloaders handload because it is interesting, less expensive than shooting factory loads and because they can often develop more accurate loads for specific guns.

The NRMA wants you to enjoy this hobby safely and this leaflet provides some basic rules observed by all top-notch reloaders. Obviously, it is not a reloading manual. You are urged to read all available books on reloading. Go to demonstrations, talk to experienced handloaders. Make yourself as knowledgeable as you can. Get all the help you can!

Basic Reloading Precautions

1. Modern ammunition uses smokeless powder as the energy source. Smokeless powder is much more powerful than blackpowder or Pyrodex. Never substitute smokeless powder for blackpowder or Pyrodex and never mix it with either.

2. Follow loading recommendations exactly. Don't substitute components for those listed. Start loading with the minimum powder charge in the loads shown.

3. Never exceed manufacturers' reloading data. Excess pressures caused by excessive loads could severely damage a firearm and cause serious injury or death.

4. Understand what you are doing and why it must be done in a specific way.

5. Stay alert when reloading. Don't reload when distracted, disturbed or tired.

6. Set up a loading procedure and follow it. Don't vary your sequence of operations.

7. Set up your reloading bench where powder and primers will not be exposed to heat, sparks or flames.

8. DO NOT smoke while reloading.

9. ALWAYS wear safety glasses while reloading.

10. Keep everything out of reach of small children.

11. Keep your reloading bench clean and uncluttered. Label components and reloads for easy identification.

12. Do not eat while handling lead.

13. NEVER try to dislodge a loaded cartridge that has become stuck in the chamber by impacting it with a cleaning rod. Have a competent gunsmith remove the round.

Smokeless Powder

All smokeless powders obviously have to burn very fast, but handgun and shotgun powders must burn faster than rifle powders. You will readily note the differences in physical size and shape of various powders, but you cannot see differences in chemical composition that help to control the rate of burning. Burn rate is also affected by pressure. "Hot primers," seating the bullet too deep, over-crimping the case on the bullet, tight gun chambers, oversize bullets, use of heavy shot loads–and anything that increases friction or confinement of the powder–will increase the pressure. Obviously this hobby requires attention to detail, patience and meticulousness to insure the safety and quality of loads produced.

Powder Warnings

1. NEVER mix powders of different kinds.

2. Use the powder ONLY as recommended in manufacturer reloading manuals.

3. Store powder in a cool, dry place.

4. If you throw or measure powder charges by volume,

check-weigh the charges every time you begin loading, occasionally during loading, and when you finish.

5. Pour out only enough powder for the immediate work.

6. NEVER substitute smokeless powder for blackpowder or for Pyrodex®.

7. Don't carry powder in your clothing. Wash your hands thoroughly after handling it.

8. Store powders in original package. Don't repackage.

9. Keep powder containers tightly closed when not in use.

10. Specific powders are designed for specific uses. Don't use them for other purposes.

11. Smokeless powder is extremely flammable. To dispose of deteriorated powders, follow recommendations in "The Properties and Storage of Smokeless Powder" — SAAMI Reprint #376-2500, which is published in some reloading guides.

12. Empty the powder measure back into the original powder container when through with a reloading session. Do not mix powders.

13. Clean up spilled powder with brush and dustpan; do not use a vacuum cleaner because fire or explosion may result.

Primers

Priming materials differ in brisance (initial explosive force) and in the amount of hot gas produced. Don't mix primers of different makes.

1. Don't decap live primers. Fire them in the appropriate gun — then decap.

2. Don't ream out or enlarge the flash hole in primer pockets. This can increase chamber pressure.

3. Over-ignition creates higher gun pressures. The best results are obtained by using the mildest primer consistent with good ignition.

4. Don't use primers you can't identify. Ask you local police or fire department to dispose of unidentifiable or nonserviceable primers.

5. Keep primers in the original packaging until used. Return unused primers to the same package. Don't dump together and store in bulk. There is risk of mass detonation if one is ignited.

6. If resistance to seating or feeding of primers is felt, STOP and investigate. Do not force primers.

7. Store primers in cool, dry place. High temperature, such as in a summer attic, causes them to deteriorate.

8. Don't handle primers with oily or greasy hands. Oil contamination can affect ignitability.

9. There have been instances of "primer dusting" in the tubes of loading tools because of vibration. Clean the machines after each use.

10. Refer to SAAMI reprint "SPORTING AMMUNITION PRIMERS: Properties, Handling & Storage for Handloading."

Handling Lead

Lead, a substance known to cause birth defects, reproductive harm and other serious physical injury, must be handled with extreme care. Handle lead bullets or lead shot only in a well-ventilated area and always wash hands after handling lead and before eating. Discharging firearms in poorly ventilated areas, cleaning firearms, or handling ammunition also may result in exposure to lead. Have adequate ventilation at all times.

Handloading Rifle & Pistol Cartridges

1. Examine cases before loading. Discard any that are not in good condition.

2. Put labels on boxes of loaded cartridges. Identify caliber, primer, powder and charge, bullet and weight, and date of reloading.

3. In handgun cartridges, the seating depth of the bullet is extremely important. Handgun powders must burn very quickly because of the short barrel. They are sensitive to small changes in crimp, bullet hardness, bullet diameter, primer brisance and especially to bullet seating depth.

4. Check the overall length of the cartridge to be sure the bullet is seated properly.*

5. If you cast your own bullets, remember their hardness, diameter and lubrication affects the ballistics.

6. Plastic cases designed for practice loads (where the bullet is propelled by primer gas only) can't be used for full-power loads.

7. Consult manufacturer regarding disposal of unserviceable ammunition. Ask your local police or fire department to dispose of small quantities.

* Accumulation of lead or grease in the bullet-seating tool may force the bullet in too far. If the bullet isn't deep enough, it may engage the lands of the barrel when loaded. This will increase the chamber pressure.

Reloading Shotgun Shells

1. Select cases that are in good condition. Be sure base wad is intact and the shells are of the same brand and type. Discard any with split mouths.

2. Check the powder bushing to be sure it is correct for the powder weight recommended. Check-weigh thrown powder charge.

3. Check shot bushing for shot charge weight.

4. Shotshell wads differ in their sealing ability. Use the load combination specified in the reloading guide.

5. For Your Safety, Please Note: you cannot substitute steel or buffered lead shot in loads recommended for lead shot only. To load steel shot or add buffer materials to lead shot, you must use different components and follow exactly the instructions provided by recognized authorities.

Prevent Missing & Double Charges

1. It is easy to double-charge if you are momentarily distracted. Use a depth gauge to check powder height in shell. A piece of doweling rod can be used as a depth gauge.

2. Observe the powder level of cases placed in the loading block. This is a way to discover any cases with missing or double powder charges.

3. Take care to operate progressive loaders as the manufacturer recommends. Don't back up the turret or jiggle the handle. Don't use a shell to catch the residue when cleaning out the powder train.

Lead Hazards In the Shooting Sports

by Robert D. Williams, Ph.D.
Director, Division of Toxicology, The Ohio State University Medical Center

LEAD IS AN integral component in the manufacture of ammunition, ranging from a relatively low amount to nearly 100 percent in shot. Lead is also present during bullet casting, reloading, and gun cleaning. Lead interacts with organic matter to produce stable complexes. Specifically, human tissues possess prominent lead-binding characteristics. Thus, with a high degree of accumulation and relatively low turnover in man, concerns over the hazards of lead exposure become apparent in the shooting sports.

Exposure to lead can occur through ingestion, inhalation, and dermal contact. In the general population, the primary route of administration of lead is through ingestion: children eating lead-based paint or drinking water contaminated by lead piping. Individuals involved in shooting sports are exposed to high lead levels through dust inhalation, particularly at indoor and covered outdoor firing ranges, or during bullet casting where inadequate ventilation exists. Although firearm instructors constitute an occupational group at higher risk, studies have demonstrated that even recreational use of small-bore rifles can produce elevated red blood cell lead concentrations and symptomatic toxicity, following a 6-month indoor-shooting season averaging only 70 minutes per week.

Higher air-lead levels have been measured in firing ranges where powder charges were employed relative to ranges where only air guns were used, which in turn were higher than archery ranges. The use of totally-copper-jacketed or solid-copper ammunition has been proposed to decrease shooting range air-lead levels, since most of the airborne lead is vaporized from bullet surfaces.

Natural sources of lead in the atmosphere represent an insignificant risk: providing lead chiefly in its sulfide form, estimated to be half a billionth of one gram per cubic meter of air. Airborne dust from the environment and gases from the earth's crust contribute to the low "background" atmospheric level. Certain areas of the world contain substantially higher than background levels of lead, e.g. cities in industrialized regions where about 98 percent of airborne lead can be traced to the combustion of leaded gasoline. Air-lead levels averaging 660 micrograms/m3, which are over one hundred million times greater than normal environmental levels, have been measured at some indoor firing ranges. One analysis of firing range dust samples revealed it was composed of 24 to 36 percent lead. Soil lead is also enriched during shooting.

Acute lead poisoning is rare and usually occurs from ingestion of lead in soluble form, not sucking or swallowing a bullet–which could lead to chronic poisoning if done long enough. The symptoms of acute poisoning include a sweet metallic taste, salivation, vomiting, and intestinal colic. A large quantity ingested may produce death from cardiovascular collapse. Survivors of acute poisoning frequently develop signs associated with chronic toxicity.

Chronic lead poisoning, or plumbism, is manifest with a variety of symptoms. Initially, the individual is tired and weak due to anemia. Subsequent neurologic problems can develop which encompass irritability, restlessness, convulsions and, in severe cases, coma. Associated gastrointestinal disorders are constipation and a metallic taste. Neuromuscular symptoms include fatigue and muscle weakness. The most serious effect of lead poisoning, which occurs more often in children than adults, is encephalopathy. The early signs of encephalopathy involve clumsiness, irritability, and insomnia, which develop because of necrosis of brain tissue. Lead sulfide may appear in the gums and gingiva of toxic individuals as a blue-to-black line of discoloration termed the Burtonian line.

Toxicity from lead absorbed by the lungs and gastrointestinal tract is cumulative. In circulation, it is primarily bound to the red blood cells. Lead accumulates in soft tissues such as liver, kidney and brain. It can remain in the kidneys for 7 years and in bone for 32 years. During steady state, blood tests are considered the best indicator of relatively recent exposure. Urine tests are also employed, although urine lead concentrations tend to fluctuate more over time. Furthermore, hair may be tested to determine long-term exposure. Chelating agents are used as a treatment to assist in the removal of lead from the body. In the event lead poisoning is suspected, it is recommended that a primary care or occupational physician be contacted.

Assistance can also be obtained through state health and environmental agencies or local poison control centers. The National Lead Information Center (NLIC) may be contacted for general information regarding household lead at (800) 424-LEAD (5323).

Precautions that reduce lead exposure while involved in shooting sports will result in significantly improved health and a more enjoyable sport. Foremost attention should be given to the presence of children. The same exposure to a child relative to an adult results in a much higher total body burden of lead due to the reduced size of the child. In 1991, as a result of a large volume of epidemiological data, the

Exposure to lead can occur when shooting in indoor ranges. Airborne lead particles are inhaled into the lungs and absorbed into the blood.

Centers for Disease Control revised the recommended concentration of lead it considers dangerous in children from 25 to 10 micrograms per deciliter of blood. A number of studies indicate that high blood-lead concentrations can hinder a child's bone growth and can induce neurological damage. Since most young children place objects in their mouths, most lead poisonings in children occur between 1 and 5 years of age. There also tends to be a higher incidence of child-related lead poisonings during the summer months. Children should be kept at a safe distance from any enclosed shooting to avoid breathing airborne lead contaminated dust or soil. Dual cartridge respirators or masks are also advisable. Furthermore, materials which may be laced with lead residue–including cartridge cases, bullets, wads, primers, shot, cleaning patches, and cloths–should be kept out of reach of children.

While cleaning any firearm, avoid contact with bore-fouling residue from oily cloths or patches, which increase the absorption of lead through the skin. Solvents such as Shooter's Choice Lead Remover or Gunslick Super Solvent effectively remove lead from gun bores. Gloves are recommended as a barrier to absorption during cleanup using this or other products. A detergent containing trisodium phosphate, available at most hardware stores, is effective at solubilizing the lead for proper removal from lead-contaminated areas. Measures should be taken to ensure that all areas—as well as tools and accessories of the loading bench, including presses, dies, scales, gauges, measurers, and funnels—are properly cleaned of lead residues. During bullet casting, an adequate amount of ventilation is required. Outside is best since vaporized lead coming off a melting pot will condense on walls and rafters and can be inhaled directly or as dust in cleaning. Smoking and eating is dangerous when handling any lead-based material because of accidental transfer from hands to mouth. After handling equipment and cleaning the area, hands should be washed.

With adequate precautions, the presence of lead while

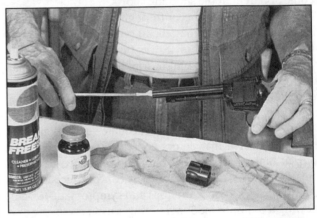

(Above and below) When cleaning firearms, avoid the fouling left on patches. The residue can be absorbed into the skin, so gloves are recommended. Also, be sure to thoroughly wash your hands and the work area when finished.

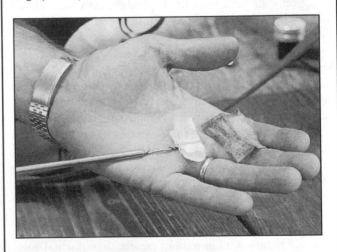

shooting, reloading or cleaning can be adequately controlled to minimize potential exposure, improving the quality of the sport and the health of each participant. Since toxicity is cumulative, periodic blood tests can provide added assurance for safety.

When reloading, only one component in the load chain is reused over and over.

The Cartridge Case

THE ORIGINAL PURPOSE of a cartridge was to facilitate quick loading and serve as a means to keep those loads consistent. The first cartridges contained charges of powder wrapped separately in paper to speed loading and eliminate the powder horn. These appeared in the late 1550s. It became apparent fairly early in the shooting game that breech-loading firearms were a lot more convenient than muzzleloaders. Soldiers especially liked the idea of not having to stand up to load while being shot at, since this interfered with their concentration. Sometimes they would forget where they were in the process, and would load a second powder charge and bullet on top of the first. At least one such soldier tamped more than a dozen loads into his rifle at the Battle of Gettysburg before tossing it away to look for something better to do than try to extract them. Several thousand rifles with multiple unfired loads were picked up after that battle.

Early self-contained cartridge cases were made of paper, cardboard, linen, rubber, collodion, even sausage skin. All were fired by a separate percussion cap. While they were more or less easy

Photo courtesy of Starline Brass

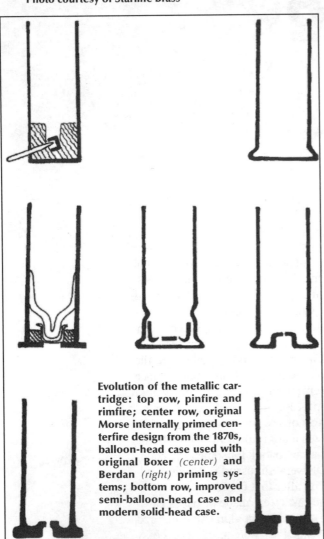

Evolution of the metallic cartridge: top row, pinfire and rimfire; center row, original Morse internally primed centerfire design from the 1870s, balloon-head case used with original **Boxer** *(center)* and **Berdan** *(right)* priming systems; bottom row, improved semi-balloon-head case and modern solid-head case.

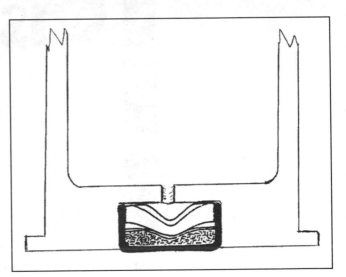

Boxer (above) and Berdan (below) systems are the ones used today.

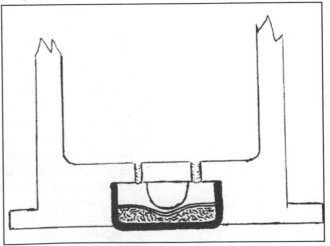

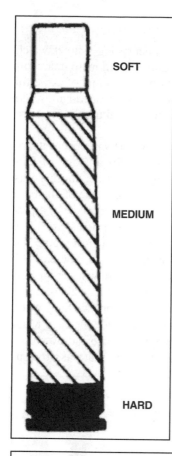

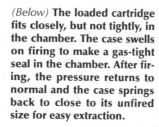

(Left) **The modern brass cartridge is made hard and thick where the greatest amount of support is needed, springy in the body for easy extraction, and soft at the mouth to ensure a good gas-tight seal when fired.**

(Right) **The parts of the cartridge case.**

(Below) **The loaded cartridge fits closely, but not tightly, in the chamber. The case swells on firing to make a gas-tight seal in the chamber. After firing, the pressure returns to normal and the case springs back to close to its unfired size for easy extraction.**

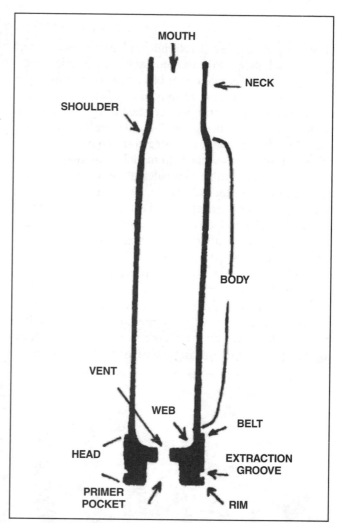

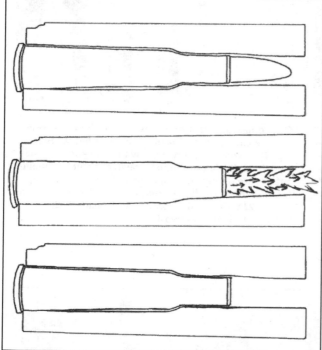

to load, those that· went into breech-loading guns still had not solved the breechloader's basic problem of gas leaks. Many attempts were made to deal with the early breechloader's nasty habit of spewing fire and smoke out of the joint between breechblock and barrel into the face of the shooter. The actions also tended to stick and eventually jam when they became encrusted with blackpowder fouling. It was

these problems that the metallic cartridge really solved, by closing the breech with a gas-tight seal and containing much of the fouling that wasn't in the barrel. At this point the cartridge became not merely a convenient package-form of ammunition, but an integral part of the firearm. By containing all the gas generated in the firing cycle it made the firearm more efficient. It also made possible the use of heavier charges generating higher pressures than could be used in a non-sealed gun. Finally, it served as a safety device by preventing gases from entering the action and destroying it.

The first commercially successful, completely self-contained metallic cartridge was invented in 1836 by Casimir Lefaucheux in France. The original style had a metal head and cardboard body, much like a shotshell. The primer was fired by a metal pin protruding above the head. The pinfire cartridge, however, had problems: It was not waterproof, and there was some gas leakage where the pin entered the case; the cartridge had to be properly oriented or "indexed" to enter the breech; if dropped it could accidentally discharge; and it was fairly expensive to produce, though it could be reloaded.

The second advance in cartridge design was the rimfire, developed in 1857 by Horace Smith and Daniel Wesson. It was based on the tiny "cap" cartridges patented around 1845, in France, by Flobert. It consisted of a copper tube closed at one end. The closed end was flattened just enough to create a hollow rim, which contained the priming material. The tube was filled with blackpowder and the open end or mouth was crimped to hold a bullet. The cartridge discharged when the rim was crushed at any point on its circumference by a firing pin. No indexing was necessary. The rim also stopped the cartridge from sliding into the barrel. The rimfire was cheaper to manufacture than the pinfire, was less susceptible to accidental discharge and could be made weather- and water-tight. The first rimfire was the Smith & Wesson Number I pistol cartridge, now known as the 22 Short. Rimfire cartridge cases could not be reloaded. During and shortly after the American Civil War, rimfires were made in sizes up to 58-caliber.

Good small designs, when made large, often don't work. This was the case with the rimfire. The larger sizes had the habit of swelling in the head area when fired if this head was not fully supported by the breech of the gun. Bulged heads jammed revolver cylinders preventing rotation. Solving this problem by making the cartridge head thicker or

harder required a very heavy hammer spring to fire it, which made the gun difficult to cock and resulted in an unacceptably heavy trigger pull. In addition, the amount of powerful priming material in the rims of the bigger cartridges would occasionally blow them off, leaving the tubular body of the case stuck in the chamber.

During and after the American Civil War, dozens if not hundreds of patents were submitted for all sorts of cartridges. One design had the firing pin inside; another was a spin-off of the rimfire, with the entire inside of the base coated with priming compound and held in place by a perforated washer. There were others with heads shaped like champagne bottle bottoms in attempts to overcome the shortcomings of the pin and rimfire designs. The basis of the solution came from George W. Morse who designed a cartridge in 1858 having a solid base with a small, separate primer in the center of the head. The primer fired when crushed against a wire anvil soldered inside the case. Mass production was impractical then, but Morse had overcome the above problems by creating a cartridge that was strong in

All of these rounds are non-reloadable for a variety of reasons. Left to right: The 12mm pinfire could theoretically be reloaded, but no components are available; tiny 230 Morris used a smaller than standard primer (not available), but new cases can be formed from cut-down 22 Hornets; aluminum and steel cases are for one-time use. "Posts" in the aluminum CCI Berdan primer pockets are battered in the first firing. The steel 7.62x39mm and 7.62x54mm Russian military cases are Berdan-primed and difficult to decap, but it can be done. The two darker cases are lacquer coated to make them function through autoloaders. This coating will likely come off in your reloading dies. In short, it's not worth the effort with Boxer brass cases becoming commonly available.

Old copper and soft brass cases from the last century and the early part of this one are a bad bet for reloading. They are often corroded by the blackpowder they contained, by deterioration through exposure to pollutants, or are simply made of poor metal and are too weak for modern smokeless pressures. *Examples include, left to right:* **22 WCF, 25-20 SS (with a newly-made 25-20 case), 38 Long, 45 S&W, and two 45-70s.**

All rimfires are essentially non-reloadable. They range from the miniscule 22 BB Cap *(far left)* to the 52-caliber Spencer round used in the Civil War.

The REM-UMC case on the left suffered near total separation due to mercury contamination. This same factor caused the one on the right to pull apart in the resizing die.

Blanks are made of substandard brass and often contain flaws, like the 223 case with the star crimp. This crimp, as with the flutes on the sides of the 30-06 dummy round, weakens the metal. These cases would likely split in the reloading die or in the next firing. In short, don't try to use brass from blanks, grenade launching or dummy rounds.

the head where strength was needed, did not require a heavy firing pin blow to discharge it, did not need to be indexed, was not susceptible to accidental discharge and could be made durable and waterproof.

In the 1870s the first really powerful cartridges were produced, based on the Morse design, with center priming and a reinforced head. The problem to be solved at this point was to come up with a design that was rugged, dependable, and that lent itself to ease of manufacture. Various folded and composite head systems were tried with limited success. The heart of the problem was to create a reliable, simple-to-manufacture primer. The problem was solved twice—by Hiram Berdan in America, in 1866, and by Edward M. Box-

er in England a year later. Berdan reduced the Morse wire to a tiny knob in the primer pocket with the priming material in a simple inverted cup above it. The ignition flame entered the cartridge case through two or three vent holes. Boxer crimped a tiny anvil in the primer cup itself with a space on either side to permit the flame to reach the powder charge through a single vent hole in the cartridge case. These are the two systems in use today. Oddly, the Boxer system became the American standard while the Berdan system found favor in Europe. The Boxer priming system with a single vent hole lends itself to easy removal by a simple punch pin, while the Berdan primer must be levered out with a chisel-type extraction tool.

Why Brass?

Early cartridges were made of copper because it was a soft, easily worked metal that could be formed into complex shapes in punch dies without becoming too brittle and splitting or cracking in the process. It had a high degree of plasticity. Among the copper cartridge's merits were that it resisted the corrosion of blackpowder and early corrosive primers; it was strong enough not to crack under the pressure of firing if well supported; and it formed a good gastight seal in a gun chamber. Copper's major failing, however, was low elasticity. When fired with a heavy charge the copper case had a tendency to stick in the chamber of a gun, particularly if that chamber had become hot and dirty with powder fouling.

Brass, an alloy of copper and zinc, possesses strengths and qualities neither element has separately. Most notable are hardness and elasticity. Modern cartridge brass (70 percent copper, 30 percent zinc) is the ideal metal for cartridges, being capable of being hardened and softened by the application of pressure and heat respectively. Thus, the head can be hardened, the body made semi-elastic and the mouth left relatively soft for a good gas seal. Such a cartridge case swells on firing to make a good gas seal in the chamber. After firing, the case springs back close to its original size, allowing easy extraction from the chamber. By the simple expedient of squeezing a fired cartridge case to its original size in a die and replacing the fired primer with a new one, it can be reused. A brass case may be used dozens of times with conservative loads. It is the most expensive component in the cartridge.

Because brass is relatively expensive, compared to other alloys, engineers have been at work to find cheaper materials that will do as well. Steel and aluminum alloy cases have been experimented with since the World War I period. In the last 20 years, advances in metallurgy and coatings have resulted in acceptable quality (for one-time use) steel and aluminum cases. Neither, however, is very suitable for reloading.

In spite of advanced heat-treating techniques, steel cases cannot be made as selectively elastic as those of brass. Steel cases tend to be rather hard and brittle. After a few resizings, the necks split, rendering them useless. To make steel

(Above) **Basic cartridge case forms include the following variations, left to right: straight-walled rimmed (45-70), straight-tapered (38-55), rimmed bottleneck (30-40 Krag), semi-rimmed straight (351 Winchester SL), rimless straight (30 Carbine), semi-rimmed bottleneck (220 Swift), rimless bottleneck (30-06), rebated head (284 Winchester), straight belted (458 Winchester Magnum) and bottleneck belted (7mm Weatherby Magnum).**

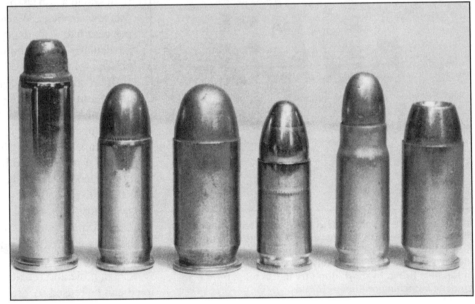

Basic cartridge forms for handguns, *left to right:* **straight rimmed (357 Magnum), straight semi-rimmed (38 ACP), straight rimless (45 ACP), semi-rimmed tapered (9mm Luger), rimless bottleneck (30 Mauser), and rebated head (41 Action Express).**

cartridges feed through various autoloading rifle and pistol actions, they are often coated with a varnish-type lubricant to keep them from sticking in the chamber when fired. When resizing these cases, this coating will tend to slough off in the resizing die and thus lose its effectiveness. Steel cases are most often encountered in military ammunition. The most common is the 7.62x39mm cartridge for the SKS and AK-47 rifles. These cartridges, in addition to being made of steel, are Berdan-primed and are thus more difficult to reload. Occasionally some steel-cased ammunition from WWII will turn up in 45 ACP and 30 M-1 Carbine. It is Boxer-primed and can be reloaded, but with good quality American brass cartridges in the above calibers now in

plentiful supply, attempting to reload this stuff isn't worth the effort. Be careful of shooting this ammunition, because some steel-case cartridges loaded with steel-jacketed bullets have been known to rust together, jumping pressures considerably when fired.

Aluminum cases in handgun calibers are manufactured by CCI as their Blazer line. These use a special Berdan primer, unavailable to reloaders, and are specifically marked NR for non-reloadable. Aluminum suffers some of the same problems as copper with its lack of spring-back, though it can be alloyed and heat-treated to make good cases for low-powered cartridges. Aluminum does not hold up well under resizing and crimping, and the cases frequently split on the

Case failures are not common, but they do happen. The nearer to the case head the rupture, the more serious it is.

This 45 ACP has been so badly battered that it will probably not go into the resizing die. The split in the body of the 22 Hornet probably resulted from too many reloadings. The tiny split on the mouth of the 44 Winchester *(center)* **could be easily overlooked. All are rejects.**

first attempt to reload them. It's not worth the effort when good brass cases are available.

The shortcomings of various early types of cases have already been mentioned, but a few points should be added. Pinfire guns and ammunition are totally obsolete; neither was made in this country and there is no reloading equipment or data available for these. Rimfire cases are primed with a wet mixture spun into the hollow rim. Owners of obsolete rimfire guns have a few of options: 1) Search for ammunition through such dealers as The Old Western Scrounger, or large local dealers who may have some in stock; 2) Polish them up and hang them on the wall.

Early centerfire cartridges are usually far too valuable as collectibles to shoot. Old cases, however, are still around and often are the only source of ammunition for some obsolete and foreign guns. Some of these cases are available from specialty suppliers and manufacturers. If vintage cases have been fired with blackpowder they are nearly always badly corroded and not safe. Copper and soft brass cases of the old balloon and semiballoon-head construction, from the last century, are too weak for use with modern smokeless loadings. Centerfire cases from the 1920s through the 1940s that have been contaminated by mercuric primers are very dangerous and should not be reloaded. This problem will be addressed in the chapter on primers.

Finally, a final word about blank cases. Even with the powder removed, these are not fit for reloading. Blanks are made from substandard cases not capable of meeting pressure and dimension standards for full-power ammunition. Attempting to remove the crimp in such a case usually splits the mouth and it's finished. The same is true for dummy cases, which contain a bullet and no powder or primer, and have flutes in the case body.

The Modern Brass Case

As firearms technology has advanced, guns have become more powerful and sophisticated. Cartridge case design has had to keep pace with this evolution. In reality, cartridges are often designed first and then guns are designed or adapted to fit them.

The basic design of the contemporary centerfire cartridge case can be one of a number of variations. The case can be: 1) straight-walled rimmed. These date from the 19th century, and include the 32 and 38 S&W revolver cartridges, the 45 Colt and the 45-70 rifle. They also include modern cartridges such as the 38 Special, 357 and 44 Magnums; 2) straight-tapered. An effort to improve extraction led to this design. It is now nearly obsolete, the 38-55 being the only current survivor: 3) rimmed bottleneck. These include late 19th century smokeless powder cartridges such as the 30-30 and 30-40, 303 British, and 22 Hornet; 4) semi-rimmed straight. These include currently-made 32 Auto and 38 Super Automatic cartridges. The semi-rimmed design was to facilitate feeding through box magazines, with a slight rim to keep the cartridge from entering the chamber; 5) semi-rimless bottleneck. Now rare, the 220 Swift is an example; 6) rimless straight. A common example is the 45 ACP; 7) rimless tapered. These are the 9mm Luger and 30 M-1 Carbine; 8) rimless bottleneck. This is an improved smokeless design from the 1890s. Most modern rifle cartridges use this design; 9) rimless belted. This design is used only on high-pressure magnum rifle cartridges such as the 458 Winchester Magnum; 10) rebated head. This one has a rimless head smaller then the body permitting a slightly increased case capacity. Examples are the 284 Winchester and 41 and 50 Action Express.

Case Selection

When buying cartridge cases for reloading, the first thing you want to be sure of is that you have the right one for your gun. Most civilian guns have the caliber marked on the barrel. Military arms, however, are not so marked, at least not very often. When in doubt, have the gun checked out by a good gunsmith. If there is no question about caliber, you want new or once-fired cases from a reputable source, marked with the headstamp of a known manufacturer and not from the "Royal Elbonian Arsenal." Military cases, referred to collectively as "brass," are often sold at bargain prices. Sometimes they are a bargain if they have been fired only once and are not battered by being run through a machinegun. The best military ammunition bargains are loaded rounds bought in bulk. That way you shoot it first. Military cases do, however, have a few drawbacks. Assuming they are not Berdan-primed, they may have been fired with corrosive primers. A wash in hot water and detergent will remove corrosive primer salts after firing.

The main problem with military cases is the crimp holding in the primer. Removing this crimp means a heavy-duty decapping pin and either chamfering the primer pocket or removing the crimp with a primer pocket swage die, as explained in Chapter 10, "Rifle Cartridge Reloading".

With the exception of new unfired cases in the box, all brass should be given an initial inspection. Bulk, once-fired, military and commercial cases may have loose debris, including primers (live and dead), rattling around inside

them that should be removed. Cases should be sorted by manufacturer and kept in separate containers. Although the dimensions for all cases are basically the same, internal dimensions (caused by varying wall and head thickness) and the size of the vent in the primer pocket will vary. Mixed cases will yield different pressures and velocities, giving less accurate shooting. Varying pressures can be dangerous if the load you are using is a maximum one. If, for instance, this load is worked up using one type of case with a fairly thin wall and thus a comparatively large internal capacity, in combination with a small vent, the internal pressure will be significantly lower than one with a thicker wall, smaller capacity and larger vent, which will be significantly higher.

Beyond separation by manufacturer, cases should be checked for splits in the neck, corrosion and any anomalies indicating pressure or headspace problems (meaning case stretching) or serious battering in the firing process that would render them unreloadable. Oil, grease, grit and dirt should be removed before reloading.

Reading Headstamps

The headstamp markings of cartridge cases contain valuable information that will prove useful when buying ammu-

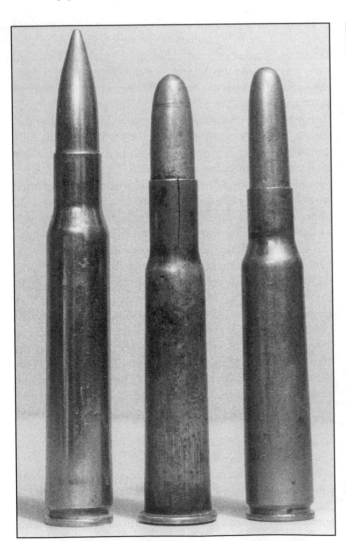

(Above) **Manufacturing defects, in this instance what appears to be poor brass, resulted in split necks in these 223 military cartridges.**

Season cracking (deterioration through exposure to pollutants in the air) caused this 1904-made 30-40 Krag case *(center)* **to split at the neck. The 7mm Mauser round** *(right)* **has hairline cracks in the deep tarnish at the shoulder. The 30-06 (left), made at the Frankford Arsenal in 1905, benefited from the advantages of good storage and is in near-perfect condition.**

What headstamps tell you. Commercial ammunition is marked with the caliber and name of the manufacturer, at least in this country. Military ammunition is usually stamped with the code of the arsenal or manufacturer and the date of manufacture. Top row, left to right: a 45-70 current headstamp, pre-WWII commercial Winchester and Remington headstamps (good candidates for being mercuric primed), and an inside-primed military centerfire from the 1880s. R indicates a rifle load, F is the code of Frankford Arsenal, 2 82 indicates it was loaded in February, 1882. Bottom row: a 30-40 Frankford Arsenal round loaded February, 1904, and a Spencer 52-caliber rimfire made by the Sage Ammunition Works.

nition and empty cases. Commercial makers mark their cases with their name or trademark, the caliber and name of the cartridge, e.g., WW 45-70 Govt. This tells you it was made by Winchester/Western and it is the 45-70 Government cartridge (originally made for the 45-caliber Springfield army rifle).

Markings on cases made for the military contain similar information, and sometimes a two-digit date of manufacture. LC is the Lake City Ordnance Plant; WRA is Winchester Repeating Arms Co.; RA is Remington Arms Co. A stamp of RA 79 indicates Remington made the cartridge in 1979. American military cases are not marked by caliber. Early cases made at the Frankford Arsenal in Philadelphia were marked, for instance, F or FA 3 05. This indicates the source and the month of manufacture (March) and the year 1905. This is not ammunition you would want to shoot, especially if it shows any sign of corrosion. American-made military ammunition used corrosive priming into the early 1950s. Different arsenals switched to non-corrosive priming at different times with all being changed over by 1954. Non-corrosive priming will require less cleaning of your gun.

Case Cleaning

Most shooters like to keep their cases shiny and bright. They look better and are easier to find on the ground.

Shined cases are less likely to collect dirt and grit and can be easily checked for damage caused by corrosion. Dirty cases can hide flaws that may run deep.

There are two basic methods of case cleaning. The first is a wet process that uses a concentrated, acid-based cleaner that is mixed with water. This must be done in a glass, plastic or stainless steel pan. Warming the pan with the cases in the mixture speeds the process. The cleaned cases must be rinsed to remove all residue and then oven-dried on "warm." Too much heat can ruin the heat-treatment of the cases. Cases should be decapped before wet cleaning.

Dry cleaning is by tumbling the cases in an abrasive cleaning media that's usually made of ground corncobs or ground walnut shells. This requires a motor-driven tumbler or vibratory tool into which the cases and media are put for cleaning. Once cleaned, cases must be wiped free of dust and any media trapped inside must be removed.

Cartridge Case and Ammunition Storage

"Store in a cool dry place" is good advice for keeping just about anything, but this isn't always possible. Depending on one's paranoia and/or notion of thrift, the decision may be made to buy a large quantity of cases. Sometimes quantity simply accumulates in the form of various loadings, always expanding with the addition of new guns to a shooting battery. Ultimately the questions arise about how long this stuff will last (both cases and finished ammunition) and how do I take care of it?

The shelf life of modern ammunition (both commercial and good handloads) is virtually indefinite if kept under ideal conditions—sealed, cool and dry. Most of us don't have this kind of storage. Experts have preached since time immemorial about the avoidance of heat and dampness when storing. Actually, heat and moisture by themselves don't do all that much damage to quality ammunition. Heat does drive off volatiles in lubricants and propellant powders, and to a degree accelerates powder decomposition. Heat and dampness together are most injurious because water absorbs pollutants and heat accelerates chemical reactions between these pollutants and ammunition. The triple threat in airborne pollution consists of acids, ammonia, and sulfur compounds. All occur naturally in the atmosphere in addition to being man-made pollutants. They are also found in a variety of household products.

It has been said that certain metals crystallize and become brittle with age. Professor Bryan Wilde, a metallurgist and director of the Fontana Corrosion Center at Ohio State University, said this was not the case. Cartridge brass has a crystalline structure. When exposed to pollutants in the atmosphere, notably ammonia, a breakdown of the alloy begins as the ammonia dissolves the copper. Acids in the atmosphere dissolve the zinc in a process known as "dezincification." In areas where the metal is stressed, like case

Liquid case cleaners contain a mild acid and require no more equipment than a stainless steel, plastic or glass bowl to soak them in. Cases should be decapped before cleaning and either air-dried or oven-dried at no more than 150° Fahrenheit.

Vibrator/tumbler case cleaners use ground corncobs or ground walnut shells to clean cases through abrasive action. This is probably the best system for cleaning large batches of cases.

necks, shoulders and crimps, the crystal edges are farther apart, thus speeding the breakdown in a process known as season cracking. Season cracking begins as tarnish, gradually turning into deep corrosion which often follows the edges of the crystals, giving the surface a frosted appearance, leading to the impression the metal is changing its structure. This phenomenon was first noted in 19th century ammunition used by the British in India, where it was exposed to the ammonia-rich fumes of cow dung and urine in a hot, humid climate.

Salts, though direct contamination, are another hazard. They occur in perspiration and are a problem mainly because they are hygroscopic—they draw and hold water, which combines with the salt to corrode the metal. Sulfur, notably sulfur dioxide (SO_2), causes tarnish when it combines with lead and copper to form sulfides. When SO_2 combines with water (H_2O) the result is sulfuric acid (H_2SO_4). Lead and lead alloy bullets are subject to damage mainly from acids. These attack lead, causing a hard white oxide crust to form, which, in rimfire ammunition, may make it impossible to chamber. Generally, the powder coating on bullets is not a problem, but it does indicate old or improperly stored ammunition/bullets. Unless the coating is excessive, such ammunition should be safe to shoot.

Pinpointing the exact reason why a particular batch of ammunition went bad is a mystery to be solved by an expert metallurgist-detective through chemical analysis and examination of cartridge surfaces with a scanning electron microscope. Manufacturers continue to come up with better priming, powder, lubricants, case materials, sealants, and packaging. What you buy represents the maker's state of the art combined with his sense of economy at the time the product was made.

Plating cases with nickel and plating or jacketing bullets with copper inhibits corrosion by acid. Non-hygroscopic bullet lubricants keep moisture away from bullets and out of case interiors. Paper boxes absorb moisture but are generally not a problem if kept dry. This boils down to the fact that if the cases/ammunition are in good shape when put away, and if kept dry and cool, they will last for years, probably decades.

Plastic boxes are good for case storage and do a good job of keeping moisture and pollutants out if they're closed on a dry day and kept closed. The cases should always be identified by maker, caliber and number of times reloaded.

A second problem that still crops up is brittle brass. After cartridge brass is formed it gets a final heat treatment called stress relief. This process involves less heat than annealing and is done to bring the brass to the optimum degree of springiness. Occasionally, a batch will get through that is improperly treated. It will perform fine when new, but after a number of years the brass will have returned to its original brittle state. This is exacerbated by the process of firing and resizing. Cases will split and sometimes burst. Any corrosion taking place will hasten this process. One advantage of the old copper cases was that they were less subject to corrosion and stress changes since they were softer to begin with.

Beyond cool and dry there isn't much to be added regarding shelf storage. For the longest run the best means is a military ammunition can with a rubber gasket, along with a fresh packet of desiccant. The can should be closed on a dry day and opened as infrequently as possible. If ammunition is stored in a can or tightly sealed cardboard container, don't break the seals (letting in pollutants) to have a look. Second floor rooms are perhaps the best for shelf-stored ammunition, avoiding attic heat and basement moisture. Cartridges should be stored away from cleaning products containing ammonia, bleaches, or acids. If it must be stored in a basement, run a dehumidifier and keep it off the floor. It is a good idea to make periodic checks of shelf-stored ammunition in non-sealed boxes—twice a year is fine—to inspect for case tarnish or a haze of white oxide forming on lead bullets.

To the above might be added a list of dumb things not to do. Slathering a gun with Hoppe's No. 9 may do well to keep it from rusting, but if this is the one kept for home defense the ammonia in the Hoppe's will spread onto the cartridges in the gun and eat right into them. The same is true for any ammonia-bearing solvent cleaner. A rust inhibitor such as WD-40 spray may work preservative magic, but WD-40 is designed to penetrate and will do so in the seams between primers and cases, eventually working into the priming compound and neutralizing it. Leaving cartridges in leather belt loops may look nifty, but if the leather has tanning salts or acids in it these will eat into the metal, etching a ring which adds nothing to the looks or strength of the case.

It should not be forgotten that cartridges are interesting and people can't seem to keep their sweaty hands off them. Ask any collector how often he wipes down his collection after showing it to friends. To prevent damage, two suggestions passed on by collectors are to treat specimens with a light coat of rust-inhibiting grease or liquid car wax. These are the best defense against repeated attacks of finger-borne corrosion. Like the guy at the gas station used to say, "Rust never sleeps."

Case Failures

In the 19th and early 20th century, case failures were an expected hazard. Today, however, the "headless" or "broken" shell extractor, once found in every shooting kit, has gone the way of the stereoscope and flatiron. Yet failures still happen and they will to you if you do enough shooting.

The quality of today's metallic cartridge ammunition is superb. Nearly two generations of shooters have grown up since the last corrosive, mercuric-primed, centerfires van-

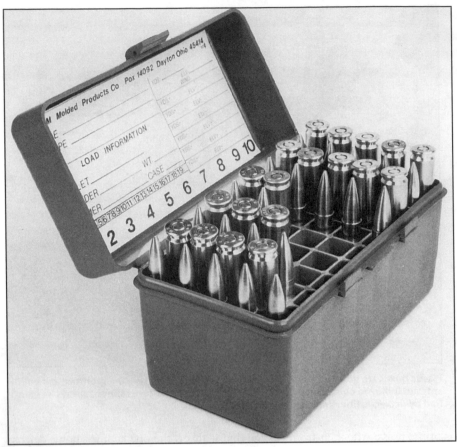

Plastic boxes are best for ammunition storage and usually come with data cards.

The old saying that lightning doesn't strike twice in the same place is just as false in cartridge case failures as it is in meteorology. The low overall incidence of case failures might lead to the belief that the one that failed was simply one bad case. Sometimes it is. If the problem rests with a defective component, given the consistency in today's ammunition, that problem may run through a case-sized quantity, possibly an entire production lot, or at least until someone in quality control realizes there is a problem and does something about it.

Split Necks

By the same token, if one case from a particular box or purchase-lot that you have been reloading develops a split in the neck, it has become brittle from resizing and the rest of the lot should be checked for the same problem. A split neck is a common failure and not dangerous to gun or shooter. Discard cases so afflicted. They are not fit to reload.

Body Splits

These are far more dangerous, with the degree of danger increasing in relation to the closeness of these splits to the head of the case. The worst instance is a separation at the case head. This allows high-pressure gas to come rushing back into the action of the gun and into your face, often damaging both. Since eyeballs and eardrums are less robust than a rifle receiver, it is imperative to wear eye and ear protection when shooting.

Longitudinal Splits

These can be a gun-related problem, namely an oversize chamber. If this is the cause, you will notice swelling of the cases and difficult extraction with normal commercial loads long before you get an actual split. If your gun is bulging cases, stop shooting! Have the gun thoroughly checked out by a very competent gunsmith. Rebarreling may be the only solution. If a case suddenly splits with a load you have been using successfully with other brands of cartridge cases, this is likely an instance of poor-quality, brittle brass. If there is visible corrosion inside and/or outside, corrosion may have helped weaken the case. Throw these away.

ished into the mists of erosive smokeless powder, and not a moment too soon. Case failures these days with new factory centerfire ammunition are virtually nonexistent.

It is in the business of reloading ammunition that most problems occur. Here, the reloader becomes the manufacturer and you must become your own quality control expert. In this role you must learn to recognize all the signs that may lead to an accident, and become an expert at "reading" cartridge cases. This is by no means as easy as it might appear, since similar failures may come from a variety of causes. Flattened, cratered and punctured primers, and gas leaks around primers, are generally signs of excessive pressure. Soft primers, stretched primer pockets caused by multiple reloading or a poor fit of the primer, however, can produce signs similar to high pressures. Swelling of the case head, often accompanied by the brass flowing back into the extractor port, are signs of high pressures, but can also be caused by soft, poorly annealed brass. Splits in cases around the head can indicate excessive headspace, which is a gun problem. Similar splits can also indicate inferior brass that contains oxides and impurities, and is sometimes recognizable by its scaly appearance. Internal corrosion from blackpowder loads or corrosively primed smokeless loads can also produce such splits. Improperly annealed brass, in this instance too hard and brittle, or brass made brittle by mercuric primers, or stressed by excessive resizing, will also show problems. That's a lot to consider in one bite, so let's move a bit slower here.

Circumferential Splits

These may be caused by poor quality, brittle brass, or brass made brittle by mercury contamination. Again, stop shooting!

If this has not happened before with other makes of case and suddenly happens on a different make or lot, it is likely caused by the above. This situation can also result from excessive headspace that is, in effect, a chamber that is too long. Chambers don't suddenly grow longer. If this is a headspace problem there will be warnings before such a separation occurs, namely stretch marks on the case as it gradually pulls apart over the course of several firings. These will often appear as bright rings and will be found on all the cases you fire in that particular gun. They will be most apparent on higher-pressure loads.

Head Separations

These can be more or less disastrous depending on how well your gun is engineered for safety, namely in terms of gas-escape ports. These allow gases flowing from the chamber, back into the action, to be directed sideways and not into your face. Contamination from mercuric primers is a likely cause of this since most of the mercury will contaminate the case area nearest the primer. Stop shooting! This batch of cases, from that box or lot, identified by the head-stamp markings, is not fit to shoot. Mercury contamination is invisible and the cases look fine until fired. Since mercuric priming was limited to non-military ammunition made from about 1928-1945 there is not that much around any more, but it can still turn up. At times these contaminated cases

will pull apart in the resizing die. This is a definite warning.

Stretched Primer Pockets

These occur after many reloadings. They are identified by gas leaks (smoke stains) around primers and by primers seating very easily, sometimes by thumb pressure alone. It's time to junk those cases when these signs appear. Excessively high-pressure loadings can also cause these symptoms. This is why maximum loads should only be worked up with new or once-fired cases. With a new case and a heavy load, such leaks tell you to stop shooting!

Primers flattened on firing also indicate high pressure, as do those that are cratered around the firing pin mark, or pierced. If these signs appear with a max load -- stop shooting! If they appear with a loading that has not produced these signs with other primers, the reason is most likely a soft primer.

Swollen Case Heads

This is nearly always a sign of very high pressure, but can also be caused by a too-soft head that was poorly annealed. If you are working up a max load, excessive pressure is the likely problem. Stop shooting! If this occurs with a load that has given no such indications and you have changed to a different make or lot of case it may be a case problem. Excessive pressures are the main culprit, and are additionally identified by cases stretching lengthwise and picking up machining impressions from the chamber walls and breech or bolt face. Such cases will stick tight to the chamber wall and give hard extraction, a definite sign of excess pressure.

In the last century, the headless shell extractor was a necessary part of the shooter's kit, given the poor quality of the cartridge cases.

Too much of either of these could be a serious problem, possibly leading to serious injury -or worse.

Understanding Pressure and Headspace

GUNS FUNCTION BECAUSE gunpowder burns rapidly to generate tremendous pressure as it is converted from a solid into a gas. This is a process called deflagration. Gunpowder burned in the air burns far more slowly than in the chamber of a gun. Inside the chamber, increasing pressure accelerates burning. As pressure increases the powder forms a churning mass.

The firing sequence begins as the primer ignites the powder. The primer contains a tiny amount of very high explosive that burns with a rapidity that far exceeds that of gunpowder. While gunpowder burned in the open produces a faint whoosh as the gas dissipates into the atmosphere, priming compound burns so quickly it will explode with great violence. This is why explosives such as priming compound, TNT, PETN, etc., are unsuitable for use as propellants. They burn so fast that before a bullet could begin to move down a gun barrel these compounds have burned completely, generating so much gas, so quickly, that for all intents the bullet is simply a plug in a closed container and the gun has become a bomb.

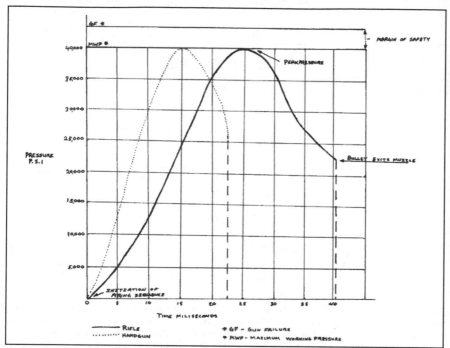

The primer is the sparkplug that starts the powder burning. Magnum primers contain more compounds and additives such as aluminum, which becomes white-hot sparks blown into the powder to give the charge even ignition. *(Photo courtesy Speer.)*

The flash hole on the case at the left was deliberately enlarged to burn a compressed blackpowder load. If this case were loaded with smokeless powder, dangerously high pressures probably would be generated.

The time-pressure curve starts at the point of ignition. In a few milliseconds, the event is over. The peak pressure is reached as the bullet is an inch or so forward of the chamber. After it has been swaged into the rifling, pressure declines and drops to zero as the bullet exits the barrel. A fast-burning pistol powder in a short barrel develops a sharp curve (broken line), while a slower rifle powder in a long barrel is flatter. The peak of the curve touches the maximum working pressure (MWP) line on a maximum load. Above this is a margin of safety area, and further above that is the point of gun failure.

The priming compound thus serves to get the powder burning. It functions much like burning balls of paper thrown into a pile of dry leaves to get the pile blazing. By throwing a greater number of fire balls into the leaf pile it will be set alight faster and more evenly than if only a few are tossed on. A magnum primer represents a high saturation of fire balls by comparison to a regular primer. By starting the fire in more places at once, the mass of powder is burned more rapidly and completely. More rapid and complete burning will generate more gas and higher pressure.

To continue the bonfire analogy, a fast-burning powder could be likened to dry leaves while a slow burning powder is more like a pile of twigs or wood shavings. The twigs take more/hotter fire balls to get them burning, but they will burn longer than the leaves and generate more hot gas more slowly. The fast-burning powder is ideal for a short-barreled gun. The rapid burn releases gas quickly, generating a high-speed movement of the bullet quickly. This sudden release of gas produces a relatively high pressure in the chamber. Therefore only a limited amount of such a powder can be used without generating dangerously high pressures.

A slow-burning powder can be loaded in greater amount. By virtue of releasing more gas at a slower rate, this works well in long barrels where the burn time is extended by the length of time it takes the bullet to travel to the end of the barrel. The slow-burning powder keeps on generating gas throughout the length of time it takes the bullet to exit. The long burn thus generates lower peak pressure and keeps the average pressure up for a longer time. Once the bullet has passed out the muzzle, further burning is pointless.

This burning process is best illustrated in what is called the time-pressure curve. A fast-burning powder such as Alliant Bullseye is intended for handguns and produces a typically short, sharp curve. A slower-burning rifle powder such as IMR 4320 produces a longer, flatter curve in a rifle-length barrel.

Of most critical interest to the reloader is the peak pressure generated by a particular load, for it is this peak pressure that will act as a hammer blow to your gun and wreck it if the peak pressure exceeds the elastic limit of the barrel/action. This will cause it to swell and eventually burst. To keep both guns and shooters from harm, arms and ammunition manufacturers design their products for a maximum working pressure. This is below the failure point by a margin of safety. Loading above this maximum working pressure will drastically shorten the life of a gun and place the shooter at significantly higher risk of a catastrophic failure every time such a load is fired.

Beyond the strength of the barrel and action, working pressure is limited by the strength of the cartridge case. The modern alloy steel in today's rifles make them capable of withstanding peak pressures of well over 100,000 pounds per square inch (psi). Even the strongest brass cartridge cases are not capable of withstanding more than 50,000 to 60,000 psi, and at pressures above that, they will swell, distort or even flow, until an unsupported point gives way and gas escapes, often wrecking the gun. Most cartridge cases are intended for pressures well below these figures.

The most obvious means of raising pressure in a barrel is to put more powder in the cartridge. This also holds true for generating higher velocity. Higher velocity means flatter shooting with less rise and fall in a bullet's trajectory,

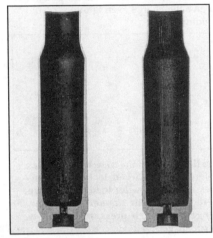

The balloon-head case on the 38 Special at left offers more powder capacity, and thus lower pressure. However, this is a weaker design than the solid-head 357 Magnum case on the right.

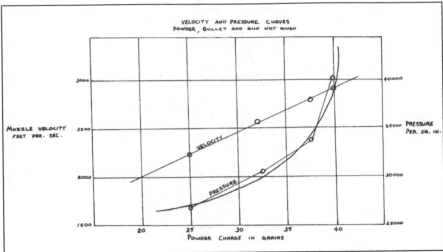

VELOCITY AND PRESSURE CURVES
POWDER, BULLET AND GUN NOT GIVEN

(Above) **The pressure-velocity curve illustrates the relationship between velocity and the pressure generated by adding more powder. As powder is added, more of the energy of the expanding gas is worked against the chamber walls and the gas against itself. Additional powder added at the top end of a load generates little additional velocity but considerably more pressure.**

The same cartridge with different internal dimensions. The smaller capacity case will generate higher pressures with the same load. Some brands have thicker (or thinner) walls, meaning different capacities. Sort your brass by maker.

and thus hitting a target at an unknown distance is made easier–ask any varmint shooter. The downside to such high-velocity loadings is the generation of very high pressures. An interesting phenomenon some shooters may not be familiar with is that as loadings are increased for greater velocity, pressures begin to go up at an increasingly higher rate. This can be most clearly expressed in what is known as the pressure-velocity curve. In conventional smokeless powder firearms, there is a ceiling on the velocity that can be achieved. This is because at a certain point, as the bullet is made smaller and lighter to achieve higher velocity, the base of that bullet has less surface area to be worked upon, and the gas in the chamber is working against the chamber walls and the molecules of gas against one another. This velocity ceiling is in the range of 11,000 feet per second (fps), and has been achieved with a steel ball blown out of a smooth-bore barrel—hardly practical. The pressure and heat generated at velocities of 5000-6000 fps will wash the rifling out of a barrel in a very few shots. A little over 4000 fps is the maximum practical velocity that can be expected to produce a reasonable barrel life–a span of a thousand shots at the very least before accuracy degrades to a marked degree. Thus, the quest for high velocity is at the cost of shortened barrel life and greatly increased pressures as the top end of the maximum working pressure is reached. This is where the last few additions of powder produce far more pressure than they add in velocity.

Other Factors Affecting Pressure
Reduced Loads

Small loads of certain slow-burning powders, well below those recommended in loading manuals, have apparently generated very high pressures. Called detonation, this phenomenon may be caused by what has been termed the log-jam effect caused by the position of the powder in the case, wherein the powder charge is forward in the case. Powder ignited in the rear slams the rest of the charge into the base of the bullet and the shoulder of a bottleneck case, resulting in a solid plug. As burning continues, pressures jump and a bomb effect is created.

The problem with this theory is that it has been very difficult to duplicate such events in the laboratory. Undoubtedly, a certain number of supposed detonations were instances of bullets fired from such reduced loadings sticking in rifle, or more likely, revolver barrels. The unwary shooter fires a second shot and this bullet slams into the one stuck in the barrel with unhappy results. Whatever the reason, there have been a significant number of accidents involving reduced loads of slow-burning powders. Thus, it is prudent not to experiment below the starting loads listed in the manuals.

With faster burning powders, it has been noted that the position of the powder charge in the cartridge case in less than full caseloads will affect pressures. If the charge is at the rear near the vent, pressures will be higher since a greater amount of powder will be ignited and is not blown out the barrel. With the charge forward, as when the gun is fired almost straight down, pressures may be lower by more than 50 percent.

Primers

Primers are the fire-starters that get powder burning. The more efficient ones, like magnum primers that burn longer

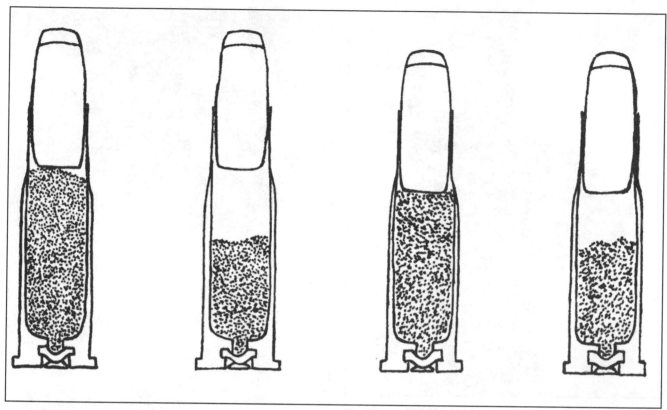

Loading density, the amount of powder and empty space in a cartridge, will affect the pressures therein, all other things being equal. The greater the density of the powder and the less space there is, the higher the pressure will be. On the left is a maximum, high-density load; next is a low-density load with the bullet seated far out. The pressure generated here would not be particularly high. Round number three contains the same load as number one, but it has been compressed by a deep-seated bullet. This would likely generate dangerously higher pressures. Round number four contains the same charge as number two, but will generate higher pressures. Case-wall thickness affects loading density by increasing or decreasing the internal capacity, a very critical point when a maximum load is used.

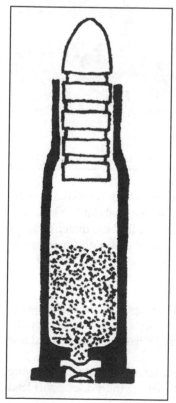

Never seat a cast bullet below the bottom of the neck into the shoulder area of a bottleneck case. The base will be melted and expanded, ruining accuracy and raising pressure.

and hotter, throw more sparks into the powder charge burning it more completely and more efficiently. This will generate more gas and, naturally, more pressure. It's best to stay with the primer types recommended by the loading manuals because pressure is affected.

Vent Hole Size

The vent bole is at the bottom of the primer pocket. Its size will affect powder burning rate by letting more of the primer flash pass into the case more quickly. A large vent, by increasing the rapidity of the burn, will raise pressures. Don't alter the size of the hole.

Case Capacity

All other things being equal, if the same amount of the same type of powder is loaded into a small capacity case such as a 223 Remington and a large capacity one such as a 45-70, much higher pressures will be generated in the smaller case. This is because there is less volume in the smaller case, thus less surface area for the pressure to work against. According to published data in the Accurate Smokeless Powder Loading Guide Number One, a load for the 223 of 23.5 grains of Accurate Arms 2495 BR powder behind an 80-grain jacketed bullet, generates an average of 51,600 psi

(Above and right) **Slugging the bore consists of carefully driving a small, soft pure lead slug down the barrel. If done from both ends, the two slugs can be compared for tight and loose spots in the barrel.**

The slug is measured from one land on one side to the land on the opposite side to find the groove diameter of the barrel.

of chamber pressure, while 66.0 grains of the same powder with a 300-grain jacketed bullet in the 45-70 generates about 22,100 psi. As mentioned in the previous chapter, some cases have slightly thicker walls and larger vents than others. Military cases are generally thicker than those made for the civilian market. This slight reduction in internal capacity can raise pressures.

Overall Cartridge Length

By making a finished cartridge longer than it should be, the bullet may rest against or even be forced part way into the rifling. This will raise pressures. If a case is not trimmed to the proper length and the case mouth extends into the rifling, the mouth cannot expand properly and the bullet will be forced through what amounts to an undersize mouth in a swaging action that will jump pressures while degrading accuracy.

Chamber and Bore Size

All American-made guns are standardized according to specifications set forth by the Sporting Arms and Ammunition Manufacturers Institute (SAAMI). Customized, foreign, and obsolete arms, however, may have dimensions different from this standard. Smaller, tight chambers and

undersize bores can jump pressures with normal ammunition. When there is a reason for doubt about the size, slug the bore with a piece of soft lead to find the dimension. It's also pretty easy to make a chamber cast with Cerrosafe or sulfur to find the exact dimensions.

Bullets

Bullets affect pressure, with the weight of the bullet having the most influence. The heavier they are the greater the pressure needed to get them moving. Beyond this is the hardness of the bullet.

Hard bronze or copper jacketed bullets require more energy to swage them into the rifling than does a soft lead

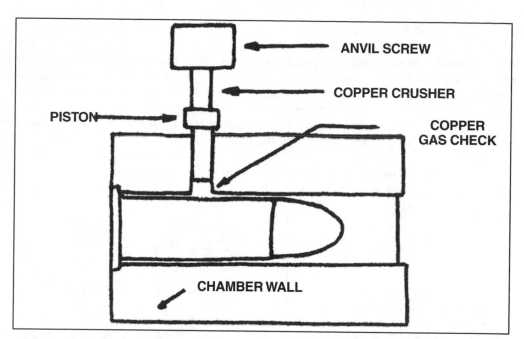

This is a drawing of a simplified crusher-type pressure gun used for measuring pressure. Pure copper and lead slugs are compressed to determine peak pressures on firing.

Diagram labels: ANVIL SCREW, COPPER CRUSHER, COPPER GAS CHECK, PISTON, CHAMBER WALL

bullet, which is more easily engraved. Finally, there is the fit of the bullet in the bore. A tight fit offers more resistance than a loose fit where gas may blow by an undersize bullet that will not obturate the bore properly. A bullet seated too deeply–below the shoulder of a bottlenecked case–particularly a lead-alloy bullet, will often expand in the case and be swaged down as it passes into the neck. This will raise pressures and degrade accuracy.

Instrumental Measurement of Pressure

Until the middle of the 19th century, the only way to test for maximum pressures was to keep increasing powder charges until the test gun blew up. It was thus assumed, at times erroneously, that similar guns would blow up with the same charge. Artillery designer Thomas Rodman developed one of the first pressure testing devices used in the U.S., in 1861. It consisted of boring a hole in a gun chamber and inserting a rod with a chisel point on the other end. A copper plate was affixed to the barrel above the chisel blade. After the gun was fired, the plate was compared to similar plates marked with chisel indentations made by known amounts of force. A year earlier, in England, Sir Andrew Noble developed a more refined device featuring a piston that fit tightly in a hole drilled in a chamber wall. A frame secured to the barrel held an anvil above the opposite end of the piston. Between the piston and the anvil, a small copper cylinder was placed. When the gun was fired, the cylinder was compressed and later compared to similar cylinders compressed by known degrees of force. The accuracy of this system depends on keeping the purity and hardness of the copper cylinders, called crushers, consistent. Calculations are affected by whether the cartridge case is first drilled, or the force needed to blow a hole in the case is factored in. Sharp pressure rises are more easily registered than more gradual ones. For shotgun ammunition, some handgun ammunition and rimfire ammunition that generate relatively low pressures, a lead cylinder is used instead of copper.

Measurements taken in this manner are expressed as copper units of pressure (CUP) or lead units of pressure (LUP). For the handloader, these can be interpreted as pounds per square inch (psi), the LUP, CUP designation simply indicating the means by which the measurement was taken.

More sophisticated systems of pressure measurement developed in this century consist of electronic transducer systems. These are of two types—piezoelectric and strain gage (yes, that's how it's spelled). The piezoelectric system, perfected in the mid-1930s, uses a quartz crystal in place of the copper cylinder, which is in a sealed tube with a diaphragm in the interior of the chamber wall. When subjected to pressure, the crystal generates electrical current in direct proportion to the amount of pressure applied. The advantage of such a system is a quick and relatively easy electronic readout and the reusability of the crystal. Disadvantages are calibration of equipment and crystals changing their value or varying in value.

The strain gage system derives pressure readings from implied information rather than direct. The device consists of a thin wire placed on the exterior surface of the chamber or around it. When the gun is fired, the chamber swells to a degree before returning to its original size, thus stretching the wire. The increased resistance in electrical conductivity of the stretched (thinner) wire during the firing sequence indicates pressure through the amount of stretch. Calibration is determined by measurement of inside and outside chamber diameters. Of the three systems, this one is of most interest to handloaders, since it is the only one that is nondestructive, in terms of not having to bore a hole in a gun chamber, and is available for home use. Such a device is the Personal Ballistics Laboratory Model 43 available from Oehler Research.

Visible Signs of Pressure

For most handloaders these are the most critical indicators of something being wrong. They are also by far the most unreliable and imprecise. There is no way to estimate pressure from observation or even physical measurement of cartridge cases or primers. Nevertheless, these components can warn of pressures that are in the danger zone.

As indicated in the previous chapter, case failures may have a number of causes, and sorting out the problem is often difficult. The only sensible way to determine whether your reloads may be too hot is to eliminate as many variables as possible, thus leaving only those cartridge anomalies caused by excessive pressure or excessive headspace. These two problems produce similar appearing but different effects. What makes them difficult to differentiate is that any problems of excessive headspace are exacerbated by high pressure! Hard case extraction is a definite sign of high pressure unless you are dealing with an oversize or very rough chamber, which is generally something you can determine by looking into it. If your handload is more difficult to extract than a factory load of the same make, this tells

These three 44 Magnum cartridges were fired under the same conditions with the pressure measured by a copper crusher. Left to right: 31,800 CUP, 39,000 CUP, and 47,700 CUP. As can be seen, there is no discernible difference! *(Photo courtesy Speer.)*

The cratered primer *(center)* appears at first glance to be evidence of excessive pressure. The actual cause was an oversize firing pin hole and a soft primer.

Was the flat primer on the left a result of high pressure or being too soft? The answer is likely high pressure since the case head also flowed into the extractor groove *(circled)*.

A pierced or "blown" primer can be caused by excessive pressure or a firing pin that is too long or too sharp. *(Photo courtesy Speer.)*

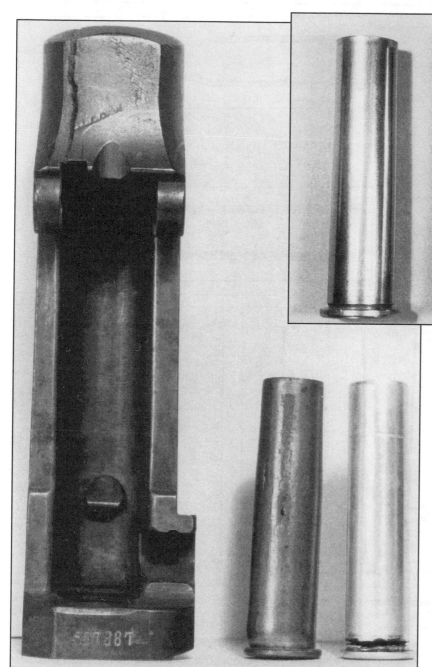

Above) **Definite signs of high pressure are obvious on these 45-70 cases. On the left is an unfired case. The center case was fired with a charge of 68 grains of IMR SR4759 powder—a 174 percent overload of the maximum loading (39 grains) for this powder with a 405-grain bullet. The barrel was bulged by this event, and the case had to be driven out with a rod. The case on the right was fired with 40 grains of Unique behind a 500-grain cast bullet. The maximum load for this bullet is 14.8 grains. This represents more than a 270 percent overload. The barrel of the gun was bulged to the point the receiver cracked. The case required considerable pounding with a hammer and a metal rod to remove it. Note the expansion in front of the solid head and stretching of the case.**

A case-head separation is the worst event, with high pressure gas blowing back into the action and often into the face of the shooter. This is why you always wear shooting glasses. The old balloon-head case on the left, combined with a double charge, cracked the rifle receiver. The case on the right suffered a nearly complete separation because of mercuric priming.

you that you have exceeded the elastic limit of the case and you are generating significantly higher pressures. A second way to check this is to take a micrometer measurement of the case-body diameter of a factory-loaded case after firing, and a handload using the same make of case after firing it for the first time. A larger diameter will indicate higher pressure than the factory load.

The flattening of primers is a sign of high pressure. However, many high-pressure rifle cartridges will show a good deal of flattening as a matter of course. Again, the critical factor is the difference between the flattening of a factory load and a handload using the same components fired for the first time. If the flattening is greater, you are getting higher pressure than the factory round and are in the upper limit of the margin of safety for your particular gun. Most factory loads are near the maximum. This information is based on the "all other things being equal" premise. Whenever you suspect something is wrong, make sure all other things are equal and you are not introducing some factor that will alter your results. Getting oil or other lubricants on cartridge cases is part of the reloading process. This should be removed before firing. Oil in a chamber or on a case will cause the case to slide in the chamber instead of expanding and sticking to the chamber wall during firing. This causes excessive back thrust of the case against the bolt. Back thrust batters the case head, often transferring impressions of machining on the bolt face to the case head. These appear, to the untrained eye, to be caused by high pressure. Battering the bolt face will also–sooner than later–increase the headspace in the gun, which is a serious problem.

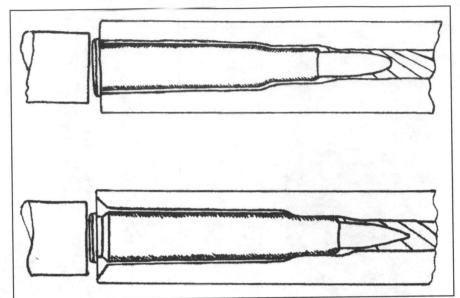

Headspace is measured between the face of the bolt and the front edge of the rim where it touches the breech on any rimmed case *(top)*. Headspace on a rimless case is measured between the bolt face and the point where the case shoulder or the case mouth contacts the chamber.

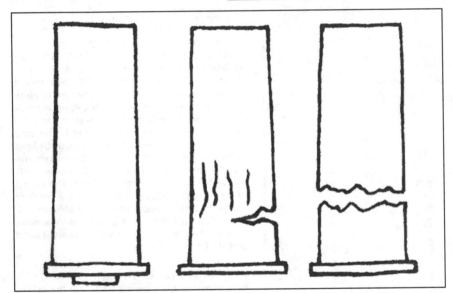

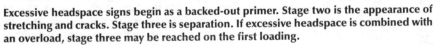

Excessive headspace signs begin as a backed-out primer. Stage two is the appearance of stretching and cracks. Stage three is separation. If excessive headspace is combined with an overload, stage three may be reached on the first loading.

Stretch marks and the crack on this case are indicative of excessive headspace. *(Photo courtesy Speer.)*

The puncturing of primers—a so-called "blown primer" where a hole is blown through the primer where the firing pin hits it—is a definite sign of very high pressure, unless you have a firing pin that is too long. Firing pins do not suddenly grow longer. Stop shooting! Before a primer blows, under pressure, there will be evidence of primers "cratering." This is where the metal in the primer flows back around the tip of the firing pin and into the hole where the pin comes through the bolt or breechblock. Cratering can also be caused by a soft primer and an oversize firing pin hole. Here again, a comparison with a fired factory round with the same components is the best way to judge differences.

Gas leaks around primers make a black soot smudge at their edges, and may be a sign of high pressure or an enlarged primer pocket. Primer pocket stretching in a case will occur after a number of loadings, particularly high pressure ones. This tells you the case is finished for reload-ing. If a leak occurs after long use, this can be assumed to be normal. When such a leak happens the first time with a new case, look for other high-pressure signs. Hard extraction, flattened or cratered primers, blown or leaky primers most often occur together.

Soot-streaking of cases when they are fired, particularly staining near the case mouth, is a sign not of high pressure, but of its opposite: low pressure. If a loading is not generating enough pressure to make a complete gas seal between the cartridge case and the chamber wall, a certain amount of gas will leak back into the chamber and smudge the case. Other than being a minor nuisance this causes no danger. It is an indication that combustion is at too low a level, owing to not enough powder or poor ignition of the powder. Such underpowered loads will tend to be inaccurate since the amount of gas that escapes will vary from shot to shot, depending on the elasticity of the individual case.

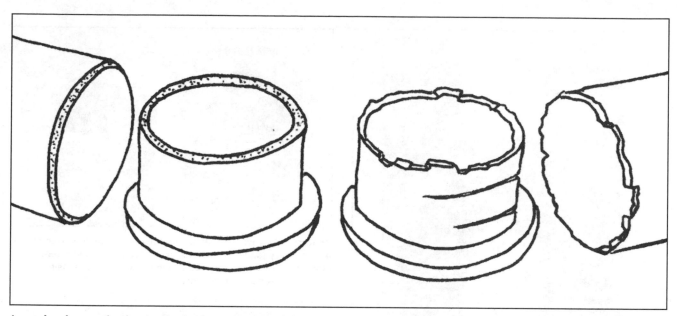

A case head separation has two basic causes. Type one is brass failure, often caused by mercuric priming contamination of brass that is otherwise weak and brittle. Type two is excessive headspace in the gun. These result in different types of fractures. Type one *(left)* is a clean break with a crystalline surface. Type two is characterized by tearing of the metal and stretch marks on the case.

Understanding Headspace

In order for a cartridge to enter and exit a gun chamber it has to be made a little smaller than the chamber, with enough room for easy extraction after it is fired. To work properly, however, the case must be firmly supported by the bolt or breechblock to keep it from rupturing under pressure. The amount of tolerance between the head of the case and the face of the bolt or breechblock is less than 0.005-inch in a good modern gun. Zero tolerance would be best, but guns and ammunition are mass-produced products and a certain amount of tolerance must be permitted for variations that are part of the manufacturing process. A tolerance of several thousandths of an inch represents the elastic limits of the cartridge case, allowing the fired case to return to close to its original size for extraction. If the tolerance is greater, the elastic limits of the case are exceeded and it will begin to deform or even rupture. This situation is known as excessive headspace.

Tolerances for headspace are set at the factory and remain in place for the life of a gun. That life is shortened by shooting high-pressure loads which batter the bolt or breechblock, gradually increasing the headspace. This problem can be corrected by a skilled gunsmith, depending on the type of gun and how bad the situation has become.

Calculating Headspace

Headspace is measured with gauges to .001-inch. In a rimmed or semi-rimmed case, the headspace measurement is between the surface of the bolt or breechblock and the point where the front of the cartridge rim makes contact with the face of the breech. With rimless cases, the measurement is between the bolt face and the point where the shoulder of the case makes contact with the counterbore in the chamber. For straight rimless cases such as the 45 ACP, the measurement is to the point where the case mouth makes contact with the front of the chamber.

Excessive Headspace

This is when the tolerances are too great. When this situation occurs, the cartridge case is held tightly forward against the chamber walls upon firing. With the case head unsupported by the bolt or breechblock, the case stretches backward under the force of the pressure inside it, until it makes contact with the bolt face and stops. Usually before this happens, the primer is pushed out of its pocket until it meets the bolt face. As pressure drops in the chamber, the case springs back and creeps back over the primer, often jamming the now-expanded primer back into the pocket. On examination, the flattened primer will appear for all the world like an example of high pressure. The reloader should make sure he has not loaded a maximum load. If this was a max load, he should try a factory cartridge for comparison. If the problem is excessive headspace the signs should be there with normal loads, and they may appear even with reduced loads although somewhat less obvious. Often, the only sign will be a primer backed out of the case.

After a case is stretched in an overly long chamber, is resized, reloaded and fired, the stretching process is repeated with the next firing. Stretch marks, in the form of shiny rings, begin to appear around the circumference of the case body forward of the head. After a number of reloadings, depending on how much stretching and resizing occurs, the case will become fatigued and rupture, blowing high-pressure gas back into the action. This often destroys the gun, and injures the face of the shooter. A combination of poor brass, a heavy load and a lot of extra headspace can bring on this condition in a single shot. Headspace problems can be created in the reloading process.

This occurs with rimless cases such as the 30-06 and 223

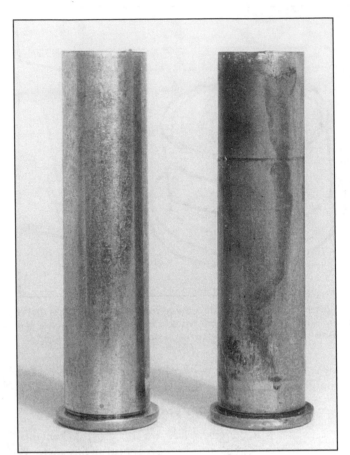

Low pressure is evidenced by the soot stains on the case on the right, which failed to make a complete gas seal when fired.

Primer pockets will stretch, as did the one on the left after a number of heavy loads. If the leak or stretch appears suddenly on a new or nearly new case, you are in the very high pressure range and should reduce your loads.

A leak around a primer indicates an expanded primer pocket. Time to discard the case.

Soft alloy bullets of lead and tin (the shiny ones on the ends) will yield lower pressures than harder alloy bullets. Jacketed bullets (third from right) create significantly higher pressures, as do heavier bullets.

where improper use of the sizing die forces the shoulder back on the case body, allowing the case to go further into the chamber than it should. The extractor hook will hold the case in the proper position for firing, but the case has now become too short and has to stretch back to meet the bolt face. If this practice is continued, it is only a matter of time until a rupture occurs with all the grief that goes with it. Any gun showing signs of excessive headspace should not be fired. Examination by a skilled gunsmith will tell you if the situation can be corrected.

Over the years,
ignition of the
powder charge
has been
accomplished in
a number of
ways. Today, big
things come from
small packages.

Primers

THE PURPOSE OF the primer is to ignite the main powder charge. This was originally done with a burning splinter or hot wire jammed into a small touchhole at the breech of the gun. Later, a smoldering rope or sparks from iron pyrites and flint striking steel were employed to set off a small charge of powder in a funnel that connected with the main charge in the gun barrel. These systems worked, but they didn't work well, which prompted a search for an ignition system that fulfilled the four criteria of today's modern primers, namely: speed, reliability, uniformity and cleanliness.

Primer Evolution

Early ignition systems failed in all the above criteria. Matchlocks were equipped with a smoldering fuse made of chemically treated rope, called a "match," which would burn out in damp weather and could be blown out by wind. With flintlocks, wind could blow the priming charge out of the pan, and wet, damp weather would saturate it with moisture to the

Modern percussion caps are essentially a primer without an anvil inside it, that part being provided by the nipple on the gun.

(Below) **Berdan** (left) and Boxer primer pockets show the differences in the systems. The ease of reloading made the Boxer primer standard in the U.S. (Photo courtesy CCI.)

point where it would not fire. Rust and powder fouling in the touchhole that connected the pan charge to the propelling charge in the barrel often prevented a successful firing, with only the priming charge burning. The expression, "a flash in the pan," is still used to describe a person or enterprise that shows promise, but fails to get past a good beginning. The flintlock system gave only reasonable reliability. A small piece of flint held in the jaws of the "hammer" (called the cock) struck a steel cover on the pan called the frizzen, knocking it open and scraping the inner side to throw sparks into the powder charge in the pan. In terms of speed it was slow. Anyone who has seen a flintlock fired is familiar with the *puff-boom!* report as the priming charge burns with a one-beat pause before the propelling charge fires. History is filled with untold numbers of targets, animal and human, who have ducked to safety during that beat—which was sometimes two beats if the day was damp and the touchhole a bit clogged.

Explosives such as fulminate of mercury and mixtures including potassium chlorate, that detonated when crushed or struck, were discovered late in the 18th century. After attempts to use them as substitutes for gunpowder failed, they received little attention until the early 19th century.

The breakthrough to improved ignition was made by a Scottish Presbyterian minister, hunter, shooter and gun buff—Reverend Alexander Forsythe. He was the first to come up with the idea of using these detonating explosives to ignite propelling charges in firearms. He received a patent in 1807 for a system that did away with the priming pan on the flintlock. This design filled the tube leading to the barrel with a percussion explosive made of sulphur, potassium chlorate and charcoal. A metal pin was inserted on top of the explosive that caused it to detonate when struck by the gun's hammer. The ignition was far faster and more certain than the flintlock. Forsythe improved his design by attaching a small iron bottle containing a supply of percussion explosive to the side of the lock. The bottle could be tipped or turned to deposit a small pellet of explosive on a touchhole, which would be struck by the hammer. The system worked effectively. However, it involved having a small iron bottle filled with high explosive very close to the firing point and to the face of the shooter. There are no reports of accidents with a Forsythe lock, but if one happened, it would almost certainly have been fatal.

The superiority of the Forsythe system was soon recognized and dozens of variations were introduced, including percussion wafers, tubes and strips of paper caps, much like those used in toy cap pistols of today. The most successful was the percussion cap, invented in about 1814 by Joshua Shaw, a British subject who immigrated to America. Shaw's system featured a small steel tube, closed at one end, about the size of a modern large pistol primer. The closed end contained the explosive held in place by a tinfoil cover, then sealed with a drop of lacquer. This made it waterproof as well as damp-proof. The cap was fitted on a short iron nipple, hollow in the center, which allowed the fire to enter the chamber of the gun. Shaw caps were on the market by 1821 and were soon adapted to sporting guns. Improvements were made by changing the cap metal to pewter and later copper. Similar caps were in use about the same time over most of Europe. The percussion cap was not adopted by the U.S. military until after the Mexican War. The military thinking at the time was that the percussion cap was yet another component the soldier had to carry and not reusable in the manner of a gun flint.

Percussion caps made the Colt revolver a practical reality, but the shortcomings of this system became apparent when repeating rifles were made using this system. A cylinder "flash over" from one chamber to the next would occasionally send a bullet coasting by the side of the gun.

Early tong reloading tools could be carried in the pocket or saddlebag. These in 32-20 (top) and 38-40 WCF from the old Ideal Company cast bullets, decapped, primed and seated bullets in blackpowder calibers.

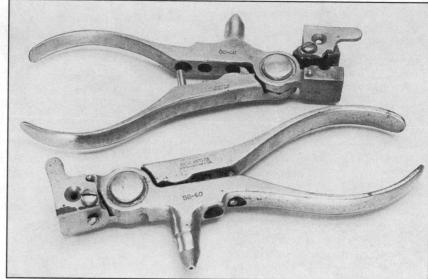

(Below) The Lee Hand Press Kit is a modern version of the old Ideal tong tool. The kit includes dies, case lube, powder dipper, etc.

With a handgun this was of little consequence since it was a one-hand weapon. With the revolving rifle such an event often amputated the fingers or thumb of the hand supporting the forend of the weapon. Revolving rifles did not gain much popularity.

Not surprisingly, the first really successful breechloaders and successful repeating arms, other than revolvers, required a self-contained, self-primed cartridge. There were a number of important steps between the percussion cap and the rimfire cartridge, but to list them here is not our mission. Suffice it to say there was a fairly logical evolution. In brief, George Morse placed a percussion cap in the head of a metal cartridge using a hairpin-shaped anvil inside the case to fire it. Hiram Berdan shortened the hairpin to a tiny knob, while Edward Boxer placed a tiny anvil inside the cap.

Center Primed

Centerfire ammunition soon eclipsed the rimfire and all the other non-reloadable types because it was reloadable. Rimfires were gradually reduced to those types that were so small that the cartridge would not lend itself to reloading. The military had great influence in ammunition development, stipulating that any ammunition developed for a

military small arm had to be reloadable. Spent cases were collected and returned to a government arsenal for reloading during peacetime. Professional hunters in the American West needed cartridges they could reload themselves with simple tools. It was this type of equipment that first appeared in the 1870s.

Early priming mixtures used fulminate of mercury or potassium chlorate, occasionally a combination of both. These fulfilled most of the criteria for good ignition: speed, reliability, uniformity, and cleanliness to some extent. While the chlorate-based primers and caps did not leave an appreciable residue, they did leave a highly corrosive deposit-potassium chloride-that would eat away a percussion nipple or the web of a cartridge. This needed to be neutralized by cleaning the gun with water that removed the salt deposit. The mercury-based compounds were both clean and non-corrosive. Their drawback came when used in combination with brass or copper primer cups and cartridge cases. When fired, the mercury would amalgamate with the copper or brass making it extremely brittle. Reloading and firing such a contaminated cartridge case can lead to a case-head rupture. In a high-pressure loading, this can wreck a gun and possibly your face. Mercuric priming was gone from commercial ammunition by about 1945, but primers made prior to this time were used by commercial reloaders for a number of years later.

Because fulminate of mercury contains free, liquid mercury, this mercury will actually migrate through the priming mixture and into the metal of the primer cup or cartridge head after a certain number of years. Ammunition primed with mercuric mixtures made in the early 1930s will probably not fire today. However, ammunition loaded with chlorate priming made during the Civil War is often still viable, so long as neither the powder nor the priming compound has been exposed to moisture. Thus, a fifth criterion should be added—long life.

From the late '20s through the mid-1930s, American

Pistol and rifle primers come in two sizes, while shotshell primers are of one size.

(Below) Pistol primers should not be used in rifle cases since they will seat too deeply, as in the case on the left. The center case shows proper seating depth, while the high primer on the right will give poor ignition and possibly slam-fire in an autoloader.

manufacturers worked to perfect a priming mixture, akin to one developed in Germany, which was non-corrosive and did not contain mercury. The basis of such priming is in compounds of lead, barium and antimony.

Early non-corrosive, non-mercuric primers did not work very well, giving uneven ignition. Priming material often fell out of the rim in rimfire cartridges as the binding material–a vegetable-based glue–deteriorated.

The Modern Primer

Modern primers of the lead, barium and antimony type fulfill all the necessary criteria for good ignition. The binders are now stable and remain so for long periods under normal "house" storage conditions, where temperatures are under 125 degrees Fahrenheit and moisture is kept at a reasonable level. The newest are the "lead free" primers of tetracene. These, however, are not presently sold as reloading components since the production demand is for use in finished ammunition. The primary use of such primers is in handgun ammunition to be fired in indoor ranges where airborne lead could present a health hazard.

Because of the difficulty of reloading them, cartridges using Berdan primers and the Berdan primers themselves have virtually disappeared from the U.S. Foreign cartridges often still use this type of priming and can only be reloaded with Berdan primers. Any attempt to convert Berdan cases to Boxer priming by drilling them in some manner will not work. Such attempts are very dangerous since they will greatly enlarge the flashhole and may damage the web. At best, such conversions give uneven ignition, at worst they can raise pressures to dangerous levels by causing too rapid a burn of the powder charge. The only current source for Berdan primers and Berdan decapping equipment is The Old Western Scrounger.

A modern Boxer primer differs little in structure from those made over a century ago. It is a brass cup containing the priming compound. A paper seal keeps the compound

in the cup and is held in place by the metal anvil made of harder brass. A better understanding of metallurgy and chemistry has resulted in a more uniform primer as well as ones that are specifically tailored to a particular type of cartridge.

Primers for pistols and rifles come in two basic sizes of Small (.175-inch) and Large (.210-inch). There also is a .317-inch primer made by CCI and used only in the 50 Browning machinegun cartridge. Small pistol primers are used in such rounds as 25- and 32-caliber handgun ammunition, while the large size is used in 41-, 44- and 45-caliber handguns. Large pistol primers are also made in a magnum variant, for use in large capacity cases using hard-to-ignite, slow-burning powders. These require a longer, hotter flame for uniform and complete burning.

Rifle primers are made in the same two diameters as pistol primers, and are designated Small and Large. They are slightly higher to fit the deeper pocket in the rifle cartridge case. For this reason, pistol primers should not be seated in rifle cases since they will seat too deeply and often give uneven ignition. Rifle primers contain more priming compound than pistol primers since they have to ignite more powder in larger capacity cases.

If you are loading both handgun and rifle ammunition, care must be taken not to mix rifle and handgun primers. If rifle primers are seated in pistol cases they will not fit

The RCBS APS primer feeder uses plastic strips instead of the conventional stacking tube, reducing the hazard of sympathetic detonation. *(Photo courtesy RCBS.)*

(Left and above) **Primers are sold preloaded in strips, but the strips can be refilled with the RCBS loading tool. You have to buy the system.** *(Photos courtesy RCBS)*

properly. They can also raise pressures to the danger point. Pistol primers tend to burn cooler, and produce more of a flame-type of explosion—good for igniting fast-burning pistol powders. Rifle primers burn longer and hotter. They often contain metallic elements such as aluminum, which act as burning sparks that are blown forward into a charge of slower-burning powder. This separates the grains, igniting them in a number of places at once, to achieve an even burning of the charge. This explosive quality is known as brisance. Magnum rifle primers have still more compound, burn longer and hotter and are used in very large-capacity cases such as the 458 Winchester Magnum. Companies such as CCI also market a benchrest rifle primer. This is simply a standard rifle primer, but made to very strict tolerances, assuring the reloader that each primer in a given lot will have a very precisely measured amount of compound, and that the diameter and hardness of all components are within very strict tolerances. These premium-quality primers give very even ignition needed for the exacting demands of the expert competition target shooter.

Shotshell primers have special characteristics needed to work properly in modern plastic shotshells. Early shotshells were made of brass and were generally of rifle-type of construction. They used rifle-style primers. Modern shells are of a composite construction with a metal head surrounding a paper, now primarily a plastic body. Inside is a base wad made of plastic or compressed paper.

Shotshells have unique ignition problems. As the mouth of the shell becomes worn and softened with repeated firing and reloading, the opening of the crimp becomes progressively easier. Modern shotgun powders require a certain amount of pressure and confinement to function properly. This decreases as the crimp softens. For proper ignition, the powder requires a very high temperature over a longer than usual burn time, but without the brisant quality of the magnum rifle powder which would tend to blow the crimp open before much of the powder was ignited. A shotshell primer produces what is often referred to as a "soft ignition."

Because of the design of modern shotshells, the primer is held in a large, longer-than-normal housing called a battery cup. This extends well into the base wad so the flame issuing from the primer mouth will not be inhibited by any part of the wad and can direct its full blast into the powder charge.

Handling and Storage

Primers are the most dangerous component in the reloading operation. They are subject to shock and explode with a violence that belies their small size. Children often have a penchant for playing with small shiny objects and primers should definitely be kept out of their hands. Primers are packaged to keep them from shock and from striking one another. Julian Hatcher, in his *Notebook*, tells of a young worker in an ammunition plant carrying a metal bucket of primers, casually bouncing it as he walked. There was a sudden, violent explosion. A part of a foot was the largest piece recovered.

Primers should only be stored in the original packaging, never in a can or bottle where they can rattle around. Automatic primer feeding devices of a tube design should be loaded with great care, because this brings a considerable number together in way that if one accidentally explodes, the remainder will go too. The explosive force of a primer is many, many times that of the most powerful smokeless powder.

Properly stored, primers do not present a particularly dangerous hazard. They will pop quite loudly if thrown in a fire, and come flying with enough force to penetrate a cardboard carton a foot or more away. People have lost eyesight from such injuries, so this is not the way to dispose of damaged, though unexploded, primers. Perhaps the best method is to load them in an empty cartridge case and snap them. If this is not possible, they can be deactivated by soaking in a strong lye solution for a week. The liquid may be flushed away with a large quantity of water. The potassium chlorate in the old corrosive primers is very water-soluble and water soaking works well with this type. We are talking here about small numbers of primers, not more than two dozen. If for some reason you should have to dispose of a large number of primers, call your local gun shop to see if they can use them.

Shelf storage should be in a cool dry place, away from containers of gunpowder and away from children's reach. To avoid an explosion hazard in case of fire, primers should not be stored in a closed heavy metal container such as a military ammunition can.

The lacquer seals used in modern primers keeps them free of deterioration from dampness, but basement storage is not recommended for any ammunition component unless that basement is kept dry with a dehumidifier. About the

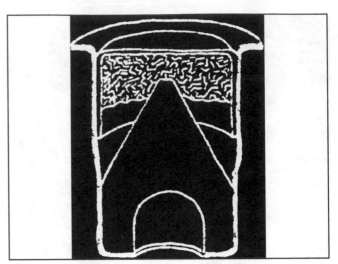

The shotshell battery cup primer comes with the primer pocket and vent as part of the unit, all of which is replaced when the shell is reprimed.

only uniquely vulnerable feature about primers is the paper seal, which could be attacked by molds under extremely damp conditions.

Three questions are frequently asked by shooters of military, foreign, and obsolete guns: (1) How can you determine if the military ammunition you are planning to shoot and reload is Berdan primed? (2) How can you determine which ammunition is corrosively primed? (3) How can you tell if a case has been contaminated by mercuric primers?

The answer to the first is fairly simple–usually. The Berdan primers are almost always of a larger diameter than the equivalent Boxer primers, although the CCI primer used in their non-reloadable Blazer ammunition is virtually the same size. Most foreign military primers are the Berdan type and are usually larger. The surest way to know is to examine a fired cartridge case and look into the case for the small twin vents that are the trademark of this system. This is not possible when buying ammunition. About the best you can do is ask the dealer if the stuff is Boxer-primed or not, and get a guarantee that if it isn't, he will take the unfired portion back.

Determining which ammunition has corrosive priming is a little more complicated. Corrosive priming was a serious problem in the early days of smokeless powder ammunition, since corrosive salts were deposited in large quantities in the barrels of guns that fired it. Blackpowder fouling, while corrosive to a degree, helped to hold these salts and the fouling was relatively easy to clean with a soap and warm water mixture. After cleaning, the bore was wiped dry and then oiled to protect it. With the introduction of smokeless powder, there was very little powder fouling in the bore. Jacketed bullets moving at high velocities left a hard metallic deposit composed of copper and nickel from the jackets. This was difficult to remove and trapped the corrosive salt (potassium chloride) in a layer between the barrel surface and the metal fouling. A barrel could appear perfectly clean but, days later, even though the bore was saturated with oil or grease, it would rust heavily under this protective coating.

Crystal Cleaner was an ammonia-based metal solvent offered by Winchester in the early days of corrosive priming. The U.S. military bore cleaner in the old dark green can combined ammonia and powder solvent in a brown, evil-smelling liquid. It did/does a good job of removing corrosive primer residue and metal fouling.

To combat this problem, cleaning solvents were developed that would dissolve this metal fouling and remove the salts from the corrosive priming. Most of these solvents contained ammonia, which readily dissolves copper and nickel. A water-based solution of ammonia does a very good job of removing both metal fouling and primer salts. Years ago, after firing a lot of corrosive ammunition, one shooter removed fouling by corking the chamber of a 303 Enfield with a rubber stopper and carefully filling the bore with household ammonia, then letting it stand for an hour or so. The dissolved salts and copper fouling were removed when the barrel was tipped. The fouling was obvious in the blue-green tint it gave to the ammonia solution. After dumping the liquid, a couple of wet patches were run through the bore, then a couple of dry patches, and the bore was swabbed with Hoppe's No. 9 solvent until everything came clean. Care had to be taken not to spill ammonia on any blued surface since it will remove the blue. He was also careful not to leave the solution too long, or worse let it dry, on any exposed steel surface since it will readily rust that surface.

Commercial solvents with ammonia, bearing names like "Chlor oil," "Fiend oil" and "Crystal Cleaner" were once marketed for cleaning up corrosive priming. They have been gone from the scene so long that few people remember their names. The U.S. military came up with its own preparation called, simply, "Bore Cleaner." This was a dark brown

CORROSIVE/NON-CORROSIVE PRIMING: U.S. MILITARY AMMUNITION
(U.S.- and Canadian-manufactured ammunition)

Headstamp	Mfr.	Changeover Date	Non-Corr. Headstamp
FA	Frankford	Oct 1951 (30)	FA 52-
		July 1954 (45)	FA 55-
DEN	Denver	All corrosive during WWII	
DM	Des Moines	All corrosive during WWII	
EC	Eau Claire	All corrosive during WWII	
LC	Lake City	June 1951 (30)	LC 52
		April 1952 (30 AP)	LC 53
SL	St. Louis	May 1952 (30)	SL 53
		July 1952 (30 AP)	SL 53
TW	Twin Cities	Dec 1950 (30)	TW 51
		Feb 1952 (30 AP)	TW 53
U and UT	Utah	All corrosive during WWII	
DAQ	Dominion (Canada)	All noncorrosive	
VC	Verdun (Canada)	All noncorrosive	
FCC	Federal	Nov 1953 (45)	FC 54-
RA	Remington	Nov 1951 (30)	RA 52-
		Sept 1952 (45)	RA 53-
WCC	Western	June 1951 (30)	WCC 52-
		Nov 1952 (45)	WCC 53-
WRA	Winchester	Aug 1951 (30)	WRA 52-
		June 1954 (30 AP)	WRA 53-
		Nov 1951 (45)	WRA 52-

All 223 (5.56mm), 30 Carbine, 308 (7.62mm), 9mm Luger and 38 Special military ammunition is non-corrosive. Exceptions are the 1956 NATO 308 Match ammunition made at the Frankford Arsenal and 30-06 Match ammunition made at the Frankford Arsenal in 1953, 1954 and 1956. All are stamped FA with the two-digit date. (This information was adapted from the NRA *Handloader's Guide*.)

(Above and below) Military ammunition generally has the primer swaged in the case with a primer crimp, which makes first-time removal a little difficult. Once the crimp is removed, however, there is no further problem.

concoction with a smell you will never forget, (although you wish you could) that combined ammonia with water-soluble oil and powder solvents. Bad as it smelled, it worked quite well.

Corrosive priming was gone from commercial ammunition by the 1930s. In the early 1950s, non-corrosive priming gradually replaced the corrosive type in U.S. military ammunition. A decade or so later, the Army switched to a newer type of bore cleaner which is sold commercially under the name "Break Free." By this time most shooters had forgotten about corrosive-primed ammunition. Today's cleaners do a fine job of removing powder fouling and preventing rust from external causes, but they do not remove corrosive potassium salt. This must be removed with a water-based cleaner since salt does not dissolve in oil.

With the importation of Russian and Chinese Tokarev, Moisin-Nagant, SKS and AKM rifles and ammunition, corrosive priming is back on the American scene. Most of the current powder solvents are ineffective in removing the corrosive salt. Probably the best way to deal with this is to get some of the old Army bore cleaner and clean with that. It is still available at many gun shops, gun shows and military-surplus outlets. Another option is to use one of the solvents that remove copper fouling. After cleaning with that, run several wet patches then dry patches until the bore is clean; then oil with a good protective oil or grease with rust inhibitors.

Identifying corrosive-primed American military ammunition is an easy matter of consulting the nearby list that was compiled by the NRA several years ago. When it comes to foreign ammunition, unless it is in the original box from a commercial manufacturer and clearly marked "Non-corrosive," assume it is corrosive, particularly if it is military ammunition, especially that from any former East Bloc country. If you wish to experiment, collect some fired cases and place them outdoors for a week or two in warm humid weather, or place them on their heads with a drop or two of water in each and let them stand over night. If corrosive salt

is present, there will usually be evidence of corrosion inside the case particularly near the vent, especially if that case is made of steel.

The question of mercuric priming is best dealt with on the basis of: If the ammunition or cases are pre-WWII and not corrosive-primed, they are likely mercuric-primed. If the ammunition is in the original box and the box declares it to be "non-corrosive, non-mercuric," and it's in good (appearing) condition, it's probably good to shoot. Keep in mind that if the old non-mercuric primers are no good, the bullets can be pulled and the cartridges can be reloaded, if you think it's worth the effort.

Oftentimes batches of old fired cases turn up and the shooter has no idea whether they are usable. If the caliber is something currently available, don't bother. The knotty problem is when such a batch turns up in some obsolete caliber, and you have one of those rifles and nothing to shoot in it. Converting some other cartridge to these is very difficult. Loaded new ammunition in these old calibers is sometimes available from companies like The Old Western Scrounger, but at considerable prices. Even at high prices, a batch of old cases might be a bargain, if they are in good condition and all the same make. If there is heavy tarnish and season cracking, forget it. If they have a scaly appearance or are stretched, bulged or otherwise show damage or distortion, forget it. This leaves the possibility of mercury contamination, which leaves no visible evidence. The only test to make the determination of mercury contamination comes from *Handloader's Manual* by Earl Naramore, published in 1937. Naramore states that you must sacrifice a case for testing. It must be carefully sectioned with a fine hacksaw. After sectioning, the cut surface it should be filed with a fine metal file to remove the saw marks, then polished on a piece of fine emery paper or crocus cloth. The polished case is then submerged for a few seconds in a 20 percent solution of nitric acid until the polished surface takes on a dull or slightly roughened appearance. Leaving the case in the bath too long will pit the surface.

After the case is properly etched, the walls can be examined with a magnifying glass for flaws in the metal. The case should be removed from the etching bath with a pair of tweezers and washed in clear water. States Naramore: "The action of the nitric acid will clean the fouling from the inside of the case thoroughly and if the surface has a silvery appearance, it is a sure indication that the case has been fired with a mercuric primer. This silver-looking coating, which is really mercury, will disappear into the brass after the specimen has stood a little while, so the condition should be looked for immediately after taking the case out of the etching solution. Unfortunately the failure of the mercury to appear does not offer assurance that the case has never been fired with a mercuric primer, but the mercury will usually show up." Naramore goes on to urge the reloader to examine the etched case for cracks or splits in the head, which can usually be seen with the unaided eye or with a magnifying glass.

Primer crimps are easily removed with this handy tool (and others), which also swages the primer pockets to uniform size.

Once you pop
the primer, you
need to fuel
the fire, and
propellants come
in many types,
shapes and sizes.

Powders

GUNPOWDER IS THE driving force that makes a gun shoot. It does this by changing from a solid to a large volume of hot gas in a very short time in what is best termed a low-velocity explosion. This works very well for propelling bullets down gun barrels without raising the pressure too suddenly, which would cause the barrel to burst before the bullet gets moving. High velocity or "high" explosives are unsuitable for use in guns for this reason.

Blackpowder and Its Variants

The original "gunpowder" is what is now referred to as "Blackpowder," and is actually a dark gray in color. Its origin dates back about a thousand years. All sorts of ingredients have been added at various times, but the basic mixture is composed of potassium nitrate (75 percent), charcoal (15 percent), and sulphur (10 percent). Many people have made blackpowder at home. This practice is not recommended simply because it is dangerous. One mistake can prove disastrous. Such a mistake cost one shooter both hands at the age of fifteen. And he considered himself lucky to still have everything else intact. For those not impressed by danger, it may be added that homemade powder is

American manufacturers and importers offer a wide variety of smokeless powder for reloaders.

never up to the standards of purity and consistency of the manufactured product. The burning rate of blackpowder is determined by the size of the granulation. Very fine powder burns very rapidly and can raise pressures into the danger zone if the improper granulation is used in an otherwise safe load. Some people say you cannot overload a gun with blackpowder. Not true.

Commercial blackpowder is mixed, then ground in a wet state to prevent an explosion. It is pressed into a cake, then granulated and sifted through screens to determine grain size. The grains are coated with graphite for ease in pouring. It is sold in four granulations: FFFFg for priming flintlocks; FFFg for handguns and rifles to 40-caliber; FFg for rifles above 40- to 58-caliber; and Fg for rifles over 58-caliber and large bore shotguns.

Blackpowder has many deficiencies. It produces a great deal of smoke and solid fouling when burned. Better than half the residue is in solid form. While most of this is blown out of the barrel, a heavy, often hard-crusted fouling is produced which will soon degrade accuracy and raise pressures unless the bore is cleaned. Blackpowder target shooters often swab their barrels after every shot to maintain top accuracy. The fouling from blackpowder is corrosive, mainly because it contains sulfuric acid. The other components are hygroscopic, which means they draw and hold water from the atmosphere—the better to rust your gun.

Because of these and other drawbacks, blackpowder was replaced by smokeless powder about a hundred years ago. With the exception of The Old Western Scrounger, no manufacturer in this country offers loaded blackpowder ammunition. Interest in shooting both muzzle-loading and blackpowder cartridge guns is increasing. For this reason, there have been efforts to develop a blackpowder substitute that will work well in the old guns and their modern replicas that will give the same performance, without the problems.

Throughout the 19th century, dozens if not hundreds of blackpowder substitutes were made and sold. Their sterling qualities are evident in the fact that none are around today. Two substitutes presently on the market are Hodgdon's Pyrodex and Triple Seven, and Goex's Clean Shot.

Blackpowder and its variants do not present any unusual problems in storage. They should be kept cool and dry since they are hygroscopic. Never leave powder containers open for any length of time since this will allow moisture to enter. Never shake any can of powder. This tends to break down the granules and alter the burning characteristics. Never have any powder near an open flame or burning cigarette, cigar, or pipe. One spark in the can and you have a very sudden, very hot fire. Always keep powder in the original container. Since blackpowder is a mixture of basic elements, its life span is indefinite. Unexploded cannon shells filled with blackpowder fired during the siege of Quebec in 1759-60, detonated with considerable vigor in the early 1970s after they were discovered during construction.

Smokeless Powder

Development of smokeless powder began in the mid-19th century, with the first really successful type being that developed by Austrian chemist Frederick Volkmann in about 1871. It was made by dissolving wood fiber in nitric acid which was later washed in water to remove the acid, then gelatinized in an ether-alcohol mixture to form a plastic colloid, now known as nitrocellulose. The powder was marketed locally and the Austrian government, in its wisdom, stuck with blackpowder and shut the operation down for not paying proper license fees.

The defining moment in the evolution of smokeless powder came some fifteen years later when the French government switched from a blackpowder single-shot rifle to a high-velocity, 8mm repeater called the Lebel. The small-bore cartridge used a smokeless powder similar to that developed by the French chemist Paul Vieille. Within about two years all of Europe had abandoned blackpowder for military rifles, and every government armed its troops with repeaters using jacketed bullets and smokeless powder. The United States was the last major power to switch to a smokeless powder repeater, when it (reluctantly) gave up the 45-70 Springfield in 1892.

Early smokeless powders were hygroscopic and, if the acid was not completely washed out, would deteriorate. Coatings were later added to make the powder more water-resistant and control burning. The power of smokeless powder was further enhanced by the addition of nitroglycerin. These two types of powder—nitrocellulose and nitrocellulose plus nitroglycerin—are the two basic types manufactured today. They are known respectively as single-base and double-base powders. All smokeless powders are coated with graphite to keep them from caking, allowing them to flow smoothly through powder measures, dippers and funnels.

The outstanding characteristic of smokeless powder is that while it is of two basic types, by changing the size and shape of the granulation the burning characteristics can be varied considerably and controlled to a high degree. This gives smokeless a tremendous advantage over blackpowder, whose burning characteristics could be only roughly controlled.

Smokeless powder varies in granule size from flakes as fine as ground pepper–used in fast-burning pistol powders—to

FFg blackpowder is a fairly coarse-grained propellant. The scale above is 1 inch divided into hundredths.

Hodgdon's Pyrodex is an improved form of blackpowder with cleaner burning characteristics.

finger-size cylinders nearly two inches long for huge naval guns. The burning can be further altered by extruding powder into macaroni-like tubes, allowing them to burn on both the outside and inside at the same time. Spherical forms can be varied to exact size, while adding various chemical coatings can control the burn rate.

Selecting the Right Powder

Modern powders are divided into three basic types on the basis of their use. These are pistol, shotgun, and rifle powders. Pistol powders are generally of the fast-burning double-base type for use in short-barreled guns. Shotgun powders are also fast burning and double-base, designed to burn completely under low pressures. Rifle powders are generally slower burning to accelerate a rifle bullet down a long barrel with maximum velocity while producing minimum pressures.

In point of fact, many powders for pistol use are quite suitable for shotguns and vice versa. Some slower burning pistol and shotgun powders will also work well for reduced velocity rifle loadings, where a light bullet and light powder charge are used.

Before buying a quantity of powder, it is a good idea to consult one or more reloading guides to see what is offered and what looks to be the best selection for your particular gun or guns. Then, buy a small can to develop your loads. If that powder proves suitable for your uses, it's a good idea to go ahead and buy larger amounts.

Storage and Handling

Modern powders are almost completely gelatinized, making them less affected by dampness. In fact, a sample of Laflin & Rand (later Hercules, now Alliant) Unique powder was placed in storage under water in 1899 to test its viability. It

The Old Western Scrounger is the only source of new, factory-made blackpowder ammunition. This lets the history buffs replicate original loads in original guns.

was last tested in 1996. It will be tested again in this century when it is expected to continue performing as well as when it was made.

As smokeless powders deteriorate, they generate small amounts of nitric acid. Stabilizers are added to these powders to absorb acid byproduct. Most powders have fifty or more years of life before the stabilizers are used up and nitric acid begins to leach out of the nitrocellulose, leaving plain cellulose and reducing the efficiency of the powder. Occasionally powder will deteriorate owing to acid residue that was not properly washed out in the manufacturing process. Such powder will take on an unpleasant acidic smell and a brown dust looking very like rust will appear in the powder. Powder in this condition will not shoot well, giving poor ignition and low power. It should be disposed of. Metal cans containing powder will sometimes rust on the interior, producing a very similar-appearing dust, but without the characteristic odor. This does not harm the powder and can be removed by dumping the powder on a flat piece of bed sheet, spreading it evenly, and gently blowing off the dust. The powder should then be placed in another container. An empty plastic powder bottle is good so long as it is clearly marked as to what it is. It is a good idea to mark containers of powder with the date of purchase and then use the oldest first. Opened containers of powder should be checked at least every year for signs of rust or deterioration if they are not being used. Sealed containers should be left sealed until they are to be used. Alcohols and occasionally camphor are

added to stabilize burning characteristics. Powder containers should be kept tightly closed to keep these volatile additives from evaporating into the air.

Smokeless powder is quite safe to handle because it is not sensitive to shock. The main caution that must be taken is to keep it from open flame or heat. It will ignite above 400 degrees F. Shelf storage is suitable, preferably on a second floor where temperatures remain most stable. Powder should never be stored in heavy closed metal containers that could act as bombs in case of a fire. Never have more than one container of powder open at a time. If there is a fire this–hopefully–limits it to one can.

Smokeless powder is toxic if ingested because the nitroglycerin component causes heart irregularity. British soldiers in WWI chewed smokeless powder from rifle cartridges to cause a brief though severe illness to get off the line, until medical authorities discovered this practice. Children have a tendency to taste things; smokeless powder should not be one of them.

Loading Density

Various combinations of bullets and powder charges can be assembled to achieve the same velocity. Some are going to be more accurate than others. Various manuals will often indicate loads that gave the best accuracy in particular guns. This is usually the best place to start developing a load, although such a combination will not necessarily be the best performer in your gun.

The chore of blackpowder cleanup is now easier with better cleaners and treated patches.

Leaving a powder measure open allows volatiles to escape and dirt to enter. Keep it capped! Never leave powder in a measure after loading or you may find yourself guessing what kind it is.

Compressed loads should be approached with extreme caution for obvious reasons.

Generally speaking, when selecting a powder there are a few rules of thumb worth following. Larger-capacity rifle cartridges, with heavy bullets, generally perform best with slow-burning powders. For best accuracy, a powder charge that fills the case with little or no air space tends to give better accuracy than a small charge that can shift position in the case. Shooters using reduced loads, particularly in rifles, get better results by tipping the barrel skyward before each shot to position the powder to the rear of the case. This can also be achieved by using wads or wads plus fillers to fill up the space, but the results are usually not as good. A filler wad should never be placed over the powder with an air space between it and the bullet. The space must be filled entirely. If there is a space, the wad will come slamming against the base of the bullet with enough force to make a bulged ring in the case and often in the chamber of the gun!

Compressed Loads

Never compress powder in a cartridge case unless such a load is recommended in a reloading manual. Compressed loads should never be more than 10 percent above the case capacity. A compression of more than this often leads to lower than desired velocities. If the compression is excessive it can actually bulge the case or cause the case to stretch in the loading process, resulting in a cartridge that is oversize or too long and will jam the gun.

Available Powders

As of this writing, smokeless powders are available from eight manufacturers or importers. These include: IMR Powder Co. (formerly DuPont and recently acquired by Hodgdon); Olin/Winchester; Alliant Powder (formerly Hercules and now a division of Alliant TechSystems); Hodgdon Powder Co., Accurate Arms, Kaltron-Pettibone, importer of Vihtavuori powder, Norma, and Ramshot.

IMR

IMR makes both single- and double-base powders of the flake type and cylinder type for a wide variety of uses.

Hi-SKOR 700-X – This is a double-base flake powder primarily designed for shotshells, but works well in many target and light handgun loadings.

TRAIL BOSS - Designed specifically for low velocity lead bullet loads, it is suitable for Cowboy Action shooting. It is primarily a pistol powder, but has some application in rifle. It is based on a new technology that allows very high loading density, good flow through powder measures, stability in severe temperature variation and additional safety to the handloader.

HI-SKOR 800-X – This is a double-base shotgun powder for heavy shotshell loads. It is also applicable to some handgun loadings.

PB – PB is a porous base, flake powder of the single-base type. It is used for many shotshell loads and in a number of handgun cartridges. PB works well in cast bullet loads.

SR 7625 – Although it carries the sporting rifle designa-

tion, its main use is for shotshell and handgun cartridges. It works well with a number of cast bullet rifle loadings. It is the fastest burning of the SR series of powders.

SR 4756 – A slightly slower burning single-base powder. It works well in some rifle cartridges, with cast bullets. The main use of this powder is in shotshells and a number of handgun loads.

SR 4759 – This is the slowest burning powder in this series. It is a cylinder powder rather than a flake type, as are the other SR powders. SR 4759 has a very good reputation with cast-bullet shooters, working well in cases as large as the 45-70. Once withdrawn, it is back by popular demand and will hopefully stay with us.

IMR 4227 – IMR stands for Improved Military Rifle. This is the fastest burning in the series. Like all the IMR series, this is a single-base powder of a cylinder type. It works well in small rifle cases such as the 22 Hornet, the 223 Remington, and even in big ones such as the 458 Winchester. It works well in heavy handgun loads and can be used in the .410 shotgun.

IMR 4198 – This powder is slightly slower burning, but works very well in small to medium-capacity cases such as the 22 Hornet and 222 and 223, where it is prized for varmint and benchrest shooting. It works well in large cases including the 444 Marlin and even the 45-70.

IMR 3031 – A favorite for the 30-30 and similar medium-capacity cases with jacketed bullets, 3031 is one of the most versatile on the market. It gives good results in cartridges as small as the 17 Remington and as large as the 458 Winchester.

IMR 4064 – Very similar to IMR 3031, 4064 has great versatility in the 30-caliber range, performing well in the 30-06 and 308. It also works well in many of the larger rifle calibers.

IMR 4895 – This medium-slow burning powder is very similar to the Hodgdon powder of the same number. It is an excellent performer in the 30-06, but works well in slightly reduced loads with cast bullets in rifles such as the 45-70. Excellent accuracy is produced in the 223 with this powder in bolt-action rifles.

IMR 4320 – Originally used as a propellant for military match ammunition, it is relatively slow burning and will produce good velocities with less recoil than the faster-burning types. It is applicable to cartridges from 22 to 458.

IMR 4350 – This is a slow-burning powder intended for large capacity cases. Its bulk fills these cases well. A favorite for the 7x57 Mauser, 30-06, 243 and 270 Winchester, 4350 is an excellent maximum load for long-range work.

IMR 4831 – Introduced in 1971, this powder carries the same number as the Hodgdon H4831, but it is not an equivalent. IMR 4831 is faster burning than the Hodgdon product! IMR 4831 is intended for magnum rifle cartridges, although it works very well in the 270 Winchester.

IMR 7828 – This is the slowest burning in the IMR series. It is designed for the 50 Browning, and large magnum rifle cartridges including the 300 and 338 magnums. It will work well in a number of African big-game cartridges. IMR 7828 is intended for pushing large, heavy bullets at high velocities, without raising chamber pressures into the danger zone.

IMR 7828SSC - This magnum rifle powder has exactly the same burn speed as standard 7828 and uses the same data. However, due to the super short kernels, metering is virtually as good as a spherical powder. This allows up to 4% more powder space in the case and in many loads yields more velocity than standard 7828.

Winchester

Winchester makes double-base powders in a spherical configuration. This "ball" powder achieves controlled burning and cooler temperatures by the use of additives. The ball shape makes it flow easily through mechanical powder measures.

231 – The fastest burning of the Winchester powders, it is for handguns and is best used for light to medium target loads. It produces excellent accuracy in 9mm, 38 Special and 45 ACP loadings.

296 – This is a pistol powder with a fine granulation. It is most useful in large-bore handguns such as the 357 and 44 Magnums. It will also work well in .410-bore shotshell loadings.

WST Super Target – WST is a shotshell propellant for Skeet and trap shooting. Its burning characteristics make it useful for 38 Special and 45 ACP as well.

WSF Super Field – WSF is a shotshell powder. It works well in 12-gauge and is the powder of choice for 20-gauge. WSF is also applicable for use in 9mm, 40 S&W and 38 Super Auto handloads.

748 – Used in military loadings for the 223 (5.56mm) rifle, this powder offers low flame temperature for increased barrel life. It is suitable for a great variety of centerfire rifle loadings in 22- through 30-caliber.

760 – Used with other Winchester components, 760 duplicates factory 30-06 loadings. Recommended for 7mm-08 and the new 30-06 Fail Safe bullet. Supreme 780, a 2008 introduction, is the same powder loaded in Winchester's factory Supreme ammunition including the 243 Win., 270 Win. and 300 Win Mag, allowing handloaders to duplicate factory loads. Its burn speed is comparable to H4831.

Alliant Powders

These were formerly made under the Hercules trademark and before that Laflin & Rand. Alliant currently offers 19 single and double-base powders. Alliant says that its Red Dot, Green Dot and Unique are now 50 percent cleaner burning than previously.

Bullseye – A longtime favorite of pistol shooters, this flake powder works well in cases as small as the 25 ACP and as large as the 44 Magnum and 45 Colt. It is a very fast-burning powder.

Red Dot – Red Dot is a flake shotshell powder that also will work well in light and medium pressure handgun loads. Some shooters have gotten good results with light cast-bullet rifle loadings as well.

Winchester has replaced metal powder cans with its new plastic packaging, which keeps volatiles in and moisture out of the powder inside.

American Select – American Select is a clean-burning shotshell powder with a burn rate between Red Dot and Green Dot. Its main use is for 12-gauge target loads, but it will work well in a variety of handgun loads.

Green Dot – This flake shotshell powder burns slightly slower than Red Dot and has an equal variety of applications.

Unique – This is a flake powder with a great number of uses. It works well in many handgun loads and is considered one of the most accurate in 44 Magnum and 45 Colt. It is well adapted to cartridges as small as the 25 ACP. It performs equally well in many shotshell loads.

E3 – Alliant's newest shotshell powder is a double-based shotshell powder designed for light and standard 12-gauge target loads. Alliant promises improved pattern consistency, better gas expansion rates, higher muzzle velocities and clean-burning performance.

Promo – For light and standard 12-gauge target loads with economy in mind.

Steel – Alliant's only powder designed specifically for loading steel shotshells, as well as 2 oz. turkey loads.

Power Pistol – As the name implies, this powder is for handguns. The primary use is for high performance loads in the 9mm, 10mm and 40 S&W. It will make good medium velocity loads for the 380, 38 Special and the 45 ACP.

Herco – This is a moderately slow burning shotshell powder with application to handgun loads. The granulation is coarse and it is best for magnum loads.

Blue Dot – This is a very slow burning shotshell powder that also works well in magnum handgun cartridges.

410 – A clean-burning powder especially for .410 shotshells.

2400 – A finely granulated powder, 2400 works well in small rifle cases such as the 22 Hornet and similar varmint cartridges. One of the older powders in the line, it is still popular for magnum pistol loads in 357, 41 and 44. It produces good accuracy in reduced cast bullet rifle loadings. Care, however, must be taken not to overload, since this

Alliant Unique powder is a powerful, fast-burning double-base propellant used in pistol and light rifle loads. It is a fine, flake powder that has been made for nearly a century.

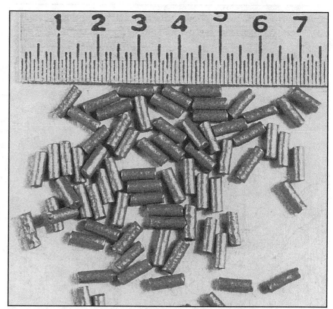

IMR 3031 powder is an extruded single-base propellant made of nitrocellulose. It has a fairly slow burning rate and has long been a standard for military rifle cartridges.

is a powerful powder that takes up very little space in large cases.

Reloder 7 – This is the fastest burning of the Reloder series. It works well in medium-capacity rifle cases of the varmint class, on up to the 458 Winchester Magnum, in which it delivers excellent accuracy with heavy bullets. Reloder 7 has been a favorite with benchrest shooters for its accuracy in the 222.

Reloder 10X – Designed for light varmint and light bullet loads in 222 Rem., 22-250 and 223 Rem , as well as benchrest loads and light bullet 308.

Reloder 15 – Reloder 15 is slightly slower burning than the discontinued Reloder 12. It works well in a wide range of rifle cases from the 223 to magnums of the 458 and 416 Rigby size. It is generally used for heavy loadings.

Reloder 19 - Reloder 19 is a slow-burning powder that works in heavy varmint cases such as the 22-250 where it yields the highest velocities. It does well in 30-caliber cases, including the magnums.

Reloder 22 - This is the slowest powder in the Reloder series. It is intended for large-capacity magnum rifle cases, although some shooters have obtained good results with this powder in the 220 Swift.

Reloder 25 – Ideal for heavy magnum rifles, Reloder 25 delivers high energy for Weatherby magnums and other large capacity cartridges.

Hodgdon

Titewad – This powder is a flattened spherical shotgun propellant that features low charge weights, mild muzzle report, minimum recoil and reduced residue. For 12-gauge only, it ideal for light loads.

HP-38 – This a spherical powder developed as a propellant for the 38 Special. It works well in a variety of medium-size pistol cartridges, producing fine accuracy.

Clays – This is a very popular, clean-burning shotshell powder designed for light 12-gauge loads. It offers soft and smooth recoil, mild muzzle report and excellent patterns.

Universal Clays – This is a flake shotshell powder with burning characteristics similar to Unique. The granulation is slightly finer. Universal Clays works very well in a variety of handgun cartridges.

International Clays – This is an improved form of the Clays formula. It yields reduced recoil in 12- and 20-gauge target loads.

Titegroup – This spherical pistol powder was designed for accuracy in large cases such as 45 Colt and 357 Magnum. Powder position in these cases does not affect velocity and performance. Excellent for cowboy action, bullseye and combat shooting.

HS-6 – This spherical powder is good for heavy shotshell loads, and works well in handgun loads in medium and large calibers when high velocities are desired.

Longshot – A spherical shotshell powder, Longshot is designed for heavy field loads in 10-, 12-, 16-, 20- and 28-gauge, and delivers magnum velocities with good patterns.

Lil'Gun – This .410 powder was designed to fit, meter and perform flawlessly in the .410 bore. It also has magnum pistol and 22 Hornet applications.

H110 – This spherical powder was developed for the 30 M-1 Carbine cartridge. It works very well in medium and large handgun cartridges. It is particularly good in magnum handgun cartridges where it will duplicate factory performance in these calibers.

H4198 – A single-base powder that produces fine accuracy in the 223 and similar small to medium rifle cases.

H322 – This single-base powder has found favor with benchrest shooters using the 222 and 6mm Remington BR.

IMR 4320 is a slow-burning single-base rifle powder for use in large-bore and high-powered rifles. The extruded grains are of a "short cut" size.

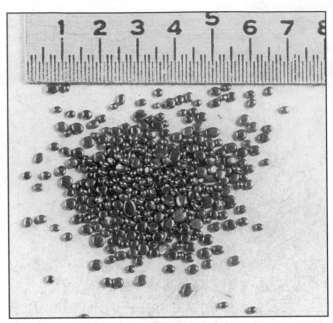

Hodgdon BL-C(2) is a spherical powder. It's a fast burning double-base powder with a well-deserved reputation for flowing very smoothly through powder measures.

It works well in a variety of 30-calibers and even in straight-walled cases as large as the 45-70.

Benchmark – As its name implies, this extruded propellant was developed for precision cartridges, and performs well for benchrest and small varmint cartridges, as well as light bullet 308 Win. loads.

H4895 - The single-base 4895 is one of the most versatile rifle powders around. It produces fine performance in calibers from the 17 Remington to the 458 Winchester Magnum. It works very well in reduced loadings, burning evenly for charges as light as 60 percent of the maximum.

H335 - This is a double-base spherical powder that produces good shooting in 22- and 30-caliber cases.

BL-C(2) - This spherical powder gives excellent accuracy in the 222 and 223, and was often used for benchrest and competition shooting.

Varget – A small-grain extruded powder, Varget is known for its insensitivity to heat and cold, which makes it a good choice for year-round hunting. Easy ignition and clean burning help produce excellent accuracy and high velocities. Fine results have been obtained in the 22-250, 308, 30-06 and 375 H&H Magnum.

H380 – This is a double-base powder that performs well in 30-caliber cases, but also does well in large-capacity varmint rounds such as the 22-250.

H414 – This works well in the 30-06 and similar 30s, particularly with lighter bullets where higher velocities are desired.

H4350 – This single-base powder is intended for large-capacity, magnum-rifle cartridges.

HYBRID 100V – A powder introduced for 2008 for use in calibers that fit H4350. Hodgdon says the powder, a small-grain part-spherical and part-extruded shape, will deliver velocities not seen before in many popular cartridges and flows smoothly through a measure.

H4831 – This is a single-base, extruded powder that gives the best accuracy with heavy bullets in 30-calibers and larger, though it is excellent in the 270.

H4831SC – This is the same powder as H4831, but has a shorter grain. The SC stands for "short cut." The finer granulation makes this powder flow more evenly through powder measures.

H1000 – This is a very slow burning single-base powder. It is another that works well with heavy-bullet loads in large capacity cases.

H50BMG – As the name implies, this is for loading the 50 Browning Machine Gun cartridge. The burn rate is very stable in a wide range of temperatures.

US869® - A 50 BMG propellant that offers significant advantages in many magnum rifle applications. A true magnum spherical rifle powder that is superb with heavy bullets in big, overbore rifle cartridges. US869 is a dense propellant that allows the shooter to use enough powder to create maximum velocities in cartridges such as the 7mm Remington Ultra Magnum, 300 Remington Ultra Magnum, 30-378 Weatherby Magnum and others. US869 is superior in the 50 Caliber BMG where it yields high velocity and great accuracy with 750 to 800 grain projectiles. This is a fine 1000-yard match propellant.

Retumbo – This magnum powder was designed expressly for very large overbore cartridges such as the 7mm Rem Ultra Mag, 300 Rem Ultra Mag and the 30-378 Weatherby Mag.

Pyrodex - This is a blackpowder substitute that offers cleaner burning characteristics and slightly less density. (See Blackpowder chapter).

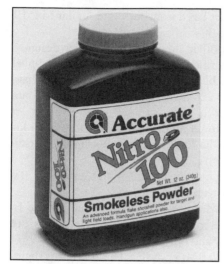

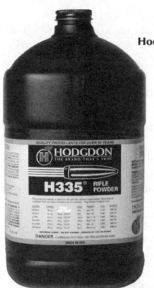

Alliant Powder packaging.

Accurate Arms' Nitro 100 is a double-base flake powder best used in shotgun target shooting. It has pistol applications as well.

Accurate Arms

Nitro 100 - This is a double-base flake powder for 12-gauge target loads. It works well in the 45 Colt and other medium to large handgun cartridges.

No. 2 - This is a fast-burning double-base ball powder for use in the 38 Special and similar medium capacity handguns. It does well in light and target loadings.

No. 5 - This is another double-base ball powder, slightly slower burning and comparable to Unique. It gives good results in a wide variety of medium to large handgun cases.

No. 7 - A double-base powder intended for 9mm Luger and similar medium to large capacity pistol rounds. It is clean burning and gives good accuracy at target velocities.

No. 9 – No. 9 is a double-base ball powder and considered one of the best for the 44 Magnum. It works very well in the 41 and 357 Magnums as well. Good results have been obtained in the 22 Hornet and the 30 Carbine. It will also work well in the 410 shotgun.

1680 – This double-base ball powder was designed specifically for the 7.62x39mm Russian cartridge. It is fast burning and delivers high velocities in the 22 Hornet. Beyond these two, its use is rather limited.

2015 – A small-grain extruded powder of the single-base type with many uses. It performs very well in small to medium rifle cases producing excellent accuracy in many 22 centerfires. The 6mm PPC and 7mm Remington have produced excellent groups with this powder. It also does well in straight-walled rifle cases.

2230 – A double-base ball powder with a fairly rapid burn, 2230 does well in the 223 and similar medium-capacity cases.

2460 – This double-base ball powder is slower burning than 2230, which extends its use from medium-capacity 22 centerfire calibers to the 308 and 30-06.

5744 – This double-base powder has a burn rate between No. 9 and 1680. It works well in pistol cases such as the 6mm TCU, 357 Magnum, 38-40, 41 Magnum, 44 Special, 44-40,

IMR powder was formerly DuPont, then later branded IMR, and now has been acquired by Hodgdon.

44 Magnum and 45 Colt. In rifles, it performs well in the 22 Hornet, 222, 25-20, 30 Carbine, 30-30, 308 and 30-06.

2495 – It is a single-base extruded powder with great flexibility and gives excellent accuracy in 22 centerfires through the 30-caliber class. 2495 works well with cast bullets and produces the best accuracy in the 45-70 with cast bullets. Reduced loadings as small as 60 percent of maximum produce consistent groups.

2520 – A ball powder with a medium-slow burning rate, 2520 gives excellent results in many medium capacity rifle cases. Fine accuracy is obtained in the 308 and 30-06. Its pressure curve makes it suitable for use in autoloaders.

4064 – This single-base rifle propellant is short cut for better metering while delivering the excellent performance. This propellant is intended to meet the needs of service rifle competitors and hunters who prefer extruded powders. Admirers of the 30-06 will especially like this propellant.

Magpro – Magpro is designed especially for the new range of very efficient short magnum rifle cartridges. Magpro has been designed to produce optimum velocities at nearly full case capacity in these calibers. Because of its uniformity of shape it has the flow required for progressive loading machines. Magpro is also a good choice for the standard magnum cartridges.

2700 – Accurate's 2700 is designed for use with heavy bullets in the belted magnum class of rifle cartridge. It works well in the 17 Remington, 220 Swift and 22250-notable exceptions to the rule.

4350 – This powder is equivalent to IMR 4350 and H4350. It has the same applications.

3100 – This is a single-base extruded powder for use in medium-capacity cases. It delivers fine performance in the 243 and 7mm Remington Magnum. It works well with heavy-bullet loadings.

8700 – This is a double-base ball powder well suited to use in medium- to large-capacity cases. Good results are obtained in the 264 Winchester Magnum, 270 Winchester, 7mm Remington Magnum, and the Weatherby 257, 270 and 300 Magnums. Good results are obtained with cast bullets, though a magnum primer is needed for consistent burning.

Solo 1000 – This fast-burning, double-base flake powder is for shotgun use. It is similar to Bullseye and has some handgun applications.

Solo 1250 – This medium- to fast-burning shotgun powder is primarily for use in 12-gauge hunting loads as well as trap and Skeet loads for the 20- and 28-gauge. It is similar to Unique and has pistol applications for medium-capacity cases such as 9mm and 40 S&W.

4100 – This powder is very similar to Accurate No. 9. It is slightly slower burning and is designed especially for the .410 bore 2 1/2-inch, 1/2-ounce Skeet load. It can be used for pistols using No. 9 data with a magnum primer.

Vihtavuori

Vihtavuori powder is made in Finland and imported by Kaltron-Pettibone. As of this writing, Vihtavuori makes twenty-two powders, both single- and double-base, for rifle and pistol use.

N110 – This is a fast-burning powder in the class of Alliant 2400, Winchester 296 and Hodgdon H110. It works well in the 22 Hornet and other small- to medium-case 22 centerfires. It serves well in the 357 and 44 Magnums and 45 Winchester Magnum.

N120 – Similar to IMR 4227, N120 is designed to work well in the 22-centerfire class of rifle cartridges. Its application beyond this, however, is limited, though good results have been obtained in the 7.62x39mm Russian.

N130 – This powder burns faster than N120. It has applications in 22 centerfires, such as the 223, and medium-capacity cases in the 25- to 27-caliber range.

N133 – The burning rate of this powder is close to IMR 4198. It works well in the 222 and 223, and good results have been obtained in the 45-70.

N135 – This powder burns with moderate speed, similar to IMR and Hodgdon 4895. It is a versatile powder with applications from the 17 Remington to the 458 Winchester.

N140 – A relatively slow-burning powder, N140 can be used in place of IMR 4320, Alliant Reloder 15 and Hodgdon H380. Best results are in 30- to 35-caliber rifle cases.

N150 – This powder has a slow burn rate similar to IMR 4350. It works well in 30-caliber and up.

N160 – This is another slow-burning powder designed mainly for magnum rifles. It works well with light-bullet loads and with heavy bullets in the 30-06. Good results have been obtained in the 220 Swift, 243, 25-06, 264 and 7mm Remington Magnum.

N165 – Slightly slower than N160, this powder is for heavy-bullet loads in the 30-06 and magnums in the 30-caliber range and up.

N170 – The slowest burning powder in this series, N 170 is suitable for large-capacity cases only.

24N41 – This powder is especially designed for the 50 BMG. This is a single-base powder like the N100 series, but the grain size is larger and burning rate slower.

20N29 – Another 50 BMG powder. This one burns slightly slower than 24N41.

N530 – A high energy powder with a burning rate close to N135. Especially for 223 Remington. Excellent also for 45-70 Government.

N540 – This is a double-base powder with a burning rate much like N140. It is designed for the 308 Winchester. A high energy powder.

N550 – Another double-base powder with a burning rate like N150, but designed especially for the 308 and 30-06. A high energy powder

N560 – The burning rate of this powder is like N 160, but it is designed for the 270 Winchester and the 6.5x55 Swedish Mauser. A high-energy powder.

N570 – New high energy powder. No information at this writing.

N310 – This pistol powder is comparable to Bull's-eye. Its fast burning rate lends itself to use in

Current label for Vihtavuori powder.

Vihtavuori N350 is a slow pistol powder for medium to large calibers. It is also suitable for shotshells.

the 25 ACP on up to the 44 Magnum, where it proves excellent for light target loads.

N320 – Suitable for shotshells and mid-range handgun loads, N320 works well in cartridges in the 38- to 45-caliber class.

N330 – The burning rate of this powder is similar to Green Dot. It performs well in pistol cartridges from 38 to 45.

N340 – This powder has a slightly slower burning rate and is similar to Winchester 540 or Herco. Good results are obtained in medium to large handgun calibers.

N350 – This is the slowest pistol powder in the N300 series, and it lends itself to use in shotshells. In this regard, it is about like Blue Dot. Use in handguns is limited to medium to large calibers like 9mm to 45 ACP.

3N37– This is not really an N300 series powder. It is used in high velocity rimfire loads and shotshells. The burning rate is between N340 and N350. Good results have been obtained in 9mm, 38 Super Auto, 38 Special and the 45 ACP. Similar results have been achieved with the 357 and 44 Magnums.

N32C – A new pistol powder. No information at this writing.

3N38 – This a powder for the high velocity loads of the 9mm Luger and the 38 Super with moderate bullet weight. Designed especially for competitive handgun shooting.

N105 – Super Magnum. This is a special powder with a burning rate between N350 and N110. It was developed for heavy-bullet loads and large capacity cases. Best results have been in magnums in the 357 to 45 class.

Norma

200 – Norma's fastest rifle powder is suitable for smaller cartridges, such as the 22 Hornet and 222 Rem. Also suitable with light bullets with low velocities for the 308 Winchester.

201 – Very good for calibers with small casing volumes relative to bullet diameter, such as 9.3x57 or 45-70.

202 – Specially produced to give maximum performance in 7.62 NATO. Also for medium calibers such as 8x57, 9.3x62 and 9.3x74 R.

203-B – Usable from 22-250 to 358 Norma. Very well suited for 6mm Norma BR and 308 Win. loaded with heavier bullets.

204 – This is a slow burning powder with good performance and high accuracy in such calibers as 6.5x55 and .30-06

MRP – A very flexible magnum powder for calibers with relatively large case volumes.

MRP-2 – A good choice for overbore calibers such as 7mm STW, 6.5-284 and 6.5-06. Fine grain facilitates filling.

URP - Proven very successful in Europe, particularly among 6.5x55 match shooters, URP is a high-energy single-base powder, with a burn rate similar to H4350, and a tad slower than Norma 203B (currently used in Norma Loaded 6mm BR ammo). That should make it ideal for the 6XC, and a good choice for 6 Improved shooters.

Ramshot Powders

Competition - A double-based, modified (flattened) spherical powder that is designed for the 12-gauge clay target shooter who is interested in cleanliness, low recoil, and consistency. Competition is a "fluffy" powder that provides a good wad-to-hull configuration and results in a tight crimp. A good choice for the cowboy action shooter.

Zip – This is a double-based, modified (flattened) spherical powder that performs extremely well in small- to medium-sized handgun cases. Clean, fast burning and consistent with a wide range of cartridges makes it a great choice for target and competitive shooters.

Silhouette - A double-based, modified (flattened) spherical powder that will allow you to make major with the 38 Super. Silhouette's low flash signature, high velocity, and clean-burning properties make it a perfect choice for indoor ranges and law enforcement applications.

True Blue – This is a double-based, spherical powder that performs extremely well in most handgun cases. The load range for True Blue is currently from the 380 Auto to 454 Casull. True Blue's physical size contributes to excellent meterability and consistency of charge weights when run through a progressive loader.

Enforcer – Enforcer is a double-based, spherical powder that produces high velocities in a wide variety of large handgun calibers. Its physical size lends itself to excellent consistency in charge weights through a progressive loader due to its meterability. Enforcer also performs well in some small rifle cases such as the 22 Hornet.

X-Terminator – A double-based, spherical powder that is designed for the high-volume 223 varmint hunter who demands a clean-burning powder that will not foul the barrel after a few shots. It meters extremely well, providing for an outstanding shot-to-shot consistency. Also does not bridge going into the small diameter necks of the 22-centerfire calibers.

TAC – A versatile rifle powder that performs well in a number of different calibers. TAC provides very high velocities in a 223 with an 80-gr. bullet and still stay within SAAMI pressure guidelines. TAC is a double-based, spherical powder providing excellent meterability and consistent charge weights.

Big Game – As the name indicates Big Game is used predominately in the 270 and 30-06 classes of cartridges but it also performs well in the short-action family of cartridges. Its performance in the 22-250 and the 220 Swift make it one of the most popular powders in the Ramshot line.

Hunter – This ball powder provides good meterability and clean burning, and produces outstanding velocity in the 257 Roberts and the new Winchester Short Magnum family of cartridges. Hunter additionally tends not to be temperature sensitive.

Magnum - 1000-yard match shooters using the 6.5x284 are having exceptional results with Ramshot Magnum. Magnum's excellent velocities, coupled with its cleanliness, make it a great choice for high-volume match shooters. Formerly designated Ramshot Big Boy.

With so many projectiles available in so many shapes and sizes, how do you find the one that's best? It depends what you're looking for.

Bullets

BUYING BULLETS FOR reloading is a fairly simple process. Most of today's guns are standardized in terms of bore diameter and rifling characteristics. If you deal with a knowledgeable dealer, a simple request for "some hunting bullets for my 30-30" will probably get you what you want. Unfortunately, there are dealers who are not very knowledgeable and even some who are mainly interested in unloading what they have in stock. Caveat emptor is still the safest position to take.

This section refers to getting the "best" bullet. The first thing you should have in mind when you go to buy bullets is a clear idea of what "best" means for your intended use. For any gun the first consideration should be accuracy. Whether it's for target or game, an inaccurate bullet is worthless. The easiest rule of thumb when it comes to buying bullets is to get what duplicates the factory loading. If you want ammunition for special purposes, which most handloaders eventually will, then you will have to do a little research. Old guns and those of foreign extraction can often be confusing in regard to what their bore and groove size

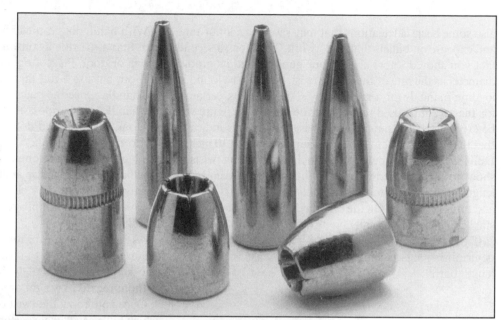

The "best" bullet for your gun is the one that shoots accurately and otherwise does what you want it to do.

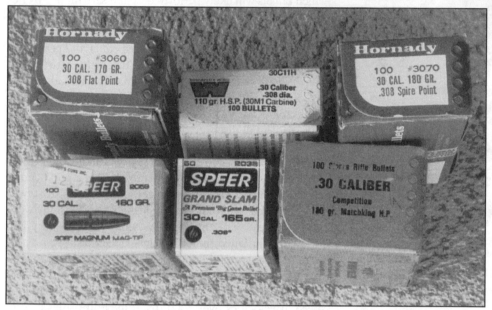

Most bullets are packed 100 to a sturdy box, with the diameter, weight and style of bullet–flatpoint, hollowpoint, etc. –marked on the box.

actually is. The best information collected over the past century indicates that the most accurate bullet is the one that exactly fits the groove diameter of the barrel. In the final analysis, this is determined by slugging the bore of your gun and measuring the slug with a micrometer or Vernier caliper and getting bullets that fit.

Proper diameter bullets can most easily be determined by reading the information on the box they come in or by measurement, if you are buying bullets in a plastic bag from someone you don't know. This can be a little confusing. For instance, 22-caliber bullets for the early 22 Hornet rifles were properly .223-inch diameter. The modern ones are .224-inch. The 223 Remington (5.56mm) is .224-inch diameter, not .223-inch! Good loading manuals usually give warnings regarding groove diameters for foreign and early rifles, especially if there is a considerable variation in these within a particular type of rifle.

The Lyman manual indicates that groove diameters on the

303 British military rifles vary from .309 to .317-inch. Put too fat a bullet in one of the tight bores, along with plenty of powder, and you can create a dangerous pressure situation, in addition to inaccurate shooting. The 303 Enfield, if loaded properly, is a fine, accurate rifle, capable of turning in some excellent groups.

Bullet Length, Rifling Characteristics

Beyond the question of bullet diameter, there is the matter of bullet length and the relationship of length to the rifling twist and how this affects accuracy. Bullets aren't identified by length, but by weight when they are sold. All other things being equal, heavier bullets of a given diameter are longer. One way to find out which bullets will work best in your gun is trial and error. Another is to limit yourself to the recommendations in loading manuals. These are only guidelines for performance for the caliber of your gun, and may or may not be satisfactory to you. Beyond this there are also some basic calculations that may save you a lot of time and expense on bullets that don't work. Therefore, a second fact you should know about your gun, beyond its groove diameter, is the rate of the rifling twist. This can be found in loading manuals for a great many standard guns, certainly for the test guns used to prepare the data. This figure will be expressed, for example, as "Twist 1:10". This indicates that the rifling spiral makes one complete turn in 10 inches. Different lengths of bullets require different rifling twists to shoot to their best advantage. If the match between bullet length and rifling is too far off, bullets may fail to stabilize and tumble in flight. On the other hand, they can be so over-stabilized they will actually break apart in flight.

If there is any doubt about the twist rate of your gun, determining this is simplicity itself, at least with a rifle-length barrel.

Good shooting only comes when you have the correct diameter and weight.

With handguns, you will have to interpolate as best you can. Stand the rifle against a plain vertical surface such as a wall or door. Place a tight cleaning patch on your cleaning rod, but use a rod that does not have a ball bearing in the handle. Once the patch is just started down bore, mark the handle and beside it make a mark on the vertical wall or door. Push the rod down the barrel, allowing the handle to turn freely. Make a second mark at the point where the handle has made one complete rotation. Measure the distance between the top and bottom marks and you know the twist rate to a very close degree. There will always be a slight amount of slippage, but this shouldn't affect your calculations.

As a rule of thumb, longer bullets of a given caliber require a faster twist to stabilize them to the point where they shoot more accurately than shorter bullets. This is true without regard to weight or velocity.

Once you know the twist of your gun, you can calculate which bullets will likely perform best and save money by not buying those that won't. There are some elaborate computer programs to do this, but there is a very simple method that works with a pocket calculator or even paper and pencil: the Greenhill Formula. The Formula for determining twist rates was the work of Sir Alfred George Greenhill, a mathematics professor at Cambridge University who later served as an instructor at the Woolrich Military Academy from 1876 to 1906. Greenhill discovered that the optimum twist rate for a bullet is determined by dividing 150 by the length of the bullet in calibers (hundredths of an inch) and then dividing again by its diameter. The number 150 is a good choice since it allows a useful margin in the calculations. Most twist rates that are close to the formulated ideal will usually work well. The beauty of this formula is that it works very well for lead or jacketed bullets. Weight does not appear to be that critical a factor. Shape and design do not seem to have that much effect either, up to velocities of 2200 fps and, to a degree, above this. To compensate for increased rotational speed at velocities over 3000 fps, some authorities recom-

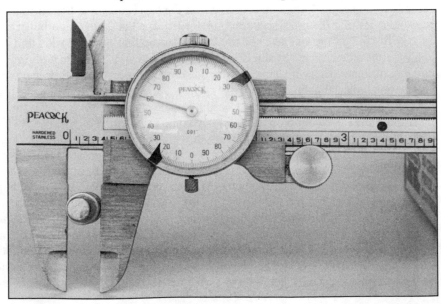

If you have any doubt about the caliber of bullets you are buying, check them with an accurate caliper and/or micrometer.

mend a slightly reduced twist rate. Although velocity does not appear to be considered within this formula, it is included in the rotation segment in a concealed form. Assume a 1:12-inch barrel firing a bullet at 1000 fps. This equals 1000 rotations per second. At 2000 fps the rotations per second double. Higher velocity yields a faster spin and is thus considered in the calculations, although it is not specifically mentioned. The most recent interpretations of Greenhill opt for a slightly faster twist with the higher velocity cartridges, in the belief that erring on the side of over-stabilization is better than under-stabilization which may result in a tumbling bullet.

The popular 223 Remington is a good candidate for study. Rifles for this cartridge are currently available with the following twist rates: 1:7, 1:8.5, 1:9, 1:10, 1:12 and 1:14 inches. To apply the Greenhill Formula using the original 55-grain bullet yields the following, for one brand of full metal jacket (FMJ) military-type bullet measuring .647-inch in length. The bullet diameter is .224-inch, which, divided into the length of .647-inch, gives 2.89 calibers long. Dividing 2.89 into 150 yields a figure of 51.90, or an ideal twist rate of

gun or having one custom barreled, if you know in advance what kind of shooting you will be doing and thus what kind of bullets you will use.

Rifle Bullets

Military surplus and military overrun bullets may be a terrific bargain if all you want is some cheap practice ammunition. Military bullets suitable for practice are of the full metal jacketed variety. They feature a solid lead alloy core with a copper, bronze or soft steel jacket and are referred to as "ball" ammunition. These bullets are made to military specifications and will produce reasonably good accuracy for preliminary sighting in and practice. The full metal jacket prevents nose expansion and is not good for hunting. Occasionally shooters have tried to make hunting ammunition out of FMJ bullets by filing the points off of the spitzer (pointed) military bullets, exposing the lead cores. This is a dangerous practice since the bullet already has the lead core exposed at the base. Opening the point often results in the core being blown right through the jacket, leaving the jacket stuck in the barrel. When the next shot hits the jacket, the

Rifling twist is important when matching bullets to a particular gun, especially with the popular 223 Remington (5.56mm). This Olympic Arms PCR-1 223 rifle comes with either a 1:8.5-inch twist or a 1:10-inch twist. Other models come in a choice of 1:7, 1:9, 1:12 or 1:14.

Ruger's Mini-14/5R 223 features a 1:9-inch twist.

one turn in 51.90 calibers. Multiplying 51.90 by the bullet diameter (.224-inch) equals one turn in 11.63 inches for this particular bullet.

The original twist for the 223-caliber M-16 rifle is 1:12 inches. In its wisdom (?), the Army decided a heavier (longer) bullet was necessary and the M-16A1 is bored with a 1-10-inch twist. The new military bullet will not stabilize in the older barrels. Bullets as heavy as 70 grains are available for the 223 Remington. For a 70-grain bullet measuring .785-inch in length, dividing by .224 equals 3.50. Dividing 150 by 3.50 equals 42.86, or one turn in 42.86 calibers; then 42.86 multiplied by .224 equals 9.60. Thus a twist of 1:9 or 1:10 inches is required to shoot this bullet accurately. There are other factors involved, such as the amount of bearing surface on the bullet, velocity and barrel length. In some cases bullets that are not well matched to twist rate can be made to function. For example, a short, 40- or 45-grain bullet, in a 223 with a fast twist of 1:9 or 1:10 inches, will perform if the powder change is cut back. By decreasing the velocity, you can keep the bullet from tearing itself apart.

Applying the Greenhill Formula can save time and money. It can serve as a useful guide when it comes to buying a

barrel is bulged and ruined. Don't try to modify FMJ bullets! Because of bullet-to-bullet weight variation, military ammunition will never produce fine accuracy.

In a worst-case scenario, a surplus bullet "bargain" could turn out to be a tracer, incendiary, explosive or armor-piercing type. Most military ammunition is identified by the color-coded bullet tips, and in the case of the tracer, by exposed burning material at the base of the bullet. There are various books on military ammunition that will tell you how to interpret these color codes on a country-by-country basis.

Surplus armor-piercing (AP) ammunition has been used for years as cheap practice fodder, mainly in military rifles. In his book *The Complete Guide to Handloading*, Philip Sharpe responded to the question of whether AP ammo did any harm to rifle barrels by conducting an experiment. He took a "gilt-edged" match rifle barrel, targeted it with match target ammunition, then fired a few rounds of armor piercing, and targeted it again with the same match ammunition, carefully cleaning between groups. His finding was that after the AP rounds, the match group had opened considerably and in spite of further cleaning did not repeat its former performance. This was with the AP ammunition of WWII, not the so-called "light armor" piercing, steel-core ammunition sold today which has a far softer steel center. Would a knowledgeable shooter put this newer kind through the barrel of a fine match rifle? No is the easy answer.

Match ammunition is full metal jacketed and of a reduced-base "boattail" design. This type of bullet has good aerodynamic qualities, producing a flat trajectory that is very desirable for hitting targets at long range. Often, these match bullets have a small hollowpoint to shift the center of gravity slightly back and improve stabilization. Match bullets often have very thin jackets and are "soft swaged" to keep the jackets smooth, flawless and of the exact same thickness. Great care is taken to ensure that these bullets are all of the exact same weight and diameter. Since this type of bullet is used for punching paper targets or knocking down metal silhouettes, expansion is not needed. Even though these bullets have hollowpoints they are not intended to expand on

more likely to intersect with vital organs, cause greater loss of blood, and result in death.

Game bullets are generally of a pointed softpoint design, known as spitzer or semi-spitzer. These hold their velocity much better than less aerodynamic designs. Also available are hollowpoint, flat-nose or round-nose designs with the lead core exposed. Attempts at improving expansion have been tried by varying the thickness of the jacket, and by making serrations in the jacket at the bullet nose to help it split open and peel back in an even pattern as the core upsets. Other modifications are hollowpoints filled with hollow copper tubes, metal or nylon plugs which are driven back on impact, expanding the bullet.

Bullets for very large, dangerous game are subject to special requirements, since they often have to penetrate a considerable amount of muscle tissue and heavy bone to reach a vital spot. Bullets for this type of hunting feature

Eagle Arms' M15A2 Post-Ban Heavy Barrel Rifle in 223 has a 1:9-inch twist.

Remington's 40-X target rifle in 223 has a 1:14-inch twist.

game and do not. They are very prone to ricochet and are not suitable for hunting.

Bullets for varmint hunting are either of flat base or boattail design and feature a tapered or spire point with the lead core exposed and swaged into a point. The jackets are thin, allowing these bullets to expand rapidly with an explosive force on woodchucks, prairie dogs and similar-size, thin-skinned animals. This design also keeps these bullets from ricocheting when they strike the ground at velocities near 2000 fps. Because of their frangibility, varmint bullets are not suitable for large game.

Bullets for medium to large game require thicker jackets to keep them together while they penetrate deep into vital areas. They are designed for controlled expansion to allow the bullet to upset or "mushroom" as it goes deeper. This makes a large wound cavity, which renders it far more lethal than a nonexpanding type or a frangible one that breaks into fragments shortly after it strikes a body

In medical terms, "lethality" is the effect of a particular bullet on a body. According to Dr. Martin Fackler - the leading wound ballistics expert in the country - bullet lethality is an easily understood concept. Lethality is determined by answering two questions: How big is the hole it produces? How deep is this hole? Bigger and deeper holes are

very thick jackets. Some, like the old RWS and contemporary Nosler Partition, have two cores with a solid web of bronze alloy running through the center of the bullet so that in section it looks like the letter H. The top half expands, but only to the center web, which insures that the base portion will stay together. Barnes Bullets offers what they call a monolithic solid, which is simply a solid bronze-alloy bullet. Speer offers a copper-alloy bullet called African Grand Slam with a tungsten carbide dowel in the center, for use on such extremely dangerous and hard-to-kill game as Cape buffalo.

Handgun Bullets

Handgun bullets for target use are often swaged from lead alloy and deliver good accuracy when properly lubricated. Their design ranges from a simple cylinder, called a "wadcutter" because it punches clean holes in paper targets, to round-nose and truncated-cone styles. Use of such ammunition in indoor ranges has raised fears of lead poisoning, since a certain amount of lead is vaporized from the bullet's surface upon firing. To counter this hazard, the "total metal jacket" or TMJ bullet was developed. The full metal jacket leaves an exposed lead base, while the TMJ covers the entire surface of the bullet. It's applied by electroplating the bullet

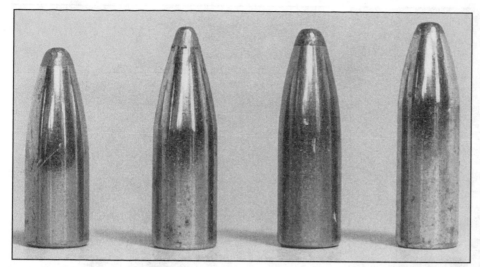

with copper. After plating, the bullets are forced through a die to bring them into perfect roundness. They don't expand as well as soft lead-alloy bullets and are thus a poor choice for hunting, but they do keep lead levels down in indoor ranges.

Hunting bullets for handguns are modifications of rifle designs, with some major engineering differences. Early attempts to improve handgun bullet lethality led to soft-point and hollowpoint designs based on rifle bullets. Results were unsatisfactory when it was discovered that these generally failed to expand and behaved no differently than FMJ types. In the last few years, new designs have emerged that will expand reliably at handgun velocities of 900 to 1600 fps. The secret to bringing this about was to design bullets with nearly pure lead cores, large hollowpoints and thin, relatively soft jackets of pure copper, copper alloys or aluminum. Serrations or cuts through the jacket and into the core improve expansion, increasing the lethality of these relative low-velocity bullets. Since most handgun hunting is done at ranges of under 100 yards, expansion is still reliable on most deer-size or smaller game animals, assuming that the handgun is a powerful one in the 357 Magnum to 500 Magnum class. Handguns of less than this performance level simply cannot be loaded heavily enough to do any serious hunting, and to try to "load them up" for this purpose is a foolish risk to both the gun and its shooter. Shooting any jacketed handgun bullet at low velocities is not recommended, particularly in revolvers. The greater resistance of the jacketed bullet to swaging in the barrel requires higher pressures than with lead bullets. Underpowered loads, particularly in revolvers with a generous gap between the cylinder and barrel, may result in a stuck bullet waiting to be slammed by the next one fired.

Handling and Storage

The care and storage of bullets is much the same as for cartridge cases or loaded ammunition. Commercially made bullets are generally packed in boxes of 100, and the boxes they come in are probably the best containers to keep them in. These are generally of plastic or reinforced cardboard

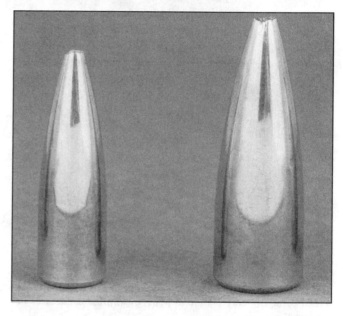

and will last a long time. Obviously, bullets should not be dropped or shaken since this will impart nicks and dents which do nothing to improve their accuracy. Lead bullets are the most susceptible to this kind of damage. The early experiments of Franklin Mann, recounted in his book, *The Bullet's Flight From Powder to Target,* demonstrated the frailty of bullets when it comes to having their accuracy severely affected by even minor damage. Bullet bases are the most vulnerable. A lead or soft lead alloy bullet dropped on a wood floor and receiving a ding on the edge of the base has just been converted into scrap. They can be used for warming and fouling shots, but their former accuracy is gone.

Perhaps the most important caution with respect to bullet storage is to be careful that bullets are not mixed up. If you are loading two very similar calibers, there is a possibility of accidentally getting a 10mm bullet in a box of 9mms of the same style and approximate weight. You would likely catch this in the loading process at the time of seating, but there are some people who might persist in attempting to jam such a bullet into a 9mm case. Perhaps more likely is confusing same-caliber bullets but with different weights. These

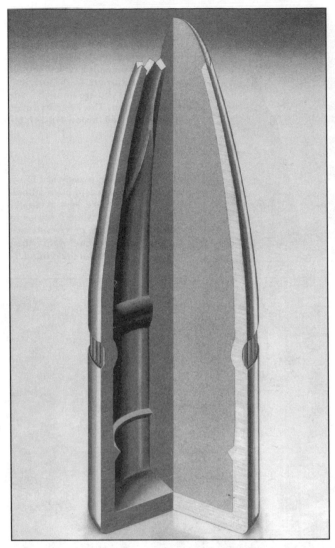

This Hornady hunting bullet features an exposed lead point and a lead core. The core is held in place by knurled cannelures in the jacket.

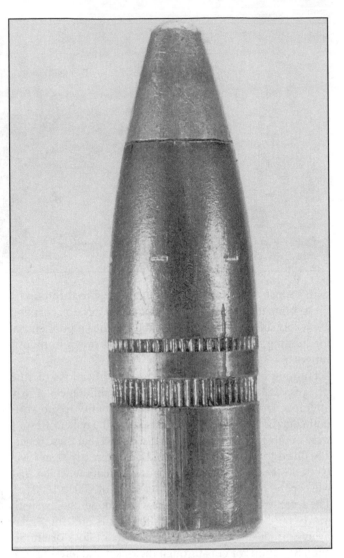

Winchester's Silvertip hunting bullet features a thin aluminum jacket over the lead point. This allows good expansion, but prevents the bullet from getting nicked and dented as the cartridge is fed through the magazine.

will seat perfectly well, but the heavier ones are going to have a higher trajectory and will land in a different place. A heavier bullet will, of course, raise pressures, and if you are using a maximum load this can have serious consequences. It is a good idea never to have two boxes of similar bullets open on your loading bench at the same time. Using boxes with snap tops or putting a bit of tape on the lid to keep it from opening accidentally is a good idea. Most people will agree, particularly after spilling a box of the 22-caliber size and picking them all up.

Buying Bullets

Most gun stores carry a good selection of bullets for most needs. The directory in the back of this book lists many suppliers of bullets of every description. As of this writing, bullets can be bought by mail. Most of the large bullet manufacturers such as Nosler, Sierra, Hornady and Speer offer reloading guides for their products. Data also is available from most smaller bullet manufacturers.

Custom bullets are supplied by small manufacturers and are often geared to special types of guns or for special types of shooting such as metallic silhouette competition. At times these makers or their jobbers will sell their bullets at gun shows where they can be bought at a lower cost and without the shipping and handling. A gun show is a good place to pick up information – and misinformation. Buying bullets in a plastic bag is a pig in a poke.

Bullet Fouling

The subject of cleaning has been touched upon in the powder and primer sections, but the main fouling problem affecting accuracy is caused by bullets. To reiterate, the problem of primer deposits is one of corrosive salts. It is very similar, in effect, to the corrosive deposits left by black-powder or Pyrodex. A water-based cleaner does a good job of getting these out of your barrel since salt and acid are readily dissolved in water and can be flushed away.

The deposit left by smokeless powder is mainly soot,

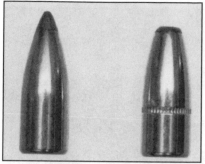

Pointed softpoint and flat-point bullets are both good hunting bullets. The pointed bullet is more susceptible to damage in feeding; the flatpoint loses velocity slightly faster.

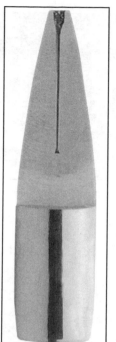

Barnes X-Bullet is a solid copper projectile designed for deep penetration, no fragmentation and good accuracy. This cutaway shows construction.

Good handgun bullet designs are the wadcutter *(left)*, so named for the neat holes it makes in paper targets, the round-nose *(center)* and semi-wadcutter *(right)*.

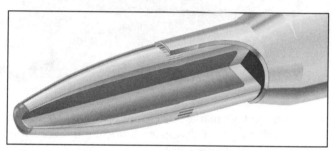

Handgun bullets designed for hunting must offer rapid expansion at relatively low velocities. To this end, they feature large hollowpoints, serrated jackets and pure lead cores.

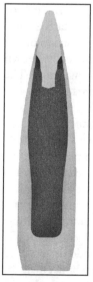

Norma's Oryx hunting bullet is a flat-based, semi-spitzer design with a thick jacket and bonded core for maximum game-stopping ability.

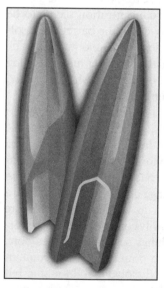

Nosler AccuBond hunting bullets include a tapered jacket, polymer tip, boattail design and a proprietary bonding process to eliminate the possibility of component separation.

Nosler's Partition bullets are designed so the front half expands in conventional manner, but only to the center. A heavy partition keeps the back half intact, retaining weight and energy, while an ordinary bullet might fragment.

Nosler Ballistic Tip and Combined Technology Ballistic Silvertip bullets utilize plastic tips and tapered jackets to control expansion on smaller big game and varmints. The tips also protect the bullet's tip from damage in the magazine.

graphite from the coating on the powder grains, small amounts of unburned powder and bullet lubricant. Often this is a varnish-like layer in the gun bore. It is not corrosive and does not draw water, nor does it tend to build up in thick deposits in the manner of blackpowder fouling. However, after a lot of shooting this fouling will begin to affect accuracy. It is easily removed by the many "nitro" powder

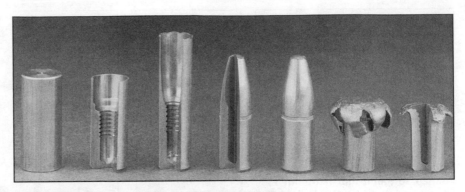

These are the steps in making one version of the Speer Grand Slam hunting bullet. A solid copper slug is punched to form the jacket. The jacket is then drawn and trimmed before the lead core is inserted. The jacket is very thick at the base to keep the bullet from fragmenting. Internal grooves and a thick base ensure the jacket does not shed the core, yet thinning the jacket in the forward portion ensures good expansion. Such bullets are for large dangerous game where deep penetration is needed.

These Speer Gold Dot handgun bullets in 38, 40 and 45 calibers evidence considerable expansion after being fired into ballistic gelatin.

solvents on today's market. These are petroleum-based and do an excellent job of dissolving lubricant and the sooty deposits of smokeless powder.

Metallic fouling is basically of two types, lead and copper. Lead fouling, known as "leading," will ruin accuracy very quickly. A poorly lubricated bullet or an over- or undersize lead bullet can deposit enough lead in a barrel with one or two shots that all those thereafter will fail to stabilize and go tumbling downrange to the extreme consternation of the shooter. Exactly what causes leading is not really known and the phenomenon may have more than one cause. The original theory was that lead bullets that were too large—or were inadequately lubricated, stripped as they passed down the barrel, and that the following bullets encountered this lead, plastered it to the bore and in the process stripped off more lead. Gradually, rough clumps of lead piled up in the barrel to the point where the rifling was so clogged that it failed to stabilize the bullets. This certainly seems possible.

This theory, however, fails to explain how undersize bullets with plenty of lubricant on them can do the same thing. The second theory holds that an undersized lead bullet will not obturate the bore fully, especially if made of too hard an alloy. Hot gases rushing by this undersize bullet melt the surface, blowing particles of melted lead down the barrel. These cool and solidify, gradually building up a layer of lead forward of the chamber, which is added to by successive bullets to the point where accuracy is ruined.

In the case of undersize bullets, recovered examples show little or no rifling marks whatsoever. The surface has a semi-melted appearance and there is often evidence of gas cutting–melted channels extending forward from the base of the bullet. Furthermore, the leading in each case is of a distinctive type.

Stripping generally happens at about the mid-point of a rifle barrel—or where the bullet runs out of lubricant—and continues out to the muzzle. The deposits are streaks and clumps usually in the corner where the land joins the groove. For some reason the heaviest concentration seems to be about three-quarters of the way down the barrel. Heat soldering, caused by gas blow-by, deposits a smooth coating of lead beginning just forward of the chamber and extending eight to ten inches. Subsequent bullets burnish this coating, making it shine and it is thus difficult to see.

In either case, the problem is to get the lead out. Nitro solvents with good lubricating qualities can flow under the lead and lift it to an extent, but the process takes days. The usual practice is to use a phosphor-bronze bore brush, saturated with solvent, and work it back and forth through the barrel, making sure not to change directions until the brush has cleared each end. Failure to do so can damage the bore surface. An overnight soak, heavily coating or filling the barrel with solvent, helps speed things on a badly leaded bore. Outers, among others, sells high-powered solvents containing ingredients which actually dissolve metal fouling, but there is still a lot of brush work to do.

Copper fouling is left by copper, brass, bronze and cupro-nickel bullet jackets, and by steel jackets plated with any of the above. Copper fouling is usually a thin wash that gradually builds into a thicker layer. Occasionally, copper alloy jackets will leave clumps of fouling which will degrade accuracy markedly and suddenly, much like leading. Removal is the same as for lead, but the process takes about three times

Speer's all-plastic snap-lock boxes keep out moisture and pollutants and prevent corrosion from getting a start on the bullets inside.

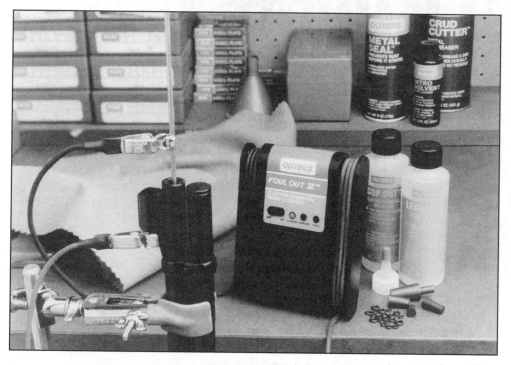

Outer's Foul Out III electro-chemical system is the easiest method of dealing with serious metal fouling problems.

as long. Ammonia-based solvents work well to dissolve copper fouling. The usual thin buildup is barely noticeable, but after it reaches a certain point, groups begin to open up—a timely reminder it's high time for a cleaning.

Outer's Foul Out III system is an advanced cleaning process for dealing with a really bad case of fouling. Foul Out works on an electroplating system. The gun barrel is plugged at the breech with a rubber stopper, then filled with a solution containing lead or copper, depending on the type of fouling to be removed. A stainless steel rod is inserted in the barrel and held in the center by rubber O-rings. Electrical contacts are attached to the barrel and the rod. A weak current passing through the solution causes the lead or copper fouling to

detach itself molecule-by-molecule to be deposited on the rod in the center. Every so often the rod must be removed and the lead or copper scrubbed off. When the solution gets weak it, too, must be replaced. The process takes a couple of hours, but it works. All fouling is removed down to the steel of the barrel. Old layers of rust and burned-on powder varnish are loosened as well. Best of all, there is no elbow-work—nothing more than a periodic inspection. For barrels that haven't been cleaned in a long time, or those that are a bit on the rough side, it doesn't get much better. When the process is complete, a few damp patches to remove traces of the solution, followed by dry patches and preservative oil, and your barrel is as clean as the day you bought it.

Homemade
projectiles have
been used
for centuries,
but recent
generations have
enjoyed many
advancements in
the art.

Casting Bullets

SHOOTERS HAVE BEEN casting bullets out of lead for hundreds of years. In the 19th century, bullet casting came into its own as a craft verging on a science. Experimenters have assembled composite bullets with hard bodies and soft/heavy noses, even going as far as pouring mercury into the mixture. Those who did that died sooner or later (more likely sooner) from the poisonous vapor. Bullets for blackpowder guns were made of lead and lead alloyed with tin. The latter gave much better results because the tin improved the quality of the cast bullet, causing it to fill the mould more completely. It was found that the velocity of lead bullets could only be raised to a certain point–about 1500 to 1600 fps. At that point lead begins coming off the bullet and gets deposited in the barrel, ruining accuracy until the lead is removed. Higher velocities with conical bullets were obtained by wrapping a slightly undersize lead bullet in a thin, tough, paper jacket (much like banknote paper), which was applied wet and shrunk to a tight fit as the cloth fibers contracted on drying. Paper-patch bullets, as they were known, produced fine

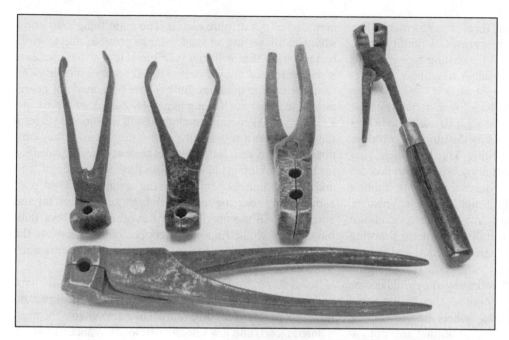

Bullet moulds from the late 18th and early 19th century cast round balls and roughly shaped conical bullets. Most had metal handles that heated up right along with the mould blocks. The finished bullet was trimmed up with a pocketknife.

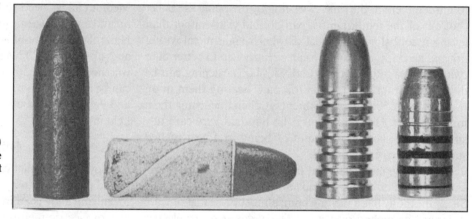

A paper-patched bullet as cast *(left)* and with the paper jacket applied. The grooved cast bullets are shown as cast and sized/lubricated.

accuracy in addition to achieving velocities close to 2000 fps. Expansion was good since the bullet alloy could be kept soft, unlike a grooved, lubricated bullet that had to be hardened to keep it from deforming from the heat, friction and pressure of high-velocity loads. When metal-jacketed bullets supplanted lead bullets for rifle use, about the time smokeless powder appeared on the scene, paper-patched bullets all but vanished, and cast lead bullets were relegated to handguns and blackpowder rifles.

The new jacketed bullets, however, were discovered to have their drawbacks: a considerably shorter barrel life caused by erosion and wear, and a hard copper fouling. This fouling was not only difficult to remove, but often covered up the corrosive salts left by primers which ate up the barrel very quickly.

Shooters began to have second thoughts about abandoning lead alloy bullets. Unfortunately, soft lead bullets and smokeless powder are not always happy together. The higher flame temperature of the smokeless powder had a tendency to melt the bases of lead bullets. Around the turn of the century, John Barlow of the Ideal Manufacturing Company–makers of bullet moulds–came up with the idea of placing a small copper cup known as a "gas check" on the bases of cast bullets to prevent this from happening. Following Barlow's death, the Ideal Company was taken over by the Lyman Gun Sight Company, which began publishing some of the first good manuals on reloading. It was not until the 1930s, however, that the basics of making good cast bullets for smokeless loadings were clearly understood.

Bullet Alloy

Hardening lead bullets with tin improved their casting quality. But tin is expensive and after adding one part to twenty parts lead, by weight, not much additional hardening was achieved. In fact, as the tin content is increased much above this point, it becomes more like solder, since the addition of tin lowers the melting point and metal fouling begins to build up in the barrel. Though antimony does not truly alloy with lead, it will combine in crystalline form and harden it to a great degree. The best hard alloys are composed of lead, tin and antimony. The tin serves to coat the antimony crystals and bond them to the lead. The antimony adds a great deal of hardness in proportion to the amount added, by weight. Tin is about twelve times as expensive as lead, while antimony is about three times as much. The addition of both metals to lead increases its fluidity in the molten state which makes it ideal for casting type metal or bullets, both of which require hardness, toughness, and precise dimensions.

When preparing or buying bullet alloy material, it is best to first consider what purpose you wish to use these bullets for, since there is no point in spending the money to produce gold-plated ammunition for plinking. Harder bullets, particularly those hardened with antimony, tend also to become brittle. Hard alloys are a poor choice for making hunting bullets since they will either drill straight through or shatter, rather than expand evenly. Hard bullets are a good choice for long-range target use or metallic silhouette shooting where velocity and flat trajectory are important and there is no need for expansion.

Bullets made of lead, tin and antimony alloy will become harder as they age. After two weeks or so, they have reached their maximum hardness. If harder bullets are desired, one way to achieve this without adding additional antimony is to harden them at the time of casting by dropping the bullet (hot out of the mould) into a pan of cold water rather than letting it cool slowly. A bullet of wheelweight metal with a normal hardness of 12.4 Bhn can be hardened to better than twice that by the above method. Similar hardening can be done by placing cast bullets in a pan, heating them in an oven to about 500 degrees Fahrenheit, then quenching them in cold water. Hot bullets must be handled very carefully since they are soft to the point of being in a near-melted state and are easily damaged.

Bullet alloys can be bought premixed from various sources, or you can buy lead, tin and antimony and mix your own. Since antimony has a melting point almost twice that of lead, it cannot be melted over an ordinary gas stove or electric melting pot. Good bullet alloys can be made from a variety of scrap materials that can be obtained at a lower cost than premixed alloys or pure metals. The main thing is to know what you are getting, at least as far as possible, and to avoid bad materials that will ruin your metal for further use. Zinc is poison to lead alloys because it will not mix properly and ruins the casting qualities. Bullets have been made of nearly pure zinc under such trade names as Zamak and Kirksite. Zinc alloys are generally too lightweight for shooting at long range. They tend to gas-cut rather badly because they cannot be gas-checked. Battery plates were at one time salvaged for bullet making. That was before they were made of lead and calcium that, like zinc, ruins the casting quality of your alloy. Babbitt, bearing metal with high amounts of tin and antimony, is of use mainly to harden other lead alloys. Babbitt contains slight amounts of copper, but this floats to the surface and generally does not cause serious problems when the metal is melted down.

Bullet alloys can roughly be classed as soft, medium, hard and extra-hard. Soft alloys are lead with about 3 to 4 percent tin or about 1 percent antimony. They are suitable for most handgun loads and low velocity rifle loads to about 1300 fps. Medium alloys need to be about 90 percent lead, 5 percent tin and 5 percent antimony, and are good to about 1700 fps. Hard alloys are about 84 percent lead, 12 percent antimony and 4 percent tin. This is the alloy used in Linotype, and it will shoot well at around or above 2000 fps. Extra-hard alloys can be anything up to 72 percent lead, 19 percent antimony and 9 percent tin. Beyond this, bullets begin to become too light in proportion to their size, and efficiency is lowered.

Mixing Alloys

Alloying and bullet casting should be done in a well-ventilated place or, better yet, outdoors. The equipment needed for mixing alloy is an iron melting pot and a lead thermometer or electric melting furnace with a thermostat, a steel spoon or skimmer to stir the metal and skim off dross. A tin can to hold the dross and an ingot mould complete the

The cast/lubricated bullet will give equal or better accuracy than the jacketed hunting bullet, while producing less barrel wear, and can be made at a fraction of the cost. At ranges of 100-150 yards, it will kill just as effectively.

Copper gas checks applied to bullets designed for them will allow increased velocities and keep hot gas from melting the bullet bases.

Block lead and tin, as well as pre-mixed alloys, ensure purity in the metal alloy. Many scrap alloys, however, may be used to make good bullets, including wheelweights, lead plumbing pipe and lead cable sheathing. Scrap 22 rimfire bullets recovered from indoor shooting ranges can also be a viable source.

This electric melting pot with bottom-pour spigot holds about 10 pounds of alloy. It's an old design that still works well.

list of basics. It is a good idea to keep the alloying operations and bullet casting separate. Alloy should be made up in 2-pound lots if you are experimenting. Once an alloy is found that suits your needs and shoots well, you can make up as much as you like-the more the better to maintain bullet weight consistency.

Cleaning scrap involves removing dirt, oxides, and such extraneous items as the steel clips on wheelweights by melting it. To keep the metal fluid and separate the unwanted material, it needs to be fluxed with a piece of beeswax or paraffin the size of the first joint of your finger. This creates smoke, which can be burned off by holding a lit match in it. The metal should be stirred with a spoon or lead dipper to work the flux into the metal and bring impurities to the top. While this stirring should be fairly rapid, it should not be so vigorous as to flip or spill hot metal on yourself. Impurities will collect on top and should be skimmed after stirring and fluxing. Fluxing will work tin and antimony into the lead that would otherwise float to the top. Do not skim off the tin, which forms a silvery gray coating on the surface. When you reach this stage, flux and stir again to blend it all together, then pour the cleaned scrap alloy into moulds for bullet casting, or for blending into a harder (or softer) alloy at another time. This final fluxing and stirring assures a consistent mixture, which should be mirror bright with a few brown spots of burned beeswax on it when in the molten state. The alloy can then be poured into a mould for small ingots for bullet making. These should be remelted in a clean pot for bullet casting. Use a scriber or magic marker to mark your finished ingots so you will know what the alloy is, since they all look pretty much alike.

The hardness of lead alloys is determined by the Brinell scale (Bhn) and is tested by dropping a known weight a known distance and measuring the impact hole. Lead testers are useful tools when making up precise alloys that will yield bullets of an exact hardness and weight. Scrap alloys are not always precise in their makeup, so they must be considered "approximate" in their composition. A quick test for pure lead is to see if you can scratch it with your fingernail. Pure lead sources from scrap include plumbing pipe, block lead and cable sheathing, although there are reports some of this may be made of a battery plate-type alloy. Scrap 22 rimfire bullets contain less than 1 percent antimony and by the time they are melted, fluxed and skimmed can be considered nearly pure lead. Tin is a component of lead-tin solder and can be bought in ingots, but it is expensive.

Small ingot moulds are the best way to store bullet alloy. To avoid mixups, ingots should be marked to identify them if different alloys are being used.

This lead and debris skimmer from Bill Ferguson easily removes clips from tire weights and similar unwanted material from the lead alloy.

A large plumber's lead pot is best for mixing lead alloys and cleaning scrap alloy, but this one from Ferguson is better suited to the bullet caster's need.

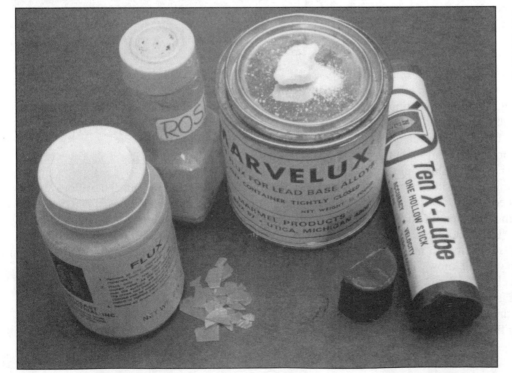

Molten metal needs to be fluxed to remove impurities and to keep tin and antimony mixed evenly throughout the alloy instead of floating on the surface. Commercial fluxes or a piece of bullet lubricant will do the job.

BULLET METALS AND THEIR RELATIVE HARDNESS

Alloy	Tin	Lead	Antimony	Copper	BHN
		— % By Weight —			
Monotype	9	72	19	—	28
Stereotype	6	80	14	—	23
Linotype	4	84	12	—	22
Electrotype	3	94.5	2.5	—	12
Tin Babbit	83	—	11	6	23
Lead Babbit	—	83	11	6	22
Tire weights	1	96	3	—	12.4
Antimony	—	—	100	—	50
Tin	100	—	—	—	7
Lead	—	100	—	—	5

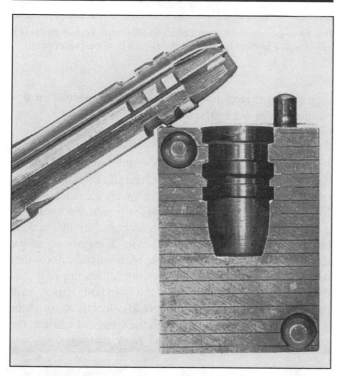

The mould cavity is given final form with a cherry, a reaming tool in the form of the bullet.

The modern bullet mould is a precision tool and a far cry from the old "nutcracker" moulds of the past. Moulds are damaged by rough treatment, and they should be kept free of rust and never battered with a metal tool.

Automobile wheelweights are a good source of alloy and can be used as is for low- to medium-velocity pistol and rifle bullets. Lead, tin and antimony alloys harden with age. The maximum hardness is reached in about two weeks. Heat-treating and quenching in cold water will harden bullets. If they are worked through a sizer, this will soften the worked surface. Tire or wheelweights, as they are often called, are now being made with slightly more lead and less antimony, and are softer, though the alloy will vary. This alloy should be tested for hardness if hardness is critical.

The Bullet Mould

The bullet mould has two equal metal blocks with a cavity in each where the bullet is cast. The blocks are aligned by pins and held together by handles much like pliers. On top of the blocks is a sprue plate with a funnel-shaped hole, through which molten metal is poured. When the pouring is complete, the sprue plate is given a rap with a wooden mallet to pivot it to one side, cutting off the excess metal, or sprue, left on top.

Bullet moulds can be made from a variety of materials and each mould maker has his preferences for his own reasons. There is no such thing as the perfect material. Custom mould maker James Andela prefers 11L17, a leaded steel of low carbon content that machines easily to a bright smooth surface. This is the same basic type used in Lyman moulds. The material cost is low, and a cold-rolled bar is virtually free of inclusions and holes, and possesses a dense grain-structure. Oil retention is low and thus the break-in time is faster than with iron moulds.

Moulds are generally made by roughing out the cavity with a drill, then cutting the impression for the bullet with a fluted cutting tool called a cherry. The cherry makes an exact negative impression of the bullet as the mould blocks are slowly pushed together on the rotating cherry.

Fine-grain cast iron is a common material with the advantages of low shrinkage and easy machinability. Iron is very stable with less inclination to warp or shrink in manufacture

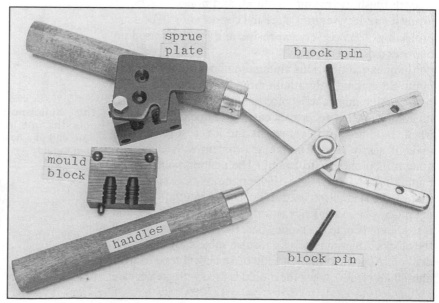

sprue plate

block pin

mould block

handles

block pin

Aluminum moulds do not require as much breaking-in as iron or steel moulds. However, the cavity must often be coated with either carbon smoke or a special compound to get good bullets.

This nose-pour mould from Colorado Shooter's Supply delivers a bullet with a perfect base since the cut-off is at the bullet nose.

or with heating and cooling. When an iron block is used in conjunction with a steel sprue plate, these dissimilar metals work well together to form a polishing action rather than a galling action where alike metals may tend to tear pieces from one another.

Brass and various bronzes (all alloys of copper) have been used for moulds with great success. They generally machine well and take a good finish. Copper alloys of all sorts have the added advantage of being highly corrosion resistant, and they heat quickly and evenly. The main disadvantages of brass and bronze are the cost of the material, which may be three times that of iron or steel. Brass and bronze are softer than steel or iron and such moulds must be handled more carefully to avoid damage. Any copper alloy (both brass and bronze) has an affinity for lead and tin and must be kept free of any acidic or similar material that could act as a flux and solder the blocks together in the casting process. Such an event usually finishes the mould. Nickel has been used to a limited extent in mould making and might very well be the perfect material, possessing the qualities of hardness, smooth finish, corrosion resistance and non-solderability, giving it an edge over iron, steel and copper alloys. The main problem is that it is very expensive, and for this reason no one uses nickel any more.

Aluminum and various aluminum alloys are widely used in mould making. Aluminum moulds require no break-in period. Aluminum's resistance to soldering, corrosion and its ability to heat to proper casting temperature quickly when combined with lightweight and low cost of material make it nearly ideal. The major problem with aluminum alloy is its proneness to galling. The melting point of aluminum (1200-1600 degrees Fahrenheit) is near enough to that of the lead alloys used in bullet making that the casting process has a tendency to anneal aluminum blocks, and thus soften them to the point where the sprue cutter will gall the blocks. Aluminum blocks are also subject to cutting and denting. Alignment pins, usually of steel, will tend to wear aluminum blocks, unless the mould is used with greater care

than an iron or steel mould. The overall useful life of an aluminum mould will be less than one of iron or steel.

Types of Moulds

The most common mould is a simple, single-cavity type that casts one bullet at a time. The next size up is the double-cavity at about the same price as a single, for small bullets. Moulds that cast up to ten bullets at a time are known as gang moulds and are used mainly by custom bullet makers because of their speed of production. They are expensive ($200). Moulds are also available with special inserts that will cast hollow-base and hollowpoint bullets in single-cavity blocks. Most moulds are of the base-pour variety with the bullet base at the top of the mould below the sprue plate. A few are nose-pour moulds with the sprue cut made at the

This hollowpoint plug fits into the nose end of a base-pour mould.

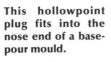

nose of the bullet. The theory behind these is that they give a more perfect base, since base regularity is the most important factor in accuracy with cast bullets. Nose-pour moulds are generally custom-made and intended for long-range, heavy target bullets.

While a bullet mould may look like a nutcracker, it is in reality a precision tool that can be easily damaged by rough handling. Dropping a mould can knock the blocks out of alignment, as can whacking it with any kind of tool. Bullets will, at times, tend to stick in one of the mould blocks when they are opened. To get the bullet to drop free, it may be necessary to give the mould a rap with a wooden rod or mallet. This should only be done by tapping the joint between the handles. Never strike the mould blocks themselves! This will ruin their alignment. By the same token, the sprue cutter plate on top of the mould should never be hit with anything but a wooden rod or mallet. A metal tool will damage the sprue cutter.

Moulds generally require a break-in period before they will cast proper bullets. The first step in preparing a mould for casting is to remove all traces of oil or grease from the blocks, particularly the inner surfaces. A solvent such as Outers' "Crud Cutter" is good for this purpose. Once the blocks are clean and the metal in the melting pot is free-flowing (650-750 degrees Fahrenheit), you can start casting. Remember, with a new mould it may take a couple hundred bullets before the good ones start coming. Patience is required. Aluminum blocks do not require breaking-in, but often need to be coated with carbon (smoke from a candle flame) or a special mould prep before they behave properly.

In a properly made mould, the blocks should make an almost seamless fit, with only a faint line where the blocks join. Operation should be smooth without the alignment pins binding or holding the blocks apart. The setting of these pins is done at the factory so they are usually in proper alignment. Occasionally, it may be necessary to adjust these pins into the blocks if they bind or the blocks do not close completely. Adjustment should never be more than a couple thousandths of an inch at a time. It should be done with the handle and sprue plate removed. Rarely will a mould be manufactured with the two blocks made of steel or iron from different lots that have a different coefficient of expansion. This would result in bullets with a larger side and a smaller side and a seam in the middle. Such a mould, along with a sample bullet, should be returned to the manufacturer for replacement.

After casting is finished, the iron or steel mould should be coated with a rust-inhibiting oil if it will not be used for weeks or months. A rusted mould is ruined if roughened or pitted. A solvent spray removes the oil when you are ready for the next casting session. Aluminum mould blocks don't require any special preservative action since they won't rust.

Bullet Casting

Bullet casting is best done outdoors or in a place where there is cross ventilation or a hood with an exhaust fan to

Bullet moulds can be warmed by placing them (carefully) on the edge of the melting pot. A pre-warmed mould will start producing good bullets before a cold one.

Best casting results can be had by holding the mould about an inch below the spigot rather than having it in hard contact.

remove lead fumes. Beyond the bullet mould, a lead melting pot capable of holding about 10 pounds of metal is the center of your activity. The best method for keeping the metal the proper temperature is to use an electric melting furnace equipped with a thermostat. A lead thermometer in a plain iron pot with a gas fire under it is less convenient, but it works. The alloy temperature can vary from about 650 to 750 degrees Fahrenheit for the alloy to flow properly. Too much heat will oxidize the tin in the alloy. The metal should be stirred frequently and fluxed every 10 minutes or so to keep the mixture constant. Failure to do this will result in bullets of uneven weight. Most electric pots have a bottom-

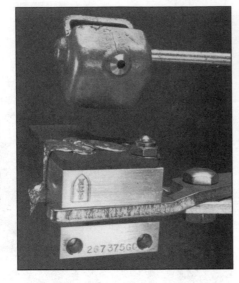

A good puddle of metal on the sprue plate helps force alloy into the mould and keep it hot so all bands in the bullet are filled out.

Never hit the sprue cutter with anything made of metal. A wooden dowel, in this case wrapped with rawhide, makes an effective cut without damage to the mould.

pour feature with a handle that releases the metal through a spigot in the bottom. This has the advantage of getting hotter metal into the mould, leaving behind any impurities that may be floating on the top.

Bullet casting, like reloading, is a solitary activity. Children especially should be kept out of the area because of exposure to lead fumes and possible spilled hot metal. A countertop, workbench, or tabletop operation is a good set-up. Some prefer to stand while casting, while others like to sit because the activity will usually go on for a couple of hours. The melting pot must have a steady base. There is nothing like a lap full of molten lead to drive this point home. The pot is the center of activity and all other components should be laid out in neat order near the pot, all within convenient reach. These include: the bullet mould; a lead dipper with a pouring spout, if you are using an open pot; a supply of alloy ingots to be added when the metal gets low; lumps of beeswax or a container of flux powder and a spoon; matches or lighter to burn off the flux vapor; a spoon or skimmer for stirring the metal and skimming off dross; a can for dross collection; an ingot mould to recover leftover alloy; a wood mallet to rap the sprue cutter and the mould joint; a tray or box lid to catch sprue trimmings; and a folded blanket or soft rug to catch the cast bullets.

A mould should be warmed up for casting. This can be done by placing it on the top edge of the electric pot or by holding it briefly in the gas flame if you are using a stove. Overheating a mould can warp the blocks and ruin it! Never dip an iron, steel or brass mould into the pot of molten metal to warm it. To do so can result in soldering the blocks together and ruining the mould. Aluminum moulds, however, can be dipped to bring them to the proper temperature.

The actual casting process should be done in a smooth rhythmic manner. If you try for quality, speed will follow. Begin by stirring the pot, and continue to do this frequently to keep the alloy from separating and to work the impurities to the top.

Lead from the dipper or from the spigot should be poured

smoothly into the mould. Some people advocate placing the spout of the dipper or spigot of the electric pot directly into the sprue funnel. This can trap air in the cast bullet and the resultant bubbles produce bullets of varying weights with different centers of gravity. Best results have been achieved by running a fairly rapid stream into the mould and allowing the metal to puddle out over the sprue plate to about the size of a quarter. This helps keep both the mould and the metal inside hot so the bullets fill out properly. Once the cast is made, cool the sprue by blowing on it for a couple seconds. The sprue cutter should then be given a sharp rap with the wood mallet to make a clean cut. The sprue plate should turn easily on its pivot, but fit flush to the top of the mould blocks to give an even base to the bullet. If lead begins to smear over the blocks, or if the cutting of the sprue tears a chunk out of the bullet base, the bullet is still too hot for cutting. Slow down and blow a little longer. The sprue plate may tend to come loose with heating and need to be tightened. Do not over-tighten. A drop of melted bullet lubricant or beeswax should occasionally be applied to the hinge on the sprue plate to keep it moving freely. Be sure not to get lubricant into the bullet cavity.

Once the sprue is removed, the handles should be pulled apart quickly. If everything is working properly, the bullet will drop free of the mould. A soft rug or towel should be used to catch the finished bullets. These should be spread apart every so often to keep from dropping one bullet on another and damaging them. Hot bullets are very soft and should be treated gently. If you wish to harden your bullets, drop them from the mould into a pot of cold water.

When the alloy level in the pot gets about two-thirds to three-quarters of the way down, it may be a good time for a break to inspect your products and replenish the pot. The first bullets will have seams on the noses and the drive bands between the grooves will not be fully filled out, with clean, square corners on the bands. This is most likely because either the metal or the mould or both were too cold for good casting. A mould that hasn't been broken in will produce similar results, often with one half being better filled

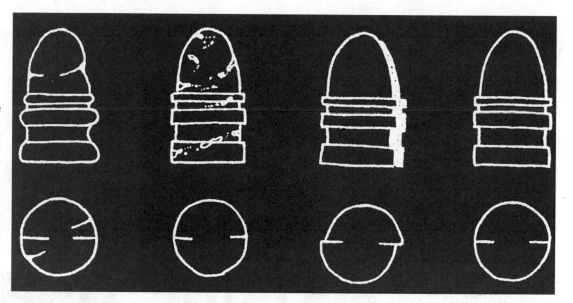

Some examples of bullet casting problems include, left to right: mould or alloy too cool; alloy has impurities; misaligned mould blocks. A good cast bullet will have all bands properly filled out and will be shiny in appearance.

out than the other. These bullets, along with the sprues, are returned to the melt pot. Expect quite a few of these in the beginning. A good bullet will be evenly filled out everywhere. Corners on drive bands will be square and the bands will be of even width all round. By rolling a bullet across a flat surface irregularities in band width may be easily seen. Discard all those that are noticeably uneven.

Irregularities, including voids (or holes) in the bullet and drive bands not completely filled out, especially in a limited area, may be caused by oil or grease having not been fully removed from that spot in the mould. Until this is completely clean, you will not get good bullets. The burned-on oil or grease should be removed with a strong solvent and a cleaning brush or wood stick such as an orange stick (available at the nail-care area of your drugstore). Occasionally lead will become stuck on the inside surfaces of the blocks, preventing them from closing properly. Any lead smear of this sort will tend to build up unless completely removed. An orange stick and, in a bad case, solvent will remove this. Never use a metal tool, acid or an abrasive to clean the interior of a bullet mould.

Just as the temperature of the mould or the alloy can be too cool for good results, it can also be too hot. Overheating oxidizes the tin and antimony, thus changing the quality of the alloy. Bullets cast at too high a temperature or from a mould that has become too hot exhibit a dull, frosted appearance rather like the surface of a piece of galvanized sheet metal. Sometimes they will have undersize drive bands as well. When such bullets appear, reduce the alloy temperature and give your mould some time to cool off. A lightly frosted bullet generally causes no problems, but it is an indication you are operating on the hot side.

Since bullet casting is a fairly messy operation, and one that requires a certain amount of preparation and cleanup, it is best to set aside an afternoon for the project. Once you get into the swing of pouring, sprue cutting and popping the bullets out of the mould, speed will come and produc-

tion can be expected to rise to 200 or more per hour for plain-base bullets. Casting hollowpoint or hollow-base bullets is more complicated, since an additional pin or post is required to make the cavity. The hollowpoint attachment goes into the bottom of the mould and turns to lock into position. Once in place, the metal is poured. After cooling, the pin is turned for removal and the bullet is then dropped from the mould in the normal manner. The extra step takes a bit more time. The secret of good production is consistency. Fluxing and stirring of the metal often is the best way to maintain a consistent alloy mixture throughout the pot. Failure to do this will start yielding bullets of varying weights, depending where you dip from the pot. Dipping serves to stir the mixture. Bottom-pour electric pots have to be stirred or the lighter metals will float to the top.

Like any other task involving hazardous material, casting should be done with a clear head, not when you are tired. At the end of the casting session an inspection of the finished bullets should be made and the obvious duds along with sprue cuttings should be returned to the melt pot. When melted, this should be poured into an ingot mould for storage. If you are using different alloys, mark your ingots with some sort of scriber to identify the alloy so you don't mix them up.

Cast bullets are far more easily damaged than the jacketed variety and must be carefully stored. Never dump or pour a batch of bullets into a bucket or box. This will cut and nick the bases and accuracy will suffer accordingly. Good methods of storage include small boxes where the bullets can be stood on their bases, packed closely together so they don't tip over. Plastic or paper boxes are far less likely to cause damage than metal containers. Proper labeling on the box is necessary to keep things straight. The same bullet cast of different alloys will have different weights and should be kept separate. If they become mixed, it's too bad because they all look alike and the only way to sort them is by weighing each one. You'd rather be shooting!

Now that you've cast a projectile to load, you can't just seat it and shoot it. There's much more to it than that.

Bullet Sizing and Lubricating

AS WITH JACKETED bullets, cast bullets and the moulds for them should be selected with consideration for the twist of the rifling of the gun you plan to shoot them in. Shorter bullets will do best in a relatively slow twist, while longer ones will require a faster twist. Beyond this is the matter of bullet design.

Cast boattail bullets will simply not work well since the unprotected, tapered base will be surrounded by hot gases and melted, with this lead then deposited on the bore of the gun. Cast bullets work best that have a flat or slightly dished base. Hollow-base bullets, in the style of Civil War Minie balls, were designed to be undersize to fit muzzleloaders and expand to bore size when fired at velocities under 1000 fps. Use of this type of bullet in cartridge guns other than handguns is not a good idea. At velocities over 1000 fps, the skirt tends to be blown out too far and may actually separate from the rest of the bullet if loaded too heavily. This can cause serious problems if the skirt remains lodged in the barrel. Accuracy in cartridge rifles is not particularly good.

Excellent accuracy may be obtained from cast bullets. Left and center are plain-base designs; the bullet on the right is designed to take a gas check.

With cast bullets, the best accuracy is generally obtained with bullets that have a relatively short ogive with the greater part of their surface bearing on the rifling. The ogive is that part of the bullet forward of the bearing surface, regardless of its shape. The greatest degree of stability is achieved with a cast bullet that has nearly all of its length in contact with the groove portion of the bore. The downside of this is increased drag and lowered velocities. Cast bullets of this design, however, are sometimes the only ones that will perform well in shallow-groove barrels. The aerodynamic shape of a bullet with a long ogive makes it a good one for long-range shooting, but such bullets are difficult to seat absolutely straight, and accuracy with cast bullets of this design is generally very poor. Much has been said in favor of "bore-riding" bullets, which offer the best compromise between the two extremes. Bullets of this design feature a relatively short drive band area with a long nose of smaller diameter that has a short taper to a point. The front portion is designed to coast along the surface of the lands–the bore–without being more than lightly engraved by them, if at all. This design provides stability without the drag encountered by a bullet with a long bearing surface, which is engraved by the rifling nearly its entire length.

Proper Bullet Size

The importance of slugging the barrel to obtain the correct groove diameter and thus best accuracy cannot be over emphasized. If a barrel is worn or of a type known to have wide variations, this is a must. While undersize jacketed bullets can give good performance in a barrel of larger diameter, undersize cast bullets will often fail to expand or upset properly, filling the grooves, particularly if these bullets are made of hard alloy. The result is considerable lead fouling and terrible accuracy, especially with deep-groove barrels. Cast bullets that are groove-size shoot best.

With every rule it seems there is an exception. In this regard there is one, and possibly others. This exception is the 45 Allin "Trap-door" Springfield. This rifle was designed for blackpowder ammunition. It features deep-groove

(.005-inch) rifling and the groove diameter may be as deep as .463-inch. A .457-inch or even a .460-inch diameter bullet is clearly undersize. If groove-diameter bullets are used in this rifle, the cartridge case will be enlarged to the point the round will not chamber! Some frustrated shooters have gone to the extreme of having their chambers reamed out to accommodate these larger bullets. The bullets worked in the sense they didn't foul the barrels, but they developed fins of lead on the rear and were not very accurate. Springfield 45 barrels were engineered to use a very soft lead-tin alloy bullet of about .549-inch diameter, which would upset as it left the cartridge case. The purpose was to design a black-powder rifle that would shoot accurately with a dirty barrel. Each bullet would thus expand to fill whatever groove space was available. These rifles and carbines will shoot very well using lead-tin bullets of a 20:1 to 30:1 alloy. Bullets with any amount of antimony in them lack the necessary malleability to expand properly and will pile up lead in the bore. If you own an old rifle with a very deep-groove barrel and find that a groove-diameter bullet expands the case to the point where it will not chamber, a soft lead-tin alloy bullet may be the only cast bullet you can shoot in it. This was a unique design, but some of the old Bullard rifles may have also used this type of boring, and there may be others.

Bullet Lubricants

Nobody actually knows how bullet lubricants work since there is no known way to observe a bullet as it is fired through the barrel of a gun. Unlubed lead alloy bullets can be fired at 600 to 800 fps without causing leading, assuming the barrel is a very smooth one. Revolvers, however, are something of an exception to this rule, probably because their bullets tip slightly or some gas blows by the bullets as they jump the gap from cylinder to the forcing cone in the barrel.

Lubricants prevent leading by reducing friction in the barrel, but they also have a considerable effect on accuracy. There are any number of lubricants that will prevent leading, but their accuracy record is often poor. Through the years

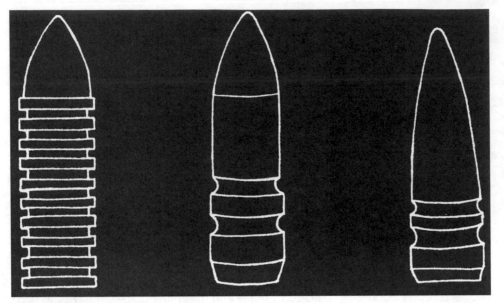

The best rifle accuracy with a cast alloy bullet is with one that has a short ogive. The bullet on the left has many lubricant grooves and will shoot well in multi-groove and shallow-groove barrels owing to good bore contact over most of its length. The center bullet is a "bore-riding" type also with a short ogive. The right bullet is of a long-ogive design. Difficulty in getting such a bullet properly seated in the case makes it a poor shooter.

any number of lubricant formulas have been tried with success rates ranging from excellent to terrible. Heavy grease of various sorts works well, as can be attested to by anyone who has shot some of the 22 Long Rifle ammunition made in the 1940s and early '50s. The problem, however, was that it would melt in warm weather and, when shot, combined readily with powder fouling to form a black greasy coating that wound up all over your hands. The use of such grease/lubricant in inside-lubricated cartridges ruined them in short order as the grease soaked into the powder and even into the primer, ruining both.

Grease/petroleum jelly in small amounts can be combined with various waxes with reasonable success to make a good bullet lubricant, but under warm conditions it has a tendency to "sweat" out of the mixture and get into the powder. Some greases will oxidize and harden over time, or evaporate to a degree. These are poor candidates for long-term storage if that is desired. Lithium-based

grease appears not to sweat out since it has a very high melting point.

Some early formulas for bullet lubricants included resin. Since this is an abrasive and not a lubricant, this is a bad idea. Tests conducted by Philip Sharpe, among others, demonstrated that resin in the mixture actually shortened barrel life.

Japan wax is obtained from an Asian sumac berry and is similar to bayberry wax. It was used in many early lubricant formulas. It has a tendency to dry over time and become brittle, at which point it loses much of its lubricating qualities. It is, to a degree, hygroscopic, which is not good if your bullets may be exposed to moisture. Sharpe found that Japan wax, when combined with copper-plated lead bullets, caused them to corrode to the point they were unshootable in a rather short time. Bullet lubricants that are hygroscopic or evaporate through time, allowing bullets to corrode, are for short-term use only. About the only

Bullets must be of the proper size and alloy to shoot well. On the left is a 45-70 rifle bullet cast of 20:1 lead-tin alloy, sized .459-inch, the proper diameter for the original 45 Springfield rifle. Next to it is the same bullet after firing. The bullet became shorter and fatter as it filled the deep-groove bore. Next is a very similar bullet sized .459-inch, but made of an alloy containing a small amount of antimony. On the far right is this bullet after firing. The hard bullet has failed to expand to fill the grooves. The rifling mark is barely visible where hot gas blew by and melted the bullet surface. The results—good accuracy from the left; a leaded bore and terrible accuracy on the right.

thing that can be done is to keep such ammunition away from heat and moisture.

Carnauba wax is a tree wax from Brazil and is the main ingredient in shoe polish. It is a hard wax that needs softening to make a good bullet lubricant. Paraffin is often included in lubricant mixtures, mainly as a stiffener. Paraffin has rather poor lubricating qualities unless heated. When subjected to pressure, it crumbles as it forms layers. It can be used in lubricants, but only sparingly.

Beeswax is hard and must be softened for bullet lubricant. In the pure form it can be used for outside-lubricated bullets, like the 22 Long Rifle, since it remains hard and will not pick up dirt and grit in the manner of softer lubricants.

Ozocerite and ceresine waxes are the same, but ceresine is the refined form, often sold as a beeswax substitute. Ozocerite is a mineral wax with many industrial uses since it is cheaper than beeswax. Candles are made of this material, often with coloring added. It is too hard to use as is and must be softened with some form of oil to make it usable for bullet lubricant.

Tallow is animal fat. In refined form it is called lard and was an early lubricant for patched bullets in muzzleloaders. The vegetable equivalent, Crisco, has long been a favorite for muzzleloader fans because it keeps blackpowder fouling soft. Tallow gets rancid and melts in warm temperatures, as does Crisco. These preclude their use in cartridge ammunition except as an additive.

Graphite is a mineral which is neither a wax nor a lubricant, but a very fine abrasive. Colloidal graphite is the finest granulation available and when mixed with waxes and oils remains in suspension. It will not burn off and has a fine polishing action and (so it has been claimed) will improve a barrel by filling pores in the metal. A little goes a long way in a lubricant, but the results have been good.

Commercial and Homemade Lubricants

Commercial lubricants are available in sticks or blocks, with the sticks being molded to fit popular sizing-lubricating machines. The ingredients in commercial lubricants can best be described as some combination of the above in varying amounts. Prices vary, though claims of effectiveness are always high. Most give good results. The formulas are proprietary and the ingredients are sometimes referred to, or at least hinted at, in their various trade names–Bore Butter, Alox, Lithi Bee and so on.

When it comes to getting a good bullet lubricant, there is no magic formula. Most of the commercial products will do the job. They have the advantage of being cast into small cakes or sticks designed to fit into sizer-lubricator machines, and some come in liquid form which can be applied by gently tumbling bullets in it, then setting them on wax paper to dry. They are clean and easy to handle.

The advantage of making up your own lubricant is two-fold - economy and versatility. Homemade lubricant is about half as expensive as the commercial product, and less than that if you make it in quantity. Versatility is probably

Liquid Alox is available from Lee and Lyman. It goes on wet and dries to a waxy finish. It works well on handgun bullets, particularly those shot as they were cast.

more important since, as is the case with bullet alloys, one formula is not suitable for all uses. Lubricant for low-velocity handgun bullets does not have to stand up to a lot of heat and pressure and can be fairly soft. A soft, sticky-type of lubricant is an absolute must for use with blackpowder or Pyrodex since the lubricant must keep the fouling soft and easy to remove. A very good lubricant of this type was developed by Spencer Wolf in his research on reproducing original ammunition for the 45 Springfield and Colt SAA revolver. The lubricant consists of beeswax and olive oil mixed in equal parts by volume. Beeswax must be melted in a double boiler to avoid oxidizing it. Overheated beeswax will turn dark brown and lose some of its lubricating properties. When Wolf was asked if there was something special about olive oil, he replied that it was on sale and was thus the least expensive vegetable oil around at the time. Presumably any vegetable oil would do. These oils blend a little better with beeswax than petroleum-based oils and show no tendency to sweat out even under warm conditions. Interestingly, the beeswax-olive oil mixture does well under fairly high temperatures. The Wolf mixture is very similar in texture to the commercial SPG lubricant and a little softer than Bore Butter. Soft lubricants are the best for cold weather shooting. Hard lubricants become harder when chilled and often fail to work causing bores to lead. Harder formulas, however, are best for shooting high-pressure, high-velocity loads. Harder lubricants generally stand up under warm summer conditions where ammunition may be heated to well over 100 degrees as it sits in a box on a loading block in the sun.

Lyman Orange Magic is a stick lubricant intended for hard-alloy cast bullets to be shot at maximum cast bullet velocities and high temperatures.

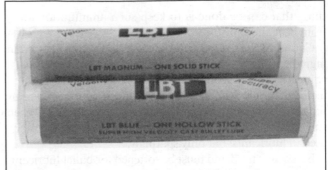

LBT Blue Soft Lube is intended for shooting cast bullets at slower velocities and low temperatures.

Lithi Bee is a stick lubricant made of lithium-based grease combined with beeswax. The mixture is an old favorite.

Taurak bullet lube is a hard grease with a high melting temperature, available in sticks from NECO.

When trying your hand at making bullet lubricant, always remember to keep records of your experiments. It doesn't get much sadder than when you stumble on a perfect formula and can't remember what went into it.

Bullet Lubrication Technique

Some bullets shoot best as cast and should be used that way if they are the proper diameter as they come from the mould. This is often the case with old guns and others that have larger groove diameters. The diameter as well as the roundness of your bullets should be checked by measuring with a Vernier caliper or micrometer.

Lubricating bullets as cast is easily done by placing them base down in a flat, shallow pan of melted lubricant, making sure that the level of the liquid covers all of the lubricating grooves on the bullets. When the lubricant hardens, the bullets are removed using a homemade tool fashioned from a fired cartridge case, of the same caliber, with the head cut off. A short case may have to be soldered or epoxied to a larger diameter case or metal tube to provide a suitable handle. Bullets are removed from the hardened lubricant by simply slipping the case mouth over the bullet and cutting it free. This is known as the cake cutter or cookie cutter method. As the tube handle fills with bullets, they are removed from the top and collected. Finished bullets should have their bases wiped free of lubricant. This is best accomplished by wiping them across a piece of cloth lightly dampened with powder solvent. They should then be placed in clean plastic boxes for storage pending loading. As bullets are run through the mixture, lubricant must be added with

each subsequent batch to keep the level at the proper height. It is best to do a full pan load each time.

Sizer-Lubricator

Sizer-lubricators are machines that perform three functions. The first is to lightly swage (or size) the cast bullet into perfect roundness; and second to fill the grooves with lubricant. The optional third is to attach a gas check. The tools cost about $125 to $175.

As they come from the mould, bullets are generally larger than required, and it is necessary to bring them to the precise size for best accuracy. This is done by forcing the cast bullet through a die, swaging it to exact diameter. When purchas-

A cake cutter, which is more of a cookie cutter, can be made by drilling out or cutting off the head of a fired cartridge case for the bullets you wish to lubricate. The bullets are placed in a shallow pan of melted lubricant and removed when it has cooled. The pan can be filled to lubricate all or only some of the grooves.

The Lee Lube and Sizing kit fits on their press. This sizing die and integral container is designed for bullets coated with liquid Alox. The pre-lubed bullets are pushed through the sizer and held in the container.

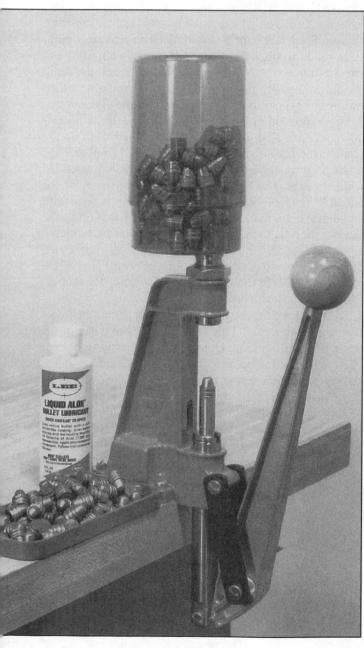

ing a bullet mould and a sizing die, it is a good idea to get a mould that will produce bullets very close to the proper final size. There will always be a certain amount of shrinkage of the bullet as it cools in the mould. If this did not happen, extracting this bullet would be nearly impossible. Moulds are sold with an indication of the cast size, but this will vary depending on the composition of the alloy that is being cast. Bullets should not be sized down much over .003-inch. Excess sizing tends to distort the bullet and adversely affect accuracy. While sizing gives a bullet a shiny mirror-like surface, it also reduces the hardness of the surface by working the metal; another reason to avoid excess sizing.

Sizer-lubricators are made by several manufacturers. They all combine the same basic features: a frame to hold the die, a handle that drives the top punch that forces the bullet through the die, and a lubricating pump that holds a stick of bullet lubricant and forces it through holes in the sizing die and into the grooves of the bullet. One nice feature of the machines made by Lyman and RCBS is that the dies, top punches and lubricating sticks are all interchangeable.

The sizer-lubricator is a bench-mounted tool for it must have solid support. Otherwise the force delivered to the operating handle would lift it off the bench or take the top off a flimsy table. The tool should be bolted to the loading bench or to a solid plank and held on a sturdy table with C-clamps. Soft alloy bullets size rather easily, while those of Linotype metal require far more force. Using these machines takes a bit of skill, much like bullet casting, but mastering it is not very difficult, and speedy production will follow once you master the basics. The first step is to be sure you have the proper top punch. A flat-point top punch will mash the nose on a round-nose bullet, and too large or too small a punch will produce its own distortions, including inaccurate alignment in the sizing die. Top punches should be matched to particular bullets. Loading manuals, particularly those dealing with cast-bullet shooting, include data on the proper top punch for various bullets. Sometimes the exact form of punch is not available. Two solutions are to get the nearest larger size and pack it with varying amounts of alu-

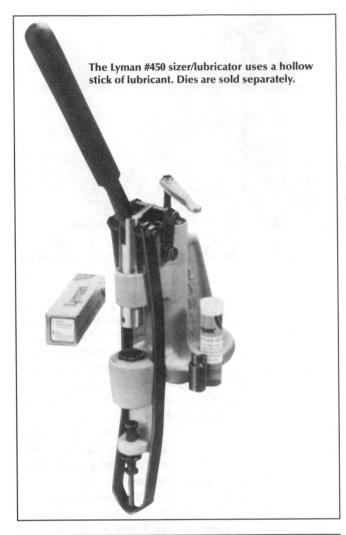

The Lyman #450 sizer/lubricator uses a hollow stick of lubricant. Dies are sold separately.

minum foil or facial tissue coated with a bit of bullet lubricant. Once this is compacted by sizing a few bullets, it will remain in place for a long time and not change shape. The other method, if the top punch is only slightly undersize, is to chuck it in a drill or metal lathe and re-contour it with a file, cutting tool or emery cloth. This may be necessary if you are using an obsolete or custom bullet mould.

Once the proper top punch is selected, the reservoir of the lubricator pump should be filled. Most take a solid or hollow stick of lubricant. If you are making your own, you can either cast your own sticks in homemade moulds fabricated from the proper size of pipe or you can try pouring melted lubricant directly into the reservoir itself. This must be done with the sizing die in the up (closed) position, otherwise melted lubricant will come welling up through the die to run all over the place. Pouring into the reservoir is difficult, particularly if it is of a type that uses a hollow lubricant stick and has a metal pin in the center. A pouring pot with a long spout is the only kind to use to avoid spilling lubricant all over. Solid lubricant is very difficult to remove–a putty knife will lift it off a flat surface. It is nearly impossible to remove from a rug. With the reservoir filled and the die in the down position, the lubricator pump handle is pushed two or three times to force lubricant into the die chamber. A bullet is seated in the center of the die and the operating handle is pulled firmly down forcing the bullet into the sizing die. Once sized, the handle is pushed back and the bullet pops up–the proper size and with the grooves filled with lubricant. The die must be adjusted, however, for the length of the bullet you are lubricating. This is done with an adjustment screw on the base of the lug that holds the die. If a short bullet is pushed too far into the die, lubricant will squirt up over the nose. If a long bullet is not seated deep enough it will not get far enough below the level of the lubricating holes in the sizing die, and some of the grooves will not be filled with lubricant.

The up stroke on the operating handle should be faster than the down stroke. This avoids having the bullet in the down position too long. Quick operation avoids lubricant building up on the base of the bullet and the face of the bottom punch where it has to be wiped off. The lubricator pump handle has to be given a couple of turns about every other bullet to keep the pressure high enough to fill all of the grooves completely. Oftentimes the bullet has to be run through the die a second time to fill all the grooves. One advantage of the Redding/ SAECO tool is that the lubricant reservoir has a spring-powered top on it, which keeps constant pressure on the lubricant, allowing the operator to lube several bullets before having to run the pump handle. This is essentially all there is to it. The trick to not smearing lube all over the bottom punch and bullet base is not to have too much pressure on the lubricant, and to bring the bullet up out of the die as quickly as possible. Always keep pressure on the handle after completing the down stroke. Failure to do so will allow lubricant to squirt in under the bullet. It is a matter of practice and developing a feel for this operation.

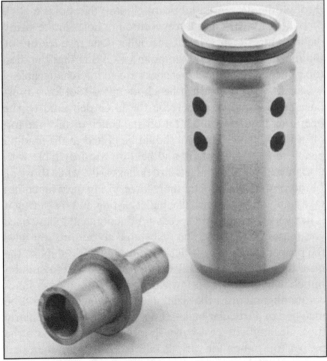

Lube/sizer dies and top punches are interchangeable between Lyman and RCBS.

A bullet pops up after having been lubricated on a SAECO machine. A solid mounting is needed to keep the machine from lifting off the bench top. Proper die adjustment is necessary to keep lubricant from squirting over the bullet nose. The small amount seen here can easily be wiped off.

Seating Gas Checks

Gas checks are intended for use on specially designed bullets. They are of two basic types: the Lyman type that is intended to drop off the base of the bullet shortly after it leaves the muzzle of the gun, and the Hornady crimp-on variety that remains attached until the bullet reaches the target. Some prefer the Hornady type since they do a better job of keeping hot gas from getting around the base of the bullet and melting channels in the bearing surface–known as gas cutting. Sometimes the drop-off gas checks do not drop off and remain on the bullet all the way to the target, making that bullet several grains heavier than the others in the series of shots and, particularly at long ranges, causing it to hit low.

Gas checks permit cast bullets to be driven almost as fast as jacketed bullets, about 2200 fps, by acting as a hard gasket at the base of the bullet. High velocities with gas-checked bullets are obtainable only with hard, tough alloys and lubricants that will stand up to high temperatures and pressures. Applying gas checks to hard alloy bullets takes more muscle than for softer ones, but can be done so long as those alloys are no harder than Linotype (bhn 22).

Seating gas checks is simplicity itself. They are placed on the face of the die punch and the bullet is seated in it. It is then pushed through the sizing die, and the bullet lubricated in the normal manner. Make sure that when the bullet bottoms in the die that it does so firmly in order to get a good fit with the crimp-on type of gas checks. When applying gas checks to soft alloy bullets, care must be taken not to apply too much pressure and flatten the nose of the bullet. The leverage on these machines is very good, allowing you to apply a great deal of pressure with minimal effort.

Bullet Inspection and Storage

Bullets should be inspected after they come out of the sizer to see that the grooves are well filled with lubricant. Sizing will not make out-of-round bullets perfect. If the grooves are wider on one side than they are on the other, this bullet was not completely filled out in the mould. These and ones with irregular drive bands should be scrapped if they are really bad, or separated for use as warming and fouling shots. Finished bullets should be loaded immediately, or stored in closed containers where they will not gather grit, lint and other foreign matter. Bullets that have been dropped on the floor and dented on the base will no longer shoot straight. Those that have rolled on the floor through primer ash, metal filings and the like should be wiped clean with a soft cloth moistened with solvent or light oil and relubricated.

Finished bullets should be weighed on your powder scale. The finest consistent accuracy is from those that are within a tolerance of +/- 0.5 grain in weight. Changes in alloy and temperature, lack of stirring and fluxing can affect weight by varying the content of the alloy in that particular bullet. By the same token, pouring technique can trap air bubbles in bullets and alter their weight. Bullets should be sorted by weight and stored and marked accordingly for best accuracy. It is best to handle finished, cast and lubricated bullets as little as possible. This keeps them clean, and your fingers won't wipe lubricant out of the grooves.

Wads and Fillers

Distortion of the base of a cast bullet, particularly a rifle bullet, is a constant problem. Smokeless powder of the

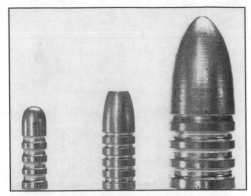

Bullets should be inspected before sizing and lubricating. Good cast bullets should have square edges and even grooves.

After lubrication, there should be no evidence of distortion or pieces of lead in the lube grooves. The accurate bullet is one that leaves the barrel evenly rifled, with no asymmetrical distortion.

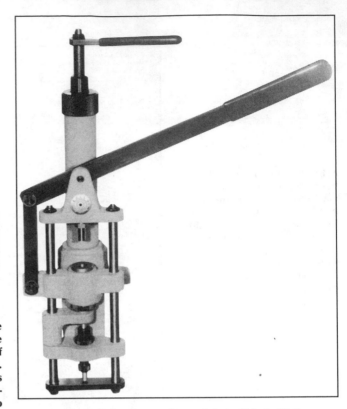

The SAECO Lubri-Sizer is a quality tool that will last a lifetime.

coarser granulations will be forced into the base of soft alloy bullets peppering them with small dents and often gas-cutting the sides to a degree. A number of strategies to overcome this problem have been tried with varying degrees of success. One thing seems absolutely clear, however: Never have an airspace between any kind of wad and the base of the bullet! This will cause that wad to come slamming forward to strike the base of the bullet and expand there. This can make a ring in the case and, in many instances, in the chamber of a rifle and ruin the barrel. One shooter had light tufts of kapok weighing about a grain, used to keep a light charge of powder in the base of a 45-70 case, make a ring in the case. These were propelled by 9 grains of Unique when they hit the base of a 150-grain bullet. Wads of felt, cork and cardboard have been used with success in straight-walled cases. Never put any kind of filler wad in a bottleneck case! All wads, however, must completely fill the void between the powder and the bullet base. Fillers between wads such as Cream of Wheat have also been tried and the results found unsatisfactory.

From time to time there is a resurgence of interest in various types of lubricating wads for use with both cast and jacketed bullets. Wax wads and grease wads have demonstrated effectiveness in improving accuracy and lengthening barrel life. These consist of a thin disc of bullet lubricant cut to exact case-mouth diameter. The lubricant is generally harder than that used in a lubricating pump. The discs are punched out of a flat sheet about the thickness of the cardboard on the back of a writing tablet. One of the better-known formulas was the development of Edward A. Leopold and was sold as "Leopold's Oleo Wads." They consisted of (by weight) 5 ounces each of Japan wax and beeswax, 2 ounces

ozocerite, and 3 to 4 teaspoons Acheson Unctious graphite #1340. According to G.L. Wotkyns and J.B. Sweany, the developers of the 220 Swift, grease wads directly behind the jacketed bullets decreased erosion and improved accuracy.

Lubricated cardboard wads were at one time loaded in rifle ammunition by UMC and Winchester for the 40-70 and 40-90 blackpowder cartridges. Bearing the above warnings in mind, those who wish to experiment with making their own wax wads will find that about the only way to get an even sheet of lubricant is to take a very clean straight-sided glass bottle, fill it with cold water and dip it straight down into a pot of melted lubricant. A deep narrow pan and a bottle that nearly fills it will be most practical. The thickness of the layer is controlled by the number of dips. When the lubricant layer on the bottle is well cooled, a straight cut is made down one side and the sheet is gently peeled off. Wads may be cut by using the mouth of a fired case from which the head has been cut to facilitate removal.

As can be deduced, the easiest and safest kind of loading for use with a wax wad is one in which the case is nearly filled with powder and the wad and bullet base gently compact the charge. Sharpe makes the point that the wad should "stay in the neck of the case." Amen to that. For reduced charge loadings you could try sticking the wad to the bullet base by either warming the bullet base and pressing the wad in place, or wetting the wad surface with a volatile solvent and "gluing" it in place with the melted lubricant. This system is not tried or recommended. Before loading any such ammunition, see how tight the bond is. If the wad drops off or can be easily removed by slipping it or tapping the bullet, don't load it unless it is supported by a charge of powder or a solid wad column of felt, cardboard or cork.

9

Reloading can
be accomplished in
any number
of ways-from
simple inexpensive
hand tools to
costly progressive
equipment. By
defining your
goals, you'll find
which is best
for you.

Tooling Up For Reloading

RELOADING BEGAN WITH relatively simple tools that could be carried in the pocket or saddlebag. They were shaped in the manner of pliers and leather punches, and were referred to as "tong tools." Manufacture of this type of equipment more or less ceased about twenty years ago, with Lyman and Lee being the only major manufacturers of this type of tool today. They are portable, cheap and capable of turning out rather good ammunition. The disadvantages are that they are slow and require more muscle power to use than bench tools. As "campfire" ammunition making became more a thing of the past, these tools have all but disappeared. They are, however, useful since you can't take a reloading bench into the woods, and there may be some instances where you might need to produce some quick loads in the field. They qualify nicely as survival equipment, too.

Whether plain or fancy, the reloading bench should have enough space for efficient tool mounting.

Today's reloader generally does not have all that much spare time and usually prefers speed in production over the option of taking tools to the field. The beginning reloader is faced with some basic issues that must be assessed when it comes time to purchase equipment. These include economy versus speed; speed versus precision; and, finally, precision versus economy. These three issues will be discussed in detail in the hope that you can reach decisions that will match your temperament and shooting habits. The beginning reloader can find himself stunned by information overload while perusing catalogs, absolutely brimming with gadgets and gizmos, all promising more/better/faster.

Basic Equipment: Getting What You Need

One way to enter the water, as it were, is to get acquainted with other reloaders and see what they use and don't use, and quiz them on the whys and wherefors of their equipment. Ask a friend if you can try his equipment. This way you can get a feel for the tools, how they work, and begin to come to some decisions regarding what you might like and what you find difficult or unnecessary.

The reloading bench is the foundation of your work area. There is no standardized design, and it may well serve a dual purpose as a kitchen counter on which reloading tools are temporarily mounted. If you must use a temporary surface of this type, your reloading press and sizer/lubricator should be permanently mounted on a solid 2x6 or heavier plank that can be securely attached to the counter top with C-

A basic reloading bench should be sturdy and have plenty of storage space. The individual design is up to the maker. This bench was built from plans formerly available from the National Reloading Manufacturers Association, which is now inactive. (See Chapter 18 for complete plans.)

clamps. The counter must have a solid top since the levering force exerted on the bullet sizer and the loading press can pull the counter top loose. If you have the space, a solid desk or workbench arrangement is best. General requirements are that it have enough weight or be attached to the floor

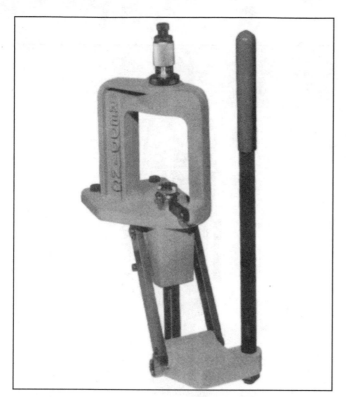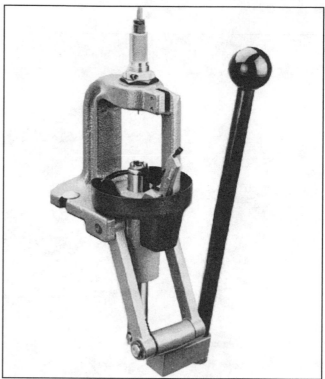

**Basic O-frame presses are reliable, rugged and easy to use.
The Redding** (*left*) **and RCBS are typical examples.**

so that it will not rock back and forth in use. It should be solid enough that the top will not pry loose under the stress of cartridge and bullet sizing. Whether or not it is to be a thing of beauty depends on how much of the public will view it, in a dining room or corner of an apartment, or if it will stay in a garage or basement area. If ammunition and powder are to be stored in the same area, the bench should in a spot that is climate controlled. It should have at least one large drawer and be close to shelving or cabinets where bullets, primers, powder, cases, loading manuals, etc., can be located within easy reach. The top should be smooth and free of cracks, holes and splinters.

While you can build a bench of your own design out of whatever scrap lumber you have at hand, an easier way is to use plans from the National Reloading Manufacturers Association. (That organization is now inactive, but you can go to Chapter 18 where your editor revisits those plans, and actually gives you the complete plans right in this book.) If you're handy with tools, you can buy all the components from your local lumber yard or building materials store for around $100 and assemble it yourself.

The NRMA bench is heavy, solid and able to support all manner of tools and presses, The plans have been around for more than 20 years, and thousands of reloaders have built them. The plans call for heavy dimension lumber and plywood, so build it where you will use it.

Once you have your bench, the next step is to choose the basic reloading tool, the heart of your operation–the press. Before parting with any money, it is best to start with the maximum amount of experience and knowledge. This returns to the above-mentioned issues of speed, economy

and precision. Your first question should be: Am I going to load for pistol, rifle or both? Shotshell reloading requires it's own special loading equipment and will be dealt with later. If the answer is to reload both handgun and rifle cartridges, then you will want to buy a press that is intended for rifle cartridges that will do handgun ammunition as well.

Economy Versus Speed

The most basic type of bench-mounted loading press is the O-frame or C-frame press, so called because the frames are shaped like these letters. Both are rugged and simple. They are also referred to as single-stage presses since they mount a single loading die in the top. Each operation-- decapping and sizing, neck expanding and bullet seating-- requires that the die be unscrewed and the next die screwed in place for each operation. Most reloaders perform each operation in batches, so you don't spend all your time changing dies. The manufacturers promise a production rate of about 100 finished rounds per hour.

Similar to these are the arbor presses, which mount a single die in the bottom. Arbor presses require a special straight-line type of die that is not compatible with the top-mounted variety used in standard presses. The price range and speed are about the same. Arbor presses are small and compact, and have the advantage of being on a flat base and not requiring permanent bench mounting. This makes them handy to take to the range where ammunition can be fabricated while you shoot. In addition to instant gratification, this portability saves time and material put into long runs of test ammunition.

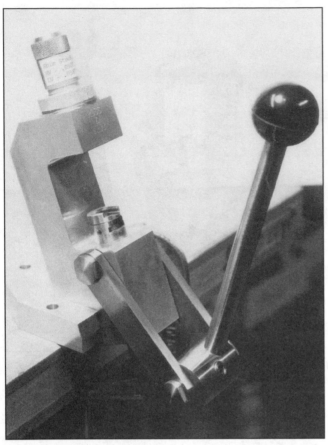

The Ross & Webb Benchrest Press is an extremely strong C-frame design for the serious reloader.

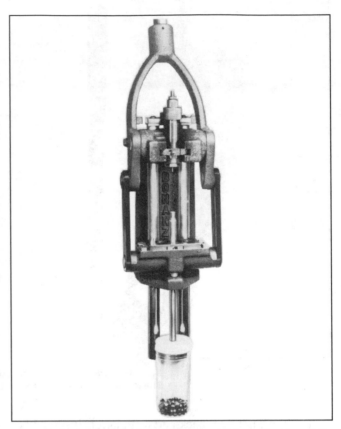

Forster's Co-Ax B-2 Press is a different wrinkle on the C- and O-frame designs. Dual guide rods offer precision alignment; dies snap in and out for quick, easy changing.

More expensive and faster are the turret and H-frame machines that allow a full three-die set to be mounted along with a powder measure. All dies are in place and the cartridge is moved from one station to the next, or the turret is rotated to bring the next die into position. Production is estimated at 200 rounds per hour, but the price is higher.

Near the top end, short of buying an ammunition factory, are the progressive loaders. These are semi-automated machines with feed tubes and hoppers that are filled with cases, bullets, primers and powder. Once the various feeding devices are filled, the operator simply pulls a handle and manually feeds one component, usually bullets or cases, inserting them into a slot on a revolving plate, and the machine does the rest, moving the case from station to station. The finished rounds come popping out at the end of a full plate rotation cycle and are collected in a convenient bin. Production rates are from about 500 rounds per hour to 1200. Plan to do a lot of shooting if you invest in one of these. You should also plan to have plenty of space since a progressive stands better than 2 feet high and weighs up to 50 pounds.

Speed Versus Precision

All of the presses mentioned will produce high quality, precision ammunition, or at least as precise as you make it, since quality control is up to the operator. Careful adjust-

The Jones arbor press is typical of the type. Arbor presses are compact and do not need to be bench-mounted, making them convenient to take to the range to assemble ammunition on the spot.

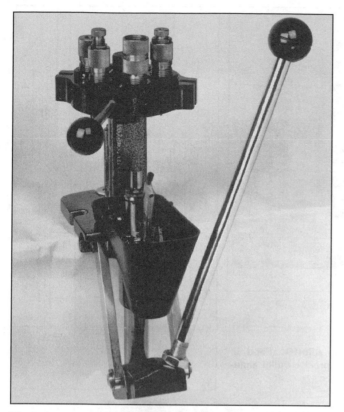

The Lyman T-Mag II is a turret press from a company that has been making this basic design for over forty years. A full set of dies and a powder measure can be screwed into the turret, and each one is then rotated into position for the next step.

The H-frame press, as typified by the CH/4D No. 444, has many followers since it holds a full set of dies and powder measure. In this system, the "turret" is fixed, thus no rotation between steps is required. The case is simply moved from station to station.

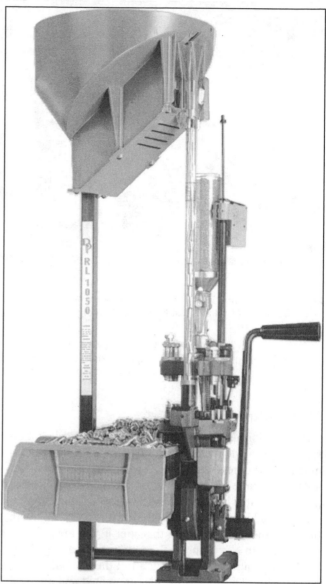

The Dillon RL 1050 will load 1000 to 1200 rounds per hour. A progressive loader of this sort represents a sizable investment and is definitely not for beginners.

ment, precise measurement, and inspecting every step in production are your job, and if you do it well, the results will show in the finished product.

Progressive loaders are designed more for speed than precision. In the case of handgun ammunition where benchrest accuracy is not expected, they are the best investment for a shooter who really burns a lot of ammunition. These are also purchased by clubs, police departments and professional reloaders who sell their ammunition. While progressives churn out tremendous quantities of ammunition, they generally require a fairly complicated set-up period, and if there is a change of caliber of ammunition, this can mean a different set of feed tubes and plates as well as dies. Because they are complicated, progressives require more tinkering and cleaning to keep them running smoothly. Automation of the process means you depend on the machine to do it right every time. That doesn't always happen.

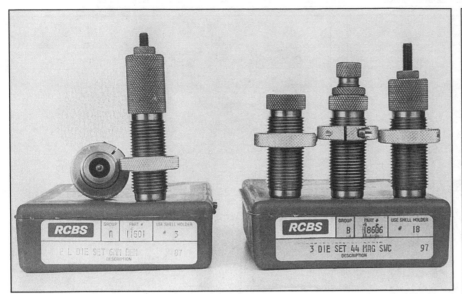

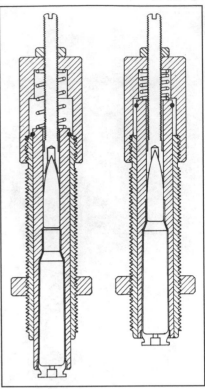

Reloading dies come in two basic formats—a two-die set for rifle cartridges and a three-die set for pistol and cast-bullet rifle loading.

Special precision dies feature micrometer adjustment and, in this example, spring-loaded sleeves for precise bullet alignment. This benchrest die set is from Forster.

Precision Versus Economy

As mentioned above, precision and economy lie mainly with the single-die and turret/H-frame (multi-station) machines. Progressives only pay when there is a demand for high-volume production of one caliber at a time. The price differential between the single-stage and turret/multi-station machines is close enough that it is probably worth the extra money to invest in the latter if you are going to do more than a very modest amount of reloading. They have the advantage of holding a full die set and a powder measure. This means the dies are seated and adjusted once, for the most part, unless you are reloading a number of calibers. The production edge will be noticed as the amount of ammunition you make increases. For a shooter reloading a single caliber—mainly for hunting—someone who does not do a lot of practice and may assemble no more than 200 to 2000 rounds a year—the best buy would be the simple, reliable O- or C-frame machine. It will do the job.

Reloading Dies

Once a press is purchased, it must be equipped with one set of dies for each different cartridge you reload. For handgun ammunition, the first die decaps the cartridge and resizes it to unfired dimensions, the second expands the case mouth, and the third seats the bullet. Rifle dies do not expand the case mouth since this is not necessary for hard, jacketed bullets. Cast bullets, however, require this expansion to keep them from being accidentally cut by a sharp case mouth.

Dies come in grades from plain to fancy. Basic die sets

of steel will last for many years and many thousands of rounds of ammunition. Using tungsten carbide or titanium nitride dies requires little or no lubrication of the cases, which speeds the loading process a bit, and they last longer than steel. Forster, Redding and Jones offer micrometer-adjustable bullet seating dies, while Harrell's Precision makes a variable base for reforming benchrest cases to near chamber dimensions. Specialty dies of this sort cost more and are worth the price if you are into competition target shooting. There are special neck-sizing dies for use with bottleneck cases that will only be fired in one particular rifle, thus there is no need to put cases through the wear and tear of full-length resizing. There are custom dies for obsolete calibers and loading cartridges as large as 20mm. Nearly anything your heart desires will cheerfully be made up by the 4-D Custom Die Co. of Mount Vernon, Ohio.

Primer Seaters and Shellholders

Primer seaters generally fit in the front bottom of the reloading press, and you will need one for large diameter primers and another for small primers. It's probably a good idea to buy both since a pair is generally quite inexpensive. Case or shellholders are needed to hold the case as it inserted into the die. One size does not fit all, but Lee and Lyman offer sets that cover most popular rifle and pistol cartridges.

A real headache is getting the primer crimp out of a military case. A number of die makers offer a useful die to remove this crimp with a stroke of the loading press handle. There is also a chamfering tool to do this, but some prefer a swager die.

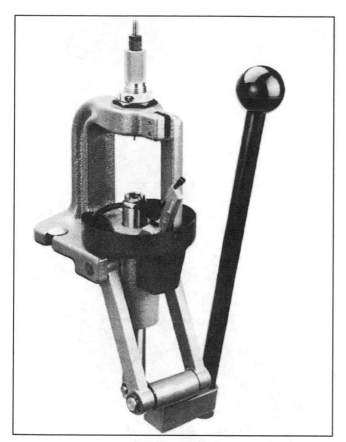

The primer seater, as shown on this RCBS Rock Chucker, is usually included as part of the press, but if you get used equipment, be sure all parts are there.

Shellholders must be purchased to fit the cartridge you are reloading. Some accept more than one cartridge, and they can be had in sets.

Problems such as crimped-in primers and stuck cases, like this one with the head torn off, require special tools such as a stuck-case removal kit.

Sizer/Lubricators

The second large bench tool you will need is a sizer/lubricator if you are planning on shooting your own cast bullets. In addition to applying lubricant in the grooves of the bullet, the sizer rounds them out to a dimension determined by the sizing die. By the use of various dies, you can control bullet diameters to .001-inch.

Small Bench Tools

These are either mounted on the bench or on the press, or are freestanding on the bench.

Powder scales are absolutely essential when working up loads, as well as for checking those that are measured with a hand dipper or metered by a powder measure. Basic balance scales will do an accurate job, but the speed advantage goes to the electronic models.

Powder measures are not an absolute necessity, but are invaluable when it comes time to get into production loading. They can be mounted on a loading press or a stand. The precision of the adjustment is not all that different. More expensive models adjust faster and a little more precisely, keep their accuracy more consistently, hold more powder and so on. The accuracy of powder-measure metering is mainly dependent on the consistency of the operator as he pulls and returns the handle.

Case trimmers are essential for keeping cartridge length consistent. Cases stretch on firing and in reloading dies, and must be trimmed back every so often. Hand-cranked models do the job, with a selection of collets and pilots available to handle most common calibers. Collets hold the case head, and pilots guide the case mouth straight against the cutter. Motorized models do the job more quickly.

Hand Tools

Case deburring or chamfering tools come with a bench mount and, in the case of the Forster case trimmer, can be purchased as an add-on feature. They are also made in hand-held versions. These are necessary to take burrs off the outside of a case mouth that has been trimmed and to chamfer (bevel) the inside of the case mouth, removing burrs that will otherwise scratch and gall jacketed bullets.

A primer pocket cleaner can be simply a flat-blade screwdriver, inserted into the primer pocket and turned several times to get the fouling out. However, all the major (and some minor) tool makers have them, and they're not expensive. The two basic types are the scraper and brush styles, and both do good work. Getting the primer ash deposit out of the pocket is necessary or the fresh primer will not seat properly. The ash build-up will either result in a high primer or one that may give poor ignition, as the firing pin blow is cushioned and the vent blocked by ash.

A steel straightedge ruler will check that your primers are seated deeply enough.

Lyman, Redding, RCBS and others offer case-care kits containing primer pocket cleaners and an assortment of case brushes to remove interior fouling, a good investment if you are loading blackpowder or Pyrodex ammunition. If you want to automate things a bit, Lyman and RCBS have a number of options to do so.

Loading blocks are the best way to keep from double-charging your cases. They come in molded plastic from several manufacturers and cost very little. You can make your own by drilling holes in a flat piece of 1-inch plank and gluing on a flat bottom. A loading block is the best way to inspect your cases after they have been charged with powder, before you seat a bullet. Double charging is very easy to do, especially when using a powder measure. If you shoot one of these loads, your gun will never forgive you.

Powder funnels cost little, and their use is only way to avoid spilling powder when you are working up loads by weighing each one. A charge drawn from a powder measure and dumped into the pan of your scale for checking is the way to maintain accuracy in your measure. If everything is working as it should, the charge in the pan is then funneled into the case. Forster offers a funnel with a long drop tube for loading nearly compressed charges.

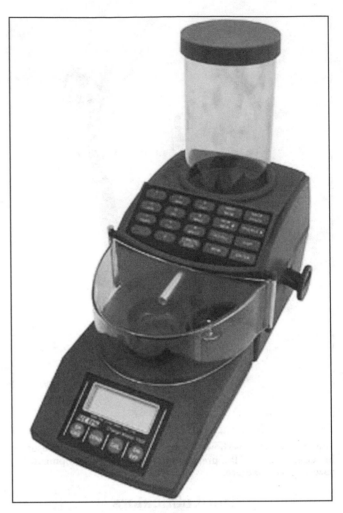

Newest, fastest and most automated powder measuring and dispensing in RCBS' arsenal is the ChargeMaster Combo, which combines an electronic scale accurate to within 0.10 grain, and an automated dispenser. You can weigh powder, bullets, cases or loaded cartridges. Just slightly more than $400.

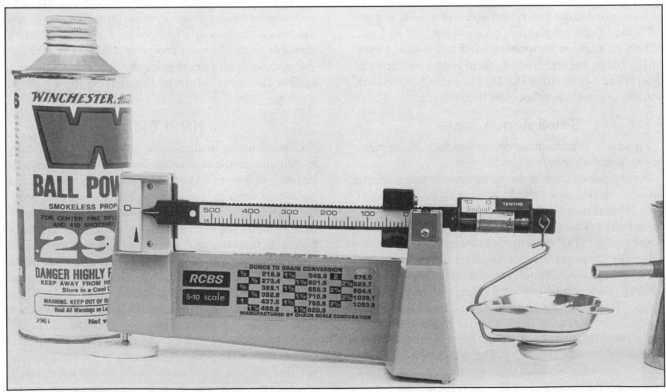

An accurate powder scale is an absolute must for working up loads. The beginner and expert should have and use this valuable piece of equipment.

A powder measure speeds production and can throw accurate loads. Precision, however, depends on the consistency of operation.

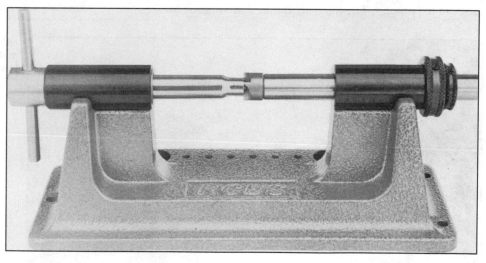

Cases stretch in firing and reloading, and every so often they will need to be trimmed to the proper length. A case trimmer requires various collets and pilots to trim accurately.

Micrometer/calipers are the best means of making all sorts of precision measurements, like case length, inside and outside diameters, case neck wall thickness, checks for bullet roundness and diameter, case swelling, etc.

Bullet pullers are there for the same reason they put erasers on pencils. Everybody, sooner or later, puts together some loads that won't fly for one reason or another and need to be taken apart. The two basic types are the one that screws into the die hole on your press and the kinetic type, which looks like a hammer. The press-mounted type is easy to use, but can mar the bullets, making them unshootable.

The kinetic model features a hollow plastic head into which the cartridge is fitted. A wad of cotton or tissue can be used to cushion the bottom of the chamber where the bullet is caught. With this addition, even very soft lead-alloy bullets may be retrieved undamaged. These are very efficient and handy tools.

Case Cleaning Equipment

Do shiny-bright cases shoot bullets straighter than tarnished ones? Case cleaning is something like car washing––you either believe in it or don't. The only real advantage of clean cases is that small cracks and flaws are more easily seen on shiny surfaces. If smokeless powder is used, most cases stay pretty clean, unless they receive a lot of handling with sweaty fingers or fire a number of low-pressure loads that fail to expand the case fully, which coats it with soot. Most cases will shine up in the sizing process, unless you only neck-size. Polishing with a cloth before you put the finished cartridge into the box will generally keep them bright for a long time.

After much use and especially after using Pyrodex or blackpowder in them, brass cases will take on the look of an old penny. Since both blackpowder and Pyrodex leave corrosive deposits (sulfuric acid), cases should be washed out soon after shooting. There are two basic case-cleaning methods, chemical and mechanical. Chemical cleaning involves washing the cases in a bath of an acid-based cleaner. The cleaner is sold as a concentrate to be mixed with water in a plastic, glass or stainless steel container. The cases are given a wash, then thoroughly rinsed. If the mixture is too strong or the cases are left in too long, these cleaners will begin etching the metal. Tarnish and dirt are removed, but the cases are left a dull yellow color. A polish is achieved by some means of buffing. Liquid cleaners are effective and require no special equipment.

Mechanical polishers are motorized tumblers or vibrators with containers into which the cases are dumped, along with a cleaning media composed of ground walnut shells or ground corncobs. Liquid polish additives are also available to speed the process. The cases are tumbled or vibrated for an hour or more and come out with a high shine. They must be separated from the cleaning media, and the media must be cleaned and replaced every so often.

Shotshell Reloading

While shotshells can be reloaded with simple hand tools, and RCBS does offer a shotshell reloading die set for use in its O-frame presses, most shotshell reloading is done on press-type machines. They are similar to the turret, multistation and semi-automated (progressive) loader designs used for metallic cartridges. Shotshells, obviously, do not require the precision alignment of bullet with case that is needed for metallic cartridges. Thus, with a decline in the need for high precision, good speed can be achieved. Precision is, of course, required in sizing, wad column seating and powder charging, although accuracy is a matter of pattern density. This is not to say that one can take a cavalier attitude when loading shotshells. A shotgun can be blown up with an overload as easily as any other gun, and with similarly disastrous results.

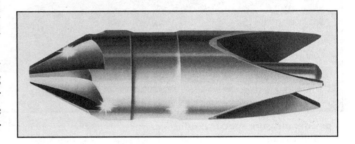

(Above and left) **A deburring tool makes bullet seating easier and lessens damage to the bullet base.**

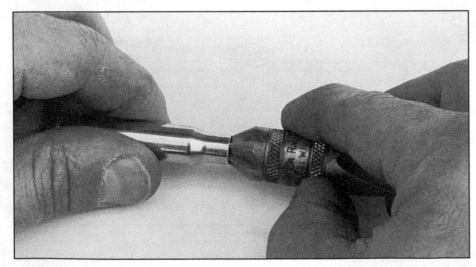

Primer pocket cleaners scour burned residue from the primer pocket. This brush-type tool works quickly.

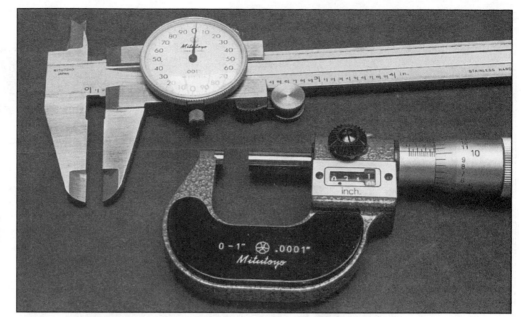

A micrometer and/or precision caliper capable of accurate measurement to .001-inch are necessary tools. Investing in good-quality equipment is worthwhile in the long run.

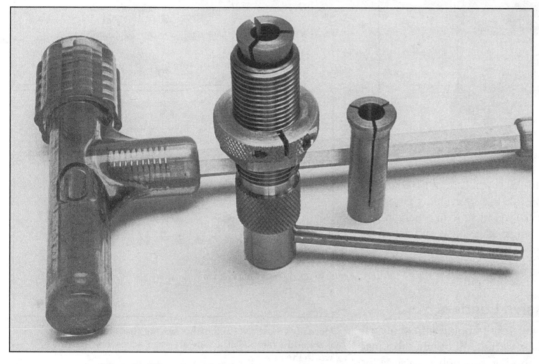

Bullet pullers come in two varieties: those that mount on the reloading press and those of the hammer-type kinetic variety *(left)*. The latter is perhaps gentler on bullets, but requires more energy on the part of the user.

Basic Equipment

If all you reload are shotshells, your needs for a bench and drawer storage are far less than for metallic cartridges. The stresses involved in sizing and reloading shotshells are less than those in making rifle cartridges. While a bench of some sort is needed, it does not have to be as large or robust. Shotshell presses do have to be firmly mounted. Overhead space is more of a consideration because many of these machines stand 2 feet high or more if you elect to attach hoppers to feed empty shells and/or wads.

Storage space is more of a concern if you are setting up for shotshell reloading, since the components are very bulky and you have more of them. Wads and shot are sold in bulk, which means finding a place to store 25-pound bags of shot and big bags of plastic shot cups. Shotshells, loaded or empty, are bulky, requiring four to five times the space needed for an equivalent amount of handgun ammunition. Shelves or cupboards are a good idea to have close to your bench.

Economy versus Speed

The same rule holds true for shotshell reloading as for rifle and pistol ammunition manufacture: Machines that turn out more ammunition faster cost more money. Because the process is somewhat simpler for loading shotshells, making ammunition goes faster. With most machines, all the necessary dies, the powder charger and the shot charger are contained in the press. With everything close together, and a need to do no more than pull an operating handle and

The Lee Load-All II (left) and MEC 600 Jr. Mark V are excellent machines for the casual shooter. The production rate is fast enough to satisfy most shooters unless they are heavily into competition trap or Skeet shooting.

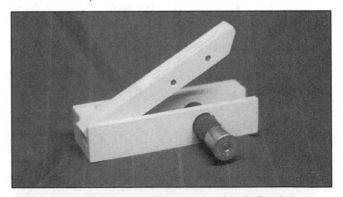

Hornady's Stack 'N' Pack makes boxing shotshells easier and is a good example of an inexpensive accessory that's well worth the money.

Precision Reloading's D-Loader does for shotshells what a bullet puller does for metallic cartridges. The case, however, cannot be saved, only the contents.

move a shell from one station to the next, even a basic machine like the Lee Load-All II will turn out 100 rounds per hour. Lee offers update kits to convert older presses to the Load-All II and conversion kits to load other gauges. Hornady offers a similar single-stage press and a conversion to progressive loader status via a kit. The MEC 600 Jr. Mark V, while a single-stage machine, is set up for speed and will double the Lee's output.

Progressive Loaders

Progressive machines are very popular with shotshell reloaders because of their output. Shotgun shooting, unlike rifle or handgun shooting, generally involves a lot of gun handling. Targets are close in the hunting field, but they're there only briefly. Practice for hunting, as well as just plain fun, is on the Skeet or trap range, and this means a lot of shooting. Developing the reflexes to become a good scattergunner requires practice, which requires a larger consumption of ammunition than for most rifle or handgun work.

Progressive machines will turn out between 300 to 400 rounds per hour. Top-of-the-line progressives like the Hollywood Automatic weigh 100 pounds and can crank out an astonishing 1800 rounds per hour, if you have the muscle to keep pulling that long. For a lot less money, the MEC 8567 Grabber will turn out 500 finished shells an hour. These numbers are production time, of course, and not counting the time spent loading hoppers, canisters and tubes with wads, primers, shot and powder. Progressive machines, because of their complexity, are more subject to problems than the simpler loaders. They require more cleaning and care as well, to keep them running smoothly.

Accessories

Unlike rifle and pistol presses, where you must buy separate die sets, shotshell reloaders come equipped with a set to load the gauge you prefer. Extra sets, of course, may be purchased, but six sets would load everything from .410-bore to 10-gauge. A great many machines come with conversion kits to upgrade performance, handle more gauges or load steel shot, which has its own requirements. There are dies to do six-fold, eight-fold or roll crimps. Most of the accessories for shotshell reloading are, therefore, add-ons to the basic press.

There are, however, several separate items that are necessary and useful. The precision scale for weighing powder and, in this case, shot is a must to work up and check loads. The same dial or digital caliper is also invaluable for checking case lengths and diameters. MEC makes a very handy metal plate gauge, cut with a dozen holes. This ring gauge allows a quick check on the diameters of all the standard U.S.-made shotshells and is essentially a go/no-go gauge for each. Hornady's Stack 'N' Pack and MEC's E-Z Pack are nifty racks for packing shotshells into standard boxes. The answer to the bullet puller is the Precision Reloading D-Loader, which allows the reclamation of shot, powder primers and wads from bad reloads. It also trims 10- and 12-gauge TUFF-type wads to length. It is a cutting tool, however, and will not save the shell itself.

Organization

Getting all your equipment organized is a key to success in reloading. Tools too close together or too far apart for convenient reach slow your work and wear out your temper. Here again, one of the best ways to get started is to see how other reloaders set things up. If possible, try their equipment to get a feel for the process. Smooth operation stems from having the right tools in the right place and components

```
CARTRIDGE_____Overall length_____

Case, make _____Times reloaded_____

Primer, make, type_____

Powder_____ Charge_____

Bullet, make, type , weight_____

For gun_____

Sight setting_____ Range Zero_____

Velocity, Chronographed_____ est_____

Date Loaded_____

Remarks_____

_____
```

A simple reloading data form can be created on a computer and reduced to stick-on labels for cartridge boxes, and/or kept in notebook form for ready reference. Accurate records are essential.

where they can be easily handled and stored. The right way is the one that works best for you.

Generally speaking, sizer/lubricators are mounted on the front of the bench. They do not need to be particularly close to the loading press since bullet sizing and lubricating is generally done as an operation separate from the actual loading process. By the same token, the case trimmer, if bench mounted, need not be near the press since this operation is generally done separately, prior to loading. The press is really the center of your operation and should have clear space around it to place boxes or stacks of primers, bullets, cases and cans of powder. You may want to try mounting tools with C-clamps to start, so a change in position to a final location and bolting down only has to be done once, as you develop a plan for working. A comfortable chair is a real asset since you will be spending many–hopefully happy and productive–hours there.

Record Keeping

The importance of record keeping cannot be overemphasized. Your load-data book of what you load and how it shoots will keep you up on what you have tried, how well it worked and, depending on your analysis and commentary, will serve as a guide to further experimentation. Without accurate records, you have to rely on that poorest of devices–memory. The type of data storage and method you choose is, again, what works best for you. A pocket recorder can be carried to the range, and notes and comments transcribed later. Some prefer data forms because they require the least work.

Record keeping includes the box in which you keep your finished ammunition. Unmarked boxes equal "mystery" loads. When working up a load, you should mark the box by indicating primer type, primer make, powder type, charge, bullet weight, alloy, lubricant and exact size. You can write on the box or use stick-on notes. Less data may be needed once you have found a load you wish to produce on a regular basis. Here again though, care must be taken to mark *clearly* high-pressure "hot" loads if you have both strong- and weak-action guns of the same caliber.

You've made
the decision to
reload, you've
collected all
the necessary
components, set up
a safe workspace
with the proper
tools, and done
the research. It's
time to get started.

Rifle Cartridge Reloading

Case Inspection

EVEN NEW AND once-fired cases should be checked over for defects. Any with splits or serious defects in the case mouth that are not ironed out in the resizing die should be discarded. Cases should be segregated by maker as determined by the head-stamp. Even though they are the same caliber, cases of different manufacture have slight differences in wall thickness and vent (flash hole) size. Mixing brands can alter velocities and pressures, and open up group size.

Full-Length Resizing

This step is just as necessary for new cases as for fired ones. If these will later be used in only one rifle, further resizing can be limited to neck-sizing only, unless heavy loads are used. Before any operation can take place on the reloading press, the die must first be adjusted to resize the case properly. For full-length resizing, with the shellholder snapped into the ram, lower the press

Empty cases should go back in the original box after firing so various brands and calibers don't get mixed.

handle completely; screw the sizer die into the press until the bottom of the die hits the shellholder. Now, raise the press handle enough so you can screw the die down about 1/8-turn more, then set the large lock ring/nut. Make further adjustments so the bottom of the expander ball is 3/16-inch up inside the die, and the decapping pin should extend 1/8-inch below the mouth of the die, which is just enough to knock out the spent primer. The best bet is to follow the instructions that come with the die set or take the time to really read a loading manual, which usually will include such instruction.

To resize a case, it must first be given a thin coating of case lubricant to allow it to work easily in the sizing die. Sizing lubricant is a special oil or grease made for this purpose.

Regular gun oil will not work. It is best applied by saturating a case lube pad with lubricant, then rolling the case over it, lightly coating the outside of the case. Too much lubricant on the outside of the case will cause dents in the walls that will flatten out on firing, but will stress the metal. Several brands of spray lube also are available, and can speed up the lubing process. On bottleneck cases, the inside on the neck should be cleaned with a brush and lubricated with a dry, case neck lubricant. Oil can run into the powder and ruin it. Neck lubricating keeps the neck from stretching unduly in the die. A light coating of lubricant is all that is needed. To begin resizing, the prepared case is inserted in the shellholder, and the press handle is pulled, to run the case completely into the die.

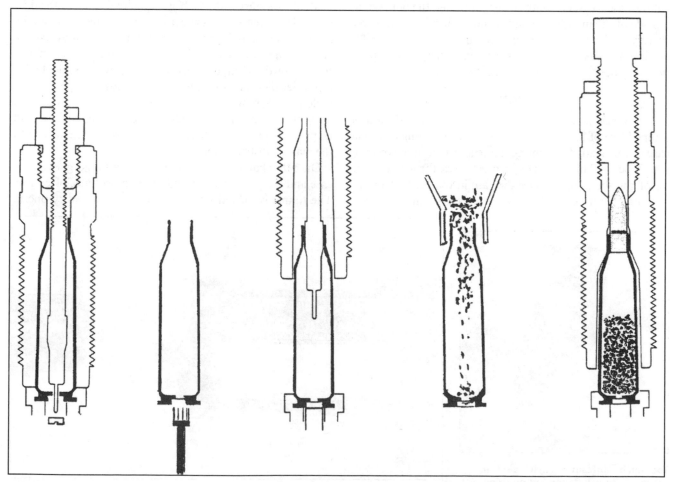

The basic steps in rifle reloading include resizing and decapping, primer pocket cleaning, inside neck expanding (done in the upstroke of the decapping process), priming, powder charging and bullet seating.

Decapping

The die should be adjusted so the decapping pin just removes the old primer, which will drop out at the end of the up-stroke. The resizing/decapping process should require a medium amount of force. If a lot of force is required to get the case in the die, you have not used enough lubricant. Back it out. If you persist, there's a good chance the case will seize in the die. If that happens, you'll need to send the die back to the maker to remove the case or buy a tool to do the job yourself.

Inside Neck Expanding

The decapping pin is mounted in a rod with an expander ball on it that stretches the case mouth large enough to accept a new bullet. This operation is completed on the up, or removal, stroke of the press operating handle.

Inspection, Gauging and Trimming

The case is now removed from the shellholder for inspection. The case mouth should be smooth and perfectly round. "Trim to length," say the books because a too-long case will enter the throat of the barrel and raise pressures as the bullet is pinched in the case. A quick check with a case length gauge or measurement with your caliper tells you if the case is too long. If the case is too long, it goes in the trimmer to cut the case to exact length. After trimming, the burr on the outside of the mouth is removed and the inside is chamfered slightly to give the bullet a smooth start. Do not cut a knife's edge on the case mouth. This trimming/chamfering operation only needs to be done when cases get too long.

Priming

If the case is a fired one, the primer pocket should be scraped free of ash with a screwdriver or cleaning tool. The case is now ready for priming. Place a primer in the priming punch sleeve. This comes up, in most cases, through the center of the shellholder. Place the case in the shellholder and pull the operating handle to lower the case onto the primer punch. This will seat the primer in the case. Enough force should be applied to seat the primer fully, but not crush or flatten it. Difficulty in seating may be experienced if you are using crimped military brass. If so, this crimp must be removed before proceeding.

After priming, the case should be checked to see that the primer is fully in the pocket. This is done by placing a steel straightedge ruler across the case while holding it to the light to see if the primer sticks up above the case head. It should not. A high primer gives poor ignition–or may not fire at all–as the firing pin simply drives it into the pocket. The primed, inspected case now goes into the loading block.

Case Mouth Expansion

This step applies only to straight-walled cases loaded with cast, lead-alloy bullets and uses the second die in a three-die rifle set. Three-die sets do not expand the case mouth in the decapping stage. The case is placed in the shellholder and run into this die, which has a stepped or tapered expander plug to open or bell the case mouth for insertion of a soft, cast bullet. This mouth expansion is done before powder charging.

Powder Charging

The case is now ready for charging. When working up a load, always start with the beginning load listed in the data manuals. Increases in powder charges should be made by no more than a half-grain (.5) at a time. Load and test fire at least ten test cartridges before going to a heavier charge. Weigh powder charges precisely on a powder scale. Using a powder measure, dispense a slightly low charge into the scale pan. A powder trickler will add minute amounts to bring the charge up to the desired weight. The scale should be properly set up and checked for adjustment according to the maker's instructions.

Once the charge is weighed, the powder funnel goes on the case and the powder is poured in, with no spills, of course. The funnel is moved from case to case until every one in

Too much lubricant will make dents in cases. These will flatten out on firing, but this works and weakens the brass.

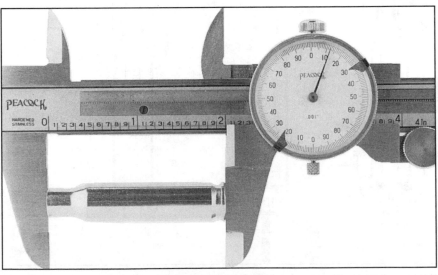

Case length should be checked after sizing and neck expanding.

Powder dippers can be purchased or homemade to pick up a fairly accurate charge of a particular type of powder. All dipped loads should be checked regularly on a powder scale.

Powder measures can be fairly accurate if operated carefully, but the loads should be weighed often, especially when making maximum loads or loading with fast-burning powders.

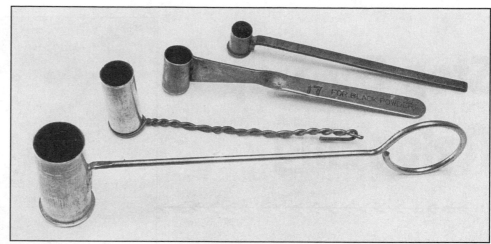

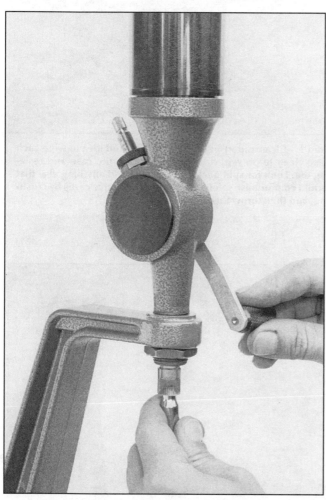

The reloader's powder funnel is especially designed to fit over the case mouth and deliver powder without spills. One size fits nearly all commonly reloaded cases.

After a powder measure is adjusted, check its accuracy, and yours, by dropping every fifth load into the scale pan for weighing. Accurate loads are within a tolerance of +/-1/10-grain (.1). Always visually check cases loaded with a powder measure in the loading block. It is very easy to pull the handle twice on the same case.

Bullet Seating

This is the final step in the loading operation. A case is placed in the shellholder, a bullet is placed in the case mouth as straight as possible, and the case is gently levered up into the bullet-seating die. Proper die adjustment is necessary so you don't exceed the maximum overall length of the cartridge as listed in the loading manual. An overly long cartridge will press the bullet into the rifling and raise pressures. The easiest way to avoid this problem is to make up a dummy cartridge. After the die is screwed into the press, adjust it so the case enters freely its full length. Gradually ease the dummy cartridge into the die and check to see it

(Text continued on page 111)

the loading block is charged. Make it a habit to check the powder level in *all* the cases in the loading block, examining them under good light, even though you are sure you did not double-charge any of them. If the powder level in any case looks suspiciously high, weigh it again.

Using A Powder Measure

The precision of mechanical powder measures depends to a great degree on the *consistency* of pulling and returning the operating handle. Use the same motion time after time.

Step-By-Step
Reloading

>>>>>>>>>>>>>>>>>>>>>>>>>>>>>>

Rifle
Cartridges

(Photos courtesy of RCBS/ATK)

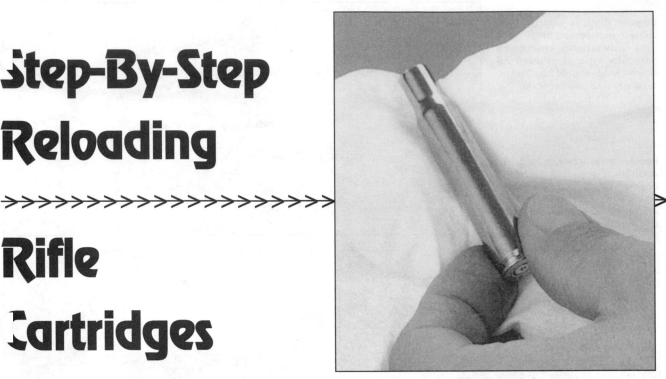

Step 1 - Clean and Inspect: It's always a good idea to wipe each case clean to prevent dirt from scratching the case and resizing die. Look for split necks, case cracks and anything else that would compromise safety. Destroy any defective cases by crushing, and then throw them away.

Step 4 - Adjusting the Sizer Die: With a shellholder installed in the ram, and the ram all the way up, thread the sizer die into the press until it touches the shellholder. Raise the press handle a little and turn the die in another 1/8- to 1/4-turn, then set the die lock ring.

Step 5 - Case Resizing: Insert an empty case into the shellholder and gently lower the press handle all the way to the bottom, running the case into the sizing die. Doing so will resize the case to factory dimensions and knock out the fired primer. Raising the press handle will lower the case and expand the case mouth to the proper dimension to hold the new bullet.

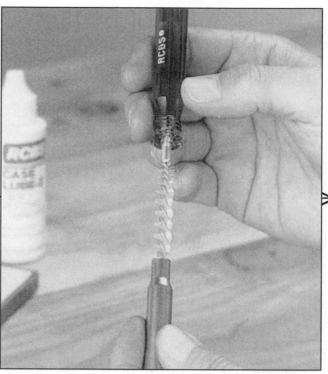

Step 2 - Lubricate the Cases: To prevent the case from sticking in the sizing die, it must be lubricated only with sizing die lube. With a bit of lube on the pad, roll a number of cases over it a few times to lightly coat the case body.

Step 3 - Case Neck Lubrication: Use a case neck brush to clean and lubricate the inside of the case neck. This will reduce resizing effort and neck stretching. Only a small amount of lube should be applied to the brush.

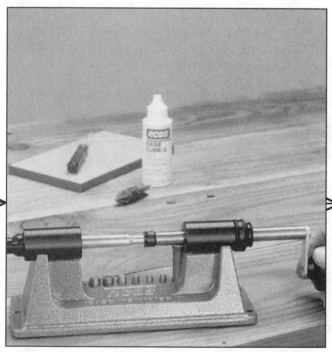

Step 6 - Case Trimming: Cartridge cases tend to stretch after a few firings, so they must be trimmed back to allow proper chambering and for safety reasons. Reloading data manuals will give the proper trim and maximum case lengths.

Step 7 - Chamfer and Deburr: After trimming, the case mouth will have a slight burr, and the sharp edge of the mouth needs to be smoothed. A twist of a simple hand tool removes the burr with one end and chamfers the case mouth with the other end for easy insertion of the new bullet.

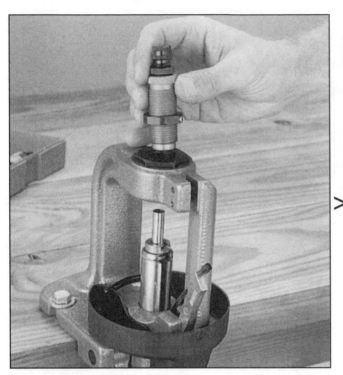

Step 8 - Case Mouth Expansion: This step applies only to straight-wall cases and is done in a separate step. Install the expander die in the press, insert a case in the shellholder and run the case up into the die. This die should be adjusted so the case mouth is belled or flared just enough to accept a new bullet.

Step 9 - Priming (A): Place a fresh primer, anvil side up, into the cup of the primer arm and insert a case into the shellholder.

Step 12 - Powder Charging (A): Look up the load in your loading manual to see exactly how much and what powder you need. It's a good idea to weigh each charge for safety and consistency.

Step 13 - Powder Charging (B): After weighing the charge, use a funnel to pour it into the case without spilling.

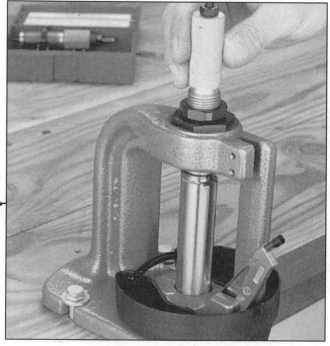

Step 10 - Priming (B): Lower the press handle and push the primer arm all the way into the slot in the ram.

Step 11 - Priming (C): Gently and slowly raise the press handle. This lowers the case onto the priming arm, seating the fresh primer. Check each case to be sure the primer is fully seated.

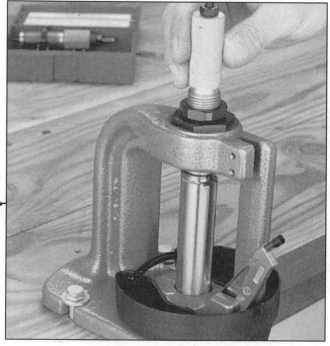

Step 14 - Powder Charging (C): Another method of charging is to use the powder measure. It dispenses a precise, uniform charge with each crank of the handle, thereby speeding up the process. Use the reloading scale to adjust the powder measure until it throws several identical charges. Then, weigh about every ten charges to recheck the weight.

Step 15 - Bullet Seating (A): Thread the seater die into the press a few turns. With a case in the shellholder, lower the press handle, running the case all the way up into the die. Turn the die further in until it stops. While using the headstamp on top of the die as a reference, back the die out one full turn and lock it in place with the lock ring.

Step 16 - Bullet Seating (B): Now, unscrew the seater plug enough to keep the bullet from being seated too deeply.

Step 17 - Bullet Seating (C): With the handle up, insert a primed and charged case in the shellholder, and hold a bullet over the case mouth with one hand while you lower the press handle with the other, easing the bullet and case up into the die. This will seat the bullet. Measure the loaded round to see if the bullet is seated deeply enough.

Step 18 - Bullet Seating (D): If the bullet needs to be seated deeper into the case, turn the seater plug down a little and run the case back up into the die. Make small adjustments and keep trying and measuring until you get the proper cartridge overall length. Once the proper setting is reached, tighten the seater plug lock ring.

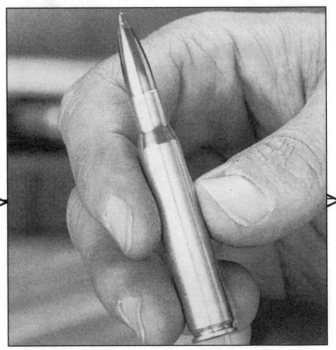

Step 19 - The Loaded Round: After wiping off any sizing lube, the first loaded cartridge is ready to be fired

(Text continued from page 105)

Seating dies have a crimping shoulder in them to crimp some hunting bullets. Never crimp bullets that do not have a crimping cannelure in them.

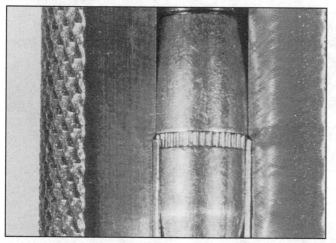

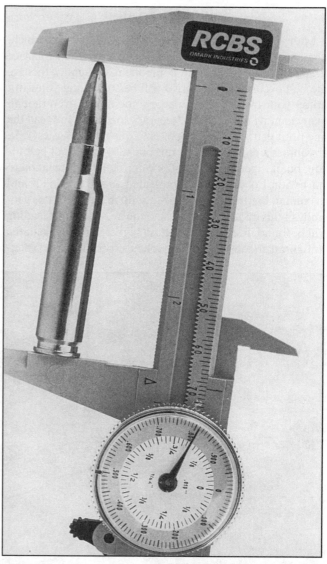

Finished cartridges should be checked to see they do not exceed overall length. If they do, the seater stem in the die can be adjusted to seat the bullets deeper.

does not pass the crimping shoulder, which turns over the case mouth. The next adjustment is to the stem of the bullet seater, which gradually drives the bullet deeper into the case. When the correct overall length is reached, tighten the seater adjustment. Keep the dummy for easy readjustment after loading longer or shorter bullets. You may want to make a dummy for every different-length bullet you load to facilitate easy readjustment. Once the die is adjusted, bullet seating is simply a matter of repetition.

Most dies have a built-in crimping shoulder to turn the case mouth over into a cannelure (groove) in the bullet. This is necessary for high-powered ammunition, particularly if it is jarred by recoil or while being fed through the magazine. Crimping keeps the bullets from being forced back into the case under such circumstances. Military ammunition that will be fed through autoloaders and machineguns is always crimped, as is much commercial ammunition. Crimping degrades accuracy and should never be attempted on bullets that do not have a crimping cannelure in them. Hunting ammunition used in tubular magazines may have to be crimped.

Easy does it is the rule for all steps. Ramming and jerking leads to damaged cases, mashed bullets, flattened primers and broken decapping pins.

The final step is to wipe off any case lubricant that may be on the case and inspect the finished cartridge with a final check for overall length. Oil left on cases will cause excessive backthrust and batter your gun. If all dies are properly adjusted and firmly in place, there should be no difference from one cartridge to the next. Place the loaded rounds in a cartridge box and mark it accordingly.

Cleaning the loading area is always a good idea. Powder should always be returned to the original container, especially from the powder measure. Powder in open containers will lose volatiles and absorb moisture. Primers can absorb moisture, and magnum and standard primers can be confused if not put back in their respective containers. Most of all, there is always the chance of confusion regarding what powder you were using when you start to work the next time.

Selecting A Load

Many people start with factory duplication loads, which, if you have already been shooting them, is a convenient place to start without varying any component. Generally, though, the best accuracy in your rifle will be something you work up on your own. This may take some doing, even though many loading manuals list "accuracy loads." If you read the fine print you will see this applies to one particular test rifle. If yours is a different make, this one may not shoot best for you, but it is perhaps the best powder/bullet combination to start with. Loading data is presented as starting loads and maximum loads with a middle ground in between. It is generally in this middle ground where the most accurate loading will be found. Rarely is the hottest, highest-pressure load the straightest shooter. Maximum loads, especially with jacket-

These offer good, cheap recreation and training without the expense, wear, noise and recoil of full-bore loads. They can be used for small game and varmint hunting at distances less than 100 yards with reasonable accuracy. Varmint loads with light bullets are practical in many 30-caliber rifles that will produce good accuracy and flat trajectory. Hunting loads are the most common for the 30s, unless you have a match rifle. For a hunting rifle, used primarily for hunting as opposed to competition, you would do best to work up the most accurate load you can from the selection of hunting bullets available.

Working Up A Load

Working up a load means not merely careful loading of ammunition, but testing it and keeping records of the

Loads should be selected from a loading manual to reflect the type of shooting you want to do. Don't experiment unless you know what you are doing.

ed bullets, shorten both case and barrel life. By working for accuracy, you start to get a clear idea of just how well your rifle will shoot. With this as a starting point, you then have a standard by which other loads can be judged.

For the most part, you will probably not have need for more than three or four different loadings, if that many. For 30-caliber rifles and up, about three different loadings will do for most of the shooting you'll be doing. On the bottom end are short-range practice loads. These are usually cast bullets driven at modest velocities of around 1200-1500 fps.

results. It also involves case inspection, looking for any signs of excessive headspace or pressures. You can use a simple notebook for records, listing loads under the name of the rifle and its caliber. Individual loads are listed under the bullet, indicating whether it is cast or jacketed, the weight, diameter and lubrication type. Next, the powder type and charge are shown. Following this is a notation on the make of case and primer type. Finally, there's a section for remarks. This includes a summary of the performance of this particular load, especially its accuracy. Ten-shot groups

The Marlin Camp Carbine in 9mm or 45 ACP is a fairly typical blowback autoloading rifle. There are a growing number of pistol-caliber carbines on the market, intended for home-defense, small game hunting and plinking.

The Ruger Mini-14 is a popular gas-operated autoloader with both civilians and law enforcement agencies.

are the accuracy test standard, although it has been demonstrated that seven-shot groups work just as well. Other remarks include the test range conditions like temperature, wind direction and velocity, and light conditions. Also noted are any indications of pressure problems. These are underlined as a warning for future reference.

Loading for Autoloaders

Since WWII, autoloaders in all calibers and types have become very popular, owing mainly to the changeover by nearly all of the world's governments to this type of rifle for their respective militaries. While all autoloaders rely on the force of the explosion in the cartridge to function the action, there are a number of differences in the ways various actions operate, and these features have a marked effect on how ammunition must be reloaded for them.

There are three basic types of autoloading actions: straight blowback (with a variant known as delayed blowback), recoil-operated and gas-operated.

Blowback actions are the oldest design, and most simple. They function by having the bolt held in contact with the barrel by a spring, thus the two are not locked together. When the gun fires, the bullet is driven down the barrel while the case is driven against the bolt face. The weight of the bolt and force of the recoil springs, and the internal pressure swelling the case against the chamber wall, keep the case from moving backward until the bullet has exited the muzzle. Somewhere around this point, as chamber pressure begins to drop, the case begins to be blown back against the bolt; the inertial force given the bolt causes it to move rearward, cocking the rifle and ejecting the fired case. Tension in the compressed recoil spring sends the bolt forward, stripping a fresh cartridge from the magazine and chambering it. This system works well with low-powered pistol-type cartridges and is used in all 22 Long Rifle and 22 WMR rifles. It was used in only a relatively few centerfire rifles, such as the obsolete Winchester 05, 07 and 10 rifles, and the current Marlin and other carbines in 9mm and 45 ACP. The system is limited to straight-walled cases because a bottleneck case would likely have its neck pulled off or have gas come rushing around it as soon as the pressure seal was broken.

Because of the necessity of equaling the forces of the forward-moving bullet with the proper amount of bolt weight and spring pressure, limitations of the system are obvious. To fire a cartridge the equivalent of the 30-06, such a system would need a bolt weighing several pounds and a very robust recoil spring. Thus, blowback autoloaders are limited to cartridges developing little better than handgun velocities and pressures.

Not surprisingly, reloads for such guns must be kept very close to factory specifications. Lower-pressure loads will not function the action, and high-pressure loads, even though the barrels can handle them, increase the velocity of the recoiling parts, battering them and causing serious damage to the rifle. Cast-bullet loads, both plain and gas-checked, work well if they are heavily crimped to provide proper burning of the powder. Slow-burning powders generally do not perform well in these rifles as they do not generate pressure fast enough to make the action function reliably.

Recoil-operated actions represent an improvement over the blowback in terms of the type and pressure of cartridge they can handle. In this system, the recoil of the rifle drives the operation. Recoil-operated systems keep the bolt and barrel locked together through part of the firing cycle. As the bullet travels forward, the barrel and bolt recoil as a unit. At about the midpoint of the operation, after the bullet has exited the barrel, the bolt unlocks from the barrel and continues traveling backward, ejecting the empty case and cocking the hammer. The bolt then strips a fresh round from the magazine, chambering it as the bolt comes forward. This system was used in the Remington Model 8 in 25, 30, 32 and 35 Remington calibers, and in the Johnson military and sporting autoloaders in 30-06. The downside of this system is the amount of recoil experienced by the shooter, which can be considerable.

Both blowback and recoil-operated autoloaders have fairly generous chambers and require full-length case resizing. Not too surprisingly, they are also rather rough on cases. Here again, the best functioning is with loadings close to factory specifications. The battering of internal parts will result from loads generating high pressures and high velocities. The best way to work up handloads for these two actions is to do so slowly, checking recoiling parts for any evidence of battering. The best loads are ones that will reliably cycle the action and no more.

Gas-operated rifles are by far the best, and most high-powered rifles made today use this system. The gas-operated system features a locked bolt and non-moving barrel, much like the accurate and reliable bolt action. They can thus fire very powerful cartridges. At some point on the barrel, forward of the chamber, there's a small hole in the barrel that taps off a small amount of gas after the bullet passes that point. The gas is trapped in a small cylinder with a piston, much like that in an engine. The piston drives a rod, which operates a camming lock on the bolt, which opens it after the bullet has exited the barrel. In some variants, the gas is directed to the surface of the cam lock to unlock the bolt. As the bolt is driven back, the case is ejected and the hammer or striker is cocked, and a spring drives the bolt forward to strip a fresh round from the magazine and chamber it. Today's high-powered autoloaders are gas-operated. The advantages are a minimum of moving parts and an action that is comparatively gentle on cases. Felt recoil is also very manageable.

The placement of the gas port is critical to reliable functioning because the amount and pressure of gas must be enough to operate the rifle, but not enough to cause damage through battering. Needless to say, the amount and type of powder used is also critical to this system's functioning. Gas-operated autoloaders are, therefore, ammunition-sensitive and will work best with loadings duplicating factory or original military specifications. Cast bullets, generally, do not work well in gas-operated guns. Fast-burning powders, such as IMR-4227, are about the only ones that will operate these actions reliably with cast bullets. Any cast bullets used in autoloading rifles should be of hard alloy, since soft bullets are often nicked and dented as they pass through the magazine and into the chamber. They are slammed up feed ramps, which will often cause them to catch and stick on something and jam the action. Because of the generous chamber proportions required for reliable functioning, cases fired in autoloaders almost always have to be full-length resized.

Ball powders tend to leave more fouling than some of the cleaner burning flake powders. The performance of ball powders in terms of reliable functioning is good, *so long as the gas port, piston and/or cam face are kept clean*. For best functioning, the powders used in reloading should be close to those used in factory loadings. Cleaning of the gas system is necessary for reliable functioning.

Reduced loads will not work reliably in any autoloader, with cartridges often getting jammed on the way out and chewed up in the process. Therefore, the range of loading options for autoloaders of any stripe is rather limited. There will usually be only a relatively few loadings that will produce good accuracy and reliable functioning. Ammunition prepared for autoloaders should be given extra care to see that all tolerances are kept close to factory specifications. Exceeding overall length will jam rifles. Cases too short and bullets seated too deeply can have the same effect. In short, ammunition preparation for successful shooting of these guns requires extra care for best results.

Testing ammunition should be done with a solid rest, firing at a known distance to determine accuracy.

Testing Ammunition

Accuracy is, or should be, your first concern. An accuracy test can consist of nothing more than plinking at a few cans at an unknown distance, but this won't tell you very much. The only meaningful test is firing from a solid rest at a known distance. This generally means getting to a target range with permanent bench installations or setting up your own range.

The best kind of shooting bench is a permanent one, with solid legs anchored in concrete.

Portable shooting benches can be homemade or you can buy one of several on the market. The type that has a built-in seat is my recommendation, since with these, the weight of the shooter serves to hold down the bench. The top either has an attached forend rest for the rifle or you can use a sandbag rest on an adjustable base.

Testing should be done on a day with good light, little or no wind and moderate temperatures. Calm conditions are generally found in the early morning or late afternoon. The place to start is with a test of factory ammunition for comparison. Really fine accuracy cannot be obtained without a telescopic sight, since this lets you see exactly where you are aiming. A spotting scope of 20x or more gives you a clear view of a distant target. A distance of 100 yards is good enough to get a fair idea of the long-range performance of your rifle and ammunition, though 200 yards is better. Most shooters use the standard of the "magic inch" at 100 yards as a benchmark by which all rifles are judged. Few hunting rifles will group this well, but will run groups of 2 to 3 inches, which is enough to kill a deer. Shoot 7- or 10-shot groups, taking your time to carefully squeeze off the shots. Be sure to clean the rifle of all copper fouling before shooting lead-alloy bullets, since they will strip lead on the copper fouling.

Shooting into turf will give you an idea of the ricochet potential of your ammunition, if this is critical. You can usually hear the results if the bullets are not ricochet-proof. For testing on game or varmint animals, there is not much in the way of practical substitutes for the real item. Ballistic gelatin is the standard by which determinations are made, but it is difficult to prepare, and it must be calibrated and used at the proper temperature.

One tissue substitute of a cheap and easy sort is newspaper, soaked overnight to get it fully saturated. Stacks of the wet paper are then put in a cardboard carton for shooting into. This is far heavier and more resistant than muscle tissue, but will give you a general idea of bullet behavior.

Packed wet snow is a fairly good tissue simulant, and if there is enough of it, you can find your bullet somewhere along a long snow loaf. High-velocity spitzer bullets are almost impossible to recover, but lower velocity cast bullets can usually be stopped within 20 to 30 feet of packed snow. These will generally be in almost pristine condition. This will give you a good opportunity to study your bullets for evidence of gas cutting and of how well they take the rifling. Large or double sets of rifling marks on the front of a bullet indicate skidding or jumping the rifling—the bullet going straight for a fraction of an inch before taking the rifling and turning, as it should. Rifling marks that are higher on one side than the other indicate the bullet was not straight in the case. Poor alignment of this sort degrades accuracy. Grease grooves that are heavily compressed and lack of lubricant will explain one cause of leading–not enough groove space and an inefficient lubricant. Bullet recovery is for those who are seriously interested, those wanting answers to questions beginning with the word "Why."

A final warning is to *always check your cases after firing*, particularly when you are testing loads that are on the high side of the pressure curve. Once you are in the field, there is a great temptation to keep shooting. If there are signs of high pressure or excessive headspace, *stop shooting*. Don't risk your eyesight and your rifle.

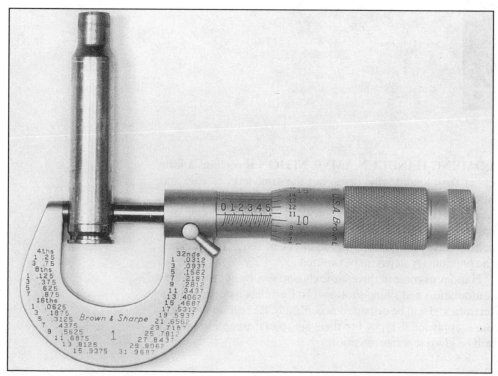

Checking a case for expansion beyond that produced by a factory load (along with stiff extraction) will give you the first indication of excessive pressures. It is a timely warning to tone things down.

Even though
your favorite
handgun digests
all types of
factory ammo,
you can
probably squeeze
out a little more
performance–and
save money, too.

Handgun Cartridge Reloading

LOADING HANDGUN AMMUNITION is perhaps a little easier than loading rifle cases, but the same level of care and attention must be given the task if good results are to be obtained. The place to begin is with once-fired or, better, new cases to work up a load. Once a load is tested and found to be satisfactory, then quantity production can begin and some of the preliminary steps can be omitted.

Handguns come in three basic classes: revolvers, autoloaders (automatics) and single-shot pistols. Each has its own characteristics and will be discussed accordingly. Basic loading procedures apply for all types, but there are special exceptions, which will be given separate attention.

Good accuracy comes from consistency in the quality of your reloads as much as it does from the gun.

Case Inspection

Even new and once-fired cases should be checked over for defects. Any with splits or serious defects in the case mouth that are not ironed out in the resizing die should be discarded. Cases should be segregated by maker, as determined by the head-stamp. Even though they are the same caliber, cases of different manufacture have slight differences in wall thickness and flash hole size. Mixing brands will alter velocities and pressures, and will open up group size.

Full-length Resizing

New cases should be sized the same as old ones, just to be sure everything is the same. Before any operation can take place on the reloading press, the die must first be adjusted to resize the case properly. For full-length resizing, with the shellholder snapped into the ram, lower the press handle completely; screw the sizer die into the press until the bottom of the die hits the shellholder. (If you are using a carbide die, as is common with handgun calibers, do not allow the shellholder to contact the bottom of the die.) Now, raise the press handle enough so you can screw the die down about 1/8-turn more, then set the large lock ring/nut. Make further adjustments so the bottom of the expander ball is 3/16-inch up inside the die, and the decapping pin should extend 1/8-inch below the mouth of the die, which is just enough to knock out the spent primer. The best bet is to follow the instructions that come with the die set, or take the time to really read a loading manual, which usually will include such instruction.

To resize a case, it must first be given a coating of case lubricant to allow it to work easily in the sizing die. Sizing lubricant is a special oil or grease made for this purpose. Regular gun oil will not work. It is best applied by saturating a case lube pad with lubricant, then rolling the case over it, lightly coating the outside of the case. Too much lubricant on the outside of the case will cause dents in the walls which will flatten out on firing, but will stress the metal. On bottleneck cases, the inside of the neck should be cleaned and lubricated with a dry graphite, or similar non-oil, case neck lubricant. Oil can run into the powder and ruin it. Neck lubricating keeps the neck from stretching unduly in the die.

To begin resizing, the prepared case is inserted in the shell-holder, and the press handle is pulled to run the case completely into the die.

Decapping

The die should be adjusted so the decapping pin just removes the old primer, which will drop out at the end of the up-stroke. The resizing/decapping process should require a medium amount of force. If a lot of force is required to get the case in the die you have not used enough lubricant, and there's a good chance the case will seize in the die. If that happens, you'll need to send the die back to the manufacturer to remove the case, or buy a tool to do the job yourself.

Inspection, Gauging and Trimming

The case is now removed from the shell-holder for inspection. The case mouth should be smooth and perfectly round. "Trim to length" say the books because a too-long case will enter the throat of the barrel and raise pressures as the bullet is pinched in the case. A quick check with a case length gauge or measurement with your caliper tells you if the case is too long. Sometimes even new ones are. If the case is too long, it goes in the trimmer to cut the case to exact length. After trimming, the burr on the outside of the mouth is removed and the inside is chamfered to give the bullet a smooth start. This trimming/chamfering operation only needs to be done when cases get too long. Do not cut a knife-edge on the case mouth, but simply remove the burr.

Inside Neck Expansion

For bottleneck cartridges, the decapping pin is mounted in a rod with an expansion ball on it that stretches the case mouth large enough to accept a new bullet. This operation is completed on the up, or removal, stroke of the operating handle.

Case Mouth Expansion

For straight-walled cases being loaded with cast, lead-alloy bullets, this step uses the second die in a three-die pistol set. Three-die sets do not expand the case mouth in the decapping stage. The case is placed in the shellholder and

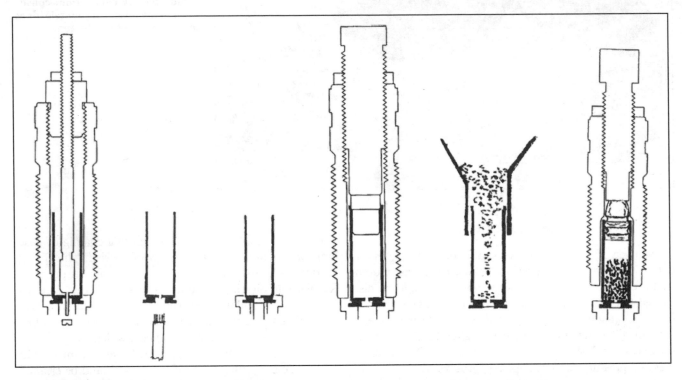

The basic steps in handgun reloading include: resizing and decapping, primer pocket cleaning, priming, case expanding, powder charging and bullet seating.

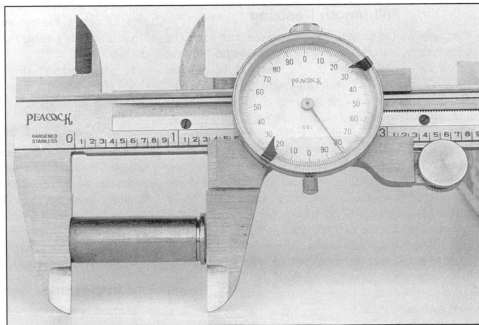

Case length should be checked after sizing and neck expanding, because the case stretches in these operations.

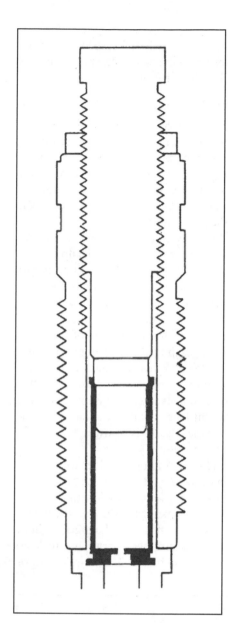

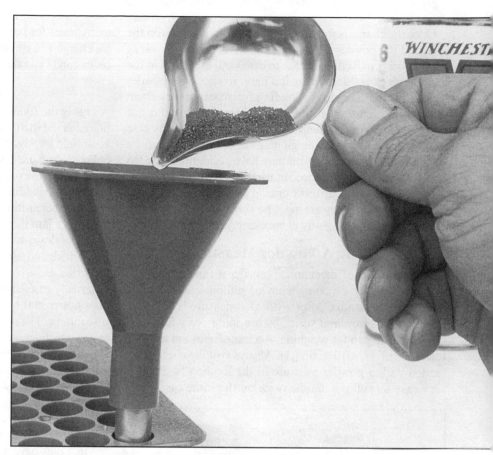

The reloader's powder funnel is especially designed to fit over the case mouth and deliver powder without spills.

Case-mouth expanding, or belling, prepares the case to accept a soft, lead-alloy bullet.

run into this expansion die, which has a stepped or tapered expander plug that opens the case mouth for insertion of a bullet. This mouth expansion is done before powder charging.

Priming

If the case is a fired one, the primer pocket should be scraped free of ash with a screwdriver or cleaning tool. The case is now ready for priming. Place a primer in the priming punch sleeve. This comes up, in most cases, through the center of the shellholder. Place the case in the shellholder and pull the operating handle to lower the case onto the primer punch. This will seat the primer in the case. Enough force should be applied to seat the primer fully, but not crush or flatten it. Difficulty in seating may be experienced if you are using crimped military brass. If so, this crimp must be removed before proceeding.

After priming, the case should be checked to see that the primer is fully in the pocket. This is done by placing a steel straight-edge ruler across the case while holding it to the light to see if the primer sticks up above the case head. It should not. A high primer gives poor ignition or may not fire at all as the firing pin simply drives it into the pocket. The primed, inspected case now goes into the loading block.

Powder Charging

The case is now ready for charging. When working up a load, always start with the beginning load listed in the data manuals. Increases in powder charges should be made by no more than a half-grain (.5) at a time and less than this for hot, fast-burning powders. Load and test fire at least 10 test rounds before going to a heavier charge. Powder charges are weighed precisely on a powder scale for working up loads. The easiest method is dispense slightly less than you want with a powder thrower, weight it in the scale pan, then bring the load to the precise desired weight with a powder trickler. The scale should be properly set up and checked for adjustment according to the maker's instructions.

Once the charge is weighed, the powder funnel goes on the case and the powder is poured in, with no spills, of course. The funnel is moved from case to case until every one in the loading block is filled. Make it a habit to check the powder level in all the cases in the loading block, examining them under good light, even though you are sure you did not double-charge any of them. If the powder level in any case looks suspiciously high, weigh it again. The balance may be sticking on your scale or you may have accidentally shifted a weight—you'd be surprised at what can happen. Mistakes with pistol powders are more critical than with slower-burning rifle powders. They are more powerful. A little too much Bullseye can go a long way in wrecking your gun.

Using A Powder Measure

The precision of mechanical powder measures depends to a great degree on consistency of pulling and returning the operating handle. After a powder measure is adjusted, check its accuracy, and yours, by dropping every fifth load into the scale pan for weighing. Accurate loads are within a tolerance of +/- 1/10-grain (.1). Always visually check cases loaded with a powder measure in the loading block. It is very easy to pull the handle twice on the same case. Since

Semi-wadcutter bullets are among the best cast revolver bullets in terms of both accuracy and killing power, which makes them suitable for both target shooting and hunting.

many loads for handguns are nearly full-case loads, a double charge will run over or fill the case to the point where a bullet can't be seated, but don't bet on it.

Bullet Seating

This is the final step in the loading operation. A case is placed in the shellholder, a bullet is placed in the case mouth as straight as possible, and the case is gently levered into the bullet-seating die. Proper die adjustment is necessary so you don't exceed the maximum overall length of the cartridge as listed in the loading manual. An overly long cartridge can press the bullet into the rifling and raise pressures in auto-loaders, or jam them. In revolvers, they will jam the cylinder. The easiest way to avoid this problem is to make up a dummy cartridge to use as a guide. After the die is screwed into the press, adjust it so the case enters freely its full length. Gradually ease the cartridge in the die and check to see it does not pass the crimping shoulder, which turns over the case mouth. The next adjustment is to the stem of the bullet seater, which gradually drives the bullet deeper into the case. When the correct overall length is reached, tighten the seater adjustment. Keep the dummy for easy readjustment after loading longer or shorter bullets. You may want to make a dummy for every different-length bullet you load to facilitate easy readjustment. Once the die is adjusted, bullet seating is simply a matter of repetition.

Most dies have a built-in crimping shoulder to turn the case mouth over into a cannelure (groove) in the bullet. This is necessary for high-powered rifle ammunition, particularly if it is jarred by recoil or while being fed through the magazine. Crimping is necessary on nearly all handgun bullets. Magnum handgun cases require heavy crimping to keep bullets from being jarred loose by recoil. No rimless auto-

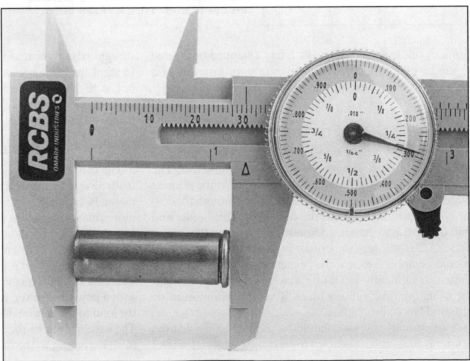

Finished ammunition should be measured to see that the cartridge does not exceed the maximum overall length specified in the loading manual.

matic cartridge such as the 45 ACP should be crimped since it headspaces on the case mouth and a crimp will allow the case to enter too deeply, giving erratic ignition.

Easy does it is the rule for all steps. Ramming and jerking leads to damaged cases, mashed bullets, flattened primers and broken decapping pins.

The final step is to wipe off any case lubricant that may be on the case and inspect the finished cartridge with a final check for overall length. Oil left on cases will cause excessive back-thrust and batter your gun. If all dies are properly adjusted and firmly in place, there should be no difference from one cartridge to the next. Place the loaded rounds in a cartridge box and mark it accordingly.

Cleaning the loading area is always a good idea. Powder should always be returned to the original container, especially from the powder measure. Powder in open containers will lose volatiles and absorb moisture. Primers can absorb moisture and magnum and standard primers can be confused if not put back in their respective containers. Most of all, there is always the chance of confusion regarding what powder you were using when you start the next time.

Selecting A Load

Many people start with factory duplication loads, which, if you have already been shooting them, is a convenient place to start without varying any component. Generally, though, the best accuracy in your handgun will be something you work up on your own. This may take some doing even though many loading manuals list "accuracy loads." If you read the fine print you will see this applies to one particular test gun. If yours is a different make, this one may not shoot best for you, but it is perhaps the best powder/bullet combination to start with. Loading data is presented as starting loads and maximum loads with a middle ground in between. It is generally in this middle ground where the most accurate loading will be found. Rarely is the hottest, highest-pressure load the straightest shooter. Maximum loads, especially with jacketed bullets, shorten both case and barrel life. By working for accuracy, you start by getting a clear idea of just how well your handgun will shoot. With this as a starting point, you then have a standard by which other loads can be judged.

For the most part, you will probably not have need for more than three or four different loadings, if that many. On the bottom end are short-range practice loads. These are usually cast bullets driven at modest velocities of around 550-750 fps. These offer good, cheap recreation and training without the expense, wear, noise and recoil of full-bore loads. They can be used for short-range target shooting where noise may be a problem. Hunting loads are really for handguns of the 357 Magnum class and up. These are near maximum pressure and velocity loadings with jacketed expanding bullets. You would do best to work up the most accurate load you can from the selection of hunting bullets available.

Working Up A Load

Working up a load means not merely careful loading of ammunition, but testing it and keeping records of the results. It also involves case inspection, looking for any signs of excessive headspace or pressures. Use a simple notebook for records. List these under the name of the gun and its caliber. Individual loads are listed under the bullet, indicating whether it is cast or jacketed, the weight, diameter and lubrication type. Next, the powder type and charge are shown. Following this is a notation on the make of case and primer and type. Finally, there's a section for remarks. This includes a summary of the performance of this particular load, especially its accuracy. Ten-shot groups are the accuracy test standard, although it has been demonstrated that seven-shot groups work just as well. Other remarks include the test range conditions like temperature, wind direction and velocity and fight conditions. Also noted are any indications of pressure problems. These are underlined as a warning for future reference.

Loading for Autoloaders

Since the 1980s autoloaders in all calibers and types have become very popular, owing mainly to the changeover by nearly all of this country's police departments to this type of handgun for duty carry. While all autoloaders rely on the force of the explosion in the cartridge to function the action, there are a number of differences in the ways various actions operate, and these features have a marked effect on how ammunition must be reloaded for them.

There are three basic types of autoloading actions: straight blowback, with a variant known as delayed blowback, recoil-operated and gas-operated.

Blowback actions are the simplest. They function by having the slide held in contact with the barrel by a spring, thus the two are not locked together. When the gun fires, the bullet is driven down the barrel while the case is driven against the face of the slide. The weight of the slide and force of the recoil spring, and the internal pressure swelling the case against the chamber wall, all keep the case from moving backward until the bullet has exited the muzzle. Somewhere around this point, as chamber pressure begins to drop, the case begins to be blown back against the slide; the inertial force given the slide causes it to move rearward, cocking the pistol and ejecting the fired case. Tension in the compressed recoil spring sends the slide forward, stripping a fresh cartridge from the magazine and chambering it. This system works well with low-powered handgun cartridges and is used in all 22 Long Rifle, 25 ACP, 32 ACP, 380 ACP autoloaders and the 9mm Makarov autoloading pistol. The system is limited to straight-walled, semi-rimmed cases because a bottlenecked case would likely have its neck pulled off or have gas come rushing around it as soon as the pressure seal was broken. Because of the necessity of equaling the forces of the forward-moving bullet with the proper amount of slide weight and spring pressure, limitations of the system

(Text continued on page 126)

Step-By-Step Reloading

>>>>>>>>>>>>>>>>>>>>>>>>>>>>>>>>>>>>

Handgun Cartridges

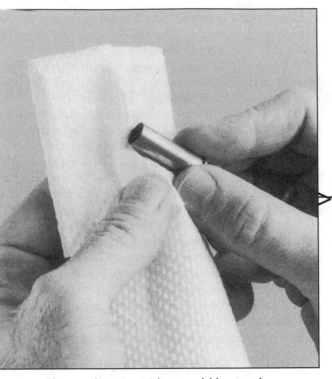

Step 1 - Clean and Inspect: It's a good idea to wipe cases clean before beginning to reload them. This also allows you to inspect them for any split necks, cracks, etc. Discard those that are damaged.

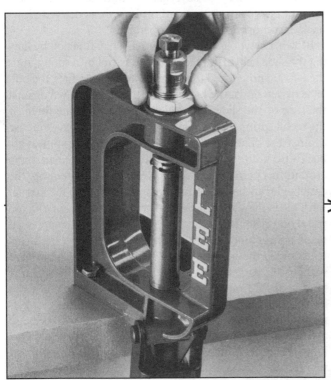

Step 4 - Adjusting the Sizer Die: Raise the ram to the top of its travel and screw the sizing die in until it just touches the shellholder. Now, slightly lower the ram and screw in the die an additional 1/4-turn. Tighten the lock nut.

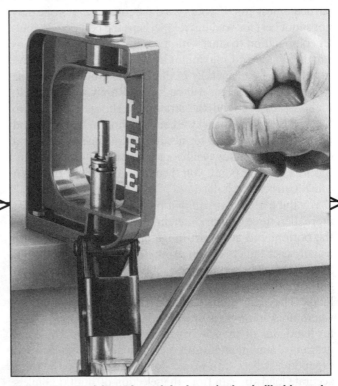

Step 5 - Case Resizing: Place a lubed case in the shellholder and raise the ram, guiding the case as it enters the sizing die. This step also knocks out the fired primer. Raise the press handle and remove the case.

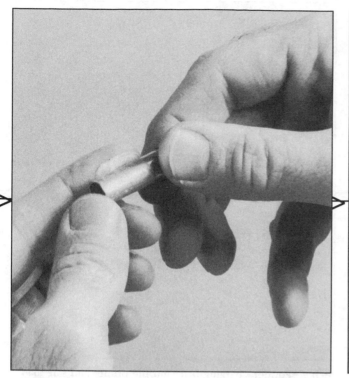

Step 2 - Lubricate the Cases: Case lube is needed when not using a carbide resizing die. Spread just a light film on each case with the fingers.

Step 3 - Installing the Shellholder: Choose the proper shellholder for the round you are loading. They usually come with the die sets. Raise the ram slightly to snap the shellholder into place with a twisting motion. Position it with the open side out to the left.

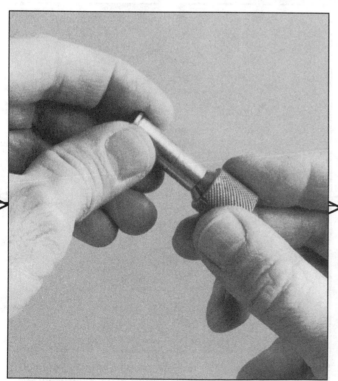

Step 6 - Chamfer and Deburr: To ease bullet entry, lightly chamfer the mouth of the case by inserting the pointed end of the chamfering/deburring tool into the case mouth and gently twisting it.

Step 7 - Case Mouth Expansion: After installing and properly adjusting the expander die, insert a case and run it into the die to bell the case mouth for easy insertion of a new bullet. Adjust the die just enough to allow easy bullet entry.

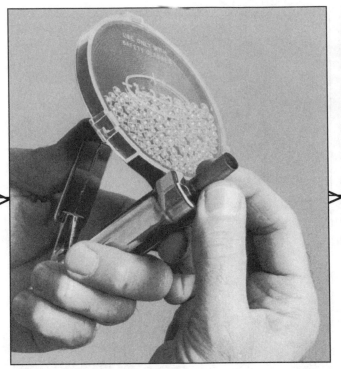

Step 8 - Priming: Installing a new primer can be done on the press or with a hand-held Auto Prime tool. After filling the primer tray, slip a deprimed case into the shellholder and press the lever to push a primer into the primer pocket. Follow the instructions that come with each tool.

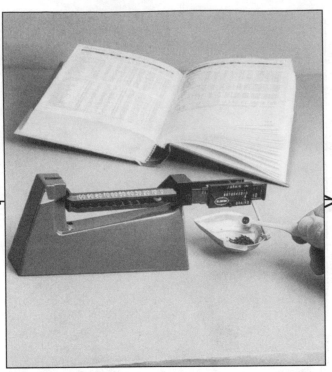

Step 9 - Powder Charging (A): Find the proper and safe load for your cartridge in a loading manual or from another reliable source, then weigh each charge on your powder scale. This is the safest method, although a bit slow, and is best for accuracy and maximum loads.

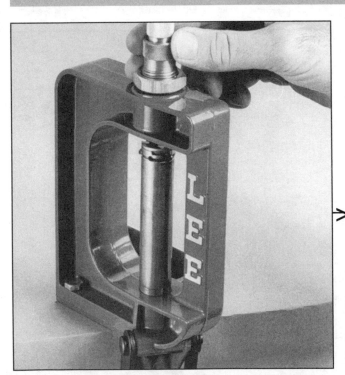

Step 12 - Bullet Seating (A): To install the bullet-seating die, place a case in the shellholder and raise the ram to the top of the stroke. Screw in the seater die until you feel it touch the case mouth. If no crimp is desired, back the die out 1/2-turn. If you want a crimp, turn it in 1/4-turn.

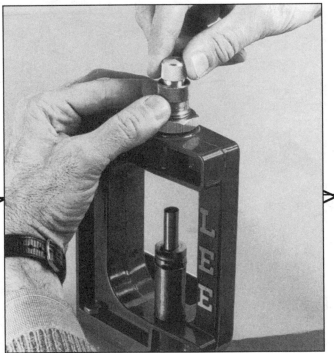

Step 13 - Bullet Seating (B): The knurled adjusting screw controls the bullet seating depth. Usually, seating to the same depth as a factory round works well. If you want a crimp, be sure the bullet cannelure is almost completely inside the case mouth. Screw the die in just enough to apply a good crimp. A little trial and error work is needed here.

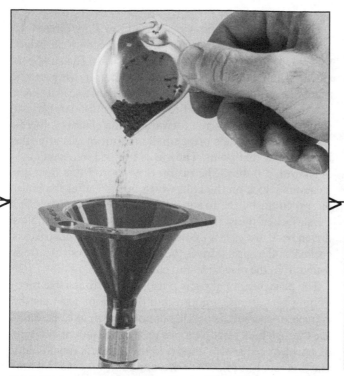

Step 10 - Powder Charging (B): Lee's expander die allows the powder charge to be dumped from the scale pan into the primed case through the die. Cases can also be set into a loading block for powder charging.

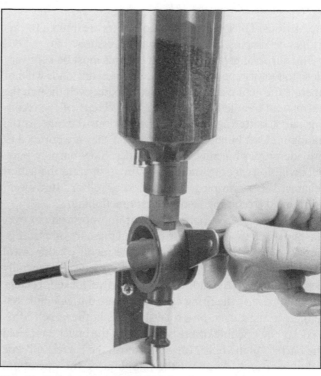

Step 11 - Powder Charging (C): Once the proper load has been found, you can dispense powder directly into the case with the powder measure. It will throw a precise, uniform charge with each turn of the handle. Check-weigh every fifth or tenth charge to be sure it is correct.

Step 14 - Bullet Seating (C): To seat a bullet, place one in the case mouth and guide it into the seating die as straight as possible. If the bullet needs to be deeper, screw in the seater plug a little bit and run the case back into the die. It may take a few tries to get the exact depth required.

Step 15 - The Loaded Round: That's all there is to loading a handgun cartridge. A final wipe with a clean cloth and the ammunition is ready to be fired. Don't forget to mark the ammo box with your load data so you can repeat the load.

(Text continued from page 121)

are obvious. Thus, blowback autoloaders are limited to cartridges developing low velocities and pressures.

Not surprisingly, reloads for such guns must be kept very close to factory specifications. Lower-pressure loads will not operate the action and high-pressure loads, even though the barrels can handle them, increase the velocity of the recoiling parts, battering them, causing serious damage to the handgun. Cast bullet loads work well if they are crimped to provide proper burning of the powder. Slow-burning powders will not generate enough power to operate the action reliably. Taper-crimping, as opposed to roll or "turn-over" crimping, is recommended for best functioning.

Recoil-operated actions represent an improvement over the blowback in terms of the type and pressure of cartridge they can handle. In this system, the recoil of the pistol drives the operation. Recoil-operated systems are generally designed to keep the slide or bolt and barrel locked together through part of the firing cycle. Some use a toggle-link system, as in the Luger, or a roller-lock, as in the Czech M52, to delay the opening of the breech until the bullet has exited the barrel. As the bullet travels forward, the barrel and slide recoil as a unit. At about the midpoint of the operation, after the bullet has exited the barrel, pressure drops, the action unlocks and the slide continues traveling backward, ejecting the empty case and cocking the hammer. The slide then strips a fresh round from the magazine, chambering it as it comes forward into battery.

This system is used in autoloading pistols using the 9mm Parabellum cartridge, 38 Super Auto, 45 ACP and similar cartridges adopted for military and police use. Battering of internal parts will result from loads generating excessive pressures and velocities.

The best way to work up handloads for autoloaders is to do so slowly, checking recoiling parts for any evidence of battering. The best loads are ones that will reliably cycle the action and no more.

Generally the only cast-bullet loads that do work are those near the maximum pressure level. While these may operate the action reliably, they may often not deliver very good accuracy, and the accurate load may not operate the action. Reduced loads will not work reliably in any autoloader, with cartridges often getting jammed on the way out and chewed up in the process. Therefore, the range of loading options for autoloaders of any stripe is rather limited. There will usually be only a relative few loadings that will produce good accuracy and reliable functioning. Ammunition prepared for autoloaders should be given extra care to see that all tolerances are kept close to factory specifications. Exceeding overall length will jam actions. Cases too short and bullets too deep can have the same effect. In short, ammunition preparation for successful shooting of these guns requires extra care for best results.

Full-length resizing is almost always necessary with cartridges used in autoloaders, since the chambers are on the large size to permit reliable feeding even when they are dirty with fouling.

Gas-operated pistols are uncommon and limited to expensive models that fire very powerful magnum cartridges that enter the lower region of rifle velocities. The gas-operated system features a locked bolt and non-moving barrel, much like gas-operated rifles, and is based on a scaled-down rifle action. They can thus fire very powerful cartridges. At some point on the barrel, forward of the chamber, there's a small hole that taps off a small amount of gas after the bullet passes that point. The gas is trapped in a small cylinder with a piston. The piston drives a rod that operates a camming lock on the bolt, which opens it after the bullet has exited the barrel. In some variants the gas is directed to the surface of the cam lock to unlock the bolt. As the bolt is driven back, the case is ejected and the hammer or striker is cocked, and a spring drives the bolt forward to strip a fresh round from the magazine and chamber it.

The placement of the gas port is critical to reliable functioning because the amount and pressure of gas must be enough to operate the pistol, but not enough to cause damage through battering. Needless to say, the amount and type of powder used is also critical to this system's functioning. Gas-operated autoloaders are ammunition-sensitive and will work best with loadings that duplicate factory specifications. Cast bullets, generally, do not work well in gas-operated autoloaders. Fast-burning powders such as IMR 4227, Herco, Unique, 2400, H 110 and AA 1680 are about the only ones that will function gas-operated actions reliably.

Any cast bullets used in autoloading pistols are best cast of hard alloy, since soft bullets are often nicked and dented as they pass through the magazine and into the chamber. Feed ramp polishing may often be necessary when using cast loads with any autoloader to avoid jams. Magazine lips that are bent or sprung are a frequent cause of jamming in autoloading pistols and should be checked for wear or damage if this problem occurs.

Loading for Revolvers

Modern revolvers are all of the solid frame type. The few exceptions are replicas of 19th century top-break guns and those old models that are still around that use this system. The top-break guns are of a weaker design and should be used only with low-pressure "starting loads" listed in the manuals, and then only if they are in good, tight condition.

Unlike the autoloader, with its box magazine, the revolver features a cylinder with multiple chambers. The mechanism in a revolver turns these chambers, via a hand or pawl that aligns each with the barrel. The relationship between this rotation and the firing cycle is referred to as timing. In revolvers where the timing is off because of wear and battering by too many heavy loads, this alignment between the chamber and the barrel may be less than perfect, poor accuracy—even badly shaved bullets—can result. To an extent, a competent gunsmith can correct this.

The revolver has a second problem—the gap between the cylinder and the barrel. The bullet must jump this gap before entering the forcing cone at the rear of the barrel.

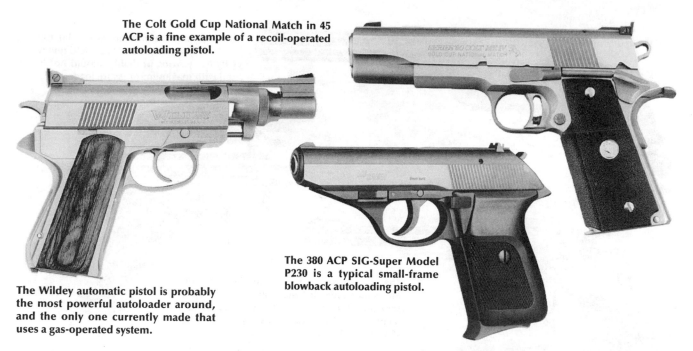

The Colt Gold Cup National Match in 45 ACP is a fine example of a recoil-operated autoloading pistol.

The 380 ACP SIG-Super Model P230 is a typical small-frame blowback autoloading pistol.

The Wildey automatic pistol is probably the most powerful autoloader around, and the only one currently made that uses a gas-operated system.

There has been much written about gas loss in the process, but the final analysis is that it isn't that much in terms of lowering bullet performance. The jump is most detrimental to accuracy because of the aforementioned alignment problems. In addition, by making this jump, the bullet gains a fair amount of speed before it hits the rifling, and may show skid marks as it moves forward for a fraction of an inch before engaging the rifling.

The throat of the revolver cylinder guides but does not really support the bullet, since it is larger than the bore diameter. Sizing revolver bullets is then something of a guessing game. The best course of action is to stick with factory diameters to start with, then experiment with different diameters after slugging the bore. The hardness of cast revolver bullets can have a decided effect on their accuracy. A fairly hard alloy (Lyman #2) generally works best, but softer alloys may be necessary to achieve proper upset and to avoid leading in some revolvers. Leading can be a serious problem in some guns, and these may require a hollow-base bullet to obturate the cylinder throat to avoid hot gas blowing by and melting the surface of the bullet. Before going to a hollow-base mould, it is best to experiment with different lubricants and alloys to see if changes in these will eliminate the problem. Different styles of bullets with larger, deeper lubricant grooves to hold more lubricant may be the answer. Failing that, buy some commercially-made hollow-base bullets or factory loads with hollow-base bullets (if available) before getting another mould. Gas checks and wax wads may come to the rescue in some cases, as will half-jacketed bullets that eliminate leading entirely.

Because they are loaded manually, revolvers work well with cast bullets, both plain and gas-checked. Owing to the recoil a cylinder-full of ammunition receives with each discharge, revolver cartridges should be crimped to keep the bullets from being pushed into the cases. Revolver cases should be full-length resized for ease in loading the gun.

One major advantage of revolvers over autoloaders is their ability to handle low-pressure/low-velocity loadings, because the action is not dependent on cartridge power for operation. These will afford economical practice with minimal wear and tear on the gun. For the same reason, revolvers can take a greater range of bullets in terms of weight and length. Bullets with a long bearing surface generally align better and produce the best accuracy. While revolvers function best with fast-burning pistol powders, the range of loading possibilities surpasses that of the autoloader.

Loading for Single Shots

These handguns are a fairly recent arrival on the shooting scene, and their use is limited to long-range target shooting and hunting. They chamber rifle cartridges and powerfully loaded handgun cartridges. Because of their solid actions and longer barrels, they generate velocities and pressures in the rifle class. These guns might best be called "hand rifles." Owing to their light weight, most cannot use maximum rifle loadings, and even with more modest pressures and velocities the muzzle blast and recoil are formidable. Most loading manuals contain special loading data for these guns. To use any of these loadings in a standard revolver or autoloader would wreck it in short order. Loading procedures for metallic silhouette guns follow rifle instructions. One of the more popular of these guns is the Thompson/Center Contender. This gun allows the use of a number of barrels, each in a different caliber. Contenders can thus shoot anything from the 22 Long Rifle on up to the 45-70, which if you want to get a real "kick" out of handgun shooting will certainly deliver the goods.

Testing Ammunition

Accuracy is, or should be, your first concern. An accuracy test can consist of nothing more than plinking a few cans at an unknown distance, but this won't tell you very much. The

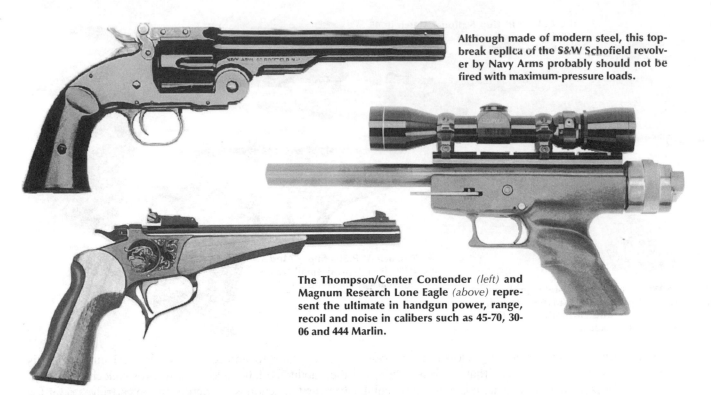

Although made of modern steel, this top-break replica of the S&W Schofield revolver by Navy Arms probably should not be fired with maximum-pressure loads.

The Thompson/Center Contender *(left)* and Magnum Research Lone Eagle *(above)* represent the ultimate in handgun power, range, recoil and noise in calibers such as 45-70, 30-06 and 444 Marlin.

only meaningful test is firing from a solid rest at a known distance. With handguns, a test range doesn't really need much more than 50 yards, since this is about the maximum accurate range of most of them, and 50 to 75 feet is the standard distance. Accuracy testing requires a solid bench installation with a sand bag or adjustable rest. If you live in a rural area or have access to a range with benches, you are set.

Testing should be done on a day with good light, little or no wind and moderate temperatures. Calm conditions are generally found in the early morning or late afternoon. The place to start is to shoot some factory ammunition for comparison. A distance of 50 yards is good enough to get a fair idea of the long-range possibilities of your handgun and ammunition if you plan to use it for hunting. Only the more powerful cartridges – 357 Magnum and up – have much use in the hunting field.

For most handguns, a 2- to 3-inch group at 50 feet is about as good as you will get. Fine target guns will shoot under an inch at this range. Metallic silhouette guns are judged and tested more by rifle standards. Shoot seven- or ten-shot groups, taking your time to squeeze off the shots. If you intend to shoot both cast and jacketed bullets, be sure to clean the barrel of all copper fouling before shooting lead-alloy bullets, since they will strip lead on the copper fouling.

Shooting into turf will give you an idea of the ricochet potential of your ammunition if this is critical. You can usually hear the results if the bullets are not ricochet-proof. Most handgun bullets ricochet very readily, even hollowpoints. For testing on game or varmint animals, there is not much in the way of practical substitutes for the real item. Ballistic gelatin is the standard by which such determina-

tions are made, but it is difficult to prepare and must be calibrated and used at the proper temperature.

One tissue substitute of a cheap and easy sort is newspaper, soaked overnight to get it fully saturated. Stocks of the wet paper are then put in a cardboard carton for shooting into. This is far heavier and more resistant than muscle tissue, but will give you an idea of bullet behavior.

Packed wet snow is a fairly good tissue simulator, and if there is enough of it you can find your bullet somewhere along a long snow loaf. High-velocity bullets are more difficult to recover, but lower velocity cast bullets can usually be stopped within 5 to 10 feet of packed snow. These will generally be in almost pristine condition. This will give you a good opportunity to study your cast bullets for evidence of gas-cutting and of how well they take the rifling. Large or double sets of rifling marks on the front of a bullet indicate skidding or jumping the rifling—the bullet going straight for a fraction of an inch before taking the rifling and turning, as it should. Rifling marks that are higher on one side than the other indicate the bullet was not straight in the case or were fired in a revolver with the cylinder slightly out of alignment. Grease grooves that are heavily compressed and lack lubricant will explain one cause of leading—not enough groove space and an inefficient lubricant. Bullet recovery is for those who are seriously interested, and those wanting answers to questions beginning with the word "Why."

A final warning is to *always check your cases after firing*, particularly when you are testing loads that are on the high side of the pressure curve. Once you are out in the field, there is a great temptation to keep shooting. If there are signs of high pressure or excessive headspace, *stop shooting*. Don't risk your eyesight and handgun.

12

Creating homemade scattergun fodder is not the same as metallic cartridge reloading. It requires different tools, components and knowledge.

Shotshell Ammunition Reloading

OF THE THREE basic types of ammunition, shotgun ammunition is perhaps the easiest to load, once you get the hang of it. Nevertheless, the same level of care and attention must be given the task if good results are to be obtained. The place to begin is with once-fired or new cases to work up a load. Once a load is tested and found to be satisfactory then quantity production can begin.

Shotshell casings are made of plastic for the most part. Since shotshells operate at far lower pressures than rifle and most handgun ammunition, they are less robust in construction. Shotshells come in six sizes or gauges. The smallest is the .410-bore which is actually .410-inch in diameter or 410-caliber. The larger sizes are listed by gauge, an old system that determined a "gauge" size by the number of lead balls of that diameter to weigh a pound. The next size up is 28-gauge, then 20-gauge, 16-gauge, 12-gauge and, finally, 10-gauge. In the bad old days

Modern shotshells, from left: 10-gauge 31/2-inch magnum, 12-gauge 3-inch, 12-gauge 2 3/4-inch, 16-gauge 2 3/4-inch, 20-gauge 2 3/4-inch, 28-gauge 2 3/4-inch, and .410 bore 3- and 2 1/2-inch.

of market hunting, the now obsolete 8-gauge, 4-gauge and even 3-gauge guns were used; the latter two were mounted like small cannons on boats for taking waterfowl. Modern shotshells, in addition to the above six gauges, are available in different lengths. Since 1933, .410 shotguns have been universally available to take the 3-inch shell, which is ballistically superior to the old 2 1/2-inch shell. The 3-inch shell should never be loaded in a gun chambered for the shorter shell. This rule applies to all gauges. To do so will result in serious pressure jumps, which can wreck your gun and your face. The shorter shell can always be used in the longer chamber, but never the reverse.

The big problem with this potential mismatching of length is that the longer shells will chamber in guns intended for the shorter load. This is because shotgun chambers are made long, allowing space for the opening of the crimp in the case mouth. A 3 1/2-inch 10-gauge shell measures 3 inches unfired, and 3 1/2 inches fired. If you have an old gun, or one of foreign make that is not marked for the length of shell it is chambered for, take it to a competent gunsmith for examination. Foreign shotguns may be chambered for shells of different lengths.

Old guns should be regarded with suspicion unless the length is clearly marked or can otherwise be identified. Old guns should also be regarded as suspect if they cannot be identified as being safe for use with modern smokeless powder. Guns with damascus barrels, identifiable by the tiger-stripe pattern in the metal, should be examined by a knowledgeable gunsmith to determine if the barrels are sound. If there is any sign of barrel corrosion from blackpowder loads used in the gun, don't try shooting it. Damascus-barreled guns in good condition should be used with blackpowder loads only, just to be on the safe, lower-pressure side. Guns designed for smokeless loads abound on the new and used market, so it's not worth the risk of blowing up Granpap's old double, let alone your hide, just to shoot the thing. Again, if there is any doubt about the soundness of the gun, don't shoot it at all.

Case Inspection and Storage

As with rifle and handgun cartridges, shotshells should be inspected for defects. Those that are badly worn around the mouth, have splits in the case walls or heads, or leaks around the primers, should be discarded. Paper shotshells are perhaps the most vulnerable of all. The bodies absorb moisture, which can also enter the seam around the primer, and moisture-swollen shells will not chamber. Before buying any old ones to shoot, if the shells can't be tested, try chambering the more suspect ones or check them with a ring gauge. Study the exteriors for bleaching or water discoloration.

Modern plastic shells don't have this problem, but in an economy move many are no longer made with brass heads. The steel heads are given a thin brass plating that will corrode quickly. The steel beneath will corrode even more quickly if exposed to pollutants. Old plastic shells that have been crimped for a long time tend to hold that crimp and reload poorly unless ironed out with a warming tool made for this purpose. A piece of metal rod or pipe of the proper diameter heated in boiling water will also serve.

Shotshells come in a wide array of colors. There is a good reason for this so you won't mix them up. Successful reloading depends on fitting all the components together correctly within the shell. There is a considerable difference in the inside capacities of various shells owing to the thickness of the base wad at the head of the shell. Matching loads to the particular brand and type of shell is critical to successful reloading. If the correct shotcup/wad is not used with the matching shell, it may be too long or too short for the shell to crimp properly. Therefore, different companies make their shells in certain colors to identify the make and further color-code these shells by gauge so they are not mixed up. A 20-gauge shell accidentally dropped in a 12-gauge gun barrel will stop about where the forcing cone is. If a 12-gauge shell is then fired, the shooter will immediately be reminded of the Big Bang Theory when the gun comes apart in the forend area. The bad part of this is the proximity of fingers

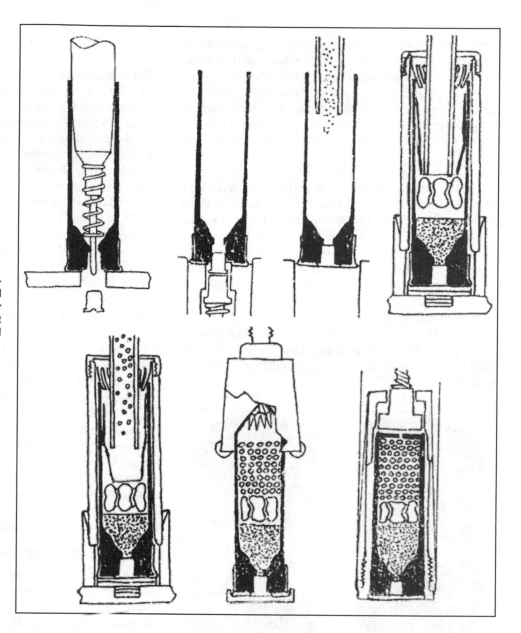

There are seven steps in shotshell reloading: resizing and decapping, priming, powder charging, wad seating, shot metering, crimp starting and crimp finishing.

and hand to the barrel that just let go. This 12/20 blowup is not uncommon, and that is why all modern American-made 20-gauge shells are some shade of yellow and all 12-gauges are usually red. Winchester uses red for all its shells except 20-gauge; Remington shells are green, 20-gauge excepted; Federal shells, including their paper-tube 12-gauge, are maroon, with the exception of the 10-gauge which is brown;

the Activ 12-gauge, which is all plastic and has no brass on it, is red; Fiocchi shells, from Italy, may be purple, blue, red, orange or brown.

Within the various makes you will find shells with different base wads, which thus require different shot cups. That is why critical inspection and storage are needed. If you are in doubt, consult a good shotshell reloading manual, such

NORMAL CHOKE PERCENTAGE	
Designation	Percentage of Pellets in 30-inch Circle at 40 Yards
Full	65-75
Improved Modified (3/4)	60-65
Modified (1/2)	55-65
Improved Cylinder (1/4)	45-55
Skeet	40-50
Cylinder	35-40

SHOTSHELL LENGTHS	
Ammo	Shell Length (ins.)
10-Gauge	2 7/8 (obsolete) and 3 1/2
12-Gauge	2 3/4, 3 and 3 1/2
16-Gauge	2 9/16 (obsolete) and 2 3/4
20-Gauge	2 3/4 and 3
28-Gauge	2 3/4
410-Bore	2 1/2 and 3

as the one put out by Lyman, which has a great many of these shells pictured in color, and of actual size. If in doubt about the proper shot cup, sacrifice a loaded one by cutting it down the middle and comparing the sectioned shell with these illustrations. The height of the brass on the outside of the head may or may not indicate a base wad of a different height, but don't count on it. Never mix components.

Shotshell Primers

Shotshell primers, while they are all the same size, do have different burning characteristics. This will radically affect pressures. The substitution of one primer for another can raise pressures as much as 2000 psi with all other components being equal. This is why when working up loads, no substitution should be made for any component listed in a loading manual. If you have several brands of primers on hand, don't have more than one box open at a time so they don't get mixed up. Primers should be seated flush with the case head. High primers can be detonated accidentally in certain guns with disastrous results. Decapping live primers is not a good idea. Either snap them in the gun or discard the shell.

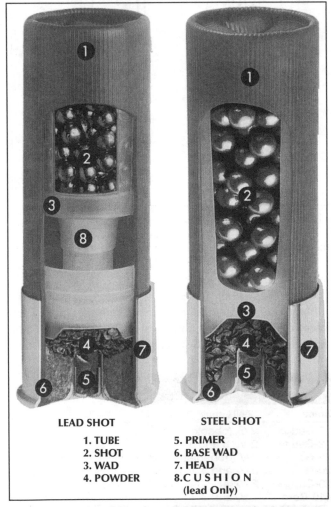

LEAD SHOT   **STEEL SHOT**

1. TUBE	5. PRIMER
2. SHOT	6. BASE WAD
3. WAD	7. HEAD
4. POWDER	8. C U S H I O N (lead Only)

There are some big differences between steel and lead shotshell components.

Shotshell Wads

Old-style brass and paper shotshells used wads of cardboard, felt and similar fibers to serve as spacers between the powder and the charge of shot. This system was used for over a hundred years. It had a serious drawback—the wads did not obturate the shell or the bore of the gun very well, and hot powder gas leaked around their edges and melted and otherwise distorted the pellets in the shot charge. Things improved in the 1940s with the addition of a cup wad over the powder to act as a gas seal. In the early 1960s, a further improvement was made with a plastic wrap being placed around the shot charge to keep it from being distorted by direct contact with the barrel.

Modern shotshells contain a single plastic wad with a cup-shaped base that goes over the powder and expands to obturate the bore. Above this is a cushioning section that compresses on firing to start the shot charge off more gently. At the top is a cup that holds the charge of shot. The sides are cut into several "petals" which open as soon as the wad exits the barrel. Unlike in the old days, when loads were assembled by adding card or fiber wads of varying thickness to get the proper height for good crimping, modern wads with shotcups are designed to hold a certain amount of shot. This way, low-volume wads with shallow shotcups are used for light field and target loads, while high-volume wads are used for heavy loads for waterfowl shooting. Attempting to over- or underload these cups gives poor results when you crimp the shell. Components should be properly matched to the shells for which they are intended, and not used in other shells.

Sizes and Types of Shot

Most shot is made of lead hardened with antimony. So-called "premium" shot is made of a harder alloy to keep it from deforming in the firing process. This is a good investment since deformed shot makes for open or irregular patterns, which translates to missed or crippled game. Sometimes hard shot is given a copper plating to make it look attractive. Whether this makes it shoot any better or not depends on your powers of imagination.

Steel shot was introduced some 25 years ago after the U.S. Fish and Wildlife Service concluded that bottom-feeding waterfowl were succumbing to lead poisoning. USFWS placed a ban on lead shot for waterfowl hunting, and thus steel shot was born. Steel shot has a number of drawbacks, the least of which is its light weight. Thus, larger shot must be loaded in greater volume to get the same weight equivalent as the old lead loads.

vWhen it comes to loading shotshells, the machines you will use have different systems from metallic ammunition loaders, and the sequence of steps will vary from one machine to another. As was pointed out in the chapter on loading equipment, shotshell loading is done on a single machine with a lot of attachments, while rifle and handgun ammunition is assembled using two or three bench-mounted tools with a number of attachments and several hand tools. Because of their relative complexity, shotshell reloading machines come with manuals that are clearly written and illustrated. They show you how to load shotshells on *that* machine. If you buy a used machine, be sure that the proper manual is with it and that the tool has all the necessary component parts. Failing this, you will have to write the company for a manual, or get someone who knows what he is doing to show you how to operate that particular machine. It is dangerous to attempt to load ammunition on a machine you don't know how to operate on an "I think I can figure this dude out" basis. Obsolete machines that may not have all their parts and manual are no bargain. Manufacturers such as Texan and Herters are out of business and spare parts, manuals and factory support are out of the question.

If you have never done any shotshell reloading it is probably best not to start with a progressive loader. These machines are the most complicated to use, and observing all the steps while determining whether or not they are being done correctly is difficult. Thus the beginner would do best starting with a basic single-stage loader such as the Lee Load-All 11 or MEC 600 Jr. Mark V. Unlike rifle and handgun loading where the manuals offer suggestions for working up loads to find an accurate one, shotshell loads are pretty much cut and dried. The manual that comes with the loader will instruct you on the use of the powder and shot bushings to be inserted in the charge bar of the machine. These must be matched to the proper type of powder and size of shot. They will dispense preset amounts of powder and shot. *Make sure you match these bushings and powders correctly!* Read the manual.

Case Inspection

Even new and once-fired cases should be checked over for defects. Any with splits or serious defects in the case mouth or body, or splits in the metal head should be discarded. Cases should be segregated by maker as determined not only by the headstamp, but by the base wad configuration. Because they wear out sooner than rifle or handgun cases, and because worn cases give different velocities as the case mouths become softer, shotshells should be carefully identified by their intended loading as well as by maker and the number of times they have been reloaded. This means careful handling when shooting so you don't mix them up, and afterwards boxing or bagging them accordingly.

Materials/Equipment Pre-Check

Make sure that your wads match the shells you are about to load. The loading manual will tell you which to buy. Select the proper primers, powder and proper size shot for your loads. Check that you have the correct bushing and shot bar in place for that combination of powder and shot, or have made the proper adjustments on the bar for those types that are adjustable. Fill the canisters on the machine. Lay out no more than 100 primers on the bench.

Shotcups/wads are designed for particular loads in specific shells. These wads hold 7/8-ounce of #7, #7 1/2, #8 or #9 shot. They are intended for use in the compression-formed plastic shells and are for target shooting.

Case Resizing and Decapping

With machines such as the Lee, decapping and primer seating are done at the same location. With the MEC, primer seating is a separate step. Place the shell under the sizing die, or slip it into the die body, and pull the handle to the bottom of the stroke. This resizes and decaps the shell.

Priming

A new primer is next placed on the primer seating station and the handle is pulled to bring the shell down onto the primer and seat it. This stroke must be firm, but not overly hard, in order to seat the primer flush with the shell head. Primers should be checked with a straightedge to assure proper seating.

Powder Charging

The case is next moved to the station below the powder container. Depending on the exact configuration of the machine you are using, the handle is pulled to bring the case into contact with the powder/shot tube dispenser. The charge bar is then pushed across the bottom of the powder container (usually to the full left position) and the powder charge will be metered into the case. *Important*: This step should be verified by checking at least ten charges on a powder scale. If you do not use a scale you have no idea whether your charges are close–or even in the ballpark. If the machine is not delivering the proper amount of powder, within a tolerance of 5 percent of the listed charge, you may have to try another larger or smaller bushing in the charge bar, or the bushing may be clogged if the powder is not dry and free-flowing. This step should be done at the beginning of each loading session and when you change to a different lot of powder. Once it is determined the charge bar is dispensing powder as it should, move on to the next step.

Wad Seating

This step may be done at the same station as powder charging or the shell may have to be moved to a new station. The wad is placed on the wad guide. The handle is pulled fully down and the wad is seated on the powder. Some powders are more sensitive to wad pressure than others, and will yield higher or lower velocities and pressures depending on their degree of compression. Red Dot is one of the more sensitive ones. The better machines have a pressure gauge on them. Note this and the wad seating height to determine that your wads are seated uniformly. If a wad goes far too deep, you have less than a full powder charge or no charge and you will have to recheck your charging operations. Care should be taken that the base cup on the wad is not caught and nicked or tipped by folds in the case mouth and descends straight onto the powder. If the seating pressure

is too high you may have too much powder or an incorrect wad for that charge, or a wad not properly matched to that case. Wad seating pressure should be at least 20 pounds. Finally, check to see that the petals of the shotcup are in full contact with the case walls so they will not interfere with shot metering.

Shot Metering

Depending on your machine, the shell may or may not be moved to another station for shot metering. Whatever, the shell is raised to the powder/shot charging tube and the charge bar is generally moved to the right across the bottom of the shot canister dropping the shot into the shell. It is important to have the proper shot bar for the load you are making. MEC tools (at least the older ones) have a different shot charge bar for each weight of shot. Other machines have adjustable shot bars or bars with powder insert bushings. Lee and Hornady machines have bushing inserts for both shot and powder.

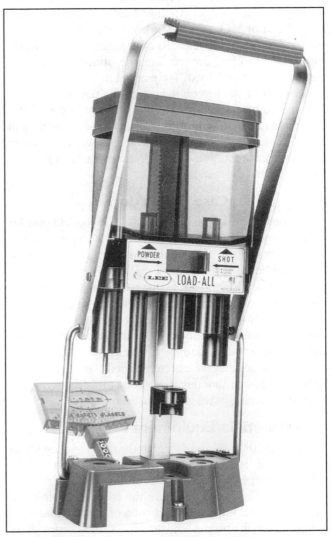

The Lee Load-All II is an excellent entry-level shotshell loader at an affordable price. It can turn out an average of 100 rounds per hour, and loads lead or steel shot.

Each shotshell load is component-specific. Primers, as well as all other components, are not created equal and should not be interchanged.

Various crimp styles, from left: an old-style rolled crimp on a paper shell with top wad; the rolled crimp, still used and necessary for making slug loads; typical six-point and eight-point crimps.

As with powder charging, shot charges must be checked on a scale to be sure they are accurate. The same five percent tolerance applies. Run several shot charges on your scale to verify that your machine is behaving properly. Occasionally a shot charge will jam or only partially

PELLET COUNT COMPARISON			
Shot Size	**12-Ga. 1⅞ ozs.** Lead pellets	**Shot Size**	**12-Ga. 1⅜ ozs.** Steel pellets
6	422	4	263
4	253	2	172
2	163	BB	99
BB	94	T	71

SHOT SIZES			
Shot Size	**Diameter** (Ins.)	**No. of Pellets/Oz.** Lead	Steel
9	.08	585	—
8½	.085	—	—
8	.09	411	—
7½	.095	350	—
6	.11	225	316
5	.12	170	246
4	.13	135	191
3	.14	109	153
2	.15	87	125
1	.16	72	103
B	.17	59	84
BB	.18	50	72
BBB	.19	43	61
T	.20	36	52
F	.22	37	40

feed, and a visual inspection of each shell you load should be made. If the shot cup is not full, return the shell to the charging position and give the charging tube a tap or two. This should cause the remainder to drop and you can move to the next step.

The loading of buckshot is a special consideration, since shot this large cannot be metered through the machine. Buckshot is loaded by pellet *count*, not by weight, and the shot have to be counted and hand-fed into the shot cup. More importantly, buckshot must be nested in layers in the cup or they will not fit properly. Some of these loads call for "buffering" with a finely ground plastic material. This should be added with each layer and the case tapped with the finger to settle it into the cup until it is level with the top layer of shot. Needless to say, buckshot loads are best assembled on a single-stage press rather than on a progressive.

Crimp Starting

Shotshells have two forms of fold crimping: six-point and eight-point. The crimp starter should be matched to the fold pattern of the shells you are reloading. Never use a six-point crimp starter on an eight-point shell and vice versa. The crimp starter is adjustable and can be raised and lowered to vary the amount of crimp start. When working with various brands of shells, a certain amount of experimentation is needed to get the proper amount of crimp start. Remington and Federal shells seem to require a little less start than Activ and Winchester shells. If your finished shells show indentations in the crimped end of the shell, the crimp starter is set too deeply and will have to be backed off a bit.

(Text continued on page 138

Step-By-Step Reloading

>>>>>>>>>>>>>>>>>>>>>>>>>>>>>>>>>>

Shotshell Cartridges

(Photos courtesy Lee Precision, Inc.)

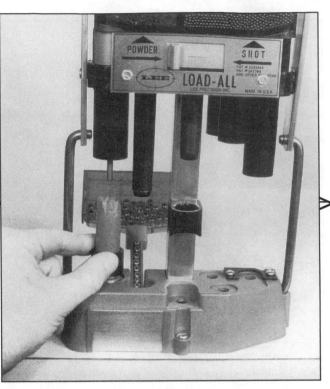

Step 1 - Sizing: Sort your hulls by brand and type, and discard the defective ones. Slip the sizing die, grooved end up, over the shell. Place the shell in Station 1 and pull down the handle. This full-length resizes and deprimes the shell.

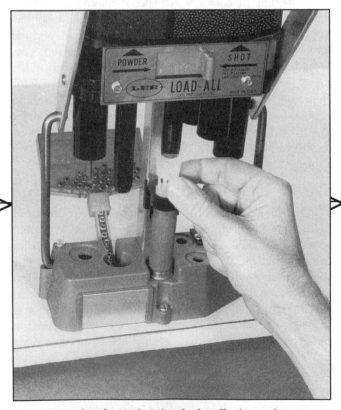

Step 4 - Inserting the Wad: Raise the handle, insert the proper wad and lower the press handle until it stops.

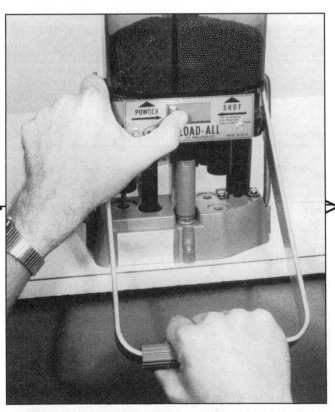

Step 5 - Shot Charging: Now slide the charge bar all the way to the left to add the shot. Raise the press handle.

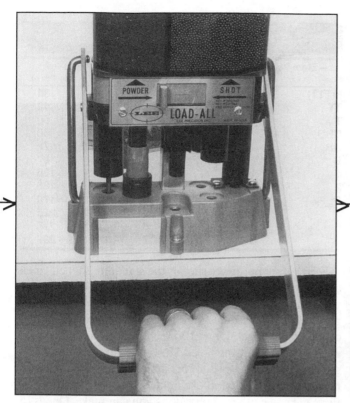

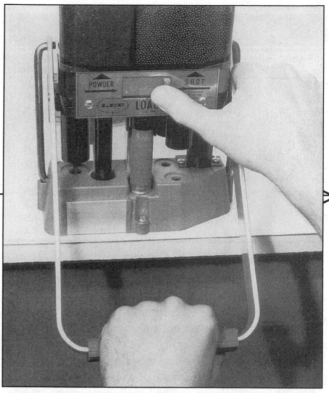

Step 2 - Priming: Place a primer in the priming pocket at Station 2. Move the shell onto Station 2 and pull down the handle. The sizing die will automatically be pushed off the shell at this station. Remove it completely.

Step 3 - Powder Charging: Slip the shell into the wad guide at Station 3, lower the handle and slide the charge bar to the right to add the powder.

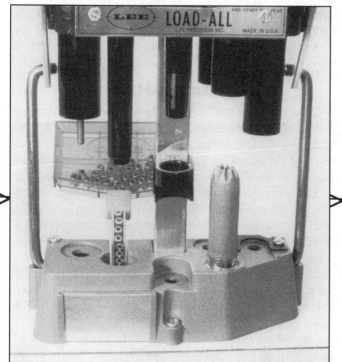

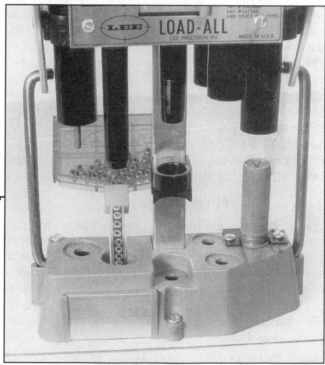

Step 6 - Crimp Start: Place the shell under the proper crimp starter, keeping an inward fold of the shell toward the front for proper alignment with the segmented starter. Pull the press handle down all the way, holding it there for about two seconds to set the plastic.

Step 7 - Final Crimp: Immediately move the shell into the shell-holder at Station 5, and pull the press handle down to complete the crimp. That completes the loading cycle, giving you a ready-to-shoot shotshell.

(Text continued from page 135

LEAD VERSUS STEEL PELLET WEIGHT			
—Lead Pellet—		—Steel Pellet—	
Size	Wgt. Grs.	Size	Wgt. Grs.
BBB	10.4	F(TTT)	11.0
BB	8.8	TT	9.6
BB	8.8	T	8.3
B	7.3	BBB	7.1
1	6.1	BB	6.1
2	5.0	B	5.0
3	4.1	1	4.3
4	3.2	2	3.5
5	2.6	3	2.9
5	2.6	4	2.3
6	1.9	5	1.8
7½	1.3	6	1.4

STEEL VERSUS LEAD PELLET COUNT			
—Steel Pellet—		—Lead Pellet—	
Size	No. Per oz.	Size	No. Per oz.
F(TTT)	39	T	34
TT	46	BBB	42
T	52	BB	50
BBB	62	B	60
BB	72	1	72
B	87	2	87
1	103	3	106
2	125	4	135
3	154	5	170
4	192	6	225
5	243	6	225
6	317	7	299

Final Crimp

The shell is now placed on the final crimp station and the handle pulled down until it bottoms. Hold the handle in this position for a second to give the crimp a firm set, then raise the handle. If the crimp is not firmly closed, this step may be repeated. Crimp depth should duplicate the original factory load. This die is adjustable and may need some tinkering to get it to accommodate the make of case you are using.

Overall length of the finished shell is critical to feeding through magazines so die adjustment must be kept to a minimum. If the problem is the center of the shell being too high or too low, you can experiment with changing the wad for a longer or shorter one or adding or subtracting shot. Adding shot should be done with caution and not done with a maximum load. A 20-gauge card wad can be added to the bottom of the 12-gauge cup to act as a filler if needed. This should be done before the wad is seated. A supply of 1/8-inch and 1/16-inch card wads is a handy item to stock.

Most shotshell loading machines have a feature to put a slight taper on the case mouth to facilitate feeding in repeating guns. Some of the more expensive loaders such as the Hornady 366 Auto and Apex machines have a third crimping feature. This rounds the front of the shell and locks in the crimp with a slightly raised ring around the edge of the crimped end. This ensures the crimp will not open through jarring as it is fed through an autoloading action.

Final Inspection

Since shotshells are made of plastic or paper and are softer than brass cartridges, it is always good practice to do a final size check before boxing them. Any case with a poor crimp that cannot be repaired in the approved manner should be junked. The same goes for one that has cracked or split in the reloading process. MEC's ring gauge is a handy item for a quick size check with a "go/no go" hole for each standard size shell.

Ammunition Testing

Because shotguns deliver a pattern of shot that is determined primarily by the choke of the barrel, testing mainly depends on duplicating factory performance. Light loads will obviously put fewer shot in the standard 30-inch circle at 40 yards than heavier loads. To check the patterning of your gun, you need a 40-yard range and a large piece of paper at least one square yard in size. Shoot one shot at the center of the target. Draw a 30-inch circle around the densest area and count the holes. Various loading manuals will give you the number of shot per ounce, so you can figure the percentage or you can make an actual count. Beyond this there are some other observations you can make. One is to see where the greatest area of density lies. It should be in the center of your point of aim and not biased to the side. The shot pattern should be more or less even within the circle. Some guns have a tendency to produce a very dense center with an uneven disbursal of hits at the edge of the circle. This may mean missed clays or crippled game. To check the efficacy of your pattern; cut a clay target-size circle (4 5/16-inch) out of a piece of clear plastic and move it around the pattern. Areas with fewer than three pellets in them are in the doubtful zone in terms of an assured kill on most birds.

Good and Bad Loads

Good loads are the ones that do what you want them to do and often the bad load is one that does not. This may be because it is inappropriate to the situation—too small shot, too light a load, not enough pattern density. These problems are rooted mainly in the lack of knowledge of the shooter and in taking shots that he should not attempt and then blaming the gun or the ammunition. There are, however, a few false notions and a similar number of hard truths that should be addressed.

Larger-bore guns kick more than smaller ones with the same loading. Not true. The recoil is mostly determined by the weight of the shot charge and its velocity. The difference in felt recoil will be affected by the weight of the gun, and a heavy gun will absorb more recoil than a light one.

Larger-bore guns hit harder. Not true. The velocity of all shotgun loads is nearly the same-in the 1200-1500 fps range. A #6 pellet from a .410 is flying as fast and hitting as hard as one moving at the same velocity from a 10-gauge, even though the .410 makes less noise.

The same shot charge from a 20-gauge and a 12-gauge

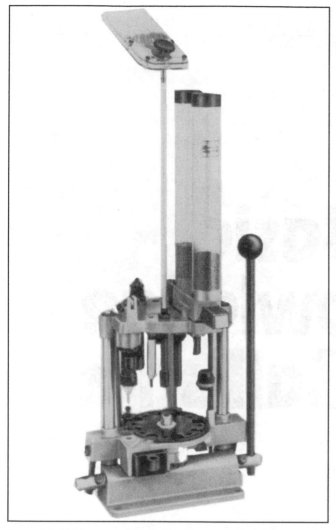

Homady's 366 Auto machine is for shotgunners who do a lot of shooting. It has a high production rate and is built of high-quality materials.

The MEC 600 Jr. Mark V can turn out an average of 200 rounds per hour. It's available in 10, 12, 16, 20 and 28 gauges.

are equally effective. This tends not to be the case. Longer shot columns tend to result in greater compression (distortion of the pellets at the back of the load) and thus produce more fliers, and consequently a less dense pattern. This probably is what led to the notion of larger-bore guns "hitting harder."

Harder shot hits harder. Not really, but hard and extra-hard shot deliver more pellets to the central pattern with fewer fliers. Heavy loads, particularly in the .410 and 3-inch 20-gauge shells, and the 3 1/2-inch 12-gauge Magnum, with their longer shot column, are most effective with hard shot.

Certain powders do not perform well at sub-freezing temperatures. This seems to be true, according to the folks at Ballistic Products. They ran tests on powder performance and concluded that Blue Dot gave significantly lower velocities at low temperatures, much more so than other powders. However, all velocities will be lower in cold conditions when the air is denser.

High-velocity shotshell loads have some fans who believe that by pumping the velocity up to 1500 fps there is some-

thing to be gained by getting the shot to the target faster. More pressure and more recoil top the list unless the shot charge is reduced. At the velocity top end, patterns get pretty ragged. Around 1400 fps, however, patterns hold well and at ranges of 25 to 30 yards are quite lethal. Unfortunately, this added lethality is at the price of ruining game meat. This is a plus in the varmint-shooting area, not so good for pot hunting. Do these loads really "reach out there and get 'em?" Not really, since pellets are very poor performers in the aerodynamic sense. The initial gain in velocity is soon shed, and at 45-plus yards this hot-rod load is not going to perform much differently than the standard factory loading. If the velocity is achieved at a reduction in the amount of shot, the situation is a little worse because of a lower-density pattern.

The main advantage of such hot loadings would appear to be in trap and Skeet shooting, where the targets are at relatively close range. Hard hitting assures more breakage and higher velocities cut lead calculation in these games of hitting them fast and hard.

A Basic Knowledge of Ballistics

Reloading involves a number of processes before the trigger is tripped, but once the powder starts burning, it's all about ballistics.

"SEND THAT GUN down to ballistics," is a throwaway line from dozens of forgettable TV cop shows. This notion of ballistics being what police crime labs do, is ingrained in the minds of an astonishing number of people.

James Hamby, as head of the Indianapolis crime lab, told of a court appearance that illustrates this point quite well. After a lengthy introduction, with explanations of his firearms examiner position, the old judge looked hard at Hamby and said. "Yeah, but what about ballistics?" It took Hamby a while to explain that "ballistics" was only a small part of the criminal investigation process, and that as an examiner he matches crime and test bullets and shell casings with particular guns, which is called "firearms examination" and has *nothing* to do with ballistics.

Calvin Goddard, the father of the field of firearms examination, later admitted that he rued the day he came up with the term "forensic ballistics." This was a hastily conceived name for the emerging science of "firearms examination" which, unfortunately, stuck in the public mind. As of this day, there is only one police organization in the country that still refers to its firearms section as "The Ballistics Lab"—the NYPD.

Ballistics, real ballistics, is the scientific investigation of the behavior of projectiles in flight. The name is derived from an ancient Roman siege machine called a *ballista*, a kind of king-size crossbow that launched spears, rocks and whatnot. The field of ballistics, in the modern sense, deals primarily with projectiles fired from guns, and is further divided into three subsections: interior ballistics, exterior ballistics and terminal ballistics. Ballistics spreads over a number of scientific fields, encompassing physics (including Newton's laws of motion), mechanics, dynamic forces, aerodynamics and the forces of air. It links up with chemistry, mathematics (including calculus), meteorology, metallurgy and medicine.

Interior Ballistics

Interior ballistics deals with everything that happens from the beginning of the firing sequence to the point where the projectile exits the barrel of the gun. The first serious use of guns was at the Battle of Crecy, in 1346, in which the English forces employed small cannons against the French. This event initiated the consideration of problems of interior ballistics—questions of pressure and velocity and pressure and gun failure—discussed in Chapter 3. It led to the investigation of propellants and ignition systems and considerations of gun barrel material and manufacture, which eventually led to the creation of the field of metallurgy. The basic questions were: how much pressure can be generated in a gun barrel and have it hold together, and how fast will a projectile be ejected? Rodman in the U.S. and Nobel in Great Britain developed the first reliable systems of pressure measurement.

Beyond the problem of establishing safe means of measuring internal pressures are considerations of increasing velocity without increasing pressure proportionally. There is the assessment of the best materials for making these projectiles, their shape, weight, strength and design, to see that they do not come apart in flight and either expand or penetrate or do some desired combination of both on reaching the target. There is the matter of material for gun barrels, the problems of barrel strength and wear. Suddenly the field of economics raises its dismal head as cost is pitted against longevity and efficiency.

Since a gun is an internal combustion, pressure-driven engine, it depends on gases from burning gunpowder to overcome the inertia of the projectile. Considerable pressure builds up (up to 6000 psi in some instances) before the inertial force of the weight of the projectile is overcome and it starts to move. The action of swaging the projectile into the rifling causes pressure to increase to the point where the peak pressure is reached. Once the swaged projectile is in motion, pressure begins to drop as the speed of the projectile picks up and the space behind it increases in volume. When the projectile is out of the barrel, pressure drops rapidly to that of the surrounding atmosphere.

Propellant materials are a major concern under the rubric of interior ballistics. These include priming materials that will burn in such a way as to provide the best possible ignition, propellants that will produce a pressure curve best suited to a particular length of barrel, and both to be of material that will work reliably under a variety of temperature conditions and not change their burning characteristics over time.

These questions and concerns have occupied ballisticians for the past 600-plus years and not all the problems have been solved yet. The 20th century probably saw the end of the evolution of guns (firearms) as we know them, and the 21st may see the practical development of electromagnetic "rail guns" capable of launching projectiles at half-again to twice, to who knows how much, greater velocity than that achieved with conventional firearms. When this comes to pass, it will probably end investigations in interior ballistics, since with rail guns, there is no interior—the projectile is launched by electromagnetic propulsive forces generated by twin rods between which the bullet travels (starting from a flat "launch pad") through the air.

Exterior Ballistics

Exterior ballistics is concerned with hitting the target with accuracy, which means achieving consistency of bullet behavior. It encompasses the study of everything that affects a bullet's flight from the moment it exits the barrel until it reaches the target. The line between interior ballistics and exterior ballistics is blurred since, from the start, the bullet is pushing air within the gun barrel, and for a short distance the muzzle blast continues the acceleration process, often causing the bullet to yaw a bit in flight until rotation stabilizes it. Things happening within the gun barrel have a great deal to do with how a projectile will behave once it has exited that barrel.

Ballistics as a science had its beginning with the publication of Nicholas Tartaglia's treatise on the flight of projectiles, published in 1537. Tartaglia was the first to calculate trajectories and to theorize that maximum range was achieved at an exit angle of 45 degrees. He was wrong in this, but correct in assuming that all trajectories were curved.

The velocity of a projectile was first measured in 1741 by Benjamin Robins, inventor of the ballistic pendulum. He fired projectiles of known weight into the weight of a pendulum, also of known weight, and measured the distance of the swing. Robbins was the first investigator to come up with a system for reasonably accurate velocity measurement to 1700 fps. Using the same pendulum, Hutton in England was the first to note that air resistance had a considerable influence on reducing velocity, and that projectiles lost velocity in direct proportion to their speed—that the higher the initial velocity, the more rapid the decline in velocity.

By the 1840s the ballistic pendulum became obsolete with Wheatstone's proposal to measure bullet flight through time as it passed through screens breaking electrical contacts. The Le Boulenge chronograph using such a system was in use in the 1860s to the 1930s, when the first all-electronic machines using photoelectric screens were perfected.

The trajectory of a bullet is the curved path it takes from the gun muzzle to the target. The basic force affecting this curve (for small arms) is gravity. Temperature, which affects air density, is a second factor. In a vacuum, the trajectory of a bullet would be affected only by gravity, and it would thus describe a flight path that would be parabolic with the angle of descent being the same as the angle of ascent. Air resistance, however, reduces velocity and thus produces a much steeper angle of descent. As this force slows the bullet and its forward velocity declines, the force of gravity predominates and the path of the bullet becomes less horizontal and more vertical.

The ballistic coefficient is a major factor in the calculation of the trajectory of a bullet. This figure is derived from the weight, diameter and form. Form is the degree of streamlining based on an ideal shape of a needle nose tapering back to a rounded body and then to a tapered base. Bullets of this "boattail" design have a high ballistic coefficient and will fly much farther than a flat-nosed wadcutter, which is nearly a perfect cylinder.

Air temperature will have a marked effect on bullet trajectory. Hot air is less dense, because the molecules are farther apart, and will offer less resistance than cold air, wherein they are closer together. A rifle zeroed on a summer day at a temperature of 80 degrees Fahrenheit will shoot low on a winter day with a temperature of 10 degrees.

Moving air (wind) serves to accelerate or decelerate the forward motion of the bullet to a degree and will affect where it strikes. Head winds will decelerate velocity and lower the point of impact. Tail winds will accelerate velocity and raise the point of impact, all other things being equal.

Lateral bullet displacement. No one knows who discovered that spin-stabilizing projectiles made a tremendous increase in their accuracy. This permitted the development of highly efficient aerodynamic designs that would fly farther, lose velocity less quickly and retain more energy than a round ball. Arms with barrels containing helical grooves (rifling) first appeared in the late 1500s. While spin-stabilized projectiles fly far straighter than round balls, the rotation is affected by the air, and irregularities on the bullet's surface, caused primarily by the rifling, allow the bullet to work against the air causing it to roll or drift in flight in the

direction it is spinning. Lt. Col. A.R. Buffington, U.S.A., developed a sight for the Springfield rifle, in 1883, which contained an automatic compensation feature for this rotational drift.

Crosswinds will have a decided effect on the lateral displacement of a bullet. The greatest displacement is when the wind is blowing at a right angle to the bullet's flight path. Wind velocity affects drift in proportion to the speed of the wind. Bullet velocity also affects the amount of drift, with the greatest degree of drift occurring when the bullet is moving at or slightly above the speed of sound. Above and below this point, wind drift is somewhat less. A bullet traveling above the speed of sound sets up a shock wave, which indicates a loss of kinetic energy caused by drag. The degree of drag is dependent on bullet diameter, velocity, air density, and the drag coefficient, which is figured from such factors as projectile shape, air density, yaw and Mach number—the ratio of the projectile velocity to the speed of sound.

Other factors affecting lateral displacement are ricochets and deflections. Ricochets are the result of bullets striking hard ground, ice, pavement or water at a shallow angle. When this occurs the bullet nearly always loses its rotational stability and tumbles in flight. Even when striking water, which most consider an easily penetrated substance, bullets will ricochet if they strike below a critical angle of entry of 5.75 degrees. Bullets striking at angles above 2 degrees will lose their rotational stability.

Deflection might be termed a lateral ricochet. For many years there have been questions raised regarding "brush busting", the ability of a bullet to hit a small branch and keep going (more or less) straight to the target. Debate over this issue had been fueled by stories of stellar performances by particular bullets which had penetrated small branches, often cutting them off in the process, then felled a game animal some distance away. There were perhaps a greater number of stories of the opposite happening, where a bullet clipped a twig and went spinning out of control, missing a large target entirely. Some investigations into deflections found support for both claims. The critical factors were the angle of contact of the bullet and the branch, and whether the bullet was damaged by the branch. If the bullet struck the branch dead center and was undamaged, it continued on a relatively straight path. If it was damaged it lost stability. If it struck to one side of dead center it would deflect and usually lose stability and tumble. The greatest degree of deflection was at the point where *half* the bullet was in contact with the branch. The degree of deflection decreased as the point of contact moved closer to dead center or toward the edge resulting in a slight grazing of the branch.

Terminal Ballistics

Terminal ballistics involves everything that happens to a bullet from the moment it reaches the target to the point where all motion ceases. The term means different things to different people. For the target shooter, punching paper or knocking over metal silhouettes is all that matters. The

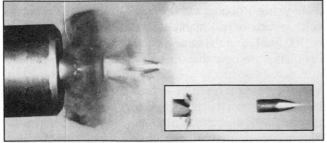

Exterior ballistics involves all that happens to the bullet from muzzle to target. Here's a Remington Accelerator leaving the muzzle at 4080 fps, and the sabot and bullet 18 inches downrange.

big game hunter is concerned with the ability of a bullet to both penetrate into a vital area, and expand, creating a large wound channel and quick incapacitation. The varmint hunter wants quick expansion on relatively thin-skinned animals to create a large wound cavity and instant death. The small game hunter needs something between these two extremes—bullets that will expand, killing quickly, but not causing the kind of disruption encountered in the varmint bullet that destroys a great deal of edible meat. For military ends, terminal ballistics includes penetration of concrete, building materials, armor plate and starting fires in fuel tanks.

Wound ballistics is a subset of terminal ballistics and is concerned with the medical aspects of gunshot wounds, including wound trauma incapacitation and treatment of gunshot wounds.

Improvements in terminal ballistics have not been as fast as those in interior and exterior ballistics, and have come about with the development of high-speed cinematography and high-speed radiography. Development of ballistic gelatin as a tissue substitute has been a particular aid to improved terminal ballistics. In the last several years considerable advancements have been made in developing bullets that will produce controlled expansion. This allows them to penetrate while expanding at a rate that will not result in breakup or in over-expansion and inadequate penetration.

A great deal has been written regarding the role of velocity, that is to say high velocity, in the area of terminal and wound ballistics. According to Dr. Martin Fackler, the leading wound ballistics expert in the country, bullet lethality is an easily understood concept. Lethality is determined by answering two questions: How big is the hole it produces? How deep is this hole? Bigger and deeper holes are more likely to intersect with vital organs, cause greater loss of blood, and result in death.

What about high velocity? In the 1960s, reports of horrendous wounds created by the M-16 rifle and, to a lesser degree, the AK-47 rifle used in Vietnam began pouring in. The wounding effects, while genuine, were presented by an ignorant press as being wholly an artifact of high velocity. As often happens, misinformation and half-truths become pillars of public opinion as they receive amplification by politicians and other public figures through the media, without scrutiny from the researcher. In the case of the velocity/lethality controversy, there is some truth to the wounding effects of hydrostatic or hydraulic shock of a high velocity bullet when it contacts an area of a body such as the liver or cranial vault. Liver tissue has poor elasticity and brain tissue behaves like a semi-fluid in a sealed container. Anyone who has seen the effect of a 3000 fps bullet on a closed container of water has a good idea of the pressure-wave effect it produces. But, this does not apply to other types of tissue with a higher degree of elasticity. While a large, instantaneous cavity is created, the resultant tissue damage of a permanent sort is minimal, not extending far beyond the path of the bullet.

In the case of extreme hyper-velocity impacts—3500-4000+ fps—both the bullet and target behave in the manner of fluids regardless of the material they are made of. This allows a 48-grain copper-jacketed bullet with an exposed lead point to knock a hole through a half-inch of steel armor plate. At less than these velocities, the softer bullet would simply splatter on the surface of the harder material.

Bullet design had more to do with terminal/wound ballistics than other factors. For the first 400 years of their existence, bullets were made of lead. The creation of the jacketed bullet in the late 19th century came as a result of the development of smokeless powder and the quest for flat trajectories, meaning higher velocities. While flatter shooting was achieved, the lethality of the small, round-nose bullets was far less than with large, soft, lead bullets of the 45-70 class. In their efforts to achieve still flatter trajectories, the Germans found that their spitzer (pointed) bullet, in addition to possessing less drag than the round-nose bullet, created a more severe wound. This design, with its long tapering point, had a heavy end and a light end and when the bullet lost stability by striking a body, the heavy rear would flip over the front causing the bullet to make a larger hole—often exiting base first as it tumbled. Soon, nearly everyone was using the spitzer bullet. The flip-over was improved by the British who filled the pointed end with aluminum and the rear with lead. Later, the Russians simply left an air cavity in the front.

The Vietnam era saw the latest improvement in the spitzer bullet that gave it much the same effect as an expanding type. By the simple expedient of increasing velocity, as in the case of the 7.62x39mm AK-47 bullet and the 223 (5.56x45mm) M-16 bullet, greater instability on impact was achieved. The 55-grain M-16 bullet, with a muzzle velocity of over 3000 fps, would often break in half at the cannelure in the middle and the two halves would shred in the body, creating a more massive wound. Even more deadly was the 7.62x51mm (308) NATO bullet made by the West German government that featured a very thin steel jacket. It was 50 percent thinner than the U.S. version and would shred in a body, causing an even more massive wound by virtue of its greater size and weight. Velocity was critical to achieving these effects, but did not cause them. Once velocity dropped below 2500 fps, lethality decreased to handgun level with equivalent-caliber jacketed bullets.

Designs for hunting bullets did not have to work under the constraints placed on nations by The Hague and Geneva conventions, which attempted to create "rules" of warfare. Hunting bullets are intended for killing, as opposed to creating casualties in war, thus they can be made of a more lethal design; i.e. to expand in a controlled manner at predetermined velocities.

Have we gone about as far as we can go along this line of development? In terms of bullet design, we probably have. In terms of making firearms capable of handling more powerful ammunition, making this ammunition more reliable and accurate, and making both more compact, there are still some worlds to be conquered.

No single book
can supply all
of the available
knowledge on
the subject of
reloading, so here's
where you can find
whatever you want
or need to know.

Sources and Resources

THE MOST DIRECT route to current information on reloading tools, accessories, supplies and reloading data is ask the manufacturers themselves, who are more than eager to provide any information you want. The major manufacturers in the reloading industry supply the bulk of tools, accessories and components, although there are many, many more companies, mail-order houses and retailers who offer their own catalogs, data books and the like. For openers, the following list of major suppliers will get you off to a fast start:

ACCURATE POWDER
Western Powders, Inc.
PO Box 158-Top of Yellowstone Hill
Miles City, MT 59301
(406) 234-0422
www.accuratepowder.com

ALLIANT POWDER
P.O. Box 6 Rt. 114
Radford, VA 24143-0096
(540) 639-8503
www.alliantpowder.com

BARNES BULLETS, INC.
P.O. Box 215
American Fork, UT 84003
(800) 574-9200
www.barnesbullets.com

CCI SPEER
P.O. Box 856
Lewiston, ID 83501
(866) 286-7436
www.cci-ammunition.com
www.speer-bullets.com

CLYMER MFG. CO.
1645 West Hamlin Road
Rochester Hills, MI 48309-3312
(248) 853-5555
www.clymertool.com
Guns tools, including reamers and headspace gauges

DILLON PRECISION PRODUCTS, INC.
8009 E. Dillon's Way
Scottsdale, AZ 85260
(602) 948-8009
www.dillonprecision.com
Reloading Equipment, Accessories and Components

FEDERAL CARTRIDGE COMPANY
900 Ehlen Drive
Anoka, MN 55303-7503
(800) 322-2342
www.federalpremium.com

HODGDON POWDER COMPANY, INC.
6231 Robinson
Shawnee Mission, KS 66202
(913) 362-9455
www.hodgdon.com

HORNADY MANUFACTURING
P.O. Box 1848
Grand Island, NE 68802
(308) 382-1390
www.hornady.com
Rifle & Handgun Bullets, Reloading Tools & Accessories

IMR POWDER COMPANY
(Now a part of Hodgdon Powder Co.
Contact Hodgdon for Information)

KALTRON-PETTIBONE
1241 Ellis Street
Bensenville, IL 60106
(630) 350 1116
www.kaltron.com
Importer of Vihtavuori Smokeless Powders and Lapua
ammunition and components

LEE PRECISION INC.
4275 Highway U
Hartford, WI 53027
(262) 673-3075
www.leeprecision.com
Reloading tools and accessories

LYMAN PRODUCTS CORPORATION
475 Smith Street
Middletown, CT 06457
(800) 225-9626
www.lymanproducts.com
Case Cleaning and Preparation Systems, Reloading Tools,
Bullet Casting, Black Powder Products

MEC (MAYVILLE ENGINEERING CO.)
715 South Street
Mayville, WI 53050
(920) 387-4500
www.mecreloaders.com
Reloading Tools and Accessories

MidwayUSA
5875 W. Van Horn Tavern Rd.
Columbia, MO 65203
(800) 243-3220
www.midwayusa.com
Major manufacturer, mail order and online provider of
shooting and reloading products.

MTM MOLDED PRODUCTS
3370 Obco Court
Dayton, OH 45414
(937) 890-7461
www.mtmcase-gard.com
(937) 890-1747 fax
Ammo cases & reloading supplies

NOSLER, INC.
P.O. Box 671
Bend, OR 97709
(800) 285-3701
www.nosler.com
Rifle, Handgun and Muzzleloading Bullets

PACIFIC TOOL & GAUGE
598 Avenue C
PO Box 2549
White City, OR 97503
(541) 826-5808
www.pacifictoolandgauge.com

PRECISION RELOADING, INC.
124 South Main Street
Mitchell, SD
(800) 223-0900
Technical Support & Customer Service
(860) 684-5680
e-mail address: info@precisionreloading.com
Shotgun, Rifle & Pistol Reloading Equipment, Components &
Supplies, Lead, Bismuth & Steel Shot Reloading Components
www.precisionreloading.com

RCBS
605 Oro Dam Blvd.
Oroville, CA 95965
(800) 533-5000
www.rcbs.com
Reloading Tools and Accessories

RAMSHOT POWDERS
Western Powders, Inc.
PO Box 158-Top of Yellowstone Hill
Miles City, MT 59301
(406) 234-0422
www.ramshot.com

REDDING RELOADING EQUIPMENT
1089 Starr Road
Cortland, NY 13045
(607) 753-3331
www.redding-reloading.com
Reloading tools, dies and accessories

REMINGTON ARMS CO., INC.
870 Remington Drive
Madison, NC 27025-0700
(800) 243-9700
Reloading Components

SIERRA BULLETS
1400 West Henry St.
Sedalia, MO 65301
(800) 223-8799 for Technical Information
(888) 223-3006
www.sierrabullets.com

STARLINE, INC.
1300 West Henry Street
Sedalia, MO 65301
(800) 280-6660
www.starlinebrass.com

SWIFT BULLET COMPANY
1001 Swift Ave. P.O. Box 27
Quinter, KS 67752
(785) 754-3959
www.swiftbullets.com

WINCHESTER SMOKELESS PROPELLANT
Hodgdon Powder Co.
6231 Robinson
Shawnee Mission KS 66202
913-362-9455
www.wwpowder.com
Ammunition and Components

KRAUSE PUBLICATIONS
700 E. State Street
Iola, WI 54990-0001
(715) 445-2214
www.krause.com
Special publications for the shooter and reloader including
Handloader's Digest, which includes a very complete
"Handloader's Library."

Handloader Magazine
2625 Stearman Road-Suite A
Prescott, AZ 86301
(800) 899-7810
www.riflemagazine.com
Wolfe Publishing A Prescott, Arizona 8630
Call Us Toll-Free 1.800.899.7810Company 2625

National Shooting Sports Foundation
Flintlock Ridge Office Center
11 Mile Hill Road
Newtown, CT 06470-2359
(203) 426-1320
www.nssf.org

SAAMI
Sporting Arms and Ammunition Manufacturers' Institute
Flintlock Ridge Office Center
11 Mile Hill Road,
Newtown, CT 06470-2359
www.saami.org

The Internet

As in all walks of life, you can find more reloading information on the Internet than you could possibly use or absorb in several lifetimes. If you search for "reloading" on Google, they serve up more than 14 million websites relating to reloading. Yahoo will give you 19 million and Lycos 1.4 million. This is fine if you have really a lot of time, but narrowing your search will yield more manageable results.

Reference Books

C.Rodney James, the editor of the 6th Edition of The ABCs of Reloading, has researched reference material for more than 40 years and offered what he considered to be the best:

"The bibliography and source references that follow are a gleaning of some 40 years of study and experience. It is both spotty and idiosyncratic, but contains those books and sources found to be worth the money and\or effort.," James noted.

Ballistics

The Bullet's Flight From Powder to Target, by Dr. Franklin W. Mann, MD. Originally published in 1909, various reprints. This is the first real book on ballistics. Even today, some 95 years after it was first published, this book contains useful information regarding bullet behavior under an astonishing number of conditions. Mann was more of a tinkerer than a scientist, but was one of those dedicated souls who set out in pursuit of that eternal quest of getting all the bullets in one hole. His experiments were often predicated on the notion of: "I wonder what would happen if...?" The good doctor had enough money to buy a lot of rifles and replacement barrels. His work with cast, lead-alloy bullets is probably second to none. His book probably raises as many questions as it answers. The second volume might have provided these answers had the manuscript not been destroyed.

Understanding Ballistics 2nd Ed, by Robert A. Rinker, Mulberry House, P.O. Box 575, Corydon, IN 47112, 1996. 373 pp. Paper covers. $19.95.

In spite of the occasional sentence that isn't a sentence, this book does an excellent job of explaining the scientific aspects of ballistics. It goes from the basic to the advanced level while keeping the math to a minimum and the explanations clear. A good glossary of ballistic terms is included.

Bullet Penetration, by Duncan McPherson, Ballistic Publications, Box 772, El Segundo, CA, 90245, 1994. 303 pp. $39.95.

This book deals exclusively with terminal ballistics with handgun ammunition. Anyone interested in stopping power, shocking power and all that, should forget anything you ever read on the subject except perhaps Julian Hatcher. McPherson, an engineer and one of the charter members of the International Wound Ballistics Association, has analyzed and scrutinized everyone's work in this area before conduct-

ing his very thorough research. The result has cleared away a number of cherished myths regarding bullet performance and the measurement of same. Though technical in nature, this work is very accessible to those without a mathematics background.

Wound Ballistics Review, edited by Dr. Martin L. Fackler, MD. Published twice a year by the International Wound Ballistics Association, P.O. Box 701 El Segundo, CA 90245-701. Four issues $40.00.

The IWBA is devoted to the medical and technical study of wound ballistics, including evaluation of literature in the field as well as encouraging and promoting new work. IWBA is an organization of medical, technical and law enforcement professionals devoted to hard research, truth telling and correction of misinformation regarding firearms, bullets, and their effects. Not surprisingly, they are engaged in battles with several popular gun magazines, the AMA, The Journal of Trauma, the federal medical establishment, and several self-styled stopping power "experts." Quite readable, very informative, not for wimps.

General Reloading

Complete Guide to Handloading, by Philip B. Sharpe. Originally published by Funk & Wagnalls.

Last updated in 1953, this massive work is dated, but contains a wealth of historical data on powder and cartridge evolution as well as the evolution of handloading. Anybody interested in the hows and whys of ammunition development will find this a treasure. Sharpe's book contains data on experiments of all sorts, many of which have a habit of turning up in contemporary magazine articles as "new" ideas and possibilities. Sharpe was a good experimenter and stands as one of the best known early experts in the field.

Principles and Practice of Loading Ammunition, by Earl Naramore, Small Arms Technical Publishing Company (Samworth), Georgetown, SC, 1954. 952 pp. One reprint by Stackpole Books.

This last of the Samworth books is now out of print, but hopefully someone will reprint it again. Naramore gets into the "science" of reloading, but does so in layman's terms, which makes this book very readable. His emphasis is on what happens to powder, primers, bullets, barrels and actions when guns are fired. His examination of all the forces at work and what they do is expressed in terms of how to deal with them in the reloading process. This is probably the best book when it comes to answering those "Why" and "What If" questions. Naramore and Mann were nearly the only author-experimenters who examined fired bullets, collected in pristine condition, and observed and deduced a good bit of information therefrom. Few writers expend this kind of time and effort on their work these days.

Handbook for Shooters and Reloaders, by P.O. Ackley, Salt Lake City, UT, 1970, (Vol. 1), 567 pp., illus. (Vol. II), a new printing with specific new material. 495 pp., illus. $17.95 each.

Ackley was one of the greats in the experimentation and development field of small arms and ammunition. A gunmaker and shooter who was also a good writer, Ackley put the better part of a lifetime of experience into these two books, which contain articles answering all sorts of questions regarding gun failures, pressure, headspace, wildcat cartridges, killing power, reduced loads, calculating recoil, bullet energy, loading data, etc.

Hatcher's Notebook, by Julian S. Hatcher, 3rd ed. 2nd printing, Stackpole Books, Harrisburg, PA 1996. 640 pp. $29.95. Julian Hatcher can be considered one of the fathers of modern firearms writing and co-founder of the field of forensic firearms examination. Hatcher was a technical editor for the *American Rifleman* and held posts as a shooter, coach and military expert that would fill an entire page. This volume is a collection of many of his best articles on military rifles, their development, autoloading and automatic systems, recoil, headspace, triggers, barrel obstructions, military rifle strengths and weaknesses, range, velocity, recoil, etc. This is an excellent companion to the Ackley volumes.

Special Reloading Topics

Cast Bullets, by E.H. Harrison, NRA Publications, Washington, DC, 1982. 144 pp. Paper covers. Out of print.

Probably one of the best books on bullet casting. It covers alloys, mould care and handling, and includes a lot of problem-solving pieces of great value when it comes to getting moulds, cast bullets and various alloys to perform the way they should. Hopefully, someone will reprint this fine volume.

The Paper Jacket (formerly *The Practical Paper Patched Bullet*), by Paul Matthews, Wolfe Publishing Co., Inc. Prescott, AZ, 1991. 75 pp. Paper covers. $13.50.

If you are interested in making and shooting paper-patched bullets this is the book you need.

Loading Cartridges for the Original 45-70 Springfield Rifle and Carbine Second Ed. Revised and Expanded, by J.S. and Pat Wolf. Wolfs Western Traders, Sheridan, WY, 1996. 188 pp. Paper covers. $18.95.

This book is an absolute must if you are going to load for one of these guns. Wolf researched the Frankford Arsenal's records and shot his way through several hundred pounds of lead to discover how to make these old guns shoot. The data is very likely to be valuable in working up loads for similar deep-groove rifles from the 1870-1890 era.

The Home Guide to Cartridge Conversions, by George C. Nonte, Jr., The Gun Room Press Highland Park, NJ, 1976. 404 pp. $24.95.

Detailed instructions on how to make centerfire cartridges for foreign and obsolete rifles and handguns from commonly available cartridges. How to fabricate ammunition for those war souvenirs you never thought you could shoot--chamber casting, fireforming—the works. Not for beginners.

Book Resources

Finding gun books, especially the out-of-print titles, is a difficult job and the costs are often high. There are a few approaches to finding these. The first involves time. This method takes you to used-book stores where you ask where the gun books are. After you get a dumb look in response to this question, you explain utilizing simple words and appropriate gestures to get across what you're looking for. They will direct you to the bottom of the back room where you will paw through a load of junk and occasionally find a treasure for $1.98. The second method is to bite the bullet (a non-lead one, of course) and negotiate with the book dealers at gun shows (who know the price of everything) and pay the going rate. Now and then a bargain can be found. A third variant is the easiest way. Send your want list to Rutgers Book Center. They have about 7000 current titles and 5000 out-of-print books. They also have a publishing adjunct, The Gun Room Press, with about forty current titles.

Another source is Ray Riling Arms Books Co., which is a major source of out-of-print books in the firearms field with more than 6000 titles. They also have a publishing arm with a few titles in print at the present time.

Just how accurate
does your hunting
load have to be?

Accuracy and the Hunter

By Dave Workman

PERMIT ME TO quickly recount a trio of hunting stories, one involving a 41 Magnum Ruger Blackhawk and a moving mule deer in the Washington Cascades, another involving a 3-point whitetail buck in the Selkirk Mountains of northeast Washington and a 257 Roberts, and a third tale about a monster 4-point muley that ended up on the business end of a Marlin 30-06 in southeast Wyoming.

Presently, you will understand something about "hunting accuracy" that may reinforce your decision to start reloading your own ammunition for the field.

I will preface my remarks by stressing that today's factory ammunition is certainly far better than factory ammunition one might have bought ten or 15 years ago, and which is still sitting in the closet gathering dust! (And, perish the thought, the same ammunition somebody might consider putting in his or her gun this fall.)

Now, all of those caveats duly recorded, the handgun buck was encountered along a road near the Cascade Crest some 20 yeas ago by odd chance. I grabbed my Blackhawk with a 6 1/2-inch barrel and factory sights and just as the buck began moving out from a patch of

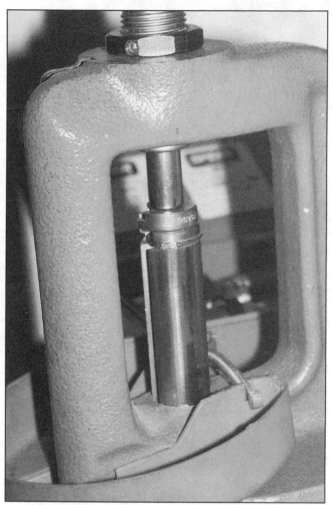

First step in producing quality handloads for your rifle is to properly re-size the brass. Author uses single-stage RCBS press to reload all of his rifle cartridges.

The case should be properly lubricated to allow it to glide into the resizing die. (Here's a tip: After initial sizing, rotate the sized case about 180 degrees and run it through the sizing die a second time.)

brush at about 35 yards downhill, I fired two shots, both handloads brewed up with Speer 200-grain hollow-point bullets ahead of 17.5 grains of 2400 (at the time manufactured by Hercules, and now available under the Alliant brand).

The bullets struck that deer about two inches apart, no small feat on a moving target in cover.

The whitetail buck was also the result of considerable luck. The deer had evidently been pushed out of its normal haunt by an early winter slash burn and quietly made its way down a ridge, suddenly appearing about 100 yards below me in the middle of an older clear-cut as it emerged from a gully. After getting over the surprise of having this buck materialize, I lifted the 257 Roberts, leveled the crosshairs right behind the shoulders and pressed the trigger. The buck took about ten steps, turned around, walked right back to the spot where it was standing when I fired, and dropped stone dead in its tracks.

The Wyoming buck made me crazy. I had fired at it in a high wind on the first morning of a hunt near Glenrock,

and missed it clean. Later that afternoon, and some distance away, I jumped the buck in a gully and as I went down for a kneeling shot in the snow, my knee landed on a concealed jagged rock and my sudden agony sent the bullet wide of the mark again! Two days later, we spotted the same animal out on a huge sagebrush flat with about 15 other deer. Through some careful maneuvering down a dry creek bed, I flanked the buck, belly-crawled about 50 yards out from the creek, took a prone rest on my backpack and put the crosshairs again right behind this buck's shoulders.

The 165-grain softpoint hit him so hard it spun him around a full 180 degrees and he dropped without taking a step. My longtime friend Rob Fancher witnessed this shot, and we paced off the distance at 200 yards across gumbo mud and snow.

So, what's the point of these recollections? Each of these animals tumbled to a carefully weighed handload. They fell "victim" shall we say, to ammunition that consisted of tumbled and polished brass, meticulously-weighed powder charges and bullets that had also been weighed on a scale to

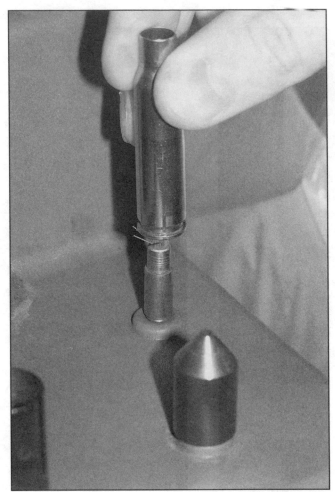

Once it is resized, the case should be given some hands-on detail. Author cleans out all of the primer pockets on his Trim Mate from RCBS.

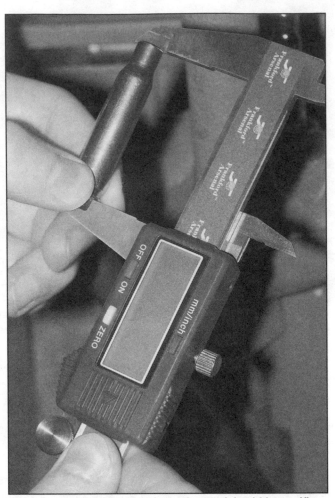

Each case should be measured to make sure it is within specifications. If not, a bit of trimming is in order. And the case mouth must be chamfered on the outside and on the inside to allow for proper bullet entry and seating.

make sure they were uniform in weight with other bullets I would use in range practice to make sure my guns all shot to point of aim.

The careful hunter who is interested in making a humane shot must first be a reasonably competent marksman. That hunter should have a well-sighted rifle or handgun, and above all, quality ammunition.

But just how precise must a hunter's shot placement be in order to assure an animal will drop without suffering, rather than limp away and never be recovered? The truth may surprise you. If you can shoot 2-inch groups at 100 yards, and don't panic when you see game, you're pretty much ready to fill the meat locker.

There was a time when it was considered "acceptable" hunting accuracy to put one's bullets into the surface of an 8-inch paper plate at 100 yards. Not anymore, and not in my book ever. Years ago, when I used to help out at my gun club on public "sight-in" days, I made a habit of asking some of the less accurate nimrods where they planned to hunt on the opener, and then I would deliberately go somewhere else. A properly-sighted rifle with good ammunition should be capable of delivering 3-shot groups within a couple of inch-

es of one another at 100 yards.

Today, thanks to modern components, new propellants and certainly the finest bullets available, a devoted handloader can develop ammunition tuned specifically to his or her gun that just might approach the kind of precision normally expected of bench-rest target shooters. That is, consistently shooting three-shot groups measuring under an inch across at 100 yards. This is commonly referred to as "minute of angle" and it refers to a rifle's ability to deliver shots on target that measure one inch across or less.

Now, should you succumb to the kind of social pressure that might be tossed your way by a pal who is a benchrest shooter, so that you demand that kind of accuracy from your hunting rifle? Nope.

Ron Reiber, product manager for Hodgdon Powder, suggested that a big game rifle needn't shoot one-hole groups time after time, and it should not be expected to. A varmint hunter who consistently is plugging away at prairie dogs or ground squirrels at ranges out to 300 or 400 yards is certainly going to want the most precise and consistent loads he can produce because even at half that range, a varmint is a very small target.

Weighing every bullet is an additional step toward producing uniform, precision loads. This Nosler AccuBond is supposed to weigh 180 grains, and sure enough, it does!

But at 200-300 yards, a buck deer or a bull elk presents a much larger target, and it is quite acceptable — and lethal — to simply be able to hit that animal somewhere in the heart-lung area to bring it down. After all, there are no degrees of dead; an animal either is or it is not, and a heart shot involves putting a bullet into a mass of tissue that easily measures several inches across.

Equally important to accuracy on a large animal, as opposed to a small one, is the energy necessary to put it on the ground. Choose a caliber capable of doing the job by delivering enough punch to stop game where it is standing.

Okay, let's get down to cases…literally. The brass case must be trimmed to the industry standard, and there is not a reloading manual I know of from any bullet maker that does not include case diagrams with dimensions. For example, I've got an old No. 10 Speer manual that shows the belted 300 Winchester Magnum case to measure 2.620 inches from the base to the mouth and I can open my current Nosler manual and find the same case measurement listed on its diagram. Not much room for discussion there.

Tumbling a case does not always polish up the primer pocket, and that's a job I do by hand. It is important that the primer pocket be clean to allow full insertion of the primer. To really make my rifle cases as consistent and certainly as clean as possible, I will finish them up by running them over my RCBS Trim Mate electric "Case Prep Center." This is one of the handiest reloading accessories I own. It is a five-station tool that allows me to chamfer the case mouth inside and out, run a brush into the case neck to remove any tumbling residue, and there is a small wire primer pocket brush that really slicks up that primer pocket.

After all the cartridge preparation is finished, it's time to complete the process by seating your bullet.

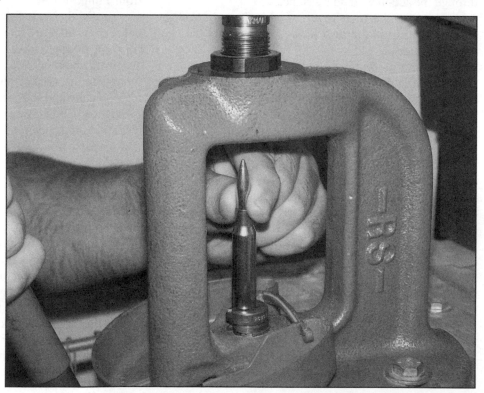

It's not enough to just reload ammunition, the proof comes at the range, well before the hunting season, when a shooter must sit down and put his work to the test.

Should you full-length resize or only partially resize? Reiber suggested at a very minimum neck-sizing even new brass, which he also de-burrs and measures to make sure it is up to spec. With once-fired brass, he will do a partial re-sizing, setting up the die so that the shell holder comes up to within about 1/8-inch from the base of the sizing die.

"Then I take the die and turn it maybe an eighth of a turn again," he detailed, "so I finally get a cartridge that runs through the action with no resistance."

He also does this to achieve a good bullet-to-bore alignment. Once all of this is achieved, he sets that die, and doesn't change it.

I full-length re-size my brass for the simple reason that I might fire it in different rifles of the same caliber, and not every rifle chamber is exactly the same. But I'm going to be as certain as is humanly possible that all of my cartridges are.

The necessity for this became obvious a couple of years ago when I purchased a new Savage rifle chambered in 308 Winchester. I have another rifle in 308 Win. and when I went to the range one afternoon, I discovered that I could not chamber some of my neck-sized cartridges. Turned out there was just enough of a difference in the chambers that the shoulders of my cases that had been fire-formed to work in the other gun, didn't chamber in my new rifle. I spent the better part of a day pulling bullets, re-sizing the brass and reloading every round. Once that was done, my fresh reloads cycled just fine, and they shot well enough on paper to satisfy me.

I don't always separate my brass by brand, though I do pay attention advisories like the one in my Hodgdon manual that cautions reloaders to reduce the listed data for the 257

Roberts by 10 percent when using +P Winchester brass. You should do likewise whenever spotting a warning like this. Other handloaders *will* separate their brass, and I will not argue with them. Whatever works for an individual is fine with me, so long as it truly does work.

One thing I will do invariably is check each cartridge case, new or fired, for length in my caliper. I have two of these tools, one a dial caliper from RCBS and the other a digital from Frankford Arsenal. Like it or not, brass will stretch ever so slightly in the firing process to the point that it will not chamber in the rifle, and may not even cycle well through the sizing or crimping dies.

A word about dies seems in order. If you are going to use more than one type of projectile, that is, one with a crimping cannelure and the other without, it is my strong recommendation to purchase a second seating die. Set one of these dies for seating and crimping your bullet with the cannelure, and set the other for seating the smooth surface bullet. I have done so for reloading the 308 Winchester, for which I will switch occasionally from a 150-grain Speer Grand Slam with a cannelure to either a 150-grain Speer boat tail or Nosler Ballistic Tip, neither of which has a cannelure. I have marked the crimping die with a blue felt tip pen so as not to confuse the two when I am reloading that particular cartridge.

Whose dies do I recommend? I can't because I use dies from at least three different manufacturers and they are all superb. What I will suggest is that if you get a second seating die for different bullets as explained above, you might consider getting a different brand than your initial set. This also helps you differentiate between the two.

Now, what about bullets? The first consideration, noted

Roger Glazier, marketing and public relations representative for Barnes Bullets, is that you use the right bullet for the job, in the right caliber. Simply put, you don't load up with thin-jacketed varmint-type bullets in .223-caliber to take on an elk, or even a deer. That's a job for a medium caliber cartridge at least, such as the .25-06 on up to even one of the .30-caliber magnums, depending upon the terrain and the particular game. You want to choose a bullet that expands properly rather than go to pieces almost immediately upon impact.

I have a personal preference for the boattail design, primarily because of its high ballistic coefficient. I'll let the Speer manual explain: Ballistic coefficient represents a projectile's ability to overcome the resistance of air in flight. In layman's terms, they fly flatter, maybe not much, but enough to perhaps make a difference at long range.

However, as noted above, I will occasionally use a non-boattail such as the Grand Slam, which also has a high ballistic coefficient and delivers good performance on game.

The best, and really the only, way to determine how well a load works is to assemble perhaps ten or a dozen rounds with a specific bullet and powder charge, and head for the range. Some guys will assemble groups of varying loads and visit the range, meticulously recording how each batch of ammunition performed in relation to the other batches. This is how they determine which load works best in their particular rifle. I did the same thing when working up loads for my 30-06.

Should you weigh each projectile? That's a personal decision. I occasionally weigh my bullets, and will select at random maybe five or ten bullets from every new box I open and pop them on my electronic scale one at a time. Occasionally I will find variations in weight of a half-grain or a bit more, but generally speaking, bullets I get from various manufacturers are pretty consistent.

Varmint shooters may want to weigh each bullet for consistency, same as they measure each powder charge sometimes down to the individual granule. When shooting at a target that may stand maybe eight or nine inches tall from a distance of several hundred yards (my personal best was a 338-yard shot a couple of years ago out on the South Dakota prairie), there is not much room for error.

What about propellants? As Bob Nosler, proprietor at Nosler Bullets observed, "Reloaders are a bunch of experimenters. They are hobbyists of the highest level. You give 'em a new toy and they love it. It's part of the whole fun of creating and engineering your own load."

Of course, Nosler is correct. Reloaders *are* experimenters, and it is because of that that we have many of the cartridges we now enjoy. I have tinkered with various powders over the years to find that "perfect load" and discovered much to my delight that with a single propellant, I can produce quality loads for my different rifles, and these loads are sufficiently accurate to put meat in my freezer. I know other guys who have actually developed whole new cartridges—they obvi-

Workman believes a chronograph is indispensable to metallic cartridge reloading, because with it, the handloader can actually measure the results of his work, and figure bullet drop and where to sight in his rifle on a target accordingly.

ously have more leisure time than I do—and the results are occasionally stunning. At other times, I must admit to wondering, "What's that cartridge do that this one doesn't?"

It's one of those "If it ain't broke, don't fix it" situations. I have settled on loads for different bullet weights using a specific powder and I have no burning desire to start messing with success. While many handloaders do like to experiment, others like me find complete satisfaction in the knowledge that a particular load for a particular rifle is going to perform as expected time after time. It does not get better than that.

On the other hand, I have found success with multiple powders for various handgun loads. For my 41 Magnum revolvers I will use 19.0 grains of H110 behind a Nosler 210-grain JHP bullet, or 17.5 grains of Alliant 2400 pushing a Speer 200-grain JHP. When I can hit a small steel plate at better than 150 yards using factory sights (no scope) with a two-hand hold, I can certainly hit something considerably larger.

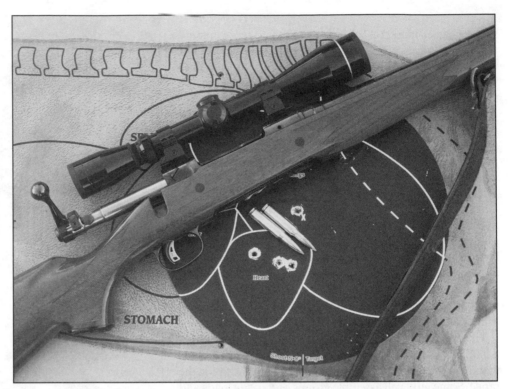

Author's Model 14 Savage in 308 Winchester produced four lethal hits on this Birchwood Casey target. The two closest were fired from a cold barrel. The one to the left was fired as barrel heated up, and the fourth, above and in the lung area, was a flyer, but still in the vital zone.

Likewise with my 357 Magnum loads, which are certainly capable of bringing down deer-sized game, will vary with the weight of the bullet I select. My favorite concoction is a 125-grain Speer JHP ahead of 17.5 grains of 2400, and it shoots accurately out of all three of my 357 Magnum revolvers. Were I going for deer, I'd go with a heavier bullet, probably a 158-grainer, and work up loads using 2400 and H110, as I trust both propellants.

This is important: Trust. If you do not particularly care for a specific propellant, *don't use it!* There are plenty of options available today, so you are not locked into one or two choices.

There are any number of reasons for handloaders to experiment with different propellants, and the most common I hear is that someone is trying to eke out an extra 50 or 100 feet per second from their loads. This is monumentally important to some people, but I am not one of them, because one may be sacrificing accuracy for speed. I have observed, on occasion, faster bullets that will not consistently zero from a particular rifle. I am confident that my rounds will strike where they are supposed to from a cold barrel.

One tool that I believe is crucial to the handloader is a good chronograph. This is a device that measures bullet speed. Why is that important? Because the velocity you get out of your gun using a specific recommended load may be different than that listed in the manual. Knowing this muzzle velocity helps you to predict a bullet's drop downrange. As a result, a person might sight his rifled in to shoot 2 to 3 inches high at 100 yards so that a 30-caliber/165-grain bullet leaving the muzzle at, say 2,700 feet per second that is dead-on at 200 yards should shoot 1.6 inches high at 100 yards. If you want to be zeroed at 300 yards, that bullet is going to

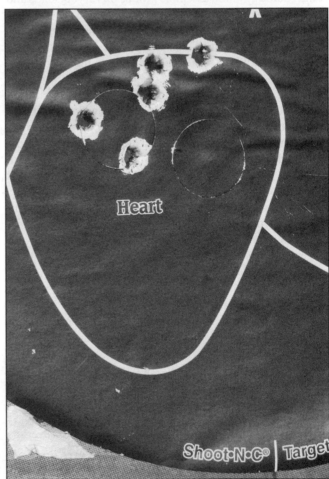

Five shots from the author's 30-06, using loads with two different 180-grain bullets. Define this target any way you want, it all comes out as a notched tag and meat in the freezer.

have to be 4 inches high at 100 yards.

My 180-grain load for the 30-06 clocking 2,685 feet per second at the muzzle shoots about 2-1/2 inches high at 100 yards from a cold barrel, putting it dead-on at about 250 yards.

And why is it important where a bullet strikes from a cold barrel? Because that's what you will be shooting through when you level the crosshairs on a live animal. With any luck, one shot is all you will need, and in order to improve the odds of that happening, a hunter who handloads his own ammunition must make the time to visit the range, as often as possible. As noted earlier, frequent shooting sessions, keeping track of your results, perhaps even keeping your targets, is a good way to record how consistently your loads perform.

It all comes together somewhere far from the loading bench, perhaps on some snowy ridge, or in a sparsely timbered canyon, or in some dense hardwood forest. This will be the ultimate test, and the only one that really counts. The cartridge will do its part if you have done yours.

If you load different bullets for the same cartridge, author suggests using two different pre-set dies and marking one so that you don't mistakenly use it to seat the wrong projectile. Here, author has his seating dies set up for (left) the 150-grain Hornady Grand Slam and (right) the 150-grain Nosler Ballistic Tip.

You might want to mark your cartridge carriers with the loading information so you will immediately know what specific load you are using.

16

Getting ready for horns on the wall, meat in the freezer.

RELOADING FOR DEER AND ANTELOPE

By Chub Eastman

WHEN THE TIME comes to start thinking about the upcoming deer and antelope season, die-hard reloaders start thinking about their magic load that will put horns on the wall and meat in the freezer. It might be a load developed from seasons past that has brought success or it might have to be a new load to replace the one they weren't quite satisfied with last season. In either case it's the vision of a big buck in the back of your mind as you start adjusting dies and prepping cases.

What makes a good load no matter what caliber or cartridge you choose is its ability to dispatch the animal quickly and cleanly with one well-placed shot. Chamber pressure must be kept at a level where it will not be a problem no matter what temperature the loads will be subject to. Bullets must be constructed to expand reliably on impact and have enough sectional density to hold together enough to penetrate to the vitals.

Bullet velocity is important to a point in the fact that it must deliver the bullet with enough impact on target to cause the bullet to perform as designed. However, velocity is not as important as accuracy. There isn't a critter that I know of that can tell the difference between a bullet launched at 2800 fps and one at 3000 fps.

Range-time is important if you are trying to get the most out of your rifle and hunting load.

After loads are developed, practice shooting positions you are likely to use in the field. The steadier the rest, the better.

A lot of handloaders, especially ones who are just starting, make the mistake of looking at a loading manual and focus on the top velocity for their cartridge. In most cases light bullets from any given manufacturer are not necessarily designed as hunting bullets to be shot at extreme velocities. An example is a 120-grain 7mm bullet loaded in a 7-08 Rem. or 7x57 might be able to perform well enough to anchor your buck with a well-placed broadside shot. How ever, that same bullet used in a 7mm Rem. Ultra Mag. or 7mm Weatherby Mag. would probably have a tendency to come apart on impact, especially if it hit bone, and not penetrate to the boiler room.

Sectional density is one of the most important considerations when making your bullet selection. It doesn't necessarily mean the heaviest bullet in a given caliber is the best choice. For deer and antelope sized game somewhere in the mid-range of bullet weights for a given cartridge would be a good choice. Most hunting bullets in this weight range are usually constructed stout enough to perform even at the hyper velocities generated by the larger magnums.

The definition of sectional density is the ratio of the bullet's weight, in pounds, to the square of its diameter in inches. To make it easy it just means the higher the number the greater sectional density a given bullet has. As a comparison a 120-grain 7mm bullet has a sectional density of .213 where as 140 - or 150-grain 7mm bullets have numbers of .248 and .266.

A good illustration of sectional density is the ping-pong ball and the rock. Both the same size but what is going to do the most damage and hurt the most; the ping-pong ball

A 140-grain Nosler Ballistic Tip loaded in a 280 Remington proved to be the perfect combination for this Texas whitetail.

The 243 Win. loaded with the 100-grain Nosler Partition is a great combination for lady shooters because of its mild recoil. Karen Lutto showed her shooting ability with her first Wyoming Antelope.

at 60 mph or the rock at 40 mph? It's obvious which will be the winner. The weight of the rock will cause more damage deeper than the ping-pong ball, which expends most of its energy on the surface and doesn't have the weight to penetrate as far as the rock does.

Today we are blessed with a selection of bullets unheard of decades ago. However, for deer or antelope-size critters the premium bullets—like the Nosler Partition, Swift A-Frame, Barnes Triple Shock or any of the bonded bullets—are not necessarily needed. Any of the hunting bullets offered by the numerous manufacturers will do the job just fine if placement is where it should be. One thing to remember is that deer and antelope are thin-skinned and only 14" to 18 inches" through the chest. A super premium bullet designed for deep penetration is really not needed. The Remington Core-Lokt, Winchester Silver Tip and bullets of this type have worked well for years on thin-skinned game.

The exception to this would be if a 224, 6mm or 25-caliber cartridge is used. Here a well-constructed premium type bullet with the highest sectional density for the caliber would probably be the best choice. Most of today's cartridges with this bore size such as the 243 Win., 257 Weatherby, 6mm Remington or 25-06 generate high velocities with a bullet that has a small frontal area and a fairly low sectional density. Consequently a Partition or bonded-type bullet is needed to ensure it stays together to give adequate penetration.

Sizing the cases has always been a controversy whether to neck-size or full-length-size. Neck-sizing cases that come from the same rifle the reloaded ammunition is to be shot in does have some advantages over full-length-sized cases. With neck-sizing the body of the case fits snugly with the shoulder of the case ensuring near perfect headspace and alignment of the cartridge in the chamber. With neck-sizing the perceived advantage is a slight edge in accuracy and extended case life. The disadvantage is the tolerances between the case and chamber are near zero. If a slight bit of grit or dirt is introduced in the chamber there is a very real chance the cartridge will not chamber or, worse, cause a problem with extraction. For normal target range work or competition shooting neck-sizing works fine and cases usually last longer as long as the loads have a reasonable chamber pressure.

However, for hunting ammunition full-length sizing is highly recommended. With full-length sized cases the outside dimensions of the case are brought to factory specifications, which are slightly smaller than the factory specifications for the chamber. Hunting rifles are subject to all kinds of environmental challenges so the chances of some obstruction getting into the action and chamber are real.

The next safeguard to ensure no problems occur is to cycle each round that is going afield with you through the action. Load the magazine as you would in the field, then cycle each round. If you don't, Murphy's Law has a tendency to jump up and bite you at a most inopportune time. It can be very frustrating if a follow-up round fails to chamber as the buck you have been chasing all day goes over the hill.

There has always been lots of discussion with hunters—

One shot from a 308 Win. using a 165-grain Swift Scirocco anchored a nice Wyoming mule deer at 225 yards at last light the last day of the season.

both experienced and neophyte—as to what the perfect shot and bullet performance should be. Some are convinced the perfect shot is where the bullet expands on impact, penetrates through the heart/lung area and stops against the hide on the far side after expending all its energy inside the animal.

The other theory is where the bullet starts expansion on impact, continues its expansion as it passes through the heart/lung area and falls to the ground after passing through the far side. The perceived advantage of this theory is now you have two holes to leave the blood trail instead of one.

Both theories will usually put meat on the table but quite a few experienced hunters lean towards the two-hole theory. If you have ever had to follow up a wounded critter you know how hard it is to follow a blood trail over uneven terrain with lots of twigs, leaves and brush on the ground. Obviously the bigger the blood trail the easier it is to follow.

It should also be understood that all animals react differently when hit. They are not much different than people as each is an individual, so a hit in the exact same spot on two different animals could result in two entirely different reactions.

Awhile back I had a conversation with a Pennsylvania deer hunter at one of the national trade shows. He was ready to retire his 700 Remington chambered for the 308 Winchester in favor of a larger caliber with more horsepower to make

sure his buck hit the ground when shot. He explained that over the past seasons he had collected his buck with a clean shot behind the shoulder and in each instance the buck dropped in his tracks. However, last season the buck ran 50 to 75 yards before he piled up. He said the range to the deer was anywhere from 60 to 125 yards. In the area he hunted a shot of 150 yards was a long shot. I tried to explain that his old 700 Remington in 308 Win. with the 150-grain bullets he had carefully handloaded for his annual deer hunt were probably as good a combination as there was for the area he hunted and the deer he was after.

I asked was the deer relaxed and at ease or was he alert and on guard with his adrenalin up? These things, besides the individuality of each animal, cause each to react in different ways. If you want to ensure the deer drops in his tracks, major bones must be hit. A shot through the spine or through both shoulders will put it on the ground before the echo of the shot has faded.

After much conversation, a cup of coffee, and a few nods of his head I think he understood what had happened and why the buck he had made the perfect shot on had gone a short distance before expiring. As he was leaving the conversation he quietly said the money he has set aside for a new rifle and set of reloading dies might better be used to replace his hunting tent that had developed a few leaks after 15 years of hard use.

Caribou can be taken reliably with the same loads developed for your deer and antelope hunt. They are roughly the same size as a big mule deer and thin-skinned.

Developing the ideal load for your rifle takes some time and effort if you want the maximum combination of performance and accuracy. Sometimes you can hit the right load the first try but usually it takes a few trips to the range to achieve what you want. As stated before, velocity is not as important as accuracy. A lot of shooters look at a reloading book and pick a given powder that develops the highest velocity, yet will not shoot to the accuracy capabilities of their rifle. With the choice of a different powder or reducing the powder charge you might find your rifle's capabilities beyond what you expected.

From experience you will find that each rifle shoots a little differently from each other even from the same manufacturer and caliber. That's why you should take your time in developing a specific hunting load for your rifle. The other benefit of range time in developing the major load is that you are practicing your shooting and becoming even more familiar with your rifle.

Practice is essential if you are going to be proficient in the field. Once you have settled on the hunting load, take a few extra trips to the range to practice. Not from the bench but from shooting positions that will probably be needed in the field such as kneeling, prone, sitting or just resting against a tree or post. I have never seen a benchrest in the deer woods, so practice field-expedient positions and shoot at different ranges to help understand the ballistics of your rifle.

Practicing at different ranges does help you understand your range limitations. Best way to determine your maximum effective range is to use a five-gallon bucket (roughly the size of the chest area of most big-game animals) and set it out at a given range. Two hundred yards is a good place to start. Keep moving it back at 30 to 50-yard increments until you can't hit it five rounds in a row. Move it back to

the last place you could hit it with all five shots and that's your effective range. Do this in one of your most steady field positions, not off the bench. Responsible big-game hunters want to adhere to the one shot – one kill mindset. Everyone's maximum effective range is a little different so don't think you have to keep up with your buddy.

Knowing and understanding the capabilities and limitations of you and your equipment can't help but make your next deer or antelope hunt a memorable one. All you will need is a little luck to go along with it to put the antlers on the wall and meat in the freezer.

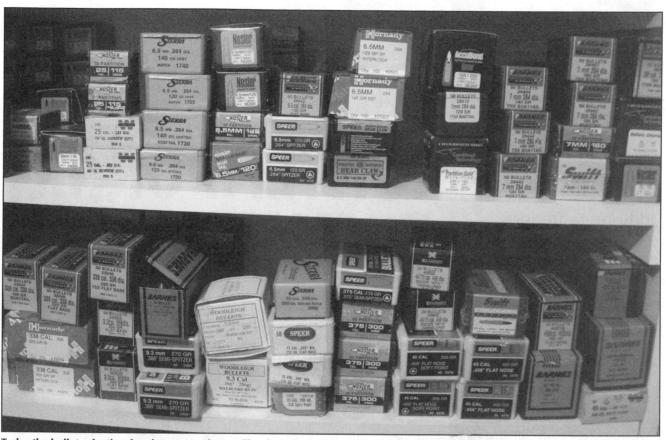

Today the bullet selection for almost any given caliber is endless. The trick is to find the one that works best for your rifle.

Murphy's Law has a tendency to raise its head at the wrong time. Make sure to cycle every round through your rifle to detect any feeding and chambering problems before your hunt.

Some new &
different offerings
in 22-caliber
varmint bullets from
Barnes and Berger.

CONTEMPORARY & UNIQUE VARMINT MEDICINE

By Mike Thomas

THERE IS CERTAINLY nothing wrong with the 22 varmint bullets produced by long-time big makers such as Hornady, Nosler, Sierra and Speer. Combined bullet selection from these manufacturers is not only complete, it is overwhelming almost to the point of intimidation for those handloaders who don't know precisely what they want in the way of a varmint bullet.

Like so many others who have handloaded ammunition for various 22 varmint cartridges, I have used quite a variety of bullets from all those manufacturers. Seldom have I been dissatisfied with regard to accuracy, velocity, and terminal ballistic performance. We have read and continue to read published reports on these bullets; needless to say they are quite popular for good reasons already mentioned.

Based on personal experience, permit me to offer some words on 22-caliber bullet designs and weights in general as a rough guide toward the selection of a suitable varmint bullet. I had been handloading for quite a few years when I read an interesting article by the excellent gunwriter Bob Hagel regarding 22-caliber bullet accuracy. I have referred to this article before and, without going into great detail, a basic observation made by Hagel was that 50-, 52- and 53-grain bullets provided somewhat better accuracy than 55-grain bullets. While the article was dated even when I read it the first time, Hagel's results were different than what I had experienced. After some careful thought, however, I realized that my own use of 22-caliber varmint bullets was, at that time, not extensive enough to make an educated comment on the subject. In defense of my own beliefs, however, I had developed some very accurate loads in several cartridges using the 55-grain Speer softpoint. Since then, I have worked with many 22-caliber varmint (and target) bullets. I have run across some exceptions, but generally speaking, I have to agree with Mr. Hagel's observations. When a 55-grain bullet does produce accuracy equal to the lighter weight bullets, more work in the way of load development is often required than is necessary with many of the lighter bullets. Keep in mind I am referring to popular 22-caliber centerfires such as the 222 Remington, 223 Remington, 22-250 Remington, the 220 Swift, and similar cartridges that normally have barrels with a 1-14 inches or sometimes 1-12 inches twist rate. The very long, heavy 22-caliber bullets available these days will not stabilize in barrels of standard twist rates. The same can also be said for some of the 60-grain bullets.

Another point worth considering when selecting a 22-caliber bullet is bullet base style: flat base or boattail? If in doubt, I always try a flat base design first. Load development with a flat base bullet is less time consuming in many––but certainly not all—applications when compared with the same for the often more temperamental boattail bullet. Depending on the rifle, of course, a flat base bullet may also be more accurate. The slightly flatter trajectory and reduced wind drift of a boattail design is wasted on most varmint shooting unless ranges are extreme, i.e., beyond 300 – 350 yards. For a rifle that will not shoot a flat base bullet accurately, which is usually not the case, then a boattail design may be the best bet. While some may not agree, my opinion was formed only after using many different bullets in many rifles.

While on the subject of bullet selection, I'll offer one more suggestion. Don't use any match bullet for varmint shooting. One is often tempted to stay with the most accurate bullet, regardless of suitability for the job at hand. I've used a bunch of Sierra 53-grain flat base match bullets. They shoot accurately in most any centerfire 22. Some gun writers have recommended these bullets for varmint shooting. (I think I may be guilty on that count also.) Sierra does not recommend them for anything but target use. Match bullets have a tiny hollowpoint. They cannot be depended upon to expand/blow up. It would also be reasonable to assume there is a greater danger of ricochet with these bullets. I have killed coyotes with the Sierra 53-grain MatchKing but stopped after I had one run off upon being hit squarely at fairly close range. He merely flinched before his escape to nearby brush where he later died.

While they may be latecomers in the highly competitive 22-caliber varmint bullet arena, Barnes Bullets, Inc. and

22-caliber hollowpoint bullets used in this article: Barnes 53-grain TSX (Triple Shock) FB, Barnes 36-grain Varmint Grenade; Berger 50-grain Varmint Match, Berger 52-grain Varmint Match, and the Berger 55-grain Varmint Match.

Berger Bullets Ltd. have each taken significant departure from traditional approaches in the production and marketing of their respective 22-caliber varmint bullets.

A recent development by Barnes is the 36-grain "Varmint Grenade". Designed to be highly frangible, it has a unique core made up of two pulverized metals: tin and copper. A gilding metal jacket of hollowpoint style, scored on the inside to promote quick expansion, encloses everything in a flat base design. Unlike some other varmint bullets of thin-jacketed construction, there are no velocity restrictions on the Varmint Grenade. In fact, Barnes furnished me with some assorted loading data that includes a 22-250 Remington load with a muzzle velocity exceeding 4,400 fps. Some 223 Remington loads approach 3,800 fps. These probably aren't the best handloads for long barrel life or the utmost in accuracy, but the Varmint Grenade will not come apart before it reaches the target when driven at such velocities. The bullet is designed for total disintegration on impact. As with other highly frangible bullets, the chance of a ricochet with the Varmint Grenade should be fairly remote.

My experience with a Barnes 22-caliber varmint bullet had been limited to the now-discontinued 50-grain Varmin-A-Tor over the past couple of years. This bullet had proven sufficiently accurate, particularly in my Ruger 77V 220 Swift, that I acquired before production ceased. The Varmin-A-Tor was a conventional jacketed hollowpoint flat base bullet with a lead core.

I first heard of the Varmint Grenade in January 2007, during the SHOT Show in Orlando, Florida. Without seeing the bullet, I tried to imagine the reasoning behind the development of such a lightweight 22-caliber varmint bullet. It had to be a very short, stubby, and ballistically inefficient

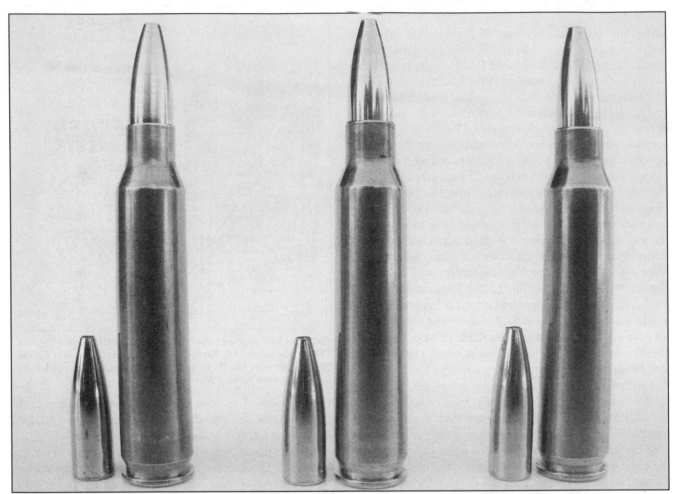

Berger Varmint Match bullets loaded in Federal 223 Remington brass, from left: 50-grain, 52-grain, and 55-grain. Bullets are loaded to a maximum overall length of 2.26 inches.

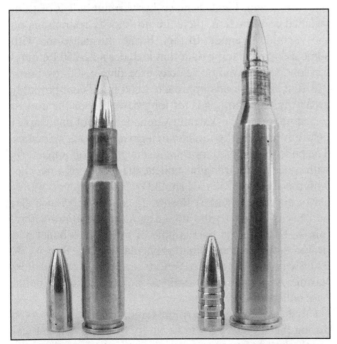

From left: Barnes 36-grain Varmint Grenade bullet loaded in Winchester 222 brass to a maximum overall length of 2.130 inches. Barnes 53-grain TSX (Triple Shock) FB bullet loaded in Winchester 220 Swift brass to a maximum overall length of 2.68 inches.

projectile. Of course, I mistakenly assumed this was a regular lead core bullet. The copper/tin core, however, weighs considerably less than a lead core and thus the 22-caliber Varmint Grenade is close to the same length as many conventional jacketed varmint bullets in the 50/55-grain weight range. The Varmint Grenade measures approximately 0.695-inch in length. Despite this, however, there is a tradeoff in the form of a considerably lower ballistic coefficient than many other conventional 22-caliber varmint bullets. While the BC of the Varmint Grenade is only .149, higher-than-normal muzzle velocities will, to an extent, offset the disadvantages of greater wind drift and bullet drop. For many varmint shooters (myself in particular) who seldom if ever shoot beyond 250-300 yards, ballistic coefficients are not something to get overly concerned about.

Barnes makes another 22-caliber bullet that, while not designed for varminting, can be very effectively used in that role. The Barnes "X" bullet has been around for a good while now. The newer Triple-Shock X Bullet is a refinement of the original and is available in all popular calibers. As reported by a Barnes technician, the 53-grain flat base Triple-Shock X Bullet is used for varmint hunting by some folks even though it was essentially developed for use on game larger than varmints, namely deer-sized game. I don't intend to open the

CCI-400 (Small Rifle) and CCI-200 (Large Rifle) primers were used exclusively by author in load development for cartridges mentioned in text.

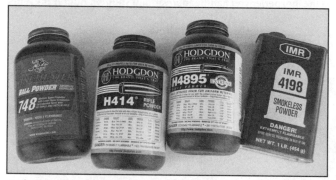

Author used the following powders in sample loads for this article: (from left) Win.748, H414, H4895, and IMR 4198. See tables for suggested loading data from Barnes and Berger.

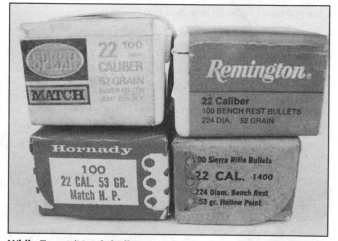

While Target /Match bullets may be very accurate and are sometimes used for varmint shooting, they were not designed with that purpose in mind. They cannot be depended upon for humane kills for reasons explained in text.

argument here regarding the use of 22-caliber centerfires for deer hunting. Regardless of one's views on the subject, lots of deer are successfully harvested annually by the various centerfire 22-calibers. I would guess the 223 Remington and 22-250 Remington are among the most popular 22-caliber rounds for such hunting.

The 53-grain TSX 22-caliber bullet shares the same all-copper construction that is used in making the larger caliber TSX game bullets. According to Barnes, the grooves in the bullet body serve as a pressure reduction measure. Conceivably, this could lead to somewhat higher muzzle velocity by the use of a slightly greater powder charge, all the while maintaining a safe and permissible chamber pressure. The Triple Shock X bullets are of solid copper hollowpoint construction and have developed quite an enviable reputation for use on game. They expand quickly and retain most of their weight. Though deep penetration is not necessary for varmint shooting, the 53-grain TSX will seldom fail to exit.

For prairie dog shooting or other types of varminting where many rounds are fired in a day, Triple Shocks may be a bit pricey. However, the handloading hunter who uses one 22-caliber centerfire rifle all year to take occasional varmints and seasonal whitetail deer may find this to be the ideal bullet if it shoots accurately in a particular firearm. There's no need to worry about the disadvantages associated with using more than one load in one rifle.

The absence of a lead core makes the 53-grain 22-caliber TSX FB a fairly long bullet, measuring about 0.800-inch in length. The ballistic coefficient is .204. Barnes recommends seating Triple Shock bullets to a depth somewhere between 0.030-inch to 0.070-inch off the lands for best accuracy, so

The available array of 22-caliber varmint bullets can be overwhelming to the inexperienced handloader/varmint shooter. Author presents a general guide to bullet selection and tips in this article.

Author at bench with his favorite long-range varmint rig: a well-used Ruger 77V in 220 Swift with factory 26″ heavy barrel. Scope is a 12X Unertl.

All test loads used by the author were prepared using a Forster Co-Ax press. A Bonanza 222 Remington benchrest seating die is in place.

some experimentation will probably be necessary to fine tune a load for most rifles. The suggested starting point is 0.050-inch off the lands.

I tried both the 36-grain Varmint Grenade and the 53-grain Triple Shock in several different loads. The test rifles used were the following:

    222 Remington – Remington Model 722, 26-in. barrel, Weaver K6 6X scope

    223 Remington – Ruger Model 77 MKII, 22-in. barrel, Burris 6X Mini Scope

    220 Swift – Ruger Model 77V, 26-in. heavy barrel, 12X Unertl scope

These rifles could best be described as "high mileage" models, though all still shoot quite accurately with preferred loads.

My handloads with both brands of bullets used CCI-400 primers for the 222 and 223 and CCI-200 for the 220 Swift. These are, of course, standard rather than magnum primers. Winchester brass was used for the 222 and Swift, while Federal cases were used for the 223.

Loads were not "worked up", save limited experimentation with a couple of different seating depths using each of the Barnes bullets in all three cartridges. Sometimes, as expected, there was virtually no change in accuracy; other times the change was dramatic. I was not accustomed to seeing recorded velocities on my Oehler 35P chronograph in

the 3,500 fps range with the 222 Remington cartridge, but such velocities are attainable with some loads using the 36-grain Varmint Grenade bullet. My Ruger 223 bolt-action displayed excellent accuracy using this bullet and Reloader 7 powder. This was a surprise to me as the old Remington 222 is usually the more accurate of the two rifles. Muzzle velocity was just shy of 3,600 fps.

The 53-grain TSX FB bullet was another story in the Ruger 223. I had a small sampling of bullets and only tried a couple of loadings using two seating depths and H4895 powder. I never did get decent 100-yard accuracy, but in all fairness, I can't pass judgment without trying more loads using other powders. The 220 Swift fared better with loads developed using my favorite powder for that cartridge, H414. Some additional fine-tuning would hopefully shrink group sizes to around a half-inch, which is what the rifle is capable of with selected loads.

Berger (now Berger Bullets Ltd.) has been in the bullet business for many years, but for quite a while catered almost exclusively to the needs of benchrest shooters. In 1990 the company began its expansion into other areas of accuracy-oriented shooting disciplines. To find a benchrest bullet manufacturer branching out in such a way is unusual in itself. It's not uncommon these days to find accuracy-oriented game hunters and varmint shooters using ammunition handloaded with Berger bullets of one variety or another. A second unique characteristic of this company lies in the fact that all the bullets manufactured by Berger are made to the same precise match grade standards as their benchrest bullets.

The sample 22-caliber caliber Berger Varmint Match Grade bullets furnished for use in this article are of 50, 52, and 55 grains. All are of flat base design. Varmint bullets have an enlarged hollowpoint opening in the nose as well as a thinner jacket wall toward the nose. These features help ensure the quick expansion necessary for instant, humane kills on varmints. Bullet bases are substantially thick to withstand high velocities. Bullet lengths and ballistic coefficients are shown here for comparative purposes:

	LENGTH	BC
50-grain Varmint Match	.715"	.199
52-grain Varmint Match	.720"	.250
55-grain Varmint Match	.753"	.250

I made up several loads with these bullets. Due to time constraints, however, as with the Barnes bullets, I did no true load development. All bullets were simply seated to maximum overall cartridge lengths, i.e., 2.130 inches for the 222 Remington, 2.26 inches for the 223 Remington, and 2.68 inches for the 220 Swift. At these lengths, bullets were still seated short of the bore lands in my rifles, but that may not be the situation in other firearms. From a safety aspect, this is certainly an important point to check before duplicating any loads.

In the 222, the 50-grain Berger was very accurate with a maximum load (for my rifle) of Winchester 748 powder and it did just as well with the old 222 Remington standard,

IMR-4198. The 223 Remington was most accurate with the 55-grain Berger and 748 powder. (Remember the rule about 50-grain 22-caliber bullets being more accurate than those of 55-grains?) In the Swift, the 52-grain version proved to be the most accurate with a near-max load of H414. The best loads in all three rifles grouped under an inch, some around a half-inch, and several groups were fired through a hot barrel.

With ample time to devote to the experimental phase of handload workup, results with both the Barnes and Berger bullets should show more than sufficient accuracy to satisfy the needs of any varmint shooter. Additionally, terminal performance should be more than adequate for the intended purpose of any of these bullets by either manufacturer.

SAMPLE LOADING DATA FOR BARNES BULLETS
(Courtesy of Barnes Bullets, Inc.)

36-gr. 22-caliber Varmint Grenade

222 Remington –Remington brass, Winchester SR primer, OAL = 2.10"

POWDER	START LOAD	MAX. LOAD	MAX. VEL.
Win. 748	25.0	27.5	3350
IMR-4198	18.0	20.0	3462

223 Remington – Winchester brass, Winchester SR primer, OAL = 2.192"

POWDER	START LOAD	MAX. LOAD	MAX. VEL.
IMR-4198	20.5	22.5	3796
RE-7	22.0	24.0	3774

22-250 Remington – Remington brass, Federal 210M primer, OAL = 2.350"

POWDER	START LOAD	MAX. LOAD	MAX. VEL.
Win. 748	36.5	40.5	4442
VARGET	36.5	40.5	4363

220 Swift – Remington brass, Federal 210M primer, OAL = 2.635"

POWDER	START LOAD	MAX. LOAD	MAX. VEL.
RE-15	36.5	40.5	4290
H414	41.0	45.0	4282

53-gr. 22-caliber TSX FB (Triple Shock)

222 Remington – Remington brass, Winchester SR primer, OAL = 2.130"

POWDER	START LOAD	MAX. LOAD	MAX. VEL.
Win. 748	22.5	24.5	3088
IMR-4895	22.0	24.0	3018

223 Remington – Winchester brass, Winchester SR primer, OAL = 2.210"

POWDER	START LOAD	MAX. LOAD	MAX. VEL.
H4895	23.5	25.5	3292
VARGET	24.5	26.5	3247

22-250 Remington – Winchester brass, Federal 210 Primer, OAL = 2.350"

POWDER	START LOAD	MAX. LOAD	MAX. VEL.
RE-15	34.5	38.5	3904
IMR-4895	33.0	37.0	3827

220 Swift – Remington brass, Federal 210M primer, OAL = 2.650"

POWDER	START LOAD	MAX. LOAD	MAX. VEL.
H380	37.5	41.5	3715
H414	38.0	42.5	3839

Note: This data is intended for use only by competent persons experienced in the proper and safe practice of ammunition handloading. Always begin load development using starting loads. APPROACH MAXIMUM LOADS WITH CAUTION. If any components are substituted for those shown, or if the overall cartridge length is changed, a reduction in starting charge may be necessary.

SAMPLE LOADING DATA FOR BERGER BULLETS
22-caliber Varmint match grade
(Courtesy of Berger Bullets Ltd.)

222 Remington

BULLET	POWDER	START LOAD	MAX. LOAD	APP. MAX.
50-gr.	H4895	20.5	23.3	3181
50-gr.	Win. 748	22.0	24.9	3337
50-gr.	IMR-4198	17.5	20.1	3216
52-gr.	RE-10X	18.5	20.7	3148
52-gr.	H322	19.5	21.8	3143
52-gr.	Win. 748	21.5	24.1	3156
55-gr.	AA XMR 2015	19.0	21.2	3047
55-gr.	IMR-4198	17.0	18.9	3029
55-gr.	H335	20.0	23.2	3074

223 Remington

BULLET	POWDER	START LOAD	MAX. LOAD	APP. MAX.
50-gr.	H4895	24.0	26.8	3311
50-gr.	RE 10X	21.0	23.5	3308
50-gr.	VARGET	25.0	27.2	3323
52-gr.	RE-12	24.0	26.6	3329
52-gr.	VARGET	24.5	26.9	3270
52-gr.	Win. 748	25.5	28.2	3418
55-gr.	BENCHMARK	21.5	25.4	3229
55-gr.	H4895	22.0	26.1	3193
55-gr.	Win. 748	25.0	27.7	3346

220 Swift

BULLET	POWDER	START LOAD	MAX. LOAD	APP. MAX.
50-gr.	RE-15	35.0	39.0	3937
50-gr.	H380	38.5	42.7	3882
50-gr.	Win. 760	39.0	43.2	3961
52-gr.	RE-15	34.0	38.6	3875
52-gr.	IMR-4064	34.0	37.7	3828
52-gr.	VARGET	33.5	37.5	3808
55-gr.	H380	37.5	41.6	3744
55-gr.	IMR-4320	34.0	38.1	3773
55-gr.	H414	37.5	41.1	3718

Note: Berger data was generated using "Quick Load" and a 24-inch barrel for the 22-2 Remington and 223 Remington, and a 26-inch barrel for the 220 Swift. Overall cartridge length for the 222 is 2.130 inches, for the 223 is 2.26 inches, and for the 220 Swift is 2.68 inches.

This data is intended for use only by competent persons experienced in the proper and safe practice of ammunition handloading. Always begin load development using starting loads. APPROACH MAXIMUM LOADS WITH CAUTION.

18

Plans for
this sturdy
reloading
platform are no
longer available,
except right here!

NRMA Bench Plans Revisited

By Bill Chevalier

I KNOW YOU'RE not keen about reading my life history, but I have to give you a small window into my adventures so you can appreciate how the plans for the National Reloading Manufacturers Association reloading bench came into being. Back in the early 1970s, our advertising agency in Portland, Oregon, was in the throes of transforming itself from an industrial agency into one dedicated to outdoor sports, mostly hunting, shooting and reloading. Through a series of circumstances, Arlen Cheney of Omark CCI/Speer, Buzz Huntington of RCBS and Charles Warren of Ponsness-Warren encouraged us to try for the NRMA advertising/PR account. So we went to the NRA convention in Washington, D.C. (they were always in Washington in those days) and presented our ideas to the association's members. The reloading industry was young enough in those days that the members consisted of some of the truly great reloading pioneers, and I have always felt privileged to rub elbows with the likes of John Nosler, (Bob's dad), Bruce Hodgon (Bob and J.B.'s dad), Fred Huntington (Buzz's dad) and Joyce Hornady (Steve's dad), among many others.

Well, the assemblage liked our DISCOVER RELOADING theme because the main thrust of the effort would be to encourage more and more shooters to (you guessed it) Discover Reloading and thereby help

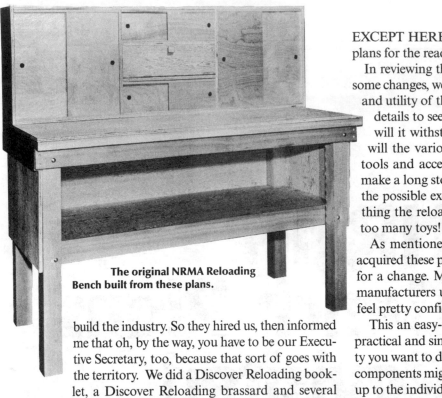

The original NRMA Reloading Bench built from these plans.

build the industry. So they hired us, then informed me that oh, by the way, you have to be our Executive Secretary, too, because that sort of goes with the territory. We did a Discover Reloading booklet, a Discover Reloading brassard and several Discover Reloading public service ads that we asked hunting and shooting magazines to run at no cost. We were always on the lookout for new materials we could offer through our ads and news releases, and that's where the reloading bench plans were born.

We put a small Reloading Bench Plans booklet together which included a list of all the materials needed including plywood, lumber and hardware, a guide to cutting the plywood and step-by-step instructions for assembly of the bench and the upper cabinet section. Our art director, Dick Cassatt, made all the necessary drawings and contributed many good ideas for construction details. Of course, we wanted to make sure all of our great ideas would work, so we set out to build the first bench ourselves. Since I'm not a woodworking guy and don't have a shop in my house, I took the plans to a cabinet shop (whose owner was the son of a gun shop owner next door) and had him accurately cut all the components, ready for assembly. I figured if I could put this thing together, anybody could. We discovered a couple of minor glitches, corrected them, and then proceeded to assemble NRMA's first reloading bench, which stands in my reloading room to this day.

For sure, we know the plans work. We built a second bench for a Discover Reloading video that starred my son, Greg, who runs the agency now. That bench is now in his garage.

The plans were well received by shooters everywhere, and we sold thousands and thousands of Reloading Bench Plans, both in their original form and as a part of a newer booklet called SET YOURSELF UP TO RELOAD.

Well, the National Reloading Manufacturers Association has recently gone inactive, their website has disappeared and all the literature is now out of print and unavailable.

EXCEPT HERE, where we have been able to resurrect the plans for the readers of this book.

In reviewing the plans to determine if we should suggest some changes, we looked at the construction, the ruggedness and utility of the bench. We also looked at the component details to see if everything is still readily available. Also, will it withstand the pressures of modern presses, and will the various storage spaces be adequate for all the tools and accessories the reloader might want? Well, to make a long story short, the bench is still good to go, with the possible exception of having enough room for everything the reloader might want. There's no such thing as too many toys!

As mentioned, probably 25 to 30 thousand reloaders acquired these plans, and there was rarely even a suggestion for a change. Many of the powder, bullet and equipment manufacturers use the bench in their catalog photos, so we feel pretty confident we're still on the right track.

This an easy-to-follow set of plans for building a tough, practical and simple bench for any kind of reloading activity you want to do. We made suggestions as to where various components might be stored, but those decisions are entirely up to the individual. The bench was designed to be extremely sturdy to withstand the pressures exerted by presses. It is a full six feet long, so there's plenty of room for both metallic and shotshell presses and other mountable accessories. In addition to the storage compartments, there is a drop-down shelf for whatever kind of powder scale you use.

While this bench was designed to be as versatile as possible, it can also be just a starting point for the imaginative builder. For instance, if you want it larger, just make it eight feet long instead of six. Or, if the height is not right, make it higher or lower just by adjusting the length of the legs. It was designed to have its main working surface at waist level for a man 6' 2" tall. Or, if you like to reload sitting on a chair or stool, figure that into your personal planning.

Speaking of size, here's an important tip: BUILD THIS BENCH WHERE YOU PLAN TO USE IT! The top of the bench is 34 inches deep and it stands over 42 inches off the floor, so if the doors in your house are around 30 inches wide, like mine are, you might have to disassemble the whole thing if your wife wants it in the dining room instead of the kitchen!

Some reloaders asked, over the years, how to accommodate a small space, such as in an apartment. You could cut the dimensions down, but be aware that the weight of the bench gives it stability, so a smaller version might have to be attached to the wall studs to make sure it can't come downv on top of you or your kids.

These plans include drawings of construction details, a materials list and a guide to cutting plywood components. If your home workshop does not include an accurate table saw that can handle a 4'x8' sheet of plywood, you might want take the materials to a cabinet or woodworking shop and get them to do the cutting according to our Guide to Plywood Cutting like I did.

The entire bench is assembled with bolts and wood screws for strength. If desired, you can sand all of the surfaces, stain it to match your preferences and add a few coats of varnish to slick it up before mounting your reloading tools.

As you will notice in the bench drawing, we have designated the left hand compartment for depriming and priming, which would include your supply of primers (ALWAYS IN THEIR ORIGINAL BOXES!), and your dies. In the middle, we show powder, a scale and a powder measure. And on the right, we have bullets, and/or shot and wads. In short, it's probably best to separate the various components, but how you do it is up to you. Notice we used sliding doors rather than hinged doors to keep the top surface unobstructed. The lower bench shelf provides a lot of room for large quantities of powder, shot, hulls, and since it is made of ¾-inch plywood like the top, it is plenty strong.

NOTE: Building materials outlets have several grades of lumber and plywood, so choose materials with the final product in mind.

One last tip before you get started: Assemble the bench section first, the upper cabinet section second, then join the two per the instructions.

MATERIALS LIST (listed for Bench section and Cabinet section)

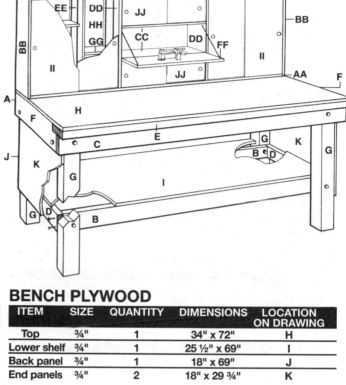

BENCH LUMBER

ITEM	SIZE	QUANTITY	LENGTH	LOCATION ON DRAWING
Top frame	2x6	1	69"	A
Bottom frame	2x4	2	66"	B
Top frame	2x4	1	72"	C
Bottom frame	2x4	2	22"	D
Top frame	2x6	1	72"	E
Top frame	2x6	2	30 ½	F
Legs	4x4	4	42"	G

Material purchase suggestion: Two 8-foot 2x4s and one 6-foot 2x4

Three 6-foot 2x6s

Two 8-foot 4x4s

BENCH PLYWOOD

ITEM	SIZE	QUANTITY	DIMENSIONS	LOCATION ON DRAWING
Top	¾"	1	34" x 72"	H
Lower shelf	¾"	1	25 ½" x 69"	I
Back panel	¾"	1	18" x 69"	J
End panels	¾"	2	18" x 29 ¾"	K

Material Purchase Suggestion: Three 4' x 8' sheets of ¾" plywood for the above items, plus those ¾" pieces required for cabinet. See Cutting Guide.

BENCH HARDWARE

12 ⅜" x 6" carriage bolts, nuts & washers

25 ¼" x 3" flat head wood screws

9 dozen ³⁄₁₆" x 1 ¾" flat head wood screws

GUIDE TO PLYWOOD CUTTING

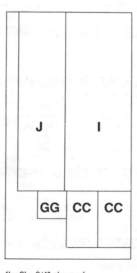

4' x 8' 3/4" plywood

4' x 8' 3/4" plywood

4' x 8' 3/4" plywood

4' x 8' x 1/4" plywood

CABINET PLYWOOD

ITEM	SIZE	QUANTITY	DIMENSIONS	LOCATION ON DRAWING
Top & bottom	¾"	2	12" x 70 ½"	AA
Ends	¾"	2	12" x 24"	BB
Center shelves	¾"	2	12" x 23"	CC
Center uprights	¾"	2	12" x 22 ½"	DD
Shelf dividers	¾"	2	10 ¾" x 22 ½"	EE
Center door	¾"	1	6 ¾" x 23"	FF
Shelves	¾"	4	10 ¾" x 10 ⅝"	GG
Cabinet back	¼"	1	24" x 72"	HH
Sliding doors	¼"	4	22 ¼" x 12"	II
Sliding doors	¼"	4	6 ¾" x 12"	JJ

CABINET HARDWARE

4 sets, each 23" long, double track for sliding doors

32' adjustable shelf track, with sufficient brackets (4 per shelf) and sufficient ½" flat head nails to affix track.

3 dozen ³⁄₁₆" x 1 ¾" flat head wood screws

2 dozen 1-inch wood screws for cabinet back

1 piano hinge, 23" long with mounting screws

1 length of light chain, 10" long, plus 2 screw eyes, for center door support

8 finger grips to fit into ½-inch holes for sliding doors

1 drawer pull for center shelf door

1 latch for center shelf door

BENCH CONSTRUCTION

STEP ONE
Saw all lumber and plywood for bench. Double check dimensions, and sand any rough edges. BE SURE TO DRILL AND COUNTERSINK ALL SCREWS.

STEP TWO
Assemble lower shelf frame. Use two 3" wood screws at each corner.

STEP THREE
Accurately saw a 3 ½" x 3 ½" notch at both REAR corners of lower shelf plywood. This will accommodate the rear 4x4 legs, which are actually 3 ½ x 3 ½.

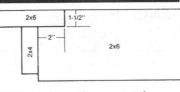

STEP FOUR
Assemble top frame. A notch must be sawn in the two 30 ½" 2 x 6 pieces that form the ends of the frame. Each notch should be 2 inches long and 1 ½" deep. This accommodates the 2 x 6 front edge support and allows for the necessary overhang. (See drawing) Use two 3" wood screws at each corner and to fasten the 2 x 6 front edge support.

STEP FIVE
A notch must be sawn into the top of both 4 x 4 front legs. NO NOTCH SHOULD BE SAWN INTO THE REAR LEGS. The notch is 1 ½" deep from the top of the 4 x 4 and 2" from the side. (See drawing) This will enable the leg to nest under the front 2 x 6 edge support.

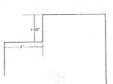

STEP SIX
Turn top frame upside down on work bench or floor and position all four legs. Using a ³⁄₈" drill bit, drill holes through frame and legs. Insert bolts, add washers and lightly tighten nuts. (See drawing)

STEP SEVEN
With bench still upside down, hold end panels against legs so they are flush against the 2 x 6 end pieces. The edge of the end panel determines the bottom edge of the lower shelf frame. Mark the legs, then drill ³⁄₈" holes for bolts in both the legs and the lower shelf frame.

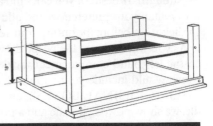

STEP EIGHT
Before bolting lower frame to legs, attach plywood shelf to frame with 1 ¾" screws. Then bolt frame to legs. Check to make sure all pieces are properly assembled, and then tighten all bolts. Turn bench right side up, and attach plywood top, end panels and back panel with 1 ¾" wood screws. Bench is now complete.

CABINET CONSTRUCTION

STEP ONE
BE SURE TO DRILL AND COUNTERSINK FOR ALL SCREWS. Assemble top, bottom and ends of cabinet with 1 ¾" wood screws. Attach plywood cabinet back to outer frame with 1" wood screws. This will automatically square up the cabinet for subsequent steps.

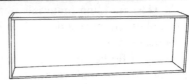

STEP TWO
Assemble center section, made up of two center uprights and two center shelves. Place a mark exactly 7 inches from the top and bottom of the uprights. This marks the location of the top of the top shelf and the bottom of the bottom shelf, creating a 7-inch center section. Measure carefully, and then assemble with 1 ¾" wood screws.

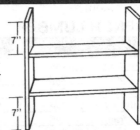

STEP THREE
Place center section in the cabinet frame. Center this section, leaving a 23-inch opening at either end. Measure carefully, then assemble with 1 ¾" wood screws.

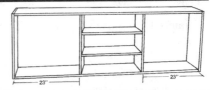

STEP FOUR
Position shelf dividers in the end compartments. When they are precisely centered, there will be an 11 ⅛" opening on either side of each divider. Measure carefully, and then assemble with 1 ¾" wood screws.

STEP FIVE
Cut shelf track to size, being careful to position track so shelf will be level, then nail into place. Add brackets for each shelf and place shelves into position.

STEP SIX
Drill ½" holes for sliding door finger grips and glue finger grips into place. Fit double track, making sure deep track is at the top and the shallow track at the bottom so doors can be properly inserted. Assemble track sections and sliding doors into place to make sure doors are captured, but can be removed if needed. When you are sure sliding doors and track fit properly, glue or nail track into place. (You may want to delay attaching track until after painting or staining is completed.)

STEP SEVEN
Attach center door with piano hinge, assembling door so it is flush with cabinet when closed. Use chain with screw eyes to hold door in a level position when open. Make sure this shelf is level for best operation of your powder scale. Attach drawer pull and your choice of catch to hold door closed.

FINAL ASSEMBLY
When bench and cabinet are complete, join them with wood screws to avoid any possibility of movement when operating reloading presses. Be sure is bench is level and rests solidly on the floor.

19

High velocity
from a compact
case and little recoil
= Fun Shooting.

Loading the Hot New Small-bore Cartridges

By John Haviland

THE HIGH NUMBER of new small-bore rifle cartridge introduced over the last few years is quite amazing. These cartridges are geared toward achieving the highest velocity possible from a compact case. Some have next to no recoil and are fun to shoot again and again while others make up into light hunting rifles for the long hike. Let's take a look what hand-loading can do for these fast-steppers.

Remington 17 Fireball

Remington's new 17 Fireball is essentially the old 17 Mach IV developed by the O'Brien Rifle Company back in the early 1960s by necking down the 221 Remington Fireball case to 17 caliber.

The 17 Fireball burns about 20 grains of powder with a 20-grain bullet to produce about the same trajectory as the 22-250 out to 500 yards. However, way out there at 500 yards, the 22-250 packs slightly more than three times the energy as the 17-caliber bullet.

Recoil is where the 17 and the 22-250 part ways. The 22-250's kick certainly isn't hard on the shoulder. But it's enough to knock back a ten pound rifle so the sight picture is lost. The recoil of the 17, though, is so gentle that even a fairly light Remington Model Seven rifle barely moves on recoil. In fact, the scope crosshairs barely jump off the target. That light

This is a lineup of new small-bore cartridges. From the left: 17 Fireball, 204 Ruger, 223 WSSM, 243 WSSM, 2.5 WSSM, 270 WSM, 7mm SAUM and 7mm WSM.

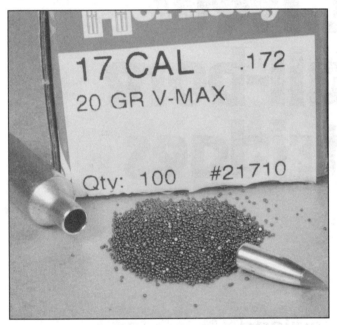

The 17 Fireball burns about 20 grains of powder with a 20-grain bullet to produce about the same trajectory as the 22-250 out to 500 yards.

Loads for the Remington 17 Fireball

Bullet (grains)	Powder	Weight (grains)	Velocity (fps)	100 Yard Group (Inches)
Hornady 20 V-Max				
	N130	16.5	3,766	1.04
	A2460	20.0	3,862	.77
	Benchmark	20.0	4,002	1.34
	H322	19.0	3,965	2.05
	H4198	17.0	4,100	1.87
Berger 25 Match				
	N130	16.2	3,520	.83
	A2460	19.5	3,611	.74
	Benchmark	18.5	3,574	.74
	H4198	16.5	3,668	.83
Hornady 25 V-Max				
	N130	16.2	3,513	1.00
	A2520	19.5	3,328	.94
	A2460	19.5	3,637	117
	H322	18.0	3,641	1.22
	H4198	16.5	3,712	1.00

204 Ruger

The 204 is another mild recoiling cartridge that is fun to shoot all day. Hornady did their homework on this cartridge because their factory loads are fast and accurate. While I was fiddling with the Varmint Hunter's Reticle in the Leupold 4.5-14x scope on a Remington XR-100 rifle in 204 I shot three-shot groups at 100, 200 and 300 yards with the Hornady 32-grain V-Max load. They measured:

- 0.926-inch at 100 yards.
- 2.355 inches at 200 yards.
- 1.759 inches at 300 yards.

Handloads did improve the accuracy of the XR-100. However, the step up over Hornady factory loads in accuracy was only a few tenths of an inch at 100 yards. Components for handloads included the Hornady 32- and 40-grain V-Max bullets, Sierra 32- and 39-grain BlitzKing bullets with Hodgdon Benchmark, IMR-4895 and Vihtavuori N135 powder.

The 204 is mild-recoiling cartridge that is fun to shoot all day. Hornady did their homework on this cartridge because their factory loads are fast and accurate.

recoil and flat trajectory make the Fireball fun to shoot, and shoot again and again.

The choice of 17-caliber bullet brands and weights are rather slim. The most common weigh between 20 and 25 grains. Berger makes 20-, 25- and 30-grain hollowpoints and Hornady makes 20- and 25-grain V-Max bullets for the 17.

The 17 Fireball's tiny diameter bullet and a small capacity case mean velocity can vary significantly with a slight change in powder weight. The Hornady 20-grain V-Max bullet had an average velocity of 3,769 fps with 18.0 grains of H322 powder. One more grain of H322 increased velocity 196 fps, to 3,965 fps. A half grain more powder increased velocity 167 fps, to 4,132 fps. So when loading this little cartridge make sure powder charges are exact, especially maximum loads.

The following are some of the best loads for a Remington Model Seven CDL with a 20-inch barrel and a Sightron 4-16x scope:

Loads for the 204 Ruger

Bullet (grains)	Powder	Weight (grains)	Velocity (fps)	100 Yard Group (Inches)
Hornady 32 V-Max Factory Load			4,038	.74
Hornady 32 V-Max				
	Benchmark	28.0	3,865	1.01
	N135	27.0	3,901	1.58
	IMR4895	28.5	3,658	1.07
Sierra 32-gr. BlitzKing				
	Benchmark	28.0	3,865	.75
	N135	27.0	3,911	.67
	IMR4895	28.5	3,667	.90
Sierra 39-gr. BlitzKing				
	Benchmark	25.5	3,453	.42
	N135	25.0	3,437	.46
	IMR4895	27.5	3,406	1.20
Hornady 40-gr. V-Max Factory Load			3,691	.66
Hornady 40-gr. V-Max				
	Benchmark	25.5	3,413	1.29
	N135	25.0	3,372	1.20
	IMR4895	27.5	3,408	.45

Loads for the 223 Winchester Super Short Magnum

Bullet (grains)	Powder	Weight (grains)	Velocity (fps)	100 Yard Group (Inches)
Nosler 40 Ballistic Tip				
	H414	50.0	4,212	.35
	H4350	50.0	4,263	.43
	H4895	43.0	4,378	.54
Sierra 50 BlitzKing				
	H4350	48.5	3,995	.35
	H4895	42.0	4,041	.85
	Hunter	50.4	4,000	94
	Varget	43.5	3,997	.47
Sierra 55 BlitzKing				
	H414	46.8	3,837	.55
	H4350	47.5	3,902	.46
	Hunter	48.0	3,787	.43
Nosler 60 Partition				
	H414	44.0	3,674	1.29
	Hunter	45.7	3,631	.88
	Reloder 19	47.0	3,658	1.92
Sierra 63 Semi-Pointed				
	BLC(2)	39.5	3,567	.49
	H414	45.0	3,688	.82
	H4350	46.2	3,775	.70
Sierra 69 HPBT Match				
	H414	44.0	3,472	.92
	H4350	45.0	3,659	.65
	H4895	36.5	3,446	.38
	Hunter	44.0	3,386	.99

Winchester 223 Super Short Magnum

This short and fat cartridge has been misunderstood since the day it was born. It was intended as a bit more of a cartridge than the 220 Swift, but in a modern design to fit on an abbreviated short action and with little body taper to the case and no aggravating rim like the Swift's. But people immediately started whining about the 223 WSSM's excessive barrel wear, even though they had never fired so much as a single round from a Browning A-Bolt with a chrome-lined bore. Browning states the 223 WSSM's bore erosion in a chrome-lined bore is on about the same level as the 22-250.

The 223 WSSM does produce impressive bullet speeds matched by no other established 22-caliber centerfire, along with excellent accuracy, flat trajectories and easy reloading. That added performance comes at the expense of burning four to eight grains more of the same powders used in the 22-250. Here are some loads fired through a Cooper Arms Model 22 that show the 223 WSSM is fast and accurate:

243 Winchester Super Short Magnum

Winchester's 243 Super Short Magnum is the velocity twin of the 6 mm Remington. Hodgdon Powder lists nearly the same powder charges for the 6 mm Remington and the 243 magnum, with both cartridges generating nearly the same bullet speeds.

A Winchester brand 243 Winchester case holds 52.8 grains of water, a Remington brand 6mm Remington case 54.3 grains of water and a 243 WSSM case 54.4 grains of water. Those weights are with the cases filled to the top of the mouth. The 243 WSSM cases are heavy. They weigh 214 grains, which is nearly 40 grains heavier than a 6 mm Remington case and nearly 44 grains heavier than a 243 Winchester case. All that brass sits in the web and case walls that look thick as a tomb door.

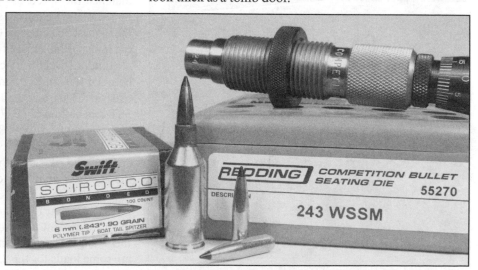

The 6mm Remington, on the left, and the 243 WSSM have identical case capacities.

The 243 WSSM cases are heavy. They weigh 214 grains, which is nearly 40 grains heavier than a 6mm Remington case and nearly 44 grains heavier than a 243 Winchester case. All that brass sits in the web and case walls that look thick as a tomb door.

Handloading the 243 WSSM was straightforward. After factory loaded cartridges were fired the cases were trimmed. They stretched next to nothing after that, even after being fired as many as five times. No cases were lost because of any type of split at the web or crack on the neck, either. The following are some 243 WSSM loads fired from a Browning A-Bolt Varmint Stalker with a 24-inch barrel:

Loads for the 243 Winchester Super Short Magnum

Bullet (grains)	Powder	Weight (grains)	Velocity (fps)	100 Yard Group (Inches)
Nosler 55 BT				
	H4895	45.0	3,979	.66
	IMR3031	44.0	3,965	.53
	W760	51.0	3,739	.27
Nosler 70-grain BT				
	BLC(2)	46.0	3,617	.73
	H4895	42.0	3,627	1.12
	Varget	43.5	3,596	.98
Sierra 75 HP				
	H4350	48.5	3,592	.79
	Varget	42.0	3,483	.60
	W760	48.0	3,483	.45
Barnes 85 Triple Shock				
	AA2700	43.5	3,086	.66
	IMR4320	40.0	3,263	.83
	RL22	49.0	3,284	.71
Swift 90 Scirocco				
	H4350	44.0	3,341	1.05
	H4831	47.0	3,287	.96
	IMR4350	44.5	3,303	1.46
Hornady 95 SST				
	AA4350	41.0	2,919	1.02
	IMR4831	43.0	3,095	.84
	Reloder 22	44.0	3,033	1.09
Sierra 100 BT SP				
	H4831	44.5	3,120	.77
	IMR7828 SSC	47.0	3,158	.53
	W760	41.5	3,012	.66
Hornady 105 A-Max				
	AA3100	42.0	2,779	1.33
	IMR4350	40.0	2,961	1.59
	WXR	42.0	2,966	1.72

With H4350 powder the 25 WSSM shoots Barnes 100-grain bullets at 3,280 fps. That's right up there with the 25-06 Remington.

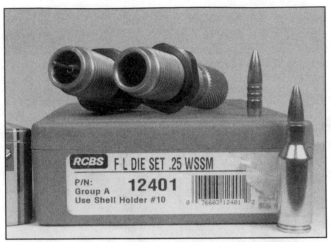

RCBS makes reloading dies for the 25 WSSM. Reloads allow shooters to shoot a much wider selection of bullets than the three bullets available in Winchester factory loads, and Winchester is the only company loading the 25 WWSM.

25 Winchester Super Short Magnum

When Winchester Ammunition introduced the 25 Winchester Super Short Magnum they stated the cartridge "... delivers the red hot, knock-down performance of the 25-06—all in a cartridge that's two action sizes smaller than the 25-06!" Those are fighting words for a longtime fan of the 25-06. But after shooting the 25 WSSM in the field and on the range, I grudgingly admit Winchester's statement is correct. In addition, the little 25 magnum accomplishes it in a light and compact rifle.

Next to no reloading data for the 25 WSSM was available when I started reloading the cartridge. Several of the reloads listed with lightweight bullets came fairly close to the speed of the Winchester 85-grain bullet load. The powder weight of a few of those loads, using powders like IMR 3031, 4064 and 4895, could possibly be increased slightly with 75, 87 and 90 grain bullets. Reloads with Hornady 117- and 120-grain bullets and IMR-4350 and W760 powders pretty well matched the speed of the Winchester 115- and 120-grain bullet loads. Relatively slower burning powders produced the highest velocities in the 25 magnum pretty much across the range of bullet weights.

Standard weight 25-caliber bullets for big game weigh between 100- and 120-grains. The Hornady 100-grain bullet reached 3,200 fps in the 25 magnum. The Hornady 117-grain SST reached nearly 3,000 fps and the Hornady 120-grain hollowpoint nearly 2,900 fps. Can't complain about that out of a 22-inch barrel.

The base of these three heavy bullets protruded into the shoulder area of the super short case when they were seated 0.030-inch from contacting the rifling. That still left plenty of room for 50 grains of powder. That bullet seating arrangement also worked out so cartridges loaded with these long bullets fit in the A-Bolt's magazine. The following are some loads for the 25 WSSM shot from a Browning A-Bolt Hunter with a 22-inch barrel and a Bushnell 2-7x 3200 Elite scope:

Loads for the 25 Winchester Super Short Magnum

Bullet (grains)	Powder	Weight (grains)	Velocity (fps)	100 Yard Group (Inches)
Sierra 75 HP				
	Hunter	51.0	3,307	.99
	IMR4064	44.5	3,349	.27
	IMR4895	43.5	3,172	.78
Sierra 87 Spitzer				
	Big Game	47.0	3,139	1.42
	IMR4064	41.0	3,029	1.10
	IMR4350	48.0	3,123	.91
	IMR4350	50.0	3,286	1.10
Sierra 90 HP Boat Tail				
	Big Game	47.0	3,149	.80
	IMR4064	41.0	3,041	.96
	IMR4350	50.0	3,289	.95
Hornady 100 SP Interlock				
	Big Game	44.0	3,017	1.08
	IMR4895	41.0	3,007	1.11
	IMR4350	48.0	3,214	2.03
	W760	48.5	3,187	1.52
Hornady 117 SST				
	IMR4064	38.0	2,781	1.14
	IMR4350	43.5	2,860	1.19
	IMR4350	46.0	2,984	1.72
	W760	45.0	2,931	1.96
Hornady 120 HP				
	Hunter	44.0	2,722	1.58
	IMR4064	38.0	2,702	1.04
	760	43.5	2,803	.54

270 Winchester Short Magnum

The 270 WSM seems to be earning the same good reputation in the game fields as its ancestor, the 270 Winchester. The 270 WSM produces good bullet and accuracy and all with fairly light recoil that won't loosen your shoelaces.

The 270 WSM is an easy cartridge to reload. The only problem I encountered was the cartridge neck was too short to properly fit in the neck of my powder funnel. When I tried to pour the first pan load of powder into a case the powder ran outside the neck. Grinding a quarter-inch off the funnel neck solved that.

The 270 WSM's neck length of 0.2765-inch is short and hunting weight bullets seated in the case stick into the pow-

der space. The 7mm Remington and 300 Winchester Magnums have even shorter necks and their bullets also protrude in powder space, but it's not a problem. Even with 0.20-inch of a bullet's base protruding into the short magnum's powder space, there's still room for plenty of powder.

The following are some loads for the 270 WSM fired through a Winchester Model 70 Classic Stainless wit a 24-inch barrel:

Loads for the 270 Winchester Short Magnum

Bullet (grains)	Powder	Weight (grains)	Velocity (fps)	100 Yard Group (Inches)
Nosler 130 Ballistic Tip				
	H4831	68	3,251	1.77
	Magnum	69	2,996	1.46
	Reloder 19	64	3,037	.62
	Reloder 22	68	3,163	1.59
Speer 130 FB				
	H4831	68	3,242	1.80
	Magnum	68	2,928	.95
	H4350	59	2,960	2.22
Swift 130 Scirocco				
	H4831	65	3,095	.93
	Magnum	70	3,013	1.92
	Reloder 22	68	3,181	1.54
Hornady 140 SST				
	H4831	66	3.165	1.10
	Magnum	70	2,958	1.04
	Reloder 22	67	3,098	1.02
Nosler 140 Ballistic Tip				
	H1000	69	3,080	1.70
	Reloder 22	67	3,136	1.13
	H4831	65	3,171	1.30
Nosler 150 Ballistic Tip				
	H4831	64	3,017	.98
	Reloder 22	64	3,030	1.26
	Reloder 25	66	2,971	1.34
Speer 150 BT				
	Magnum	69	2,972	.88
	H1000	66	2,889	.67
	Reloder 22	64	2,922	1.71

7mm Winchester Short Magnum

Winchester's 7mm short magnum duplicates the performance of the standard length 7mm Remington Magnum because both have nearly the same powder capacity. Near as

The Nosler 130-grain Ballistic Tip bullet reached 3,251 fps in the 270 WSM with 68.0 grains of H4831. The 270 WSM's neck length of 0.2765-inch is short and hunting-weight bullets seated in the case stick into the powder space. But that's no problem because the case contains plenty of room. (150-grain Nosler shown here.)

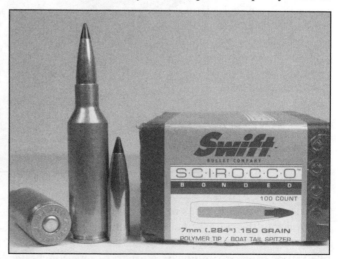

With heavier bullets, like the Swift 150-grain, the 7mm SAUM shot best with relatively slower burning powders like H1000.

Redding makes reloading dies for the 7mm SAUM Remington.

RCBS makes reloading dies for the 7mm WSM.

I could weigh, a Winchester brand 7mm Remington Magnum case holds 85.1 grains of water right up to the top of the case mouth and a Winchester 7mm WSM case holds 81.3 grains of water. Hodgdon Powder lists charges of about two grains more of its powders for the 7mm Winchester compared to the 7mm Remington, with light-weight bullets like the 140-grain. With heavier bullets, like the 160-grain, Hodgdon lists one to two grains more powder for the 7 mm Remington. Ramshot Powders lists one to two grains more powder in the Winchester magnum for all bullet weights compared to the Remington magnum.

I loaded the 7mm WSM with a variety of Hodgdon and

Ramshot powders and discovered the velocities for the 7mm WSM pretty much mirrored the velocities from my records on the 7mm Remington Magnum.

Ramshot Magnum powder performed the most accurately across the board of bullet weights, and usually with the highest velocity. Magnum started Nosler 175-grain Partition bullets out of the barrel of the Sisk rifle at 2,912 fps and grouped three bullets slightly under one inch at 100 yards. The same load in the Winchester Featherweight lagged about 50 fps, but grouped the Partitions in 0.47-inch. Actually, all seven powders listed in the load tables produced good accuracy and velocity with one or more bullets.

Here are some loads for the 7 mm WSM fired through a Sisk Rifles with a 23-inch Lilja barrel:

Loads for the 7mm WSM

Bullet (grains)	Powder	Weight (grains)	Velocity (fps)	100 Yard Group (Inches)
Nosler 140 Ballistic Tip				
	H414	61.0	3,224	.93
	H1000	71.5	2,904	1.21
	H4350	61.5	3,024	.91
	Magnum	76.5	3,172	2.01
	Retumbo	71.5	2,877	1.02
Sierra 150 HPBT Match				
	Hunter	64.5	2,981	1.14
	H414	59.5	2,947	1.10
	H1000	71.5	2,918	.96
	Magnum	76.0	3,110	.63
Nosler 160 AccuBond				
	Hunter	62.5	2,937	.61
	H414	57.0	2,865	1.33
	H1000	69.0	2,856	1.45
	Magnum	75.0	3,071	1.92
Sierra 168 HPBT Match				
	Hunter	61.5	2,896	1.14
	H4831	63.0	2,940	1.29
	Magnum	73.5	2,984	.54
Nosler 175 Partition				
	Hunter	60.0	2,796	.78
	H4831	57.0	2,638	1.23
	Magnum	72.0	2,912	.98

7mm Remington Short Action Ultra Magnum

Opinions floating around the shooting sports world hold the 7mm Remington Short Action Ultra Magnum doesn't quite measure up to other 7mm magnums. That's unfortunate because the Remington 7mm SAUM's performance is right up there with several other 7mm magnums and delivers it in accurate and compact rifles.

Remington's 7mm short magnum is a 404 Jeffery (or Remington 7mm Ultra magnum) case shortened to 2.035 inches. A 7mm SAUM cartridge with an overall length of 2.80 inches just fits in the magazine of a Remington Model Seven action, which is actually a bit shorter than a Remington Model 700 short action. The case has a body length of 1.458 inches and a neck length of 0.311-inch.

In comparison, the Winchester 7mm Short Magnum is based on the same case. But the Winchester case has a length of 2.10 inches (.065-inch longer): a 1.648-inch case body and a neck length of 0.243-inch. Total case capac-

ity is nine percent less for the 7mm Remington short compared to the 7mm Winchester short. However, because of the Winchester's smidgen longer case and case body and shorter neck, the Winchester case has 13 percent more powder capacity than the Remington case when a bullet like the Hornady 162-grain SST bullet is seated in both cases. Still, the Remington short magnum is loaded with only nine to three percent less powder than that loaded in the 7mm Winchester.

The 7mm SAUM shot well with a variety of powders. With 115- and 120-grain bullets Hodgdon 414 and IMR-4350 produced the highest velocity. With heavier bullets, though, the relatively slower burning powders provided the highest velocity. Reloder 22 had a slight edge in accuracy and velocity over all the other powders. Here's what the 7mm Remington Short Action Ultra Magnum turned in with a variety of bullets and powders fired through a Remington Model Seven SS Magnum with a 22 inch barrel:

Loads for the Remington 7mm SAUM

Bullet (grains)	Powder	Weight (grains)	Velocity (fps)	100 Yard Group (Inches)
Speer 115 Hollow Point				
	Big Game	58.0	3,191	1.15
	H414	63.0	3,323	.80
	IMR4350	64.0	3,328	1.45
Nosler 120 Ballistic Tip				
	Big Game	57.5	3,113	.79
	H414	64.5	3,360	1.03
	H4831	67.0	3,211	57
	IMR4350	64.0	3,333	1.00
Nosler 140 Ballistic Tip				
	H414	60.0	3,074	1.34
	H4831	64.5	3,070	1.09
	IMR4350	60.0	3,003	1.46
Sierra 140 Boat Tail				
	H414	60.0	3,023	1.24
	H4831	64.5	3,015	1.11
	IMR4350	60.0	2,981	.76
	Reloder 22	64.0	2,948	.56
Sierra 150 HPBT Match				
	H414	57.0	2,886	1.12
	H4831	61.5	2,890	1.47
	H1000	68.0	3,006	.81
Swift 150 Scirocco				
	H414	57.0	2,848	.88
	H4831	61.5	2,906	1.26
	H1000	68.0	2,951	1.12
Hornady 154 SST				
	H414	57.0	2,838	1.10
	H4831	60.0	2,829	1.91
	H1000	68.0	2,953	1.66
	IMR4350	56.5	2,803	2.10
	R19	61.0	2,898	1.93
	Reloder 22	63.0	2,963	.97
Nosler 160 AccuBond				
	H4831	60.5	2,823	1.46
	H1000	67.0	2,887	1.41
	IMR4350	56.0	2,820	1.86
	H4831	60.5	2,857	1.39
Nosler 175 Partition				
	H1000	65.5	2,769	.61
	IMR4350	54.5	2,667	1.64
	Reloder 19	58.0	2,664	1.26
	Reloder 22	59.0	2,719	.63

There was a time when almost any handload could outshoot a factory round. That is absolutely no longer true.

Cloning Factory Ammo

By Charles E. Petty

I THINK IT is both accurate and fair to say that handloaders drove the factories to improve their product both in terms of accuracy and bullet selection. If you look at old ammo catalogs you'll see that most cartridges only had one or two bullet weights and styles. The bullets were the company's standard with identifiable trade names and they established brand loyalty with good advertising and word of mouth.

But in the years after World War II, companies with names like Nosler, Speer, Sierra and Hornady offered shooters bullets you couldn't get in factory ammo. Of these, John Nosler's famed Partition bullet must surely have been a prime mover for it quickly built a stellar reputation as a game bullet and only handloaders could have it. Of course that was good for handloading and many hunters started the hobby just so they could have access to those bullets.

Some of you may remember back in the '60s and '70s when the best way to get brass was to shoot factory ammo and the industry liked it that way. You "could" buy new brass but it was packaged in boxes just like ammo and savings were small.

The tide began to turn in the '70s when Federal introduced their "Premium" ammo, first with Sierra and then Nosler bullets. It was a huge success for Federal, so much so in fact that they have even changed their entire

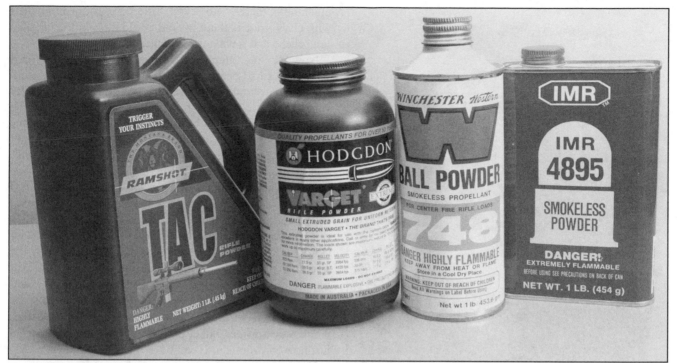

The reloader has far fewer choices in powders than do the factories.

brand name to "Federal Premium." Although I'm sure the ammo industry might not say so, I can't help but believe that while they generally sneered at handloaders they must have seen the effect on their market share and taken steps to correct it. Then again I have surely seen disdain for handloaders expressed by top ammo executives who couldn't imagine why anyone would go to all that trouble.

But the simple fact is that every American ammo manufacturer now has ammo with a "prestige" bullet or, in some cases, the choice of several and you no longer "have" to reload to have access to the latest bullet technology. Nor is it any longer a given that handloads will outshoot factory. In fact it is now sometimes really hard to get them to even equal factory. The handloader's incentive is now largely financial. After all, the factories charge pretty dearly for their top-of-the-line stuff.

I've often talked about the merit of trying to duplicate factory ammo but the topic given me here is another challenge altogether. In science a "clone" is an exact, gene-for-gene, carbon copy of another creature, so to clone ammo would mean to duplicate every aspect of the factory load. Velocity and bullet are pretty easy but accuracy is something else again. Let me tell you a story.

One of my favorite rifle subjects is the tactical or "sniper" rifle specifically the 308 Winchester. Over the years I have tested quite a few and mostly have shot best with Federal's 168-gr. Gold Medal match load. That has been the case with my Remington 700 P that has been tweaked and loved on. It has had its action trued, barrel re-crowned, trigger slicked, and has been glass-bedded too. It displayed a preference for the 168 gr. Federal load and since everyone knows good handloads are better, I set out to beat Federal at their game.

The biggest mystery about most factory ammo is the powder used, and the factories have a much wider choice than you and I. Powders that reloaders can buy are called "canister" powders and are often blended so that the 4895 you buy today will produce the same results as the batch you bought ten years ago. Factories are not so constrained because they can and do pressure test ammo several times during the day and can make adjustments if needed to stay within the pressure and velocity parameters for any given load. They buy "commercial" grades of powder that may have the same name or number we know but that can differ in the burning characteristics, sometimes quite a bit. In some cases powder manufacturers will even craft a very specific powder to meet a special need. Typically commercial powders are packed in 50 lb. drums and big companies often buy in tractor-trailer loads of 40,000 pounds or more. One of the interesting things about the powder business is that none of the ammo companies make their own anymore. Back when Remington was owned by DuPont there was an incentive for them to use their company's powder... same for Winchester but now both of those are owned by other companies. Alliant Powder is owned by ATK, which also owns Federal. Alliant's manufacturing, at least from the handloader's perspective, is largely limited to handgun powders. The fact is that a lot of the powder used in this country is imported from Europe, Canada, South Africa and Australia.

None of the ammo companies are going to make an on-the-record statement of what powder and charge they use but I was able to learn that Federal had several "qualified" powders for their 308 Match ammo including both 4895 and 4064. Of course this wasn't exactly a surprise since both are very popular with reloaders but with that information I set

If we are really trying to duplicate a factory load we have to use their primers.

out to copy Federal. We know that they use the Sierra 168-gr. Match King bullet and Federal GM primers and their own brass so this should be an absolute cakewalk. Sometimes being wrong is good experience.

I began by acquiring a good baseline of results with the factory ammo including extensive chronograph data and accuracy results with my Remington. Then I began handloading using Redding Competition dies and both 4895 and 4064. I used once-fired Federal brass and went through all the rigmarole "said" to be vital to loading good ammo. The primer pockets were uniformed and cleaned shiny new, flash holes were deburred and all the cases trimmed to a standard length, their mouths painstakingly chamfered and deburred. Of course I had the great Sierra bullets, Federal's match primers and the patience of Job.

It wasn't hard to work up loads that duplicated the velocity of the factory ammo. I did that by loading groups of five rounds, varying the weighed powder charges by one grain—later, half a grain—until my ammo came in at 2700 fps, the average velocity for the factory ammo. My loads used the same OAL as the factory ammo which put the bullet further off the rifling than I would have liked but my job was to equal the factory ammo, not change it. Over the course of many rounds my rifle had averaged 0.541-inch five-shot groups at 100 yds. with the factory loads and my wonderful handloads did 0.763-inch.

I suspect by now you are asking how could that be? You may also expect that it is a complete mystery to me. I've seen the ammo loaded at the factory and it is done on the same

machines—there is no secret little back room populated with elves—nor is there pixie dust floating in the air. The tired cliché… it is what it is… applies here.

Now the only thing I did different was to use once-fired brass, but it had been fired in the same rifle and just neck-sized so that should have given me an advantage. It is pretty common to see a slight improvement in accuracy on the second loading of new brass since it is fire-formed to the gun. Of course I did not give up. Next I took some more once-fired brass, sized it, went through all the other stuff, and then carefully turned the necks just enough to remove any irregularities—and there were some high spots—loaded and went back to the range. This time my results were equal to, or slightly better than, the factory.

Right about now it might be easy to jump to the conclusion that it is impossible to "clone" factory ammo. By the scientific meaning—strictly speaking—it is very difficult because we simply don't know—or have access to—"exactly" the same components. We all know there can be some variation from one lot to another in any component whether it is powder, primer, bullet or brass but it is less understood just how convoluted this can be.

None of the ammo companies make powder anymore so they have to buy it somewhere. Actually there are only two manufacturers of smokeless powders in the United States: Alliant in Radford, Virginia, and St. Marks Powder Co., in St. Marks, Florida. St. Marks is the former Olin (Winchester) plant that is now owned by General Dynamics. But there are numerous offshore sources and the ammo companies can—and do—have powders crafted for specific applications we know nothing about.

All the major ammunition manufacturers make their own primers and, generally speaking, the primers you and I can buy are the same—but the factories also have the ability to

The great Nosler Partition bullet was responsible for many hunters becoming reloaders.

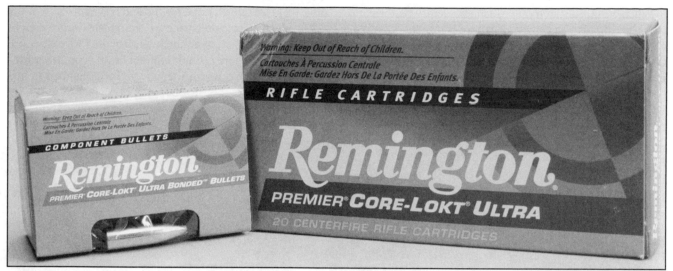

Major manufacturers now make their own specialty bullets and sell them as components, too.

make a special primer if they need it...maybe they need just a little more (or a little less) oomph for one specific load. If so, it is a relatively simple matter to tweak the primer chemistry just a little to fit a special need.

Bullets are yet another difference. You and I would usually think that if it says "Remington" on the box the bullet is made there too, and it usually is—but it doesn't have to be. After all, there are companies like Hornady, Sierra and Speer who make good bullets and sometimes they're cheaper to buy. Sometimes too there is a competitive advantage to be gained by telling everyone you use a Sierra Matchking or Nosler Partition in your ammo.

So, for the sake of discussion, let's take a slightly lenient interpretation of "clone" and say "duplicate." Not too long ago the Lyman Reloading Manual had the practice of indicating a "factory duplicate" load in their data. I really found this helpful because very often that was all I needed to do with a handload.

There is only one way to really achieve that goal, though, and that is to chronograph the factory ammo and see how fast it goes and how well it shoots in your specific gun. Modern electronics make it perfectly reasonable for every serious reloader to have a chronograph and if you think about the costs of shooting gear, chronographs are among the least expensive. You can buy a perfectly functional chronograph for less than a hundred dollars and a really fancy one for less than the cost of a good scope. You will be surprised at the differences between "real" and published velocity numbers, and the velocity measurement process is a great addition to the hobby.

Trust me on this: the data printed in the ammo catalogs is obtained with test barrels under controlled conditions and you will not get that. Duplicating factory ammo is simply impossible without a chronograph. The loading manuals can be misleading, too. I can't begin to count the number of times a shooter at the range has asked me to chronograph one of his handloads. I'm usually glad to do that as long as it sounds reasonable but, almost without exception, they

Sometimes the bulletmaker's name on the box is a selling point, such as Winchester's use of Nosler bullets. Federal's famous Gold Medal rifle ammo uses Sierra bullets. Barnes has one of the best game bullets around with the solid copper X-Bullet, which was recently improved and renamed Triple Shock.

will tell me the chronograph is wrong because, "The manual said it was..." Well, my chronograph is rarely wrong but they have sometimes missed the fine print in the manual that told about all the components and the length of the test barrel. Chances are the handloader has differences in some or all of those elements.

When we talk about trying to achieve factory performance from handloads, the success or failure involves not only the components we use but also the equipment and "how" we do the job. Reloading gear is almost always a lifetime investment so it's a good idea to buy quality in the beginning. I think presses should be heavy as hell and of cast iron that will never flex. and always move in a straight line. If the press doesn't put the brass in the die the same way every time, there isn't much hope for the end product.

The electronic scale is one of the greatest advances in reloading ever. They save time by the ton and while they are not necessarily more accurate than a beam type, the convenience they offer is worth the money. I also happen to like the powder dispensers, not because I believe you gain anything by weighing charges to the nearest microgram, but again because of convenience. While the dispenser is doing

A sturdy press is the first requirement for good handloads. It is much easier to prime cases with a separate tool; either hand- or bench-mounted.

its thing I can be doing something else, like seating bullets.

I like neck-sizing and have come to favor the bushing-type dies where they are applicable, and benchrest seating dies so I can ensure the bullet is seated as straight as possible. Anything that gives more precision in the loading process is likely to find a way to my bench, but as much as we'd like to think so, there isn't very much about shooting that is an "exact" science.

Every component of the shooting equation has a built-in set of variables and we can see this every time we chronograph a string of shots. It is so rare as to be almost unheard of to ever get exactly the same speed from two shots in a string, and that is why we really must rely on average velocities to make decisions. We often get lots of statistical information from our chronograph but the number that gives us the most useful information is Extreme Spread (ES); the difference between the slowest and fastest shot in the string. Everyone talks about Standard Deviation (SD), but it really doesn't tell us anything we can't get from ES and only begins to be meaningful when we have large sample sizes and history.

Our attempts to duplicate factory ammo do not have to turn into back-breaking projects. We already know which brass and primer to use, and unless a specialty bullet is required we can usually find the exact product in bulk form from one of the component sellers like Midway USA. That lets us narrow things down to just finding a powder and even though we probably don't know what is used in the factory ammo we can turn to one of the major loading manuals for help. All we need to do is check the book to see what powders come close to the velocity we've found for the factory load. Since the broadest data often comes from bullet companies we may not have loads for the exact components we want but it is almost always safe to begin our quest with the "starting" load shown that comes closest to matching our target.

Of course we know the rules about "working up" to maximum loads but let me offer another hint. It's pretty rare these days to shake a round of factory rifle ammo and hear powder rattle around. The reason is that they know that most consistent performance is usually obtained with a powder charge that fills the case, leaving very little air space when a bullet is seated. It is my practice to avoid anything other than very light compression of the powder charge unless there is something that suggests results from greater compression will be superior.

You may have noticed that I haven't mentioned anything about powder burning rate. Burning rate charts can be confusing or get us in trouble. Just because one powder is right next to another on the chart doesn't mean the two are going to behave in the same manner when we load them. Perhaps they will, but there are no guarantees. Nor will the chart give any hint about how a load might shoot for you.

The most important thing for us reloaders to remember is that it is pretty tough to "improve" on factory ammo. Making bullets go faster does not automatically make them better and we first need to worry about actual velocities in our own real guns.

Practical loading procedures do not need to be modified and, while competition dies are nice, we can load perfectly good ammo with standard dies of good quality. I am concerned, though, about the average reloader's... how can I put this nicely... "cheapness" that often involves using brass picked up by the side of the road or maybe at Civil War bat-

Digital scales and powder dispensers greatly improve speed and accuracy when charging cases.

Lyman's combination scale pan and funnel is a wonderful gadget to have.

tlefields. While it is certainly possible to find nice once-fired brass discarded at the range, there is also the chance that it was left behind because it was no longer any good. I know the cost of brass is a major expense in reloading and going up at alarming rates, but how can we hope to equal the factory's efforts if we don't start with brass of known heritage?

One critical issue for us is the determination of overall cartridge length. The industry has a set of voluntary standards that are established to be sure that everyone's ammo will fit in everyone's gun. Length standards are often limited by a gun's magazine and leave us little maneuvering room, but very often we have room to make the round a little longer and this frequently helps accuracy. It becomes a trial

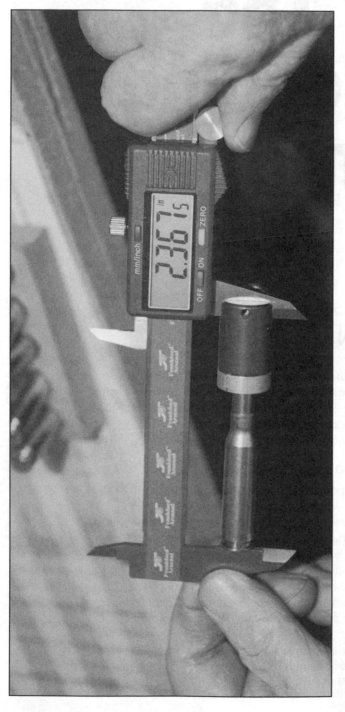

and error procedure and we already know about those, but unless our rifle's magazine limits us we can often find better accuracy by adjusting OAL.

In order to find out how we're doing in our search for better ammo we have to develop a testing procedure and ensure that all our loads are treated the same way. There is plenty of debate over how this should be done but the procedure is only going to be worthwhile unless we do it the same way each and every time. The shooter needs a good rest and has to remember not to flinch or jerk the trigger.

Accuracy shooting is the best way I know to learn about something called "random distribution," or the Bell Curve. The guy who goes out and fires two shots and proclaims he has found the Holy Grail is doomed to disappointment if he ever uses that load again. We need to find a way to balance a reasonable expectation of valid results against the onerous and expensive chore of shooting hundreds of rounds to obtain a statistical certainty that we have the right answer.

There is no single "right" way to test. Rifles with skinny barrels can start to throw flyers as they heat up and large bore, high-capacity cases will heat a gun faster than smaller cartridges. Heat per se is not the villain; rather it is how the barrel responds. We know that steel expands as it gets hot and tubes warp so we can see shifts in point of impact due to the effects of heat. The conclusion here is that we want to shoot the minimum number of shots that will yield the needed information. For sporter rifles the trend now is toward three-shot groups while heavy-barrel varmint rifles more often get five-shot groups.

The condition of the bore is also important and common practice is to begin with a clean cold barrel and fire one or two fouling shots before record groups are fired. I think a minimum is three groups and we should base our judgments only on the average of all three. In my practice I begin by looking for clues so I'll pick several powders that seem promising and load sets of three with the starting load, the maximum and one right in the middle of the spread. Chances are that one or two powders will show better accuracy and that preliminary information can be used to determine what powder deserves further work. Then I'll take the charge that came close to the desired velocity and shoot the required three groups. Of course we have already chosen the load we're trying to clone and will use its case, primer and bullet so the only major variable at this point is powder.

The process is intended to narrow our choices with as little shooting as possible, but I've learned through sometimes-painful experience that a load that looked wonderful today can be positively awful tomorrow. Thus, if the load is something that may be used a lot I'll shoot it on several different days, preferably with a wide range of temperatures and weather conditions. It's really hard to find a load for all seasons.

Getting the right overall length can be critical 20-10 Benchrest seating dies help ensure straight-line seating.

Make better
handloads,
Be more
productive.

New Gear For The Reloading Bench

By JOHN HAVILAND

THE FOLKS WHO manufacture reloading equipment are hard-core reloaders themselves and are always on the lookout for new wares to help hobbyists produce better handloads, spend more productive time at the loading bench and learn more about handloading.

Let's take a look at some of these new products.

Books and CDs

Books and CDs by the experts are the best way to enjoy and learn more about reloading.

Lyman's *Reloading Handbook, 48th Edition* is unique because it provides loads with bullets from a variety of bullet companies and cast bullet loads. In addition to loads for the latest magnum cartridges the Handbook also provides loading information for obsolete cartridges like the 25-20 WCF and 38-40 WCF and smokeless powders loads for old blackpowder cartridges like the 40-65 Winchester and 50-70 Government. Chapters in the Handbook cover articles by gun writers on loading accurate ammunition to pressures and bullet flight.

The Lyman *Shotshell Reloading Handbook, 5th Edition* devotes 230 pages to reloading data for cases, wads and primers offered by all leading manufacturers from the .410-bore to the 10 gauge. In addition, the latest and

New reloading gear helps you shoot your best, whether it's off the bench at the range or in the field.

most popular powders from Alliant, Hodgdon, Accurate, IMR, VihtaVuori, Ramshot and Winchester are included.

The Shotshell Handbook includes an expanded section on loading nontoxic shots like bismuth, Hevi-Shot and steel. To accompany the nontoxic loads are four articles that cover the development, history and use of nontoxic shots. Other chapters contain tips on using shotshell loading machines, case identification and slug and buckshot loads.

Sam Fadala wrote Lyman's *Black Powder Handbook, 2nd Edition*. This manual includes thousands of pressure-tested loads using Goex and Elephant brand blackpowders, Pyrodex RS, Select and P, Pyrodex Pellets for a large assortment of round balls, conicals and sabots. Down-range velocities and energies are also given for each load.

Fadala covers such topics as choosing your muzzleloader, building the best loads, propellants, ignition and maintenance. In addition, blackpowder cartridges are well covered with the help of Mike Venturino. There are also hundreds of pressure-tested blackpowder loads for such cartridges as the 45-90, 45-100, 45-110 and 45-120. Cowboy action calibers such as 44-40, 45 Colt and 44 Special are also covered in both handguns and rifles.

The Speer *Reloading Manual #14* has been updated to include loads for all the new super short, short and ultra magnums. It contains a very interesting chapter on black-

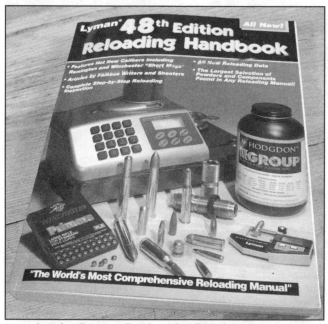

Lyman's *Reloading Handbook, 48th Edition* is unique because it provides loads with bullets from a variety of bullet companies, and cast bullet loads. In addition to loads for the latest magnum cartridges, the *Handbook* also provides loading information for obsolete cartridges like the 25-20 WCF and 38-40 WCF and smokeless powders loads for old blackpowder cartridges like the 40-65 Winchester and 50-70 Government.

Wolfe Publishing has gathered all *Handloader* magazines from 1966 to the current issue and put them on collections of DVDs

Wolfe Publishing has also put some difficult-to-find classic books on firearms and reloading on CD.

Rifle Bullets for the Hunter, published by Ballistic Technology, is a definitive study on rifle bullets.

powder cartridge performance, advanced loading techniques, progressive reloading equipment and short- and long-range ballistic tables out to 500 yards for all of the Speer bullets containing trajectories, retained velocity, energy and time of flight.

Wolfe Publishing has gathered all its *Rifle* magazines from 1969 to the latest issue and its *Handloader* magazines from 1966 to the current issue and put them on collections of DVDs. With a click of the computer mouse you can find what yesterday's masters such as Wooters, Hagel, Zutz and Waters wrote about rifles, handguns and shotguns and what today's experts such as John Barsness, Mike Venturino and Brian Pearce think about modern firearms and reloading.

Wolfe Publishing has also put some difficult-to-find classic books on firearms and reloading on CD. Stuart Otteson's *Bolt Action Rifle Volume 1* and *2* is a must for students of the rifle. Otteson covers popular bolt-action rifle models by exploring their history and design, strengths and weaknesses and illustrating their nuances in drawings.

The "Art of Bullet Casting Collection" CD contains articles on bullet casting from issues of *Rifle* and *Handloader* magazines on basic to advanced bullet casting, as well as the *Bullet Making Annuals 1* and *2* and *Cast Bullet Special Edition* that cover techniques and tools to cast and swage bullets.

The Bullet's Flight, by Franklin Mann details Mann's experiments with rifles and ammunition and the ballistics of small arms. Firearms Pressure Factors unravels the mysteries of internal ballistics rifles, shotguns and handguns with an in-depth study of velocity and pressures. *The Gibbs' Cartridges* explores the Rocky Gibbs' line of cartridges from the 1960s that created quite a controversy with their front ignition technique.

Rifle Bullets for the Hunter, published by Ballistic Technology, is a study on rifle bullets. The book contains background chapters about the history of bullets, theories of stopping power and testing rifle bullets. Seven gun writers cover bullets for varmints, deer and big game and cast bullets, solids and muzzle-loading bullets.

Lee Precision

Knowing the hardness of your lead alloy is an immense help in developing an accurate cast bullet load. The Lee Lead Hardness Testing Kit is an easy method of helping determining that hardness. The Kit contains a calibrated ball indenter that screws into a reloading press, a V-shaped cradle to hold a bullet, a 20-power microscope and a conversion chart.

A bullet must have a flat filed on its side to accept a hardness impression from the indenter ball. The bullet is placed flat up in the cradle that snaps in a reloading press shell holder. The press ram is raised to contact the bullet with the indenter ball and then raised slowly until the indicator rod is flush with the top of the indenter tool. That position is held for 30 seconds to get the proper impression on the bullet. The diameter of the impression is then determined by looking at it under the microscope that has a scale of 0.002-inch divisions.

The chart converts the diameter of the indentation on the bullet to a Brinell Hardness. In the case of a bullet cast from wheel weights and 2 percent tin, the indenter ball left a 0.060-inch diameter depression. According to the chart, that meant the metal had a BHN of 14.3. That hardness sounds close, as the tin added to the wheel weights somewhat hardened the alloy.

Lyman

Lyman's 1200DPS III Digital Powder System combines a precision electronic powder scale and an automatic powder dispenser into one product. The new DPS dispenses powder twice as fast as the original DPS and features an Auto-Repeat Setting enabling you to throw a precise charge automatically each time the pan is put in place. This scale has the capacity to store up to 100 favorite loads that are easily recalled by cartridge, specific powder and weight. Powder weights are accurate to plus or minus 0.1-grain.

The 1200 DPS PC Interface accessory allows transferring memory directly from a computer to the DPS Powder System. This interface also has a separate Digital Reloader's Log for storing thousands of loads in standard reloader's log format with a section for comments.

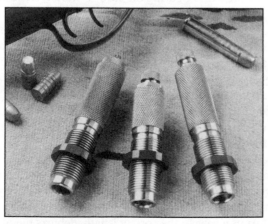

Lyman Classic Dies.

A kit is also available to upgrade DPS I and DPS II to perform just like the DPS III.

I've found electronic dispensers require at least 20 seconds to measure 70 or more grains of powder. That adds up to a lot of time if you're loading 50 or more cartridges. To save time, I set a manual powder measure to dump powder a few grains light of the intended weight, pour the powder into the pan of the electronic dispenser and let the electronic dispenser dribble in the last bit of powder.

The Lyman E-Zee Flo powder trickler features a vertically adjustable base that adapts to even the highest platform. The powder trickler tube has an extension that has enough reach to use with electronic scales that have a wide platform base.

Lyman's 1500 grain scale features an electronic scale that comes with a removable powder trickler that works in right or left hand mode. The 1500 is accurate to 0.1-grain, features a fold-back dust cover and handy storage tray that stows an included calibration weight, AC adapter and cleaning brush. The scale also works with a 9-volt battery for use at the range.

The 1000 XP is accurate to 0.1-grain over the full range of its 1,000 grain capacity. The scale works with a 9-volt battery or with AC adapter and includes a calibration weight, powder pan and AC adapter.

The Lyman Power Trimmer uses a175 rpm motor in 110 or 220 volts. Included are nine pilots for most the most popular calibers. Trim lengths of cases are uniform with a fully adjustable setting. The cartridge case lock and unlock is quick to use with just a twist of a handle. The trimmer includes two cutter heads, a set of primer pocket brushes and a safety guard over the cutter.

Lyman has been in the bullet casting business since its Ideal Reloading Tool Company was founded in 1884. Lyman's new 4500 Lube Sizer for cast bullets features a solid one-piece bottom casting that can be used as it is with soft lubes or with a built-in heating element for lubricating bullets with hard lubes. A longer handle with a ball knob provides more leverage for sizing and lubricating the largest bullets. The 4500 also comes with a gas check seater and stick of lube.

RCBS

I've been using an RCBS Rock Chucker Supreme press for a couple years and it has been a great press for loading everything from the short 17 Fireball to long magnums. However, to prime cases on the press required inserting one primer at a time with my fingers in the seating stem. RCBS has speeded up the priming process with

a Rock Chucker Supreme Auto Priming Unit that uses a tube feed. It eliminates the need to handle primers and has a 100 primer capacity. The Auto Prime body attaches to the press at the same place as the standard priming arm and operates with a push bar, and comes with a Large and Small primer pick-up, feed tubes and primer seat plugs.

The Gold Medal dies are the latest in a long line of dies that started when RCBS's founder Fred Huntington began

The RCBS Trim Pro 3-Way Cutter trims a case to the correct length, deburrs the outside of the case mouth and chamfers a slight angle on the inside of the case mouth—all in a single step.

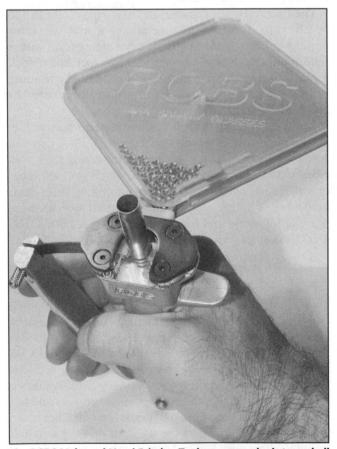

The RCBS Universal Hand Priming Tool uses one pinch-type shell holder to prime most all handgun and rifle cases. That saves using a separate shell holder for cartridges with different rim sizes and taking the tool apart and putting it back together every time you want to prime cases.

making his own bullet swaging dies in 1943. A popular varmint to shoot in the West was the rock chuck, so Huntington called his dies the Rock Chuck Bullet Swage, or RCBS. Demand grew for his dies and soon the RCBS line expanded to include reloading dies and the Bullet Swaging & Reloading press.

Huntington's first general purpose reloading press was the Model A introduced in 1949. It was built with Huntington's patented compound leverage system that removed some of the strain of swaging bullets and forming cases.

The Junior press was introduced in 1963. This smaller press was much more affordable, especially for handloaders just entering the game. A Junior was my brothers' and my first reloading press and we used it to load tens of thousands of rifle and handgun cartridges. The last cartridge I loaded on that Junior press was a 7mm Winchester Short Magnum. Bullet run-out of that cartridge was 0.002-inch, which shows the press ram is as tight and perfectly aligned as the day we bought it.

Precise alignment of the ram and reloading dies is essential on a press. That is insured several ways on the Rock Chucker Supreme press. The Supreme's 1-inch diameter ram is centerless ground, or ground from two sides at once, to make sure it's round. Once inside the press frame, the ram has 12.5 square inches of bearing surface to help it remain in alignment with the reloading die. Drilling the holes in the press for the ram and the reloading die so they are straight with one another is critical for alignment.

The RCBS Piggyback 4 is a great accessory for the Supreme press for those who want to step up to a progressive press, but lack the cash or bench space for another press. The Piggyback 4 attaches to the top of the Supreme press and handles cartridges in length up to 30-06.

The Piggyback 4 uses Automatic Priming System's primer strips to continuously feed primers during loading. The APS plastic strips isolate the primer under the force of being seated in the case. That's a good safety feature because if a primer fires somehow during loading, its flame cannot reach other primers and touch off a whole tube or tray of primers.

Assembling the Piggyback 4 kit, installing it on the Supreme press and figuring out how to work it smoothly to load 38 Specials took about one hour. The piggyback held the sizing die, case mouth expander die, powder measurer, powder checker die and bullet seat die. All I had to do was set a fired case in the first station and a bullet on the case charged with powder, pull the handle down and back up, rotate the Star Wheel to advance the cases and watch the loaded cartridges pile up in the bin. When I was finished, I unscrewed the Piggyback from the Supreme press and stored it in under my bench.

The RCBS Trim Pro 3-Way Cutter has been on the market for a couple years now. I don't know how I ever got along without one. The 3-Way Cutter replaces the regular cutter head on any of the RCBS case trimmers. All in one step it trims a case to the correct length, deburrs the outside of the case mouth and chamfers a slight angle on the inside of the case mouth. That saves untold hours of work doing the separate steps deburring and chamfering cases.

Complete 3-Way Cutters are available with one pilot of popular calibers from 17 to 37. Chamfer pilots of different calibers are available so you can use just one 3-Way Cutter head for trimming cartridges of different calibers. However, adjusting the deburring blade on the cutter head to remove the correct amount of brass takes quite a bit of time and trial and error.

The Universal Hand Priming Tool uses one pinch-type shell holder to prime most all handgun and rifle cases. That saves using a separate shell holder for cartridges with different rim sizes and taking the tool apart and putting it back together every time you want to prime cases.

The VLD Deburring Tool has a longer nose and puts a deeper bevel and more of an angle on the inside of case mouths so long and tapered very low drag bullets seat easier in cases.

The Hand Case Neck Turner Kit is a precise way to turn cases necks to the correct thickness. It come with a Quick Change Case Holder to hold cases with different head diameters and a cutter that adjusts neck rim thickness and how far down the neck the cutter reaches. Pilots are available from 17 to 50 caliber.

Gold Medal Match Dies are RCBS's newest dies. The Gold Medal's sizing die is either a full-length or neck-sizer with changeable neck bushings of various diameters. Inserting the correct neck bushing for your cases reduces work-hardening of brass and prolongs case life. These neck bushing dies also improve accuracy if case necks have been turned to a uniform thickness and the cases fired in a correspondingly dimensioned chamber.

The Gold Medal seat dies have a micrometer-adjustable bullet seating plug and a window on the side of the die to insert a bullet. An O-ring holds the bullet in and aligns it in a sliding guide so the bullet enters the case mouth straight.

Redding

The Model 2400 Case Trimming Lathe uses an extended cast iron frame to accept today's long magnum cases up to 3.25 inches in length. A push button chuck lock simplifies fastening and removing cases and helps align the case mouth and trimmer pilot. A micrometer helps adjust case trim lengths by as little as .001 of an inch. The Model 2400 Case Trimming Lathe is supplied with a universal collet, replaceable titanium nitride coated cutter, 22, 24, 25, 27, 28 and 30 caliber pilots, two neck cleaning brushes and large and small primer pocket cleaners.

While you're preparing cases, use the Primer Pocket Uniformer to square up primer pockets and make sure they are all the same depth. The Flash Hole Deburring Tool removes burrs on primer flash holes inside the case.

The Case Neck Gauge is a quick way to sort cases by neck wall thickness and uniformity. This tool has a dial indicator accurate to 0.001-inch that allows you to accurately measure neck wall thickness of cartridge cases to determine uniformity, and whether the case requires neck-turning to 'true' its neck wall thickness.

Two mandrel sizes are supplied to allow measurement of all cases from 17 to 338 caliber and including cases with small (0.060-inch) flash holes. The Gauge's base can be clamped right to the edge of a reloading bench. Pilot stops of 22 and 30 caliber are supplied with the tool and fit inside new and resized case necks and will not pick up imperfections at the case mouth, resulting in accurate indicator readings.

The Redding Deluxe Die Set includes both full-

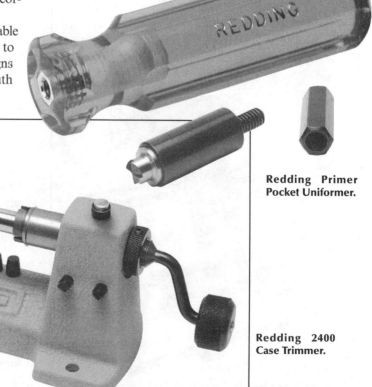

Redding Primer Pocket Uniformer.

Redding 2400 Case Trimmer.

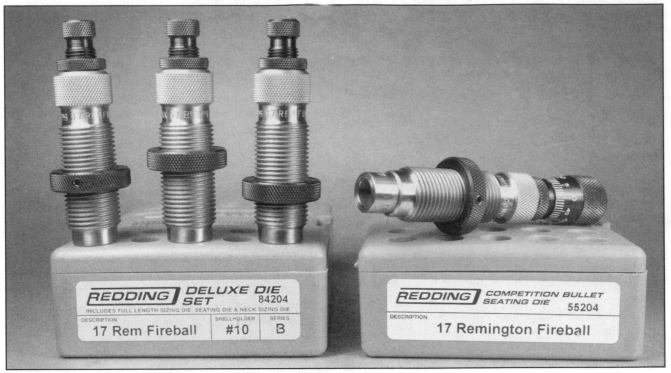

The Redding Deluxe Die Set includes both full-length and neck-sizing dies and a seating die.

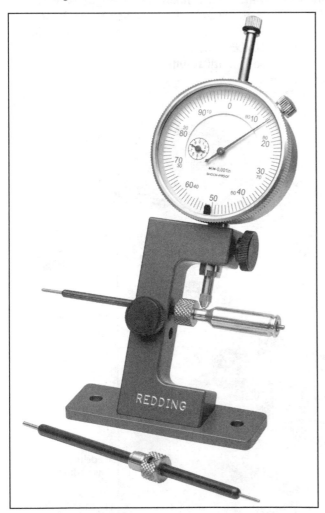

Redding Case Neck Gauge.

length and neck-sizing dies and a seating die. While loading the new Remington 17 Fireball with the Deluxe set I used the neck-sizing die to size just the case necks for three loadings. That saved having to apply and remove sizing lubricant, and kept the cases just the right size to fit snugly in the Remington Model Seven's chamber. After many loadings, though, some cases expanded enough that, to fit in the chamber, a bit of a push down on the bolt handle was required to chamber them. That sort of torque on the action can cause a bullet to fly wide of aim. Then I switched to the full-length sizing die to reduce the cases bodies and set the shoulders back so they fit easily in the chamber.

While you're at it, buy a Redding Competition Bullet Seating Die. The case chamber of the Competition Die is so tight that oversized brass may not fit in the die. A sliding sleeve in the top of the die aligns the case neck with a sliding bullet seating stem and, once again, tolerances are so tight oversized bullets may not fit in the die. The micrometer bullet seating adjustment on the top of the die adjusts bullets seating depth 0.001-inch with each increment on the barrel. That takes the guesswork out of seating bullets that last little bit to achieve an exact cartridge length.

Forster

In one step the Forster Precision Plus Bushing Bump Sizing Die sizes the outside diameter of a case neck and sets the correct amount of headspace in line with the case's centerline. The die is easy to adjust and prevents overworking necks, allowing you to control the amount of neck tension for your bullet seating. The bushing in the die is adjustable to allow you to partially or totally resize the length your case necks to an exact diameter.

As famed writer
Robert Ruark
advised long ago,
"Use Enough Gun."

AMMO FOR THE BIG BOYS

By Chub Eastman

A LONG TIME ago a famous outdoor adventure writer, Robert Ruark, wrote a book called *Use Enough Gun*. (Safari Press) It was a great classic read about one of his numerous trips to the Dark Continent and contained his experiences with game animals both large and small. Quite a bit of the text was on critters that had a bad temper and would just as soon see you in the happy hunting grounds in the sky as look at you. Even though the book was written many decades ago when the modes of transportation and safari camps were a lot more primitive than they are in this day and age, the animals pursued and collected are the same. Same tenacity for life, same bad attitude and the same tendency to charge rather than run away when provoked or cornered.

After finishing the book it is easy to understand the reasoning Ruark used when it came to the title. He related that for the smaller plains game most any reasonable rifle and ammunition combination would get the job done in good fashion. However, when it came to the "Big Boys" and the ones that can hurt you, he came to the conclusion something bigger was needed to handle the situation at hand.

With the exception of elephant and rhino, the game he encountered in his adventures are not that much different in size, and sometimes attitude, than big game we have on the North American continent. Our North

This great 8x6 New Mexico bull elk dropped in his track from a Kimber 325 WSM and a 200-grain Nosler AccuBond.

This nice 6x6 bull elk from British Columbia fell with one shot from a 338 Win. Mag with a 250-grain Swift A-Frame.

American bison are near the same size as a cape buffalo, lions and leopard are similar in size and attitude to our grizzly and cougar and the eland and kudu have a lot of the characteristics of a bull moose and elk.

His conclusion to *Use Enough Gun* rings true to any responsible hunter who goes afield in pursuit of our North American species as it does someone planning a trip across the pond. This is especially true when it comes to the big critters. As a hunter you have the responsibility to use equipment that is capable of dispatching the game you pursue quickly and humanely. *Use Enough Gun* is still available through Amazon.com and other places.

I've been asked and have heard the question asked to experienced big game hunters and outfitters what rifle/cartridge combination they should bring on their elk, moose or big bear hunt. If you read between the lines when the answers are given you will come to the conclusion there is no such thing as being over gunned. Most will suggest a 7mm Mag., any good 30 caliber, .338 or larger if you can shoot it well. I have never heard an outfitter suggest a .270 Win. or something smaller. If a client insists on a rifle/cartridge like this they make it very clear that the heaviest premium bullets be used.

I know I'm stepping out on a limb with that statement and am sure there will be a few comments about 30 years of one shot kills with their magic .270 Win. and I know that a .270 Win. will kill an elk properly if the bullet is placed perfectly. In that case a .243 Win. will do the same thing. The .270 Win., .243 Win. and smaller cartridges are good deer and antelope medicine. However, and that's a big however,

American bison are tough and tenacious. It took two shots from a 338 Win. Mag. using the 250-grain Barnes –X-Bullet.

Good friend John Barsness collected his meat for the winter with his 9.3x62 and a 285-grain Nosler Partition.

with elk, moose and bears you are pursuing an animal that is three to four times as big as a large whitetail buck. The hide is thicker, muscle tissue is thicker and denser especially with the big bears and the skeletal structure and density is in proportion to the size of the animal.

I have a good friend and hunting partner who hunts with a .280 Rem. which is just slightly larger than the .270 Win. with powder capacity near identical. He has elk horns hanging from almost every wall in his house. But, he is a dedicated, patient and very good game shot who will not pull the trigger until the animal is broadside with the heart/lung

area exposed. Even then he will very rarely take the shot if the range is much over 100 yards. I have seen him pass up shots 99% of other hunters would have taken only because he didn't feel confident enough the shot would be on target. That's elk but when it comes time to head north with a moose tag and the real possibility of grizzly in the area the .338 Win. Mag. with 250 gr. Nosler Partitions comes out of the gun cabinet.

Another instance that happened to me a few years ago convinced me big bullets with a high sectional density are a lot better than relying on velocity and hydrostatic shock

Craig Boddington used a Krieghoff 500x416 with Nosler's 400-grain Partition to put a ton of Australian water buffalo on the ground.

Lars-Olof Swanteson from Sweden only uses one rifle for all his big-game hunting. His 40-year-old Krieghoff double chambered for the 9.3x64 loaded with the 286-grain Norma Oryx was more than enough for this British Columbia grizzly.

to get the job done. I was in Northern British Columbia on an elk and moose hunt with friends from Sweden. We were hunting with an outfitter buddy who had a very large area out of Fort Nelson, BC. By chance I had a grizzly tag besides elk and moose just in case we had a bear problem during the hunt.

When the hour long bush plane flight from Fort Nelson landed at base camp, the first thing the outfitter asked was if one of us had a grizzly tag. I said, "Yes" and he promptly took me aside and said he needed help as a grizzly had been raiding one of his out camps and the cook was ready to quit unless something was done. After a short conversation with my hunting partners it was decided I would be back at base camp the next day and they had time to unpack, get their gear ready and have a relaxed dinner.

All I had time to do was grab my rifle, ammo and day pack before we were in the air headed for his out camp twenty miles away. When we landed one of the guides had the horses saddled and we were on the trail twenty minutes after landing.

The guide knew approximately where the bear should be back of camp. After about an hour ride we were in an area of small hills with patches of dense timber that bordered a large flat area of nasty muskeg with chest high brush you couldn't walk through without a machete. The only change in the landscape was a twenty foot wide strip through the middle that had been cleared by a seismograph crew years before.

After hours of scouring the surrounding hills for sign we stopped at the edge of the muskeg flat and decided to take the cut line the seismograph crew had left back to where we had left the horses. It was going to be dark soon and this was the fastest way.

As we were discussing our next move the damnedest racket of roars, jaws snapping and brush being thrashed broke the silence. Couldn't tell where it was coming from but knew we didn't want to be in this area when the sun went down so we headed the cut line as quickly as we could. If you have ever encountered a muskeg flat you can understand the pace was not too fast.

We had stumbled and sloshed approximately two hundred yards from the tree line when that sixth sense tells you something isn't right and puts the adrenalin on overload. We both froze in our tracks and turned to the right just as a loud "whoof" and what looked like an elevator emerged out of the brush fifteen paces away.

This was not the time where hunter and guide discuss strategy, it was the time where two guys were in trouble and the only thing that happened was pure reaction. What seemed like minutes was actually milliseconds as both rifles went up and discharged so closely together it probably sounded like one shot. The bear disappeared and there was no sound. I racked the bolt so fast and hard on my old Model 70 I'm sure that piece of brass is still in orbit. It was just a practiced reaction that would have not done much good as the bear was too close if a second shot was needed.

There is a large selection of premium bullets from most all bullet manufacturers, just pick the one that shoots best in your rifle.

Premium bullets come in all configurations but all are designed to achieve maximum penetration. L/R: Nosler AccuBond, Nosler Partition, Barnes-X, Barnes Triple Shock, Swift A-Frame, Swift Scirocco, Hornady Bonded, Woodleigh Bonded and Norma Oryx.

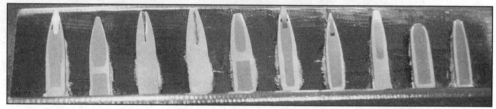

After what seemed like hours and we could breathe again we separated about twenty feet apart and slowly started through the brush to see what happened. When we were close enough to see through the brush we saw the bear was down and not breathing. The relief that flooded over both of us was almost bad enough we might have to change our underwear and my hands were shaking so bad I couldn't get a cigarette lit.

The lesson learned was the fact that bigger is better for big critters. My Model 70 was chambered for 338-06 with a 250 Gr. Nosler Partition. My guide's rifle was a Ruger Model 77 chambered for .270 Winchester loaded with a 150 Gr. Nosler Partition. Both shots hit the bear in the center of the chest not an inch and a half apart. When we performed the autopsy to see what happened, the 250 Gr. 338 Partition had hit the heart and lungs and severed the spine before stopping just under the hide on his back. The .270 150 Gr. Partition went through the breast bone, hit the heart and was lodged in the top of one lung. The .270 Win. was a kill shot but did not immobilize him. At that close range, 15 measured paces, there would not have been enough time for a second shot even though the pump was stopped and the air let out of him.

Where he fell was right on top of a moose carcass he was feeding on and the roars and noise we had heard was a fight he had just had with another grizzly. When he stood up in front of us I'm sure his thoughts were that we were next.

As a side note the outfitter purchased five all weather stainless .338 Win. Mags. and three boxes Federal Premium ammunition with 250 Gr. Nosler Partition for each. Numbers were painted on the stocks and one was put in each of his five out camps with instructions that guides were not to leave camp without one in their saddle scabbard.

Big critters need firepower with stay-together type premium bullets that give the maximum penetration. Not every opportunity presented for the shot is perfect. In a lot of cases the bullet must have enough weight and sectional density to plow through a lot of hide, meat and bone before it gets to the vitals. Even then it has to have enough energy left to do the damage it was designed to do.

Unlike deer, antelope or caribou, the big animals, especially moose, are relatively unaffected by the shock of a bullet strike. The metabolism and body size of each has a lot to do with how each animal reacts. Thin skinned game such as deer and antelope usually react dramatically and leave no doubt of a hit. Elk will vacate the area when hit but mostly to get away from the sound of the shot. Moose are really different as they are almost impervious to shock. I have seen moose hit square through the boiler room when feeding in a meadow and only raise his head to see where the shot came from and then go right back to feeding until his legs buckled and fell over with the browse he was feeding still in his mouth. A grizzly and even black bear will snap and bite where the bullet hit, acting more like he was just stung by a wasp.

Torb Lindskog, President of Norma, collected this nice Swedish bull moose with his O/U 9.3x74R using the factory 286-grain Oryx bullet.

We are blessed today with a bullet selection for almost every caliber that will get the job done on the Big Boys. There are numerous styles and configurations but all have one thing in common and that's penetration. Most every bullet manufacturer has developed a premium type bullet for big game. Some are a partition style where a partition separates the front half on the bullet from the back that stops the bullet expansion from going any further, therefore retaining most of its weight. Bonded style is where the lead core is actually bonded to the jacket so when expansion occurs the lead core cannot separate from the jacket. Another bullet developed is pure copper with a hollow point to start the expansion. With this style weight retention is near 100%. Each manufacturer has a different approach to their premium bullets. They vary in jacket thickness, position of the

partition, bonded, front section solid copper with a rear lead core and one just the opposite with the lead in the front half and rear solid copper. They all work, they are all designed for maximum penetration which is what is needed for the Big Boys.

Many premium bullets available for reloading are now loaded in higher end factory ammunition, including Winchester Supreme, Federal Premium, Remington Premier and Black Hills Gold.

Remember that accuracy is more important than velocity. If the bullet goes in the wrong place it doesn't matter how good it is. The other thing to remember is the cost of a premium bullet is a very very small price to pay when you consider the cost of license, fuel, food and camp.

And lastly *Use Enough Gun.*

You want safe,
accurate handloads,
so which information
will get you
the best results?

Whose Loading Data Should You Use?

By Dave Workman

PERHAPS THE MOST perennially loaded (no pun intended) question that beginning, and even some seasoned, reloaders ask is "Whose reloading data should I trust?"

The easiest answer to that is to begin with eliminating sources of information you probably should *not* trust in your quest for the "perfect" handloads for your particular firearm. First on the list: Don't simply walk, *run* from some of the data you might see on the Internet offered by somebody who posts information under an alias like "Nitro Burner."

Instead, the responsible reloader, whether a veteran at the game or a novice, should invariably go with the experts; that is, follow the reloading data found in published reloading manuals from companies that manufacture bullets and propellants.

End of story, right? Not hardly. It is a bit more complicated than that, and for good reason. There are a lot of reloading components on the market, and there are several quality reloading manuals available, and this may come as a complete surprise to some folks but the data is not necessarily interchangeable. You should not substitute one powder for another, and the same goes for bullets that may weigh the same and even look similar.

Don't take my word for it. Instead, pay attention to what the bona fide experts say.

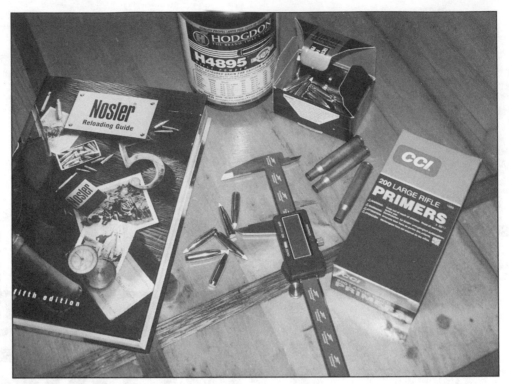

Quality reloads depend on good information. If you use bullets from Nosler, for example, consult the Nosler reloading manual, make sure you have the right propellant for the job, and always rely on good primers, like the ones from CCI.

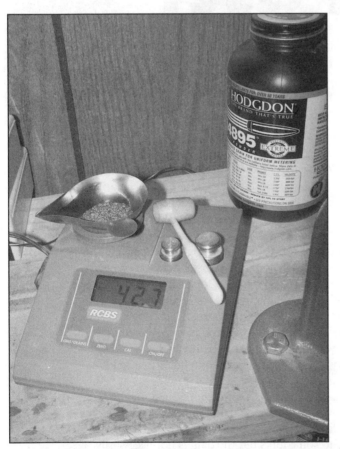

Before weighing a powder charge, place your pan on the scale and zero it. That way, the only weight that registers will be that of the actual powder charge, in this case, 42.7 grains of Hodgdon's H 4895. Author strongly recommends using an electronic scale, which gives accurate readouts.

"There is some excellent data out there," acknowledged Bob Nosler, whose father, John, founded the Nosler Bullet Company in Bend, Ore. What this guy doesn't know about the manufacturing of bullets probably has not yet been discovered. He understands bullets inside and out.

His advice: "Use the data supplied by the specific bullet maker, and use the data provided by powder manufacturers as long as it is for a specific bullet. The data that I don't care for is data that is not specific, but generic. I think a person would be wise to start conservative."

That is, begin with the lightest generic load recommended for a specific weight of bullet, and work up gradually, watching for signs of excess pressure.

Hornady's Steve Johnson concurs on this advice, and he added this tip: "Pay attention to what they (loading manual authors and technicians) use for components."

Johnson stressed that it is important to look for different details, particularly to see whether the recommended load in one manual has used one brand of primer and whose brass is used, while the load in another manual uses a different primer and brass.

For example, Johnson noted, if you were to crack open a Hodgdon loading manual or their magazine-like *Annual Manual*, looking for specific data for a particular bullet, and then consult a Hornady manual for the same projectile, the recommended loads might vary by one or two grains of powder, because the Hodgdon technicians may have used a different primer, or different brass, or both.

You see, in the reloading game, all things are not equal, and if a reloader approaches this subject as if one size fits all, the result could be disastrous.

Different types of projectiles will invariably require different data for reloading. Author is a fan of the 41 Magnum, and from left-to-right are the Nosler 210-grain JHP, the Speer Gold Dot and Speer's 200-grain JHP.

Workman uses a single-stage press to reload all of his rifle cartridges, such as this 308 Winchester. This time, he's topping off with a Nosler 150-grain Ballistic Tip.

Left to right are three 100-grain bullets that reloaders might select for use in any number of 25-caliber cartridges, such as the 250/300 Savage, 25-06 Remington, 257 Roberts or the 25 Winchester Super Short Magnum. Left-to-right, the Speer boattail, Nosler's Ballistic Tip and Sierra's hollowpoint. Note difference in length, and bearing surface.

Now, here's a dilemma Workman confronted: the obvious difference in design and bearing surface for two superb bullets for the 45 ACP cartridge. On the left is Nosler's 185-grain JHP, and on the right is the Barnes 185-grain all-copper hollowpoint. They weight the same, but that's about it.

My longtime friend and one of the genuine gurus of handloading is Allan Jones, now retired from Speer, but author of that company's past three loading manuals. He put it in simple, blunt terms: "It used to be that bullets were bullets, and they were all built pretty much the same, but not anymore."

Today, if one takes a careful look at bullet construction from one company to the next, there are enough significant differences between similar-looking projectiles that it is imperative to "go to thc source."

"Go to the prime source of data for a particular bullet, and that is the maker of that bullet," Jones stated. "I believe loading data has become more brand-specific because bullets are made differently. We see different pressures for the Speer Gold Dot, for example, than if we shoot a (similar) bullet from a different manufacturer."

Sierra's Carroll Pilant, that company's sage promotions manager, added, "We recommend people use the data from the company whose bullets they are using."

And here's an example why: Pilant noted that the famous Barnes X-Bullet may bear some resemblance to a Sierra projectile, but they may have a longer bearing surface (the bullet surface that actually comes in contact with the bore) and that can translate to a significant change in pressure if you were to use a propellant charge recommended for a Sierra bullet to propel a Barnes projectile.

For the record, I have shot bullets from Barnes, Sierra, Speer, Hornady and Nosler, and if one were to consult different reloading manuals, one will find different recommendations for propellant charges that may vary by as much as one or two grains even though the bullet weights are identical.

But there is good news this year. The Barnes solid copper bullet has gone through another evolutionary step, and the X-Bullet has been replaced by the new Triple Shock X, a projectile that has grooves cut on the shank to improve expansion and also reduce bearing surface. According to Ty Hearing, Barnes' customer service director, the new Triple Shock X loading data will be much closer to data for other bullets of the same weight.

In January 2008, Barnes was scheduled to publish its new loading manual with fully-updated data based on this improved bullet design, said Roger Glazier, public relations and marketing representative for Barnes.

Here's just one example of the variances that illustrates the dilemma for handloaders in terms of varying data: Loading the 308 Winchester with a 165-grain bullet.

In *Speer Manual No. 13*, the data on Page 282 lists a maximum charge of 49.0 grains of IMR 4350 for a muzzle velocity of 2,751 fps (fps) using their superb boattail, and notes that this is a compressed load. However, Nosler's Fifth Edition manual for their 165-grain Ballistic Tip, which is also a boattail, lists a maximum load of 50.0 grains of the same propellant on Page 302. That is also a compressed load, producing a muzzle velocity of 2,792 fps.

Not only should you have the manual on hand for the brand of bullet you're using, but have a reliable cross-reference from the powder company! Hodgdon's *Annual Manual* looks like a magazine, but it is loaded with current data.

What did you learn just now by reading the above paragraph? That guy Workman has more than one reloading manual at his disposal! Darned right I do, and in that mix you will find the most recent Hornady two-volume set, plus a Lyman manual, a manual from Sierra and a hardcover manual from Hodgdon Powder, along with the aforementioned *Annual Manual* on a shelf right next to my reloading bench. I keep a Barnes manual at the office unless I need it at home, along with an older Speer manual, and I consult them faithfully and frequently.

Am I deranged? No, just careful. My rifles and handguns are valuable investments, and so are my fingers, hands and eyes, and I don't care to risk any of them by goofing around at the loading bench, mixing and mis-matching data that should be used for one maker's specific bullet, substituting it for the data for somebody else's product.

It is imperative to have the most up-to-date manuals available, said Hornady's Johnson.

"Everybody thinks data is more conservative now than it was 20 years ago because everyone (in the industry) is scared of lawsuits," he said. "That's not correct. Actually, the data is so much better today than it was 20 years ago, because we are relying on more accurate equipment."

Hornady now uses a device called a "strain gauge" to measure the radial expansion of a barrel chamber when a cartridge is fired. This measurement may be in the hundred/thousandths of an inch, but it is critical to accurately measuring chamber pressure. Johnson said this device didn't exist when some earlier manuals were written.

"The data in the days of old; we didn't really know what we had," Johnson acknowledged. "We were safe, but we've gotten a lot better technology."

Perhaps the "text book example" (or in this case, the loading manual example) would be to compare the data found in Hornady's Third Edition manual published in 1980 to data in the Sixth Edition, published in 2003. On Page 170 of the earlier edition, Hornady lists a maximum charge of 49.8 grains of IMR 4064 powder for the 270 Winchester using Hornady's 130-grain No. 2730 Spire Point bullet. Open the Sixth Edition to Page 277 and look up the data for that same bullet, and now the maximum charge is 48.6 grains of IMR 4064, yet both loads are supposed to deliver 3,000 fps muzzle velocity.

Just to show that Hornady is not alone in its updating of data, recall my reference above to the .308 Winchester load listed in the *Speer Manual No. 13* (my most recent edition) listing a maximum charge of 49.0 grains of IMR 4350 for a muzzle velocity of 2,751 fps using the 165-grain boat tail bullet. Journey back to 1979 and *Reloading Manual No. 10*, and on page 226 of that relatively ancient volume, you will find that the maximum recommended load in those days was 52.0 grains of IMR 4350 for a muzzle velocity of 2,755 fps.

"The bottom line," Johnson observed, "is that if somebody has a 10-year-old loading manual, it's time to go spend $30 on new manuals."

Bob Nosler does not entirely agree that yesterday's data is obsolete, insisting, "Some of that ten-year-old data is good stuff."

"There are a lot of guys who stay with a good load, and that load doesn't change from year to year, or from book to book," he said, reminding me that I am a living example. Bob knows me, and he knows my gun preferences, particularly for one cherished bolt-action rifle in my gun safe.

I have been using the same two loads for a prized 257 Roberts built on a Mauser 98 action with a Douglas barrel, for the past 20 years. This particular load is topped with the 100-grain Nosler Ballistic Tip and it has served me faithfully. The load consists of 37.0 grains of IMR 4895 for a muzzle velocity of 3,120 fps and Nosler lists that load as its recommended maximum and most accurate with that powder. It has worked well enough to put both mule deer and Western whitetail bucks in the meat locker for me, and one does not argue with venison on the table, or little tiny groups on a 100-yard target!

As it happens, that 100-grain Nosler has the identical ballistic coefficient and sectional density as the 100-grain Speer boattail, and I have discovered much to my satisfaction that the same powder charge behind that bullet also produces remarkable accuracy, though the bullets have a slightly different point of impact.

Now, there is more. It's that "other" load I was talking about: 37.0 grains of H4895, which is not the maximum generic load listed in Hodgdon manual No. 25 for 100-grain bullets. Hodgdon says a maximum load of 38 grains of H4895 is acceptable for a listed muzzle velocity of 2,990 fps. Also, it lists a maximum 37-grain load of IMR 4895 producing a generic muzzle velocity of 2,826 fps, roughly 300

fps *less* than the velocity listed in Nosler's manual.

It can take a few years for any company to update its hardcover reloading manual, but Hodgdon's *Annual Manual* addresses that timeliness problem by actually coming off the press every year with updated information on literally thousands of loads. I have found this handy magazine-size reference guide to be invaluable and educational.

Chris Hodgdon, the third generation at this family-owned powder company, told me that the philosophy behind the *Annual Manual* was straightforward and remarkably simple: "Our theory is that reloaders are looking for the most updated information they can find, especially concerning the new cartridges. When a hard-bound manual is introduced, it is already out of date because they are behind in listing some of the news cartridges that are introduced."

That said, he insisted that the hard cover books are "great resources" for updated information on existing cartridges.

The *Annual Manual*, Hodgdon said, provides information at a reasonable price, and with a particular focus. For example, the 2007 edition concentrated on the 50 most popular cartridges among shooters today, including the newer "short-fat magnums" such as the 223 WSSM, 243 WSSM and 24 WSSM. The 2008 edition will have a different focus, but you can bet that the data will be up-to-date and reliable.

Hodgdon technicians, just like the specialists at Speer, Hornady, Nosler, Barnes and Sierra are continually doing research on their loading data. At Sierra, Pilant told me, "We're constantly working on more data. That is a long, drawn-out process."

Nosler confirmed that the same philosophy is at work at his Bend, Oregon plant, especially because it seems as though every year, someone is bringing out a new cartridge and bullet makers simply have to keep up.

"There are a lot of new products out there," Nosler

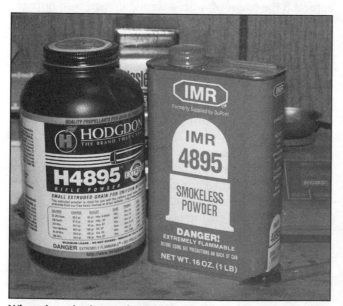

Whopping mistakes can be made by people who think one powder with the same numeric designation as a propellant from another manufacturer will deliver the same results. Loading data can vary by as much as two or three grains!

Serious handloaders will brew up cartridges for whatever rifle and/or handgun they might have in their gun safe. Author keeps his dies on a shelf below his bench, in their original boxes. Note that he has dies from several manufacturers, and he trusts them all.

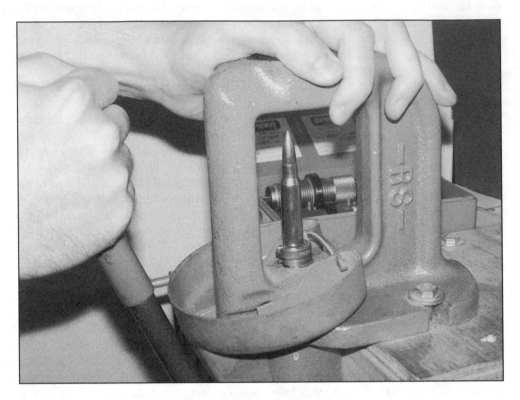

One other thing you'll find in a loading manual is data for overall cartridge length. Make sure you have this small detail in mind so that when a cartridge comes out of the press, bullets (like this 150-grain Speer) are seated to the proper depth.

observed, "a lot of new cartridges, a lot of new propellants and a lot of new bullets. We, as a company, have to stay on top of that. It's like keeping a checkbook balanced. If you don't stay on top of it, you get behind so quick that you can't ever catch up."

Nosler confessed that he still personally helps out with shooting for data if things get backed up. I suspect he enjoys it quite a bit.

Reloading technicians develop loads for different types of bullets of the same weight by selecting the bullet with the greatest amount of bearing surface, working up the powder charges based on that bullet's performance. The wisdom of this is that other bullets in the same weight class, but of different design, will perform with the same powder charges at lower pressures, but with nearly identical velocities.

Selecting powders is another part of the process. Pilant noted that at Sierra, technicians will select from the most popular propellants, and include any new ones that may have been recently introduced, work up data on all of them and then select perhaps a dozen of the most consistent loads for inclusion in their manual.

One benefit of the *Annual Manual* is that it includes loading data for three different brands of propellants: Hodgdon, IMR and Winchester. Hodgdon markets all three brands, and it specifies which company's bullet it uses. For example, on page 73 of the current *Annual Manual*, there are 76 different loads involving seven different bullets from five different manufacturers. In this case, the Hodgdon, IMR and Winchester powder data should be used in cross-reference with data from such bullet makers as Speer, Barnes, Hornady, Nosler and Sierra.

While it is true, as noted above, that I have long ago found a pet load for my 257 Roberts and I stick with it, I am not so stubborn that I am not willing to adjust my loads based on new information. No matter how much experience someone has at the loading bench, you should be equally open-minded. One is never too old to learn.

Some years ago, when I first started shooting a 41 Magnum revolver, I used a load suggested by the late Elmer Keith using then-Hercules 2400 powder, and found them to approach the realm of a fire-snorting dragon with horrible recoil when pushing a 200-grain Speer hollow-point bullet, at least in my revolvers. At the time, I consulted Speer *Reloading Manual No. 10* (which I still have) and found the maximum recommended charge of 2400 was 18.5 grains, using a CCI No. 350 Magnum Large Pistol primer, for a muzzle velocity of 1,384 fps out of a Model 57 Smith & Wesson with a 6-inch barrel, one of the guns I was shooting at the time, and still own. (I also own a pair of Ruger Blackhawks in that caliber.)

That load still seemed a bit hot for my six-guns, with some cases showing flattened primers, so I backed off a full grain after some experimentation, reducing the load to 17.5 grains. That worked like a champ behind the Speer 200-grain bullet.

Lo and behold, *Speer Manual No. 13* recommends a maximum load for that same 200-grain bullet today as 16.8 grains of 2400, now made by Alliant, for a muzzle velocity of 1,311 fps. This particular load does not suggest a magnum primer.

Now, suppose you want to switch bullets, and go with the slightly heavier and much different-shaped Nosler 210-grain

JHP. A quick check in Nosler's fifth edition manual shows a maximum powder charge of 16.7 grains of 2400 for their 210-grain, .410 bullet, for a muzzle velocity of 1,500 fps. Even a casual glance at the Nosler and Speer bullets shows just how different they are, with far different bearing surfaces, not to mention a difference of 10 grains in weight.

Aha, there is more to this puzzle! Look at Hornady's sixth edition loading manual and the data for *their* 210-grain XTP jacketed hollowpoint lists a maximum load of 20.0 grains of 2400 to produce a muzzle velocity of 1,350 fps, out of the same Model 57 S&W wheelgun. If I opt for H110, the Hornady manual lists a maximum load of 22.7 grains, while my 19.0-grain load is a half-grain below the minimum listed in their chart!

You can consult the Sierra manual and find two separate listings for the 41 Magnum, one for revolvers and the other for single-shot handguns such as the Thompson/Center Contender and Encore. The revolver load, once again, was tested in a Model 57, and the maximum suggested load of Alliant 2400 for the Sierra 210-grain hollow point is 18.9 grains for a muzzle velocity of 1,200 fps. That same bullet, pushed by a charge of 19.0 grains of 2400 out of the Thompson/Center gun generates 1,550 fps from the muzzle.

Quite a difference, all around, eh? Now do you see the importance of following loading data from the manufacturer of a particular bullet or powder? The caution could spare you a damaged firearm.

Now, we've just discussed a single cartridge and all the available variations in data from one source to another. Same or similar bullet weights and bullet types, same test gun, same propellant, but because different companies manufactured these bullets, the data is remarkably varied. It all boils down to the specific bullet design, and that brings us back around to the subject of bearing surface.

According to the now retired, but still very savvy Allan Jones, "Bearing surface is a 'heavy hitter' influence on pressure." What may seem like the slightest difference in bearing surface between bullets can translate to a significant increase in chamber pressure. This is yet another reason that careful reloaders should have more than one, and perhaps a minimum of three different reloading manuals as reference guides.

Here's another example of the importance of having more than one reference. The 30-06 Springfield is quite possibly the most popular big-game rifle cartridge today, and it has been around for 100 years. In the early days, bullet choices were very limited, but today, every bullet maker produces several types of 30-caliber projectiles that work very well in this cartridge.

Once again, depending upon whose bullet a reloader uses, the data can vary enough to make a significant difference in chamber pressure if someone starts substituting components. Let's look at data for IMR 4064, a very popular propellant among reloaders. The Hornady manual on my desk lists a maximum load of 49.2 grains of 4064 behind their 180-grain boattail bullet for a muzzle velocity of 2,700 fps, which is rounded off, according to Hornady's Johnson.

Now, take a look at the Nosler manual for a 180-grain Ballistic Tip, and there you will find a maximum recommended powder charge of 47.0 grains of IMR 4064, for a muzzle velocity of 2,580 fps.

But reach for the *Speer No. 13 manual*, crack it open to page 298 and you will find their recommended maximum load for a 180-grain Speer boattail bullet being 50.0 grains of 4064, resulting in a muzzle velocity of 2,756 fps.

And data for the new Barnes Triple Shock X 180-grainer shows a recommended maximum load of 48.0 grains of 4064 for a muzzle velocity of 2,639 fps.

In addition to the dilemma of similar-looking bullets of the same weight producing far different results, the reloader also must be aware that some reloading propellants have similar designations, but they are not the same. This is most prevalent in powders produced by Hodgdon and IMR. Examples that come to mind are IMR 4895 and H4895, IMR 4831 and H4831, and IMR 4350 and H4350. Adding to the confusion is the presence of AA 4350. While the powders with identical numeric designations often show *similar* loading data, they are not the *same* in any given manual.

Try this example: in just the Hornady manual, data for the 30-06 cartridge using Speer's 190-grain spire point boattail bullet shows a maximum load of 51.8 grains of IMR 4350, a maximum of 52.0 grains of AA 4350 and a maximum of 52.8 grains of H4350.

Jump down to the 220-grain Hornady roundnose bullet for the same cartridge and you find a maximum load of 53.8 grains of IMR 4831 listed, while the maximum recommended charge of H 4831 is 56.6 grains! Because these powders have different burn rates, albeit slight, it is imperative to use the data for the specific powder.

This is where the powder scale is critical, because you must weigh your powder charges for consistency, and to make sure your loads do not exceed the recommended charge weight in grains. I use an RCBS electronic scale, and I strongly encourage every handloader to invest in one of these because they are so precise.

To further insure that your loads are consistent, be sure to re-size your brass, trim to recommended length according to the case dimensions in your loading manual (that's probably the one feature that is consistent between all reloading manuals!) and clean it in a tumbler.

Are you sufficiently confused? Good, because confusion makes one more careful and attentive, and when you are producing your own ammunition for use in your personal firearms, the ultimate responsibility for safety rests entirely on your shoulders. There is no room for foolishness, and failure is not an option.

Fortunately, every reloader has a tremendous "support staff" consisting of every technician at every bullet and powder manufacturing company in the nation. These folks are the experts, and if you follow their advice, using *their* data for *their* products, it is hard to imagine ever going wrong.

Whether you load for rifle, revolver or pistol like the 45 ACP Colt Commander show here, paying attention to details and following recommended loading data from a good manual can produce this kind of result on the range. Now, it looks like five holes, but author put six rounds into this target from 25 yards for a test he did in Krause's, *Gun Digest, The Magazine* a sister publication to the ABC's of Reloading.

We have an absolute
embarrassment of
riches when it comes
to the number of
smokeless powders.

The Lowdown on Powder Burn Rates

By R.H. VanDenburg Jr.

SO WHAT IS the story on the burn rates of all these powders? Most hand-loaders realize that in addition to the great number of powders available, the percentage actually useful in any particular cartridge is actually quite small. Why that is and what it means to us is what we are going to take a look at.

Most powders, and all we are concerned with, have nitrocellulose as a base component. Nitrocellulose is manufactured by treating (nitrating) cellulose, the principal component of wood pulp or cottonseed linters, with a blend of nitric and sulphuric acid. Water is used as a control agent. After a lengthy and detailed process, the result is nitrocellulose in a bulk or cake-like form. As something of an aside, a portion—and it varies from company to company—of the nitrocellulose used in the manufacture of smokeless powder is recycled material recovered from surplus military powder.

The bulk nitrocellulose then must go through a series of treatments before it becomes smokeless powder. The treatments are twofold: a physical one to determine the final shape and size of the individual powder granules, and a chemical one to further control the final product. Separately and together these treatments determine the end result in terms of usefulness, of applicability, of safety, of the rate at which the powder releases its energy when confined and, ultimately, the name on the can we purchase at our friendly gun or sporting goods store.

The many reloading manuals help us understand powders and their relationship to other components, to the cartridge and ultimately to their burn rate.

Older books on reloading often discussed powders in some detail and gave load data, but rarely mentioned burning rates.

The physical treatment is usually referred to as the geometry of the power: its physical size and shape. Most of our powders are extruded, a process whereby the nitrocellulose is forced through a die or plate with holes, creating spaghetti-like strands which are then cut to length. If the resulting lengths are shorter than the diameter, the powder is referred to as flake powder. If the lengths are the same as or longer than the diameter, the resulting powder is referred to as extruded, or in the vernacular, "stick" powder. Alliant's handgun and shotgun powders such as Bullseye and Red Dot are examples of flake powders. IMR 3031 and 4350 are examples of extruded powders. Flake and extruded powders, in addition their length and diameter can be further distinguished by the presence or absence of perforations. The recently released IMR Trail Boss, a very bulky handgun powder aimed at the Cowboy Action shooting market is one exception. Trail Boss has a relatively large single perforation, making its granules resemble tiny donuts. The reason for its bulkiness is to preclude double charging a case. Cowboy

Action shooters frequently strive for a quick recovery time between shots and gravitate toward light bullets, low velocity and small powder charges. The perforation offsets the large granules by increasing the surface area and speeding up the burning rate. In spite of its bulk and size, Trail Boss is faster burning than Bullseye. Interestingly, virtually all flake powders once had a perforation. Hercules old-timers such as Sharpshooter and Lightning and such current stalwarts as Red Dot and Herco all originally had a perforation. In the case of the latter two, changes in manufacturing technology in about 1969 resulted in the simple flake form we now recognize as almost universal.

Another flake powder that employs a different manufacturing process is frequently referred to as "sheet cut." Here, wet nitrocellulose is poured onto a flat surface to the required thickness and then dried. Once dry the sheets are cut at a slight angle lengthwise and crosswise, resulting in parallelogram-shaped granules. In years past most, if not all, Alcan powders were so made. Powders of this type are

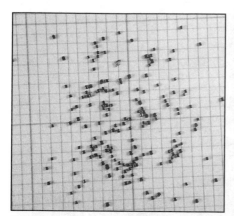

Spherical powders are most commonly used with metallic cartridges. Frequently at the slower-burning end of the scale, all are double base.

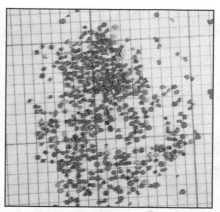

Flattened ball powders are usually paired with handgun and shotgun shells as they tend to be fast burning and prevent migration in loading.

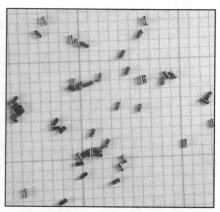

Extruded powders are most frequently associated with rifle cartridges. They can both be single- or double-base and come in a variety of lengths and diameters.

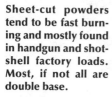

Sheet-cut powders tend to be fast burning and mostly found in handgun and shotshell factory loads. Most, if not all are double base.

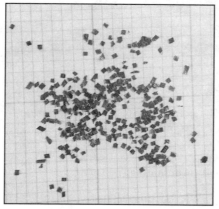

Flake powders are extruded and then cut into very short lengths. Used primarily in handgun and shotshell applications, they can be single- or double-base.

still manufactured in Europe and are currently used, among other places, in Baschieri & Pellagri shotshells, which are imported by Kaltron Outdoors of Bensenville, IL.

In addition to those extruded powders having no perforations or a single perforation are those with multiple perforations. Examples of extruded powders with multiple perforations are some of the Hodgdon Extreme series. In most instances, perforations, whether single or multiple, are not readily visible due to subsequent surface coatings.

The last commonly seen powder shape is spherical. Usually referred to as ball powder because each granule resembles a tiny ball, the term "Ball Powder" is a registered trademark owned at various times by Western Powder, Winchester Ammunition, Primex and General Dynamics. Various manufacturers refer to this type of powder as Ball Powder, spherical powder or ball propellant, all of which mean the same. In everyday use, we find there are two spherical powder types, one that retains its spherical shape, and the other that has been passed through rollers creating what is known as a flattened ball. The standard spherical shape is best in metallic cartridges where powder migration cannot occur. Flattened ball is usually preferred in shotshells to minimize migration of the powder from below the overpowder cup to the compressible area of the plastic wad where its purpose is lost. Such migration typically occurs in transport. A flattening of the balls also serves the same purpose on some

automated loading machines where the migration or escape of powder around the powder dispensing stations can create problems of cleanup and safety.

The chemical treatments to which nitrocellulose must be put to produce safe, salable and useful smokeless powders are varied. Untreated nitrocellulose would suffer a short shelf life, be very hygroscopic, susceptible to static electricity, lack fluidity, exhibit a strong muzzle flash and be unsuitable for general transport.

Perhaps the most well known chemical treatment is the addition of nitroglycerin.

This changes what we refer to as single base powder into double base powder.

Nitroglycerin, where it is used, performs two very important functions. It adds to the energy level of the powder and reduces the natural porosity of the nitrocellulose to make it less susceptible to absorbing moisture from the atmosphere. There are other methods available to address the moisture situation, of course, but nitroglycerin is an obvious solution where increased energy content is desired. Most powders developed as handgun or shotshell propellants are double base as are all spherical powders. The nitroglycerin content of such powders tends to run from a low of 4-5 percent in some rifle powders to as high as 40 percent in some handgun powders.

When a single base propellant is desired, the hygroscopic

Burn rates help to determine a powder's suitability for use in rifle, handgun or shotshell reloading.

nature of the nitrocellulose still needs to be addressed. The addition of such agents as dinitrotoluene or trinitrotoluene is frequently employed. All powders are manufactured with a prescribed moisture level. The purpose of such additives is to minimize the possibility of the level changing over time due to exposure to the elements.

Another common additive is graphite. This is applied to the surface of the granules through tumbling to improve fluidity, meaning the granules flow easily through automated ammunition loading equipment, our own powder measures and into the case or shell. Even of greater importance is graphite's ability to prevent buildup of static electricity and its potentially dangerous consequences.

While the physical geometry of powder granules serves to control the rate at which powder burns and creates the gases that propel the projectile, further control is available through the use of chemical agents. Usually this involves the surface treatment of granules to retard initial burn rate. The effect is to allow the gases to be produced more slowly while overcoming the inertia of the projectile at rest. Later in the cycle, as the powder burns past the surface treatment, the rate increases to keep up the pressure in the rapidly expanding chamber.

Other chemical additives are needed to maintain stability in transport, insure a stable and long shelf life and control muzzle flash. In some powders a decoppering agent is employed to help reduce the level of metal fouling left in the bore after firing.

What all this means to us is that each combination of case or shell capacity, bore size, projectile weight, allowable flame temperature, pressure limitation, expected velocity and a host of other variables could, indeed, call for a different rate of energy release and therefore a different powder. That a fast-burning powder suitable for the miniscule 25 ACP may also serve well in the 45 Colt and the 12-gauge shotgun, but not in the 9mm Luger, or that a slow-burning powder suitable for the 30-338 Weatherby may be totally unsuited for almost anything else, only adds to the fascination of it all and makes it such a rewarding field of study. That perhaps a dozen or so companies worldwide are vying for the same market only compounds the subject and gives us multiple powders suitable, but not interchangeable, for any conceivable component mix.

While this somewhat simplistic overview doesn't do justice to the actual complex and sophisticated nature of powder manufacture, let's turn to how powders available for reloading are presented to the shooting public. But first we need to define a couple of terms. In *Handloader* magazine, No. 4, November-December 1966, the late and noted ballistician, Homer S. Powley, inventor of the famed slide rule-type computer bearing his name, defined burning rate as "the rate at which the surface of a powder granule moves toward the center of the web as the solid powder transforms the gas at the surface." Powley went on to quantify this as typically 0.0004-inch per second per pound per square inch (psi) for a single base powder and 0.0006-inch for a double base.

Limited application powders such as these tend to be extremely well-suited for their particular niche: very large case capacity rifles; steel shot loads in 12-gauge shotshells and lead bullets in some handgun and blackpowder rifle cartridges at Cowboy Action and target velocities, respectively.

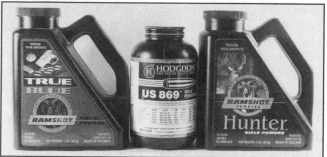

Three spherical (ball) powders: True Blue for big-bore handguns such as 44 Magnum; US869, a very slow-burning powder for large case capacity rifle cartridges; Hunter, a medium-burning rate powder, is excellent in cartridges of '08, '06 and WSM range of case capacities.

Medium-to-slow burning extruded powders: IMR 4007SSC and Hodgdon 4831SC are single-base; Alliant Reloder 22 and Norma MRP2 are double-base.

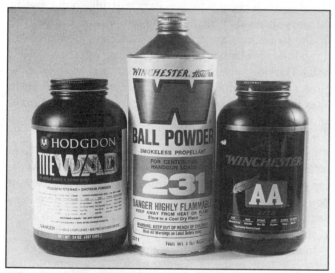

Some very fast-burning powders for shotshell and handgun reloading. All are flattened ball, double base.

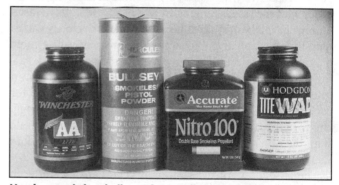

Handgun and shotshell powders: Bullseye and Nitro 100 are double-base flake types; Titewad and AA Lite are flattened ball.

Later, Powley defined the quickness of a powder as "how fast a charge containing hundreds of granules develops its pressure because of the transformation of solid to gas. He further stated that quickness can be determined in a test pressure bomb (closed bomb test) to give relative values so we can say that one powder is faster or slower than another. Then, in the context that as handloaders we use different types of powders from many different sources, "Talking about burning rates and getting this confused with relative quickness and the muzzle velocity developed devolves to a comparison of apples with oranges with lemons."

The treatment of powders in print has evolved over time by necessity. The earliest reference to rating powders by their burn rate or quickness puts the date at 1907, apparently in Europe. The earliest American treatment of powders usually included a brief discussion of each powder—there weren't many back then—and perhaps some specific load

data, without any reference to burning characteristics. The great handloading books of the early and mid-20th century followed that lead. J.R. Mattern's *Handloading Ammunition* (1926) Earl Naramore's *Handloader's Manual* (1937) and *Principles and Practices of Loading Ammunition* (1954), Philip Sharpe's *Complete Guide to Handloading* (1937, et al) and Col. Townsend Whelen's *Why Not Load Your Own* (1957) all offered a discussion of DuPont and Hercules powders and some load data but no chart or reference to comparative burning characteristics. The Ideal and later Lyman manuals did the same, adding other powder lines as time went on. It wasn't until the 48th Edition (2002) that a Burn Rate Chart (97 powders) was included.

The first appearance of a Burn Rate Chart in a handloading manual found to date was in the first *Sierra Handloading Manual* (1971), in which a chart of 71 powders appeared. It was identified as the ARA Burn Rate Chart, referring to the

American Reloaders Association, an industry trade group. The ARA subsequently gave way to the National Reloading Manufacturers Association, now inactive.

The *VihtaVuori Reloading Manual*, 3rd Edition (2000) includes a Burning Rate Chart of 107 powders, but also rates its own powders according to relative quickness. N110 is assigned the arbitrary value of 100; faster-burning powders have correspondingly higher values and slower powders correspondingly lower.

The *Norma Reloading Manual* (2004) describes each of fits powders (from fastest to slowest) including their composition, but does not rate them according to quickness. The manual does, however, offer a most interesting Burn Rate Chart of rifle powders from the most popular makers. The chart was developed by the manufacturer of Norma Powders, Bofors, also a Swedish company, and was arrived at by charging a 308 Winchester case with 43.2 grains of each powder, capping it with a 143-grain FMJ bullet and firing each load in a pressure barrel. Pressure and velocity were measured and recorded. IMR 4350 was assigned a value of 100 for each measurement and all other powders assigned values as they compared with IMR 4350. The powder closest to IMR 4350 on the fast side was VihtaVuori N160 with a pressure of 107.5 and velocity of 102.l. Closest to IMR 430 on the slow side was Rottweil R904 with values of 99.1 and 101.0, respectively. The chart is presented in relative pressure order with the values ranging from 849.8 to 38.7. It is a fascinating chart as you study it because while the velocity values tend to follow, relatively speaking, the pressure values, there are many exceptions. It also seems, based on our stated definitions, to be more of a relative quickness chart than a burn rate chart, given that the exact same conditions existed for each powder. The text introducing the chart quite tellingly states that while this chart may not be any more accurate than the others, it does provide more information and does relate to at least one real world situation.

The Hodgdon Powder Company is perhaps the leader in providing a burn rate chart as it is closing in on 200 powders. The order in which the powders are presents ostensibly is fastest-to-slowest. There is no formula or relative quickness comparison to determine the order but rather an intuitive assessment based on years of experience gained in the laboratory developing metallic cartridge load data. In a sense, because it does not rely on any one particular set of circumstances, it is likely more generally reliable than any other. Still, neither this nor any other chart is linear, i.e., some adjacent powders may be very close in burning speed while other adjacent powders may be quite far apart. Probably the Norma chart reflects these better than any other.

VihtaVuori, in its *Reloading Guide for Centerfire Cartridges,* takes another approach in listing powders vertically, from fastest-to-slowest, by brand. Further, the vertical spacing attempts to align powders of similar burn speed so the chart can be read horizontally. The chart clearly states, however, that it is for reference only and cannot be used for powder substitution.

Another interesting aspect of all this is how producers of reloading manuals and guides present their load data. Frequently there is some statement in the text that powder data are presented from fastest to slowest, but a check with their own or someone else's burn rate chart suggests that sometimes this is not the case. The reason, of course, is that relative positions of powders aren't set in stone and can vary as the component mix changes.

Speer reloading manuals used to list powder data based on the maximum powder charge, in descending order, which would generally equate to a slowest-to-fastest presentation. In the 13th Edition, however, this changed to listing powders by the maximum velocity produced, from highest to lowest.

Shotshell reloading manuals, on the other hand, are very difficult to discern because data are generally presented by case make and length, shot weight and velocity levels. Within all this, data usually appear to be presented, but not always, in fastest-to-slowest order.

The *Nosler Reloading Guide*, the latest I've seen is the 5th Edition, takes a different tack. The maximum velocity produced by each powder (within each cartridge/bullet weight category) is divided by the maximum powder charge. The resulting quotients are arranged in descending order giving the powder presentation a more-or-less fastest-to-slowest order. Harking back to the Norma chart and examining the Nosler data for a number of different categories might help to explain how the order can change from one condition to another. Order of relative efficiency might be a good way to describe the Nosler approach.

In its *Reloader's Guide*, Alliant Powder presents its load data vertically with all relevant powders appearing across the top of each page and the data appearing below the relevant powder. All metallic data are maximum charges. Reloaders are instructed to cut powder charges by 10 percent to arrive at starting loads. Shotshell data are to be used as listed.

In the end, while all powders are designed to accomplish a specific task, many of them turn out to be quite flexible in their usage. It is not possible for any list or chart to accurately portray powders in any order that is not dependent on such variables as case volume, projectile diameter or weight or any number of other factors.

Given Powley's definitions, what we, and the industry, refer to as Burning Rate Charts really aren't, nor are they Relative Quickness Charts. The name will have to do, though, as they do give us some sense of "fast" and "slow" and the relative meaning of each. Our best use of all listings or charts is as a general overview of what powders are available and their likely use. As always, reloading books, manuals and guides with their attendant laboratory-developed load data are the only reliable source for our handloading efforts. For those interested in a more detailed look at powders, their manufacture, composition and use, the European manuals such as the Norma and VihtaVuori books tend to provide more information than their American counterparts.

Loading
techniques
from bunnies
to bruins.

Blackpowder Cartridge Hunting

By Mike Nesbitt

MOST OF THE time when our discussions turn to hunting with blackpowder cartridges, we're talking about going for big game with some pretty big ammo. While those big guns for big game are certainly there, more variety can easily be found in our blackpowder cartridge loading and shooting. Looking back over the years that I've used and enjoyed reloading and hunting with blackpowder, the variety is the key that kept it all very interesting.

One of the accepted generalities about loading blackpowder cartridges is that the case must be filled with blackpowder so there is no air space left in the loaded cartridge. That is most often the way it is but that isn't completely necessary. In other words, there are some outstanding exceptions to that general rule.

Starting in the mid-1880s, there was the "short-range load" which first appeared for the 32-40 and the 38-55 cartridges. The short-range 32-40 used a 98-grain bullet over 13 grains of loose blackpowder. For the 38-55 the short-range loading used a 145-grain bullet over just 20 grains of blackpowder. The intended purpose for those loads was to take small game or perhaps for a finishing shot on a big-game animal at very close range.

Short-Range Loads

Those short-range loads are rather easy to reload for, especially if you have the mould for the proper bullets. Lyman made the bullet moulds for those bullets

Author uses jar lid while lubing short-range bullets in melted grease. These bullets, for his 303 Savage, are then "cake-cut" out of the solidified lube using a modified cartridge case.

Five of the 303 Savage short-range loads gave a fair group, just a little high, when tested on a small target.

One shot from Mike's old 303 Savage, using short-range loads, took this snowshoe rabbit.

for many years but they are not available new today. The old Lyman/Ideal mould number for the short-range 32-40 was #31950 and for the 38-55 it was #37583. Those are mentioned just in case you might find one; for a few years the bullets from these moulds were advertised for use in either 31- or 36-caliber cap & ball revolvers.

The rifle I've used short-range blackpowder loads in the most was my old 303 Savage. Yes, the 303 Savage was one of our early smokeless cartridges but for a short time factory blackpowder ammo was available with two different loadings. One of those loadings used a 100-grain lead bullet over 10 grains of loose blackpowder and that was called the "303 Savage Miniature." The other blackpowder loading in the 303 Savage was a "full load" that had 40 grains of "black" under a full-metal-cased 190-grain bullet.

I took a special interest in duplicating the old 303 Savage miniature loads soon after I was lucky enough to find one of those bullet moulds. This mould is just about as old as the catalog being mentioned and it is marked "Ideal MFG Co. – New Haven, CT – Savage .303". I also found an 1894 Winchester reloading tool for 303 Savage. Those tools combined, with comments on reloading found in an old 1903 Savage catalog, gave me the data I needed. In that catalog it said if proper smokeless powder was not available for short-range loads, simply use 10 grains of loose blackpowder.

Having the old bullet mould and the equally old Winchester loading tool allowed me to handload my 303s just the way a woodsman would have about 100 years ago. First, the bullets were cast by using the pot and dipper method, using a fairly soft lead alloy. These short-range bullets did not have to be very hard. After casting the bullets, maybe 35 or so, attention was turned to lubricating them. The bullets would be loaded and fired unsized but they needed to be lubricated. Bullets were simply placed on their bases in a jar lid, then the lid was placed in a small cast iron skillet just to assure even heating, and the skillet with the jar lid was put on the stove.

Preparing The Lube

As the lid holding the bullets warmed up, chunks of cold grease were dropped on top of the bullets. My grease was a combination of beeswax, deer tallow, and bear oil—left over from making lube for loading paper-patched bullets. Those little chunks of lube melted quickly and soon enough the bullets were all standing in a pool of liquid grease. Enough

A 5-shot group fired with the Model '92 in 44-40 at 50 yards wasn't the tightest, but all scored 10s.

One shot through the neck with a 44-40 hollow-point cast bullet did in this Oregon buck.

grease was added so the lubricating grooves on the bullets were well-filled. Then the skillet, with the jar lid and the bullets, was set aside to cool.

While the greased bullets were cooling, I made a "cake-cutter" to remove the greased bullets from the cake of hardened grease. An old 32/40 case became the basis for this tool and the base was drilled out so the bullets could be pushed clear through. Also, the mouth of the 32/40 case was chamfered slightly, just to sharpen it, and the cake-cutter was ready to use. When the 32/40 case was pushed down over a bullet, it cut the lube, freeing the bullet. The lubricant stayed in the bullet's grooves, of course, and the unsized bullets were ready to load.

The Winchester loading tool seated the bullets very well, with a good crimp, too. I charged the primed cases one at a time with 10 grains of GOEX FFFg right out of my powder horn. The powder was simply poured into my adjustable Haddaway powder measure so those powder charges were measured by volume and not by weight. Then each powder charge was poured into the empty but primed case with the powder measure's funnel. Bullets were seated to the standard depth; the old Winchester loading tool is essentially non-adjustable and the bullets could not be seated deeper than the standard depth. Priming was done with the Winchester loading tool as well, using CCI standard Large Rifle primers.

I used my old 1899 Savage saddle ring carbine for the shooting tests. That carbine had a real good barrel and was equipped with a tang peep sight, making it very capable of accurate shooting. I couldn't think of a more appropriate rifle for shooting these 303 Savage short-range miniatures.

Small Game

After trying the short-range loads on a target positioned approximately 50 feet away, I was satisfied with their grouping and was ready to try the loads on small game. Luck was

A variety of loads in 45-70 cases. L/ R: A "collar-button," 330-grain hollow-point (2 bullets on their sides and 2nd one standing), 45-70- 405 load, 45-55-405 "carbine" load, the big 45-70-500 load, a 45-75-420 Sharps and a 45-70-500 Sharps.

with me because that was accomplished the very same day as the shooting test. A snowshoe rabbit hopped out on the trail and then disappeared. I followed with the 303 carbine held ready. The snowshoe was sitting still just beyond a small bush. His coloring didn't hide him and the Savage's ivory bead found its mark on the rabbit's head.

You might say that 'rabbit test' proved positive, the rabbit died. The 100-grain cast bullet from the 303 Savage hit right where it was supposed to and there was no meat damage at all. That short-range load did its job and nothing more.

Now, while most of you won't have a 303 Savage, let me point out that the loading just described can be used with the same excellent results, by using the Lyman/Ideal bullet #3118 (now listed as #31,1008), in the good ol' 30-30.

Another short-range bullet that certainly deserves attention is the old "collar button" for the 45-70. This little bullet weighs the same as a round ball of the same .457-inch diameter, about 144 grains. The name "collar button" comes from its shape, very short and deeply grooved to hold a lot of lubricant, and to extend its length and bearing surface

A tight 5-shot group fired at 50 yards with an 1886 Winchester take-down, using 330-grain hollow-point cast bullets over 70 grains of GOEX Cartridge powder.

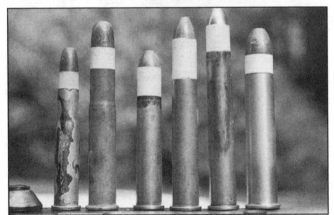

Paper-patched loads, L/R: 40-70 Sharps Bottleneck, 44-90 Sharps, 45-75-420 Sharps 2.1-inch 45-90-500 Sharps 2.4-inch, 45-105-500 Sharps 2 7/8-inch (Quigley cartridge) and the "Big 50" Sharps 2 1/2-inch.

against the bore. No one can present a complete and full description of loads for blackpowder 45-caliber rifle cartridges without prominent mention of the collar button.

Reduced loads in the 45/70 had and still have several purposes which include hunting small game and for gallery practice. In the old days some National Guard units used reduced loads in their Trapdoor Springfields for indoor target practice. The benefits of using reduced loads should be obvious; the economy of the light charges, and the drastic reduction of blast and recoil. The reduction of recoil is one of the most significant characteristics and allows all of us, inexperienced shooters and old timers alike, better control of the rifle and easier concentration.

The original loading for the collar button bullet in the 45/70 case was only 5 grains of loose blackpowder. That load was more than sufficient for target practice at distances of 25 or 50 feet. While that distance might seem terribly short, these light loads provided excellent practice.

Ray Rapine saw a need for the collar button bullet again and his version is just a little heavier than the original, about 150 grains, mainly because the lube groove on the new bullet is not as deep as the original style. This is a very light bullet for the 45/70.

Just as soon as I got my Rapine mould for the collar button bullet, that mould was put to good use. Some wheel weights were melted, and the casting was done using the good old pot and dipper method. My heat source was just a simple small fire. While this casting method, or using a fire as a heat source, does not seem to work the best for casting large quantities of bullets, it sure worked fine for me and soon there were about thirty shiny new collar buttons ready for the next steps.

Those bullets were sized and lubricated in my RCBS sizer, sized to .457-inch and lubed with BPC lube from C. Sharps Arms. Then they were loaded in new Federal 45/70 cases, seated over 10 loose grains of GOEX "CARTRIDGE" powder. I wanted just a little more "steam" for my loads than what the original 5-grain loading could give. With those steps completed, the collar button loads were ready for shooting at the range.

The rifle that has eaten these collar button loads the most is my good old Sharps Model 1874 by C. Sharps Arms, a 45/70 with a 30-inch half-round barrel. I also have tried them in my Model 1886 Winchester, although the collar button bullet is so short that the cartridges must be loaded single shot in those repeating rifles; they can't be fed from the magazine. Actually, my 1886 Winchester handles the collar button loads better than my Sharps because the Sharps has its chamber throated for use with paper-patched bullets, so the short collar button has a bit of a jump to make before entering the barrel's rifling.

With either of my rifles, the collar button loads have some real potential for small game. The average velocity with the 10 grains of loose CARTRIDGE powder is only about 450 fps. That works out to about 65 foot-pounds, so I think we can agree the collar button loads in the 45-70 are not too powerful for small game.

What the collar button does is greatly increase the range of use for rifles of 45/70 or similar caliber. There is no better load for introducing a youngster to shooting the blackpowder cartridge rifles and the light collar button loads make these otherwise big booming rifles excellent for small game. I hope to harvest some grouse and rabbits, maybe trying some interesting recipes, while using the 45-70 on big-game hunts. As a final comment about the collar button bullets, let me just say, "Small game, look out!"

Full Loads For Big Game

Now let's talk about some big-game hunting with some blackpowder full loads. There's variety in the full loads too, but we'll talk in detail about only a few of them.

To start our discussion on the full-power blackpowder loads, let's begin with an old favorite of mine, the 44-40. I've had a few 44-40 rifles but the only one I have now is a Model 1892 Winchester carbine. A lot of handloading gets done for that carbine and it did its best to show me that it has plenty of power for deer hunting.

For bullets I always use those I've cast from my double cavity Lyman mould for #427098. This is the same as the original Ideal bullet for the 44/40. And, because my mould is double cavity, I had one of the cavities hollow-pointed. That way each time I fill both cavities, I'd get one solid bullet that weighs about 215 grains and one hollow-point bullet that weighs about 205 grains. I do believe that mould is still avail-

able from Lyman but a custom machinist must be found to have one cavity fitted for hollow-pointing. Incidentally, I've done my best shooting with the hollow-point bullets.

With 40 grains of GOEX FFg, the solid-nose bullet went over the chronograph screens at 1,250 fps out of the carbine's 20-inch barrel. The hollow-point bullet, being 10 grains lighter, was a little faster at 1,270 fps.

The deer this carbine anchored for me was a fair-size fork-horn buck, a blacktail taken in western Oregon. The deer was only about 30 yards away and my bullet, one of the 205-grain hollow-points, took the buck high in the neck. That shot broke the spine but the bullet did not go all the way through.

The bullet was recovered, broken into two major pieces and there were clear indications of bullet expansion. The spine was not shattered like it often is after being hit with a high-velocity bullet, but it was badly broken.

Another hollow-point bullet that I will give a lot of credit to is the 330-grain Gould Express bullet for the 45-70, Lyman's mould #457122. This bullet is my choice for use in my 45-70 Model 1886 Winchesters. In those lever guns this bullet performs very well, although I have never personally taken a head of game with it. I was, however, on hand when a partner took a fine black bear in British Columbia with one shot while using this bullet over 70 grains of GOEX Cartridge powder in his Model 1885 High Wall single shot made by C. Sharps Arms. That bear was hit hard through the chest and it traveled a very short distance.

Loading the soft (wheel weight lead alloy) cast bullets over a full 70-grain charge of blackpowder in the 45-70 requires compressing the powder before seating the bullet. Using the bullet to compress the powder usually deforms the soft bullets. Instead, I use the expander die, which does not have a de-capping pin, to seat a card disk (punched from single ply cardboard such as tablet-backing or "shoe box") over the

Rolling the moist paper patches onto the smooth-sided bullets. At the left is a brass pattern for cutting the patches.

powder, compressing the powder to a depth needed for seating the bullet. Then the bullets are easily seated, making sure they sit all the way down on the card wad. This works very well and the bullets are not deformed at all.

When seated over 70 grains of compressed GOEX Cartridge powder, the 330-grain bullet leaves a 26-inch barrel at about 1,370 fps and is accurate. Other bullets are always being tried in my 1886 Winchester rifle but the 45/70/330 with the old Gould hollow-point is my standard load.

This brings us to the 405-grain bullet, generally the standard slug for the 45/70. The military used the 405-grain bullets in loads for their Trapdoor carbines with 55 grains of powder, but all the sporting loads I know of with this bullet used a full charge of 70 grains. Lyman's mould #457124 casts the old style 405-grain round nose and that weight is when the bullet is cast with pure or nearly pure lead. With harder alloys the bullet weighs about 385 grains. This bullet has always performed very well and I use it over 70 grains of GOEX Cartridge powder in my Model 1886.

The Sharps

Now let's talk about some of the loads for the single-shot rifles such as the Sharps. The first one I'll mention is my favorite, using the 420-grain paper-patched bullets which I cast in Rapine's mould to duplicate the old 45/75/420 Sharps loading. With the Sharps loads the bullets do not have to be seated as deeply as for use in a repeating rifle and the same 45/70 case is used. This is my usual load for my 1874 Sharps by C. Sharps Arms with the 2 1/10-inch chamber. That's also the Sharps that gets used the very most—the rifle, loads and bullets are all highly recommended.

That's the rifle I got my biggest bear with while on a hunt in British Columbia in 1996. The first shot was from the front, into the chest at only 40 yards. That hit rocked the bear back but it recovered and began to climb a large evergreen tree. While it climbed, it exposed itself for another good shot so one more 420-grain paper-patched bullet was sent in its direction. Shortly after getting hit the second time, the bear died and fell to the ground. My two hits were only

Author used his Sharps '74 with 45-75-420 paper-patched loads to bring down his biggest black bear, taken in northern British Columbia in 1996.

two inches apart and what kept the bear alive after the first hit is a mystery to me.

The first critter to be "tagged" by me using a rifle firing a blackpowder cartridge was a blacktail doe. That rifle was my Gemmer-Sharps chambered for the "Big .50" Sharps cartridge. I still use that rifle now and then with the cartridges loaded with 500-grain paper-patched bullets over 100 grains of Cartridge powder. There is also another Sharps in my cabinet, a Model 1874 heavy-barrel rifle chambered for the long 45 2 7/8-inch cartridge. That rifle usually eats 500-grain paper-patch bullets propelled by 105 grains of GOEX Car-tridge powder. No game has been taken, so far, with the big 45-105-500 but it certainly is calling for its turn.

Now, I know this story is not as detailed as it could be. My intention was to show how much variety blackpowder loads can have. Very few of the old blackpowder cartridges were produced with just one loading. The ammunition makers at the time made a good variety available for each caliber and shooters had their pick of loads. Today we have the advantage of duplicating those old loads by handloading, so we can enjoy the wide variety in blackpowder cartridge shooting.

A 5-shot group 50-yard group fired with the big 45-105-500 Sharps with paper-patched bullets.

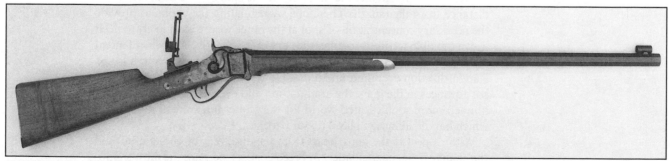

This Sharps Model 1874 has a 32-inch long heavy barrel in 45-caliber with a 2 7/8-inch chamber. Weighing 13 pounds, it was built by C. Sharps Arms, and is a very accurate shooter.

Shotshell
components and
techniques can help
you tailor loads
for the patterns you
want to create for
your kind of shooting.

Controlling Patterns With Handloads

By R.H. VanDenburg Jr.

AS ANY STUDENT of the shotgun over the past century and a third knows, the way in which we regulate the performance of our guns is through the use of choke. Choke, or a constriction or reduction of the diameter of the barrel interior at its muzzle, provides us with some measure of control over the shot charge after it leaves the barrel. While the range of useful constriction is relatively small, within that range the greater the constriction, i.e. the smaller the muzzle opening is relative to the interior of the barrel, the smaller the diameter of the swarm of shot at any given distance from the muzzle. Therefore, by regulating the choke to provide the necessary concentration of shot at the range we are most likely to need it, we are able to produce guns that are quite effective at their intended purpose. Such a set of circumstances logically would have led to a lot of standardization over time, and it did. However, in the last half-century or so, advances in the guns, the ammunition and even the shot have created a much more sophisticated world for the scattergun student and one in which handloading can play a major part.

With respect to the guns, apart from the discovery of choke itself and the change from muzzleloaders to breechloaders, perhaps the most significant change has been the development of screw-in, interchangeable choke

Fast-burning powders such as these help spread patterns.

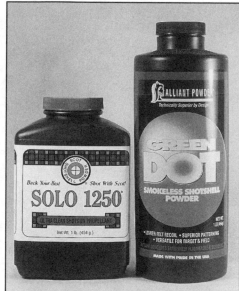

Solo 1250 has a reputation for placing more shot in the annular ring than most when used with relatively open chokes; Green Dot for holding tight center densities.

tubes. Such devices do not make a woodcock gun out of one designed for waterfowl hunting, nor yet a Skeet gun out of a trap gun, but they do allow for a certain amount of tailoring of our ammunition to the task at hand.

When it comes to ammunition, the changes over the years have been as profound as the changes in the guns themselves. From the loose components of the muzzleloader to the brass or paper hulls of early self-contained ammunition to the modern plastic shells and wads; from blackpowder to smokeless; from lead to non-toxic shot, change has been inexorable.

To further complicate matters, there are millions of shotguns around with fixed chokes, many of which were made when shotshells contained a built-up wad column of card and felt or other filler wads. The internal dimensions of forcing cone and choke frequently differ from guns made in the plastic wad era. Many of these older guns tend to shoot differently, as if they had maliciously, and unknowingly, received a tighter choke when modern ammunition is fired. The situation is always safe, assuming we're talking about a gun proofed for smokeless powder, but the performance may not be what was expected. Likewise, modern guns with their typically longer forcing cones and often less constriction rarely handle built-up card as ammo well. All of which serves to underscore the fact that through handloading we can tailor our shotshells to perform as we want in our guns.

To understand how, we first need a way to measure performance. Shotshell and shotgun performance is determined through a process of patterning. This involves firing the gun at a large sheet of paper at a known distance, drawing a circle around the bulk of the holes made by the shot passing through the paper and ascertaining what percentage of the total number of pellets are represented by the holes in the pattern sheet. Industry standards dictate that the measured distance at which the patterning is done is 40 yards for all gauges except the .410 bore, which is done at 25 yards.

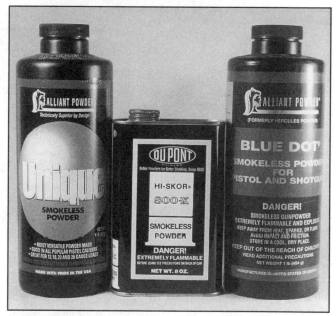

Unique, 800-X and Blue Dot, all slow burners in the 12-gauge, tend to retain high core count.

The circle is fixed at a diameter of 30 inches—20 inches for the .410—and is drawn to encompass the largest number of pellets possible. While this is done by glance, it is easier than one might think. By patterning a number of shells and determining an average we tend to overcome shell-to-shell differences as well as any errors in circle placement. Absolute figures have tended to change over time but we generally rate performance according to the following percentages:

Cylinder: 35 percent or less
Skeet: 35 to 45 percent
Improved Cylinder: 45 to 55 percent
Modified: 55 to 65 percent
Improved Modified: 65 to 70 percent
Full: 70 to 80 percent
Extra Full: Above 80 percent

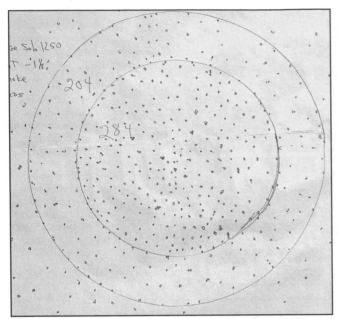

Solo 1250 at 25 yards shows high annular ring count.

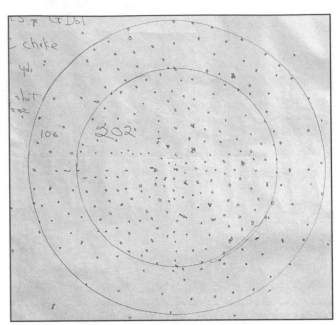

Green Dot at 25 yards puts high pellet count in the 20-inch core.

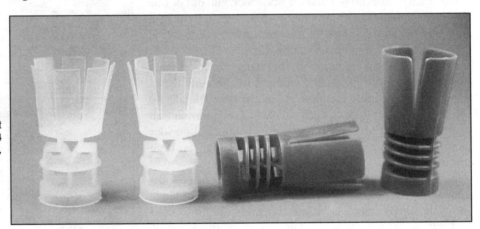

Windjammer target wad with its eight petals drops away quickly; Federal 12S4 works will with heavier hunting loads, holding tight center density.

It is perhaps unfortunate that we have grown to identify shotgun performance in this manner as it tends to obscure what we are really attempting to do. No one builds a gun expressly to put half of the shot charge in a 30-inch circle at 40 yards. If that was what we wanted we would just cut the shot charge in half and put 'em all in the circle. That's not possible, of course. What we really want is to evenly distribute enough pellets of sufficient size to ensure a clean kill in as large a circle as possible—and 30 inches is a reasonable standard—at a range at which we are most likely to shoot our target. If that likely range is 20 to 25 yards it may well be that only half of the pellets will remain in a 30 inches circle at 40 yards, but the latter was never our goal. But we do need standards and the current system seems to work.

A more sophisticated examination of our patterning is necessary to properly evaluate our shotshells but is beyond our scope here. A simple expansion of the concept is to include a 20-inch circle concentrically drawn within the larger one, giving us a core and an annular ring. This helps us to establish the actual, useful pattern width at that yardage. In testing. we should always attempt to pattern our shells at

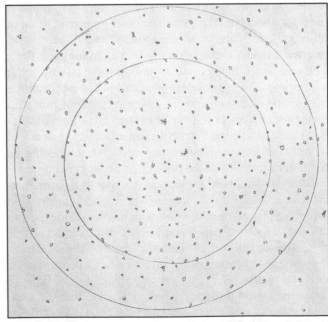

Sixteen gauge spreader load from tight modified barrel shows good distribution at 25 yards.

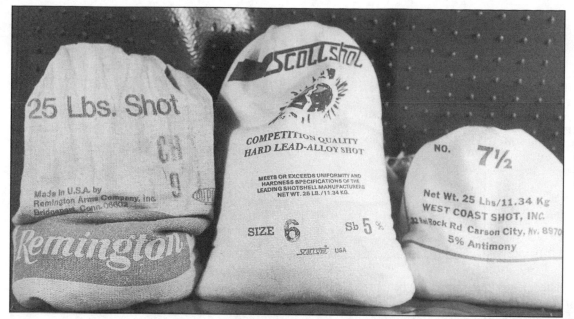

Shot hardness and size can influence pattern width and density.

Small shot on left will open faster, better at close ranges; larger shot on right holds tighter patterns, retains energy for longer ranges and bigger targets.

Spreader loads using "B" overshot card wads with "X" inserts help to create wide patterns at close range.

the range at which we will likely employ them as well as both shorter and longer ranges while paying particular attention to both core density and their degree of coverage in the annular ring. It is only in this way do we get a mental picture of actual shot dispersion as the yardage changes.

If our patterning does not reflect the result we want and choke substitution is not practical or possible, such as with a fixed-choke gun or a second shot from an autoloader, we can exert further influence on our patterns through hand-loading and our knowledge of how components affect patterns.

We know, for example, that soft shot, that is, shot with an antimony content of, say, 1/2 to two percent, deforms more upon firing and through travel down the barrel than does harder shot with an antimony content of five or six percent. The deformed shot then tends to disperse more and more quickly upon hitting air resistance. This can be useful at close ranges but rarely beyond 20 to 25 yards. Hard shot, on the other hand, retains its shape better and tends to create tighter patterns at all ranges until it, too, disperses beyond usefulness. Plated shot, assuming high-antimony

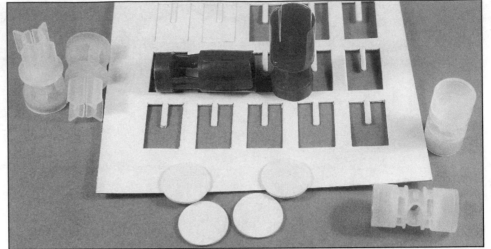

The handloader has a variety of aids to assist in opening patterns: "B" cards, "X" inserts, PC Post wads, BPI spreader wads, brush wads, among others.

shot was what was plated, tends to perform even better than unplated hard shot. The plating, nickel or copper, creates a more slippery surface, allowing the pellets to shift around more and avoid bridging or jamming together, during their travel through the forcing cone and choke. Shot size also offers some measure of control, within reason of course, as the larger the pellet the less it is affected by travel down the barrel and by air resistance once escaping the muzzle. In the former case it's because a smaller percentage of its surface comes in contact with the bore or other pellets and in the latter because its heavier weight is better able to overcome ordinary air resistance.

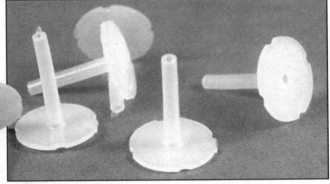

Shooter's Edge compressor inserts look like post inserts but serve to tighten patterns by holding a strong core count.

We also know that the faster we drive our shot charges, regardless of the pellet size, the greater the effect of pellet deformation and air resistance. Hence, the higher the muzzle velocity, the faster the pattern will open up.

When it comes to powders, there are also rules of thumb, arrived at through decades of experience and testing. Faster burning powders, relatively speaking, tend to open patterns; slower powders tend to tighten them. This is due to the abruptness, or ease – again relatively speaking – with which the shot charge is propelled up the barrel. Still, some powders have developed reputations for conspicuous behavior. In the 12-gauge, Accurate's Solo 1250 has long been touted as a powder that will place a significant percentage of its pellets out in the annular ring of our circle, even at relatively close ranges, creating wider, more useful patterns. This characteristic is more apparent with open chokes, improved cylinder and Skeet. Alliant's Green Dot, on the other hand, is known for tightening chokes, which is, concentrating more of the pellets in the core of the pattern and fewer in the annular ring at close ranges, resulting in a pattern that will be most useful at longer ranges. Alliant's Unique and IMR's 800-X appear to possess similar characteristics. Green Dot's performance seems to hold true regardless of choke or gauge but is restricted to target loads of no more than 1-1/8 ounces of shot weight.

Generally speaking, any given combination of gauge,

choke, muzzle velocity and shot weight will allow some tailoring of the pattern through our selection of powder and shot.

Primers can be a source of manipulating patterns as well but perhaps with less latitude. Once again, generally speaking, the effect of primers of different strength, or brisance, on fast burning powders, and by extension their patterns, is negligible. Conversely, the influence of primer strength in igniting larger quantities of slower burning powders can be significant. Hotter primers tend to ignite the powder charge more quickly, giving higher pressures and velocities and more open patterns. Milder primers do the opposite: igniting the powder charge more slowly, resulting in a milder shove down the barrel, lower pressure and velocity and tighter patterns. Problems can arise, however. Some powders can be difficult to ignite and switching to a milder primer from a hotter one in a published load can result in erratic ignition and performance. Cold temperatures can compound this. On the other hand, substituting a hotter primer in a published load developed with a milder one that was already near the maximum allowable pressure for the gauge could easily push the load over the limit, creating an unsafe and, possibly, unstable load. Here high temperatures can magnify the problem. A careful perusal of published data will often show the primer substitution in another load along with any necessary change in powder charge.

Wads, too, can have an effect on shotshell performance. There are two schools of thought. One, that "soft" wads designed for target payloads and velocities will compress more readily, absorbing the shock of ignition, thereby minimizing shot deformation and allowing a greater percentage of the shot to be controlled by the choke. The other, that "harder" wads will have thicker petals and therefore do a better job of protecting the shot as it travels down the bore, resulting in the same thing. The former probably has more adherents but the astute handloader will test both theories because other variables may also influence results.

That said, there are other wads specifically designed to affect performance. These include brush wads (without petals), spreader wads, post wads, steel shot wads and many others. Then there are aids designed to influence performance that we add to our initial recipe. Examples include "B" or "X" wads of paper or plastic composition designed to act a spreaders, creating very wide patterns at close range. Others are designed to have a tightening effect, such as compressors or buffers, to hold patterns together for shooting at longer range.

The hull can also influence patterns. More spacious hulls tend to require a heavier powder charge to develop the same velocity as a load using a smaller-capacity hull, thereby offering a bit more flexibility and frequently better crimps. Worn hulls that have been reloaded many times, and therefore are candidates for field use where they will most likely be lost, tend to produce less pressure and velocity, and tighter patterns, than loads put up in new or once-fired hulls. This is due primarily to weakened crimps. Many modern compression-formed hulls and a few other top-of-the-line offerings, however, show amazing wear resistance.

These, then, are the principles. Let's look at some examples. A popular choice among trapshooters involves selecting different powders to control performance. For 16-yard singles and the first shot on doubles, we use a fast powder to fill out our circle at about 30 to 32 yards.

Remington STS hull (12 gauge 2 ¾-inch)
Remington 209P primer
Remington Fig 8 wad
1 1/8 ounces hard lead shot
18.0 grains Red Dot
Velocity: 1145 fps
Pressure: 9200 psi

For the second shot on doubles and for handicap yardage, the load is changed to a slower powder to help hold patterns together longer as the shots will be taken perhaps 10 yards further on:

Remington STS hull (12-gauge 2 ¾-inch)
Remington 209P primer
Remington Fig 8 wad
1 1/8 ounces hard lead shot
19.0 grains Green Dot
Velocity: 1145 fps
Pressure: 7300 psi

To avoid confusion, the Red Dot loads could be put up in the green STS hulls; the Green Dot loads in the gold Nitro 27 Handicap hulls. The principle could apply to any brand of hull, of course, and we could also go to a slightly larger shot size for the Green Dot load, from 8s to 7 1/2s, for example.

The same principles apply in the field. Our first shot at upland birds will likely be taken at close range. Assuming an open choke, at 25 yards we can expect good annular ring coverage with this load:

Winchester AA hull (12-gauge 2 ¾-inch)
Winchester 209 primer
Windjammer wad
1 1/8 ounce small lead shot
24.0 grains Solo 1250
Velocity: 1200 fps
Pressure 7400 LUP

Our second shot, either from the other barrel or, if a pump or autoloader, from the same barrel will be at a target a bit farther off. To hold a tighter center density for those shots, this load has proved useful:

Remington Premier or STS hull (12-gauge 2 ¾-inch)
Remington 209P primer
Remington Fig 8 wad
1 1/8 ounces small lead shot
21.0 grains Green Dot
Velocity: 1200 fps
Pressure: 8800 psi

Of course, our patterning, our quarry and how closely the birds are holding may show that the Solo 1250 is appropriate for both shots. For Western quail hunting scenarios, maybe the Green Dot holds more promise. We may also assist the Green Dot load by going up a shot size, from 9s to 8s, say.

Patterning may show we're still not getting the shot spread we want with the first shot. We can frequently increase patterns a good 10 inches or more at 25 yards by building a scatter load. Here we use special techniques or components. The options are nearly endless. The aforementioned brush wad, which has an over powder cup and a cushioning section but no petals to protect the shot can perform well in some instances. Better, perhaps, are two "B" card wads as used in Remington factory spreader loads to separate the shot charge into three segments or a wad favored by Winchester which divides the shot into four sections. Both were popular with built-up card wad loads and work well today when positioned over a brush wad. Another option includes a plastic "X" insert, which can be placed onto any normal plastic wad load. It, as do all the inserts, takes up the space of about 1/8 ounce of shot. A combination that has served well in a number of guns is this one:

Federal Gold Medal hull (12-gauge, 2 ¾-inch)
Federal 209A primer
Federal 12S4 wad
X-Stream insert
1 1/8 ounces small lead shot
19.0 grains Red Dot
Velocity: 1200 fps
Pressure: 10,000 psi

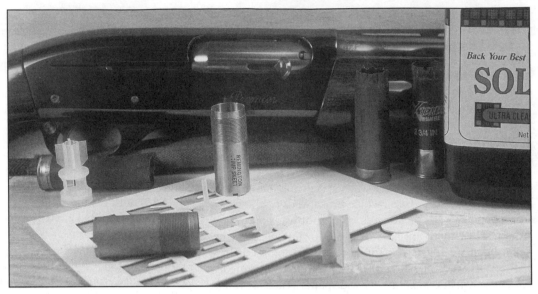

Between interchangeable choke tubes and hand-loading wiles, we can tailor our gun's performance to our needs.

The 12S4 wad, which is designed for 1¼ ounces of shot, is substituted for the 12S3 in the published data. The X-Stream Spreader Insert, available from Ballistic Products of Corcoran, MN, as are any number of specialty shotgun reloading products, is inserted into the 12S4 wad., reducing the capacity to 1 1/8 ounces. The original published powder charge was 19.5 grains, but the above gave the published velocity.

Sometimes we may be faced with the opposite problem. Our open-bored quail or grouse gun may be pressed into service in the cornfields in search of pheasant. Our shots will be longer, the shot charge heavier and the shot size larger. Our stated principles call for hard, large shot and slow-burning powder. Here's a load that has proved to be up to the task:

Remington STS hull (12-gauge 2 ¾-inch)
Winchester 209 primer
Federal 12S4 wad
1¼ ounces lead shot
24.5 grains 800-X
Velocity: 1275 fps
Pressure: 10,600 psi

The above have all dealt with our most popular gun, the 2 ¾-inch, 12 gauge. The same principles for manipulating patterns apply regardless of shell l length or gauge. Of course, what constitutes a slow powder in the 12 gauges will likely be a fast powder in the 20 gauge.

A pet 16-gauge, a vintage Fox that has a propensity to throw extremely tight clusters of shot from its more open modified barrels has responded well to this load:

Fiocchi plastic hull (16-gauge 2 ¾-inch)
Fiocchi 616 primer
G/BP Sporting 16 wad with
X-Stream Spreader Insert
7/8 ounce lead shot
23.0 grains Herco
Velocity: 1230 fps
Pressure: 9800 psi

The load was originally developed for the Ballistic Products Disperser-X, a one-piece plastic wad with a built-in X

divider. That product is no longer available but the above is an admirable replacement.

IMR's 700-X is a fast powder in the 20 gauge. It seems to display the characteristics we want when trying to gain a few more inches of pattern width at short ranges. This one has expanded a Modified choke to Improved Cylinder in a couple of guns:

Federal plastic hull (20-gauge 2 3/4–inch)
Remington 209P primer
Windjammer wad
7/8 ounce small lead shot
14.5 grains 700-X
Velocity: 1200 fps
Pressure: 11,300 psi

Another trick to control 20 gauge patterns with heavier shot charges is to turn to the three-inch shell. Most modern field guns are chambered for the longer length. This technique allows us to use slower powders generating lower pressure, higher velocities and generally improved patterns. This is especially true when attempting to duplicate the 1 1/8 ounce baby magnum factory loads:

Federal plastic hull (20 gauge, 3-inch)
Remington 209P primer
Remington RXP20 wad
1 1/8 ounces lead shot
21.1 grains Longshot
Velocity: 1230 fps
Pressure: 9900 psi

We could go on with more gauges and examples, but you get the idea. None of this is license to arbitrarily make component substitutions, other than shot size and hardness, in published data but to encourage the broader review of published data with an eye to selecting loads that incorporate the principles that are likely to give us the desired results. The principles enumerated are sound, but each barrel can be a law unto itself. The willingness to do the heavy lifting associated with patterning our shotshells and selecting the components to meet our needs can, and will, pay dividends.

Effective loads for ducks, geese and pheasants.

Non-Toxic Shot

By Tom Roster

EVERYONE KNOWS YOU can reload lead shot, but can you reload nontoxic shot?

I'm here to tell you that yes, you can definitely reload nontoxic shot. But, you cannot reload every one of the nearly 13 nontoxic pellet types now available in factory ammunition.

To be reloadable, a nontoxic pellet has to be first, available for sale and secondly, there must be data developed for it. In the case of hard nontoxic pellets it should also be added that there also must be available suitable reloading wads to properly contain the pellets and prevent barrel scoring from pellet to barrel interior contact.

As this is written the above provisos leave us with three nontoxic pellet types: steel shot, HEVI-Shot®, and bismuth shot. In the future other nontoxic pellet types may spring onto the shotgunning scene and become reloadable.

Reloading Steel Shot

Without doubt the nontoxic pellet type sold the most in factory ammunition and which is also the most reloaded is steel shot. It's also the least expensive of all the currently available nontoxic pellet types out there. And what is more, with the burgeoning economies of India and especially China pur-

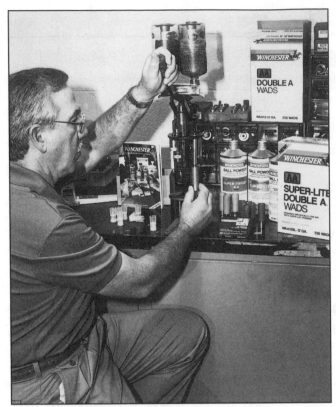

Single-stage reloading tools are the most useful for reloading non-toxic shot types including steel, HEVI-Shot and bismuth.

chasing more and more lead on the world market for car batteries thus exponentially driving up the cost of lead and therefore lead shot in recent years, steel shot may very well become less expensive to reload than lead shot! So, let's get a handle on how steel shot shapes up to lead.

Steel Shot Is Different

Steel shot differs substantially from lead shot in terms of hardness. Lead shot is quite soft. On the Diamond Pyramid Hardness (DPH) Scale, soft lead or hard lead shot will test about 30-35 DPH, while properly annealed steel shot will test 90-95 DPH. Steel shot, even of the proper hardness level, is about three times harder than lead shot. Steel shot also differs substantially from lead shot in terms of density. For a given volume, steel shot will weigh lighter than lead shot. As a rule of thumb, steel shot is about one-third lighter or weighs only about 60 percent as much as lead shot for the same volume.

As a result: **When reloading steel shot you cannot use the same shot bar or bushing used to throw lead shot or vice versa.** This is true for two reasons. First, a lead shot bar, for example, which throws 1-1/8 ounces of lead will not throw 1-1/8 ounces of steel. It will throw only 7/8 ounces of steel. A cavity designed to throw 1-1/2 ounces of lead would be needed to throw 1-1/8 ounces of steel. Secondly, when a bar designed to load lead or any other soft shot type is moved to dump the lead shot charge, frequently (and unknown to the reloader) one or more of the soft lead pellets are sheared off at the top of the shot cavity. This prevents jamming. Unfor-

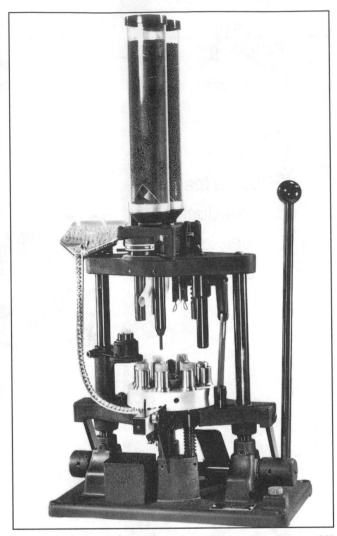

Progressive reloading presses such as this Ponsness-Warren 800 model are excellent for reloading lead shot and non-buffered bismuth loads. For any steel, HEVI-Shot or buffered shotshell loads, however, single-stage presses are much more useful.

tunately, this shearing will not happen with hard steel shot pellets. Instead, the bar will definitely jam. To alleviate this problem most reloading tool manufacturers have built a soft compressible rubber insert into the top edge of the shot cavity of their steel charge bars. This is especially true in MEC presses. This feature allows hard pellet types such as steel to compress into the insert during bar travel and thus allows the bar to travel across without jamming.

Steel Shot Wads

Because of steel shot's hardness special wads must be loaded to prevent barrel damage. A steel shot wad, unlike a lead shot wad, must absolutely prevent the hard steel pellets from contacting the barrel interior. It does this by completely containing all the pellets of the steel shot charge in a large capacity shotcup featuring very thick, very dense petal walls. The petal walls so constructed will not allow the pellets to rub-through to contact the barrel interior as they often do in a shotcup or shot wrapper used for loading lead shot. Additionally, a steel shot charge must never extend above the top of the shotcup as it often does in heavy or magnum lead loads. Such shot would make direct bore contact and cause extensive scoring and erosion. This requires careful selection of the plastic resin and the radius design of the bottom of a steel shotcup to allow the pellets during combustion to compress into the base of the wad, yet still be released upon muzzle emergence.

Thus while a steel shot wad when examined looks simple, it is far from it. I'm aware that there are several different brands of wads being sold for steel shot reloading. I have conducted extensive destructive tests searching for barrel damage with Precision Reloading steel shot wads. The data I acquired have convinced me Precision Reloading wads will definitely prevent barrel damage when reloaded with either steel or HEVI-Shot. Other steel reloading wads may do as well, but I have no empirical data as yet to convince me. So I'm going to focus on the wad brand, which I know for certain is an acceptable wad for reloading steel and other hard shot types.

Steel Is Less Forgiving

Because during combustion hard steel pellets do not compress like soft lead pellets and because steel shot wads sold for reloading by and large do not contain a cushioning section, chamber pressures build up very rapidly in steel shot loads. As a consequence and as a general rule slower burning propellants must be used when reloading steel as compared to lead in order to keep chamber pressures down. The lack of compressibility of steel shot and its attendant wad also makes steel shot loads much more sensitive to component substitutions or deviations from loading data. **Never substitute any component for the exact components listed for any given steel shot recipe detailed in this article.** In fact, this goes for any published steel shot reloading recipe regardless of source.

Because steel shot is less forgiving it is also more likely to develop dangerous pressure levels as the result of an overcharge of powder or shot than would a lead load. As a general rule of thumb, when loading steel shot the reloader is encouraged to throw a powder and shot charge as close to the exact weight of powder and shot called for in each recipe. **The acceptable range of variation is plus or minus one-half grain from the powder charge weight and plus or minus 25.0 grains from the shot charge weight. Failure to do so could result in dangerous pressure levels, which could result in serious injury or death to persons and damage to firearms and property.**

The Hand-Weighing Method

The best reloading presses for reloading steel shot are single-stage tools. However, many reloaders elect to throw steel shot charges by hand rather than using a bar or bushing. They choose to weigh out each shot charge on their reloading scale. This is an excellent way to do business, but of course, is much slower than throwing shot charges with

A properly designed wad for reloading hard shot types such as steel or HEVI-Shot contains the entire shot charge from the moment it exits the hull until the time it exits the muzzle. This high-speed photograph captures a properly designed hard shot wad of Roster's patented design at the moment of muzzle emergence. Note that the shot is set back inside the shotcup so that most of the shot is recessed about 1/8" below the top of the wad and none of the pellets are escaping ahead of the wad. If hard steel or HEVI-Shot cannot contact the inside of the barrel, it cannot score it, period.

Generally speaking, slower-burning propellants are necessary when loading hard steel or HEVI-Shot in order to keep chamber pressures within voluntary safe limits. Some of these include Hodgdon's HS6 and Alliant's Blue Dot. Others include Hodgdon's Longshot, Alliant's STEEL, and IMR's SR-4756, 800-X, and IMR-4227.

a bar or bushing. Be advised that whenever loading a steel shot pellet size larger than No. BB (.180") all shot charges with these large pellet sizes should be hand-weighed.

Sensible Steel Reloads

There are all manner of steel shot reloading recipes out there. They run the gamut from very slow, very heavy loads to very light, hyper velocity loads. My extensive testing and experience with steel shot for taking ducks, geese and pheasants over the past 25 years – some 150,000 rounds-plus of experience – has taught me clearly that both extremes are ineffective.

My empirical testing tells me clearly that steel shot load velocities are most serviceable in the 1300 to 1400 fps range. Anything faster is really unnecessary. But hey, if it makes you feel good, fine. But to keep pressures within safe limits all high velocity steel loads have to be loaded with less than standard weight shot charges.

I have also learned that for successful bagging of ducks, geese and pheasants no one needs a steel pellet any larger than two pellet sizes greater than what would be used if lead shot were being fired. I have never found that the advice often hyped that to compensate for steel's lightness a steel pellet three times or even larger than a lead pellet is needed. If you follow this unscientifically tested, unproven advice, you will end up with a tiny shot charge substandard in pellet count and thus generally a pattern too thin to insure a sufficiency of pellet strikes on birds. This will increase rather than decrease wounding losses. Generally my research clearly indicates that steel BBBs and Ts are needed for pass shooting of large Canadas and steel BBs are excellent for all geese over decoys. For the large and medium-sized duck species steel 2s and 3s are most effective with steel 4s and 6s indicated for teal-sized ducks. For pheasants nothing is more effective than a steel No. 2 with a steel No. 3 a close second.

Proven Steel Shot Reloading Recipes

When all is said and done the following steel shot reloading recipes have proven themselves lethal for ducks, geese and pheasants when the appropriate steel shot sizes are loaded for the game bird being considered. They also use hulls featuring long reloading life, lots of volume, and good crimping characteristics.

3-1/2" 10 gauge Federal plastic hull with paper basewad
Fed. 209A primer
36.5 grains Alliant STEEL powder
Precision Reloading TUPRW105 wad + 20 ga. 1/8" fiber or felt wad
1-1/2 oz. (656.3 grains) steel shot
Velocity: 1343 fps; Pressure: 10,380 psi
Note: You can go up to 1-5/8 oz. (710.9 grains) of steel with this load but minus the 20 ga. insert wad and the powder charge must be reduced to 32.5 grains of Alliant STEEL for 1246 fps at 10,650 psi.

3-1/2" 12 gauge Federal one-piece plastic hull
Winchester 209 primer
35.5 grains Alliant Blue Dot powder
Precision Reloading TUPRW1235 wad + 20 ga. 1/8" fiber or felt wad
1-1/2 oz. (656.3 grains) steel shot
Velocity: 1300 fps; Pressure: 13,900 psi

3" 12 gauge Federal one-piece plastic hull
Federal 209A primer
30.0 grains Alliant STEEL powder
Precision Reloading TUPRW123 wad

1-1/4 oz. (546.9 grains) steel shot
Velocity: 1300 fps; Pressure: 11,500 psi

2-3/4" 12 gauge Federal Gold Medal plastic hull
Winchester 209 primer
25.0 grains IMR SR-4756 powder
Precision Reloading TUPRW12 wad
1-1/8 oz. (492.2 grains) steel shot
Velocity: 1365 fps; Pressure: 11,400 psi

Reloading HEVI-Shot®

HEVI-Shot is a very unique projectile. Its basic properties must be understood by the shotgunner to make sense of reloading it.

The principal attraction of HEVI-Shot is that HEVI-Shot pellets sold for reloading feature a density fully 10 percent greater than lead. While this makes for very promising lethality, the high tungsten content of HEVI-Shot pellets makes them about twice as hard and twice as expensive as traditional steel pellets. As a result of its physical properties, HEVI-Shot demands proper containment during bore passage to absolutely prevent pellet to bore contact. As previously discussed any bore contact by a pellet as hard as steel shot (and even more so with HEVI-Shot) will result in scratching and erosion of the barrel interior.

After extensive testing I have determined that the steel shot type wads being sold by Precision Reloading (P.R.) with the addition of P.R.'s very fine bead, plastic spherical buffer (PSB) provide an extremely high degree of barrel protection when reloading HEVI-Shot – **without** the addition of a shot wrapper or any other protective components. The HEVI-Shot recipes which follow result in virtually no pellet rub-through in the wad walls and no HEVI-Shot pellets riding above the top of the shotcup during bore passage. Thus barrel scratching and erosion are eliminated.

Because of HEVI-Shot's greater density than lead shot, just as with steel shot there is a volumetric difference when loading HEVI-Shot versus lead. A given charge of HEVI-Shot pellets will take up less space in the shotshell than a comparable weight shot charge with lead shot. As a result, when compared to lead shot there will be slightly fewer HEVI-Shot pellets in a given load weight. This means, for example, that a 1-1/4 oz. charge of No. 4 HEVI-Shot will have slightly fewer pellets in the shell than a 1-1/4 oz. charge of No. 4 lead shot.

Also, because of HEVI-Shot's high density and hardness, like steel shot it has a greater proclivity for raising chamber pressures than does a soft shot type such as lead. This is compounded whenever a buffer is added to the shot as buffers also tend to raise chamber pressures. Thus you will note that the load weights featured in the HEVI-Shot recipes below are not the maximums featured in many factory HEVI-Shot loads. Rather, to keep chamber pressures within SAAMI recommended limits with the powders currently available for reloading, mid-weight shot charges are used.

Finally, high velocities are not needed for good lethality

HEVI-Shot is denser than lead, harder than steel shot and is unique in that its tungsten-composite pellets are decidedly not round, yet pattern beautifully. HEVI-Shot can be reloaded without concern for barrel damage so long as the reloader uses a properly designed wad for reloading hard shot. A buffer also helps.

with a high density pellet such as HEVI-Shot (12.0 grams/cc). Velocity levels no higher than 1200 fps are perfectly satisfactory with any shotshell projectile possessing a density of 11.0 grams/cc (the density of lead shot) or higher. Therefore, you will also find that the recipes below generally fall into the 1200 to 1350 fps range. No hyper-velocity loads are featured.

Adding Buffer

Buffer helps reduce pellet rub-through. There are several methods of adding a buffering substance to a shotshell load. Of these, the one I find most reliable and which consistently results in filling all the interstices among the pellets is vibration. I recommend that the Precision Reloading PSB buffer I stipulate for the loads that follow be added **only** by the vibration method.

Adding the buffer by vibration is fast and simple. After assembling the load according to the published recipe and before applying the crimp-start, heap the recommended weight of buffer on top of the shot charge. Then, apply vibration to the outside of the hull. The vibration source can be any vibrating instrument – electric scissors, electric razor or other vibrating device which when pressed against the exterior of the shotshell hull in the vicinity of the shot charge or the base of the shotshell causes the buffer to sift down into the shot charge. **When the sifting action is complete the buffer should just cover the top layer of pellets.** Then, the crimp-start and crimp-finish should be applied in the normal manner.

The goal after dropping the shot charge is to add the buffer in such a way that all the air spaces among the pellets become occupied, but not to disrupt the resting position of the pellets. The proper method is to add just enough vibration so that the pellets remain touching one another and perhaps, spinning slightly, while the buffer gently sifts its way into every nook and cranny among the pellets. Care must be taken not to over-agitate the shot charge. The pellets in the shot column must never be jumping up and down while adding the buffer. Rather, the pellets must be left in contact with one another both vertically and horizontally while the buffer works its way into the shot charge. This results in maximum crimp space.

A drop of candle wax, nail polish or shellac-like glue can be added to the top of the crimp to achieve a waterproofing effect and to help retain the buffer. You may also add a thin, frangible overshot wad such as Precision Reloading's Tight Seal on top of the shot before crimping.

Just as when loading steel shot, single-stage reloading tools allow the quickest and most practical reloading of HEVI-Shot loads, especially those that call for a buffer. The reason is that after throwing the shot charge most reloaders prefer to remove the shotshell from the loading tool to add the buffer and apply the vibration for thorough and successful sifting action into the shot charge. On Ponsness-Warren tools, leave the shell in the sizing die and apply vibration either to the outside of the die or press the base of the shell and die against the vibration source.

The addition of a buffer to bismuth shot loads helps reduce brittle bismuth pellets' proclivity for fragmenting during combustion and bore passage. When loading HEVI-Shot, however, frangibility is not an issue but buffer still helps. Adding buffer to HEVI-Shot loads helps prevent the pellets from rubbing through the petals of the shotcup during bore passage. Buffer is not needed when loading steel shot.

Loading Tips

Because HEVI-Shot pellets are primarily more tear drop-shaped than round and also quite disparate in actual diameter per given shot size, the reloader may experience difficulty in throwing accurate charges of HEVI-Shot through traditional reloading presses. If it is desired that a reloading press with the standard bar or bushing cavity setup be used to throw HEVI-Shot charges, please be advised that the reloader will have to employ a press adapted with parts for reloading steel shot. Standard lead shot bars and bushings will not be capable of shearing off HEVI-Shot pellets, so special "steel shot" bars, bushings and sometimes even drop tubes must be used.

Even when using those presses adapted for steel shot, the reloader may well find throwing consistent and accurate charges of HEVI-Shot to be very troublesome. The solution – as time-consuming as it may seem – is to weigh out HEVI-Shot charges with a standard reloading scale. This is the recommended procedure for top-drawer HEVI-Shot reloads. The same weighing procedure will be necessary for throwing accurate charges of PSB buffer.

Preferred Shot Sizes

My extensive empirical tests of HEVI-Shot performance have proven HEVI-Shot to be the most lethal projectile shotgunners can currently reload for taking ducks, geese and pheasants. For geese – all species – you really do not need a HEVI-Shot pellet larger than No. 2 except for extreme pass shooting distances. Then and only then would a No. B (.170") or BB (.180") HEVI-Shot pellet be necessary.

For ducks the best all-around HEVI-Shot pellet is a No. 5 (.120") if you can find them. HEVI-Shot 4's will cleanly kill all sizes of ducks at all ranges while HEVI-Shot 6's will do the same on all ducks at over-decoy ranges. For pheasants HEVI-Shot 5's or 4's are the most lethal pellet sizes at all distances, with HEVI-Shot 6's indicated for pheasant shots at less than 40 yards.

Proven HEVI-Shot Reloading Recipes

3-1/2" 10 gauge Federal plastic hull with paper basewad
Winchester 209 primer
37.0 grains Hodgdon Longshot powder
Precision Reloading TUPRW105 wad + 1/2" 20 ga. fiber or felt wad + 45.0 grains PSB buffer
1-5/8 oz. (710.9 grains) HEVI-Shot
Velocity: 1240 fps; Pressure: 10,900 psi

3-1/2" 12 gauge Federal one-piece plastic hull
Winchester 209 primer
33.0 grains Hodgdon Longshot powder
Precision Reloading TUPRW1235 wad + one ½" and one 3/8" 20 ga. fiber or felt wad + 45.0 grains PSB buffer
1-1/2 oz. (656.3 grains) HEVI-Shot
Velocity: 1220 fps; Pressure: 13,310 psi

3" 12 gauge Federal one-piece plastic hull
Winchester 209 primer
29.0 grains Hodgdon Longshot powder
Precision Reloading TUPRW123 wad + 3/8" 20 ga. fiber or felt wad + 40.0 grains PSB buffer
1-1/4 oz. (546.9 grains) HEVI-Shot
Velocity: 1270 fps; Pressure: 10,900 psi
Note: This load may be loaded with 1-3/8 ounces (601.6 grains) of HEVI-Shot in the same hull but using the Fed. 209A primer, 41.0 grains of Alliant STEEL powder and only a very thin thickness of 20 ga. fiber or felt wad in the PR TUPRW123 with no buffer for 1400 fps at 11,400 psi.

2-3/4" 12 gauge Federal Gold Medal plastic hull
Winchester 209 primer
27.0 grains Hodgdon Longshot powder
Precision Reloading TUPRW12 wad + ¼" 20 ga. fiber or felt wad + 35.0 grains PSB buffer
1-1/8 oz. (492.2 grains) HEVI-Shot
Velocity: 1330 fps; Pressure: 11,400 psi
Note: This load may be loaded with 1¼ ounces (546.9 grains) of HEVI-Shot in the same hull but using the Fed. 209A primer, 32.5 grains of Alliant STEEL powder and only a very thin thickness of 20 ga. fiber or felt wad in the PR TUPRW12 with no buffer for 1375 fps at 11,400 psi.

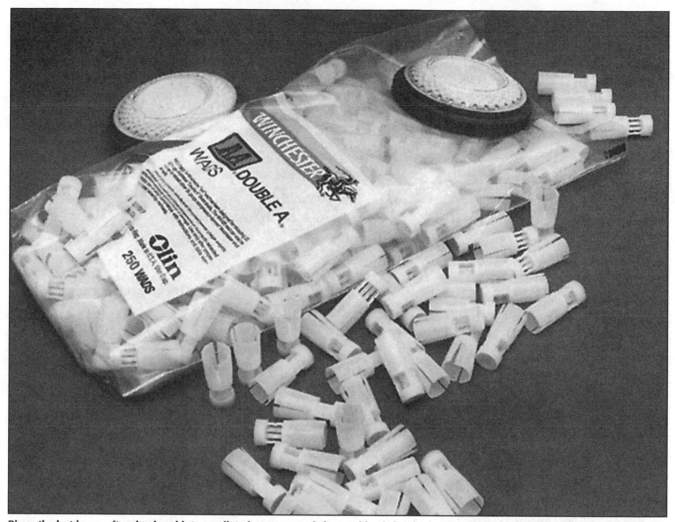

Bismuth shot is as soft as lead and intermediate between steel shot and lead shot in density. Bismuth can be reloaded in virtually any lead shot wad. As a result bismuth can be reloaded in all the gauges and shell lengths.

For many more HEVI-Shot reloading recipes, please contact Tom Roster for a copy of his 20-page *HEVI-Shot Reloading Manual* at $12.95 ppd, phone 541/884-2974.

Reloading Bismuth Shot

Bismuth shot is an interesting nontoxic pellet. As a raw material bismuth is almost as dense and soft as lead, but strangely it is very brittle. Bismuth could never survive as an ammunition projectile material in its pure state because the projectiles would bust into pieces during combustion and bore passage. So when used for ammunition projectiles bismuth is alloyed with tin to reduce its proclivity for being frangible. In pellets the addition of tin is significant enough that a bismuth-tin pellet ends up being about intermediate in density between lead and steel shot for the same pellet size. This means that just as with steel shot and HEVI-Shot, a bar or bushing which throws a given weight of lead shot will not throw the same weight of bismuth shot.

Because bismuth shot is so soft, there is no barrel scoring issue when shooting it. As a result, no special wads are required such as with steel and tungsten composite pellets. Bismuth can be loaded in lead shot wads in all the gauges.

And, any reloading tool suitable for loading lead can be used to reload bismuth shot.

Eley in England loads all of the world's bismuth pellets and bismuth factory ammunition. Any bismuth factory ammunition or bismuth pellets sold for reloading in the U.S. are imported from Eley. This was true even when the Bismuth Cartridge Company in North Hollywood, California, was still functional. That company has now gone out of business and so the future availability of bismuth shot for reloading in the U.S. is in doubt.

In terms of lethality and because of the fact that a bismuth tin pellet is less dense than lead but more dense than steel, as a general rule of thumb those hunting ducks, geese and pheasants with bismuth shot should use a pellet size one shot size designation larger than what would be used if firing lead shot. For large geese bismuth No. BB's (.180") are needed. Use nothing smaller than No. 2 bismuth for medium-sized geese. For large ducks bismuth No. 3's are best, 4's second best. For medium size ducks bismuth 4's or 5's are indicated and small ducks can be taken nicely with bismuth 6's. For pheasants the best all-around bismuth pellet would be a No. 3.

Because of its greater density than steel, bismuth pellets – like HEVI-Shot – do not benefit from high velocity. In fact, any effort to load bismuth shot at high velocities results in a greater number of bismuth-tin pellets busting apart when they are launched. Buffering bismuth loads greatly helps reduce the frangibility problem, which always exists to some extent in any bismuth shotshell load.

Reloading data is provided below for those who have acquired or can still find existing stocks of bismuth shot for sale.

Proven Bismuth Shot Reloading Recipes

3-1/2" 10 gauge Federal plastic hull with paper basewad
CCI 209M primer
41.0 grains Alliant Blue Dot powder
Precision Reloading TUPRW105 wad + 1/4" 20 ga. fiber or felt wad + 34.0 grains PSB buffer
2 oz. (875.0 grains) bismuth shot
Velocity: 1200 fps; Pressure: 11,000 LUP

3-1/2" 12 gauge Federal one-piece plastic hull
Winchester 209 primer
39.0 grains Alliant Blue Dot powder
Precision Reloading TUPRW1235 wad + 1/2" 20 ga. fiber or felt wad + 32.0 grains PSB buffer
1-7/8 oz. (820.3 grains) bismuth shot
Velocity: 1220 fps; Pressure: 13,800 psi

3" 12 gauge Federal one-piece plastic hull
Winchester 209 primer
29.0 grains IMR SR-4756 powder
Precision Reloading TUPRW123 wad + 1/8" 20 ga. fiber or felt wad + 30.0 grains PSB buffer
1-5/8 oz. (710.9 grains) bismuth shot
Velocity: 1200 fps; Pressure: 11,000 LUP

2-3/4" 12 gauge Winchester AA or Remington STS hull
Winchester 209 primer
26.5 grains IMR 800-X powder
Winchester WAA12F114 or Remington SP 12 wad + 27.0 grains PSB buffer
1-1/4 oz. (546.9 grains) bismuth shot
Velocity: 1295 fps; Pressure: 10,500 LUP

2-3/4" 16 gauge Winchester compression-formed or two-piece plastic hull
Winchester 209 primer
27.0 grains Hodgdon HS-6 powder
Remington SP 16 wad + 26.0 grains PSB buffer
1-1/8 oz. (492.2 grains) bismuth shot
Velocity: 1200 fps; Pressure: 10,200 LUP

3" 20 gauge Federal plastic with paper basewad hull
Federal 209A primer
44.0 grains IMR-4227 powder
Winchester WAA20F1 wad + 24.0 grains PSB buffer
1-1/8 oz. (492.2 grains) bismuth shot
Velocity: 1291 fps; Pressure: 11,400 LUP

2-3/4" 20 gauge Federal plastic with paper basewad hull
Federal 209A primer
23.0 grains Alliant Blue Dot powder

Winchester WAA20F1 wad + 21.0 grains PSB buffer
1 oz. (437.5 grains) bismuth shot
Velocity: 1185 fps; Pressure: 11,800 LUP

2-3/4" 28 gauge Remington STS one-piece plastic hull
Winchester 209 primer
13.0 grains IMR 800-X powder
Remington PT 28 wad
3/4 oz. (328.1 grains) bismuth shot
Velocity: 1155 fps; Pressure: 10,400 psi

3" .410 Winchester AA or AA HS hull
Winchester 209 primer
12.0 grains Alliant 410 powder
Winchester WAA410HS wad
5/8 oz. (273.4 grains) bismuth shot
Velocity: 1200 fps; Pressure: 12,400 psi

2-1/2" .410 Federal plastic with paper basewad hull
Winchester 209 primer
13.0 grains Alliant 2400 or 12.0 grains Alliant 410 powder
Federal 410SC wad
1/2 oz. (218.8 grains) bismuth shot
Velocity: 1250 fps; Pressure: 11,400 psi
Note: This recipe only works with size No. 7-1/2 or smaller bismuth shot. When loading No. 6 or larger bismuth shot, drop only 7/16 oz. (191.5 grains) bismuth shot.

To Order Components

To mail order components listed in the recipes above, please contact Precision Reloading in Mitchell, South Dakota USA at 800-223-0900; www.precisionreloading.com; E-mail: info@precisionreloading.com.

For many more bismuth shot reloading recipes, please contact Tom Roster for a copy of his 24-page *Buffered Lead and Bismuth Shotshell Reloading Manual* at $12.95 ppd, phone 541/884-2974. Many more recipes are available for reloading HEVI-Shot and bismuth shot in Tom Roster's *Buffered Lead and Bismuth* and *HEVI-Shot Reloading Manuals*.

To Reach Tom Roster

For any problems or questions you may have in assembling any of the steel, HEVI-Shot or bismuth loads above, or for answers to questions about reloading recipes published in any of Tom Roster's reloading manuals, please contact Tom at 1190 Lynnewood Blvd., Klamath Falls, Oregon USA 97601, 541/884-2974, FAX 541/882-6184; E-mail: tomroster@charter.net.

WARNING: The technical data provided herein was derived from a specific set of circumstances and conditions developed and practiced by the author. It is intended to be used only as a supplemental guide to the established safe practices of the remanufacture of ammunition, not necessarily explained herein in its entirety. Due to the variation of shotguns, reloading equipment, components, and practices of individuals, neither the author nor the publisher accepts responsibility for any bodily injury or equipment damage resulting from its use.

Sometimes you'll
want to shoot
your chronograph,
but in certain
situations it can
be your best friend.

Do You Need A Chronograph

By Mike Venturino
Photos by Yvonne Venturino

MY FRIEND CLINT Smith, director of Thunder Ranch, the world class shooting school, told me recently that he put a bullet right square through his chronograph. It wasn't an accident. It had given him fits, refusing to function when he needed it so he put it out of his misery. Personally, I often brag that someday if and when I get to retire, I'm going to pile all my chronographs and cameras on top of a huge pile of smokeless powders and light it all off.

Why this sort of hostility? Because chronographs can be cantankerous beasts. I would term them the mules of electronic instruments. If it's too bright out they might not work. If it's too dark out they might not work. If you live in the south and the sun is far to the north they might not work. If you live in the north and the sun is far to the south they might not work. Just once forget to have extra batteries along and that insures the one in the machine will go dead before you're finished shooting. If you absolutely need the data of the current string in the chronograph's memory that will also assure that its battery will die before you can retrieve it.

The author's chronograph set up allows him to change the screens to align with targets at various distances.

If your chronograph has a paper feed you can be sure that sometime it will jam, requiring you to take the thing apart to free it. You can also count on losing any screws you took out of it in order to get the paper un-jammed. If your chronograph is the type that the entire instrument sets out in front of the gun, be sure it will eventually be shot. Most likely not by you but by someone who asks to try just one of their handloads "so they will know." If your chronograph has the photo-electric sensors called various things like "skyscreens" that set out in front of the gun then be sure they will eventually be shot too – most likely by someone who asks to try just one of their handloads "so they will know."

If someone does manage to check a load without shooting your machine, or even if they let you do the shooting because you tell them the last guy you let shoot over your chronograph blew it to pieces, then be prepared for them to go off in a huff when their loads' velocities are much lower than they brag to their buddies. They'll say your chronograph is faulty.

So if chronographs can be such a pain, then why have I not been without at least one since 1973? Because early on I decided to spend my life as a gunwriter. Without some sort of data to present, a gunwriter's credibility can get strained. Do you want to read that a bullet is traveling somewhere between 800 and 1000 fps, or that it's going precisely 916 fps on the average and only varied 21 fps in a five shot string? Are professional gunwriters then the only shooters who

need chronographs? No; they can be pretty handy – when they work – to many types of shooters.

Who doesn't need a chronograph is perhaps an easier question to answer. I feel that hunters who only shoot factory ammo don't need chronographs. They just need to sight their rifles in at known distances, and check their bullet's drop between say 100 and 300 yards. If they don't handload there's not much they can do about their loads anyway, except try a different one. Checking one load's drop against another's between, again say 100 and 300 yards shows which load will suit their needs most. In the past factory ammo varied all over the map in regards to its actual ballistics compared to published velocities. Nowadays speaking in overall terms it is pretty good: especially the premium stuff.

Back in the spring of 2006 I went over to Thunder Ranch in Oregon for Clint and me to celebrate our mutual birthday. Born on the same day/same year, we make it a habit to get together then and shoot – a lot. That year we had access to a rancher's property that was overrun with their little Beldings ground squirrels. Overrun to the point that in five days I fired over 1700 rounds, and had just as much shooting on Friday afternoon as I had enjoyed on Monday morning. Since my new Savage Model 11F 223 Remington arrived shortly before leaving on the trip, only nine rounds had been fired through it for zeroing the 4.5-14X Leupold scope. Black Hills factory loads with bullet weights ranging from 40 to 77 grains were taken along and none had been

This is another view of the author's adjustable stand for chronograph screens.

Shooters who must set their chronographs up at various locations must rely on either photography light stands *(left)* or camera tripods. Note the light stands hold the Oehler three-screen bar for their Model 35P and the camera tripod holds the two foot screen bar of the PACT Professional Model chronograph.

The author is fond of PACTs Model IV speed-shooting timer because it can also serve as a chronograph.

The Oehler Model 43 Personal Ballistics Lab is the Cadillac of all chronographs, and meant for the serious experimenter.

clocked for velocity. That didn't hurt things a bit and that week was the most enjoyable varmint shooting I have ever done.

Plinkers don't need chronographs. It doesn't matter how fast a bullet goes through a soda can or block of firewood. There's nothing wrong with plinking. I'm so busy most of the times I don't get to do it much anymore, but its loads of fun. But, as long as the ammo functions the firearms then who cares about its ballistics?

Big-game hunters don't need chronographs, even if they are handloaders. What for? Again their most important factor is trajectory and of course their rifles' grouping abilities. The first can be ascertained by shooting the rifles on paper at known distances, and the latter can be ascertained in the exact same way. In fact I think a chronograph can be a detriment to hunters, if they get "velocity-happy." That is they get the mindset that the faster a bullet goes, the better it is for hunting purposes. Brothers and sisters, velocity doesn't

kill big-game animals. Destruction to their vital organs by the bullet passing through their bodies kills them.

I got "velocity happy" as a young fellow fresh moved to Montana and going out for pronghorns the first time. Everyone had told me that most shots at pronghorns would be long ones, so I worked with my old Model 54 257 Roberts until I had the 100-grain Sierra spitzer doing a full 3200 fps, which you might recognize is par for the larger capacity 25-06 cartridge.

First morning out I got a good shot at a buck at about 150 to 200 yards and the bullet made a loud "*whop*" sound on hitting him. Also it fell in its tracks. Elated, I started towards him but to my amazement he regained his feet! I let loose with several more shots hitting him in various places. It wasn't pretty but he didn't get away. Later, upon skinning him out, I found the first 100-grain Sierra bullet had landed exactly where aimed; at the point of the shoulder. It had flattened to the size and thickness of a dime and then slid under his hide, traveling up and over his neck stopping under the skin on the other side. It had done virtually no damage at all because it was going too fast.

After that I slowed my 100-grain Sierra bullets down to about 2900 fps and got through and through penetration on more pronghorns, and some mule deer too. Better yet, I eventually switched to a 117-grain bullet and never retrieved a spent one because they all penetrated completely. The last two antelope I shot were with a Browning Model 1885 single-shot 270 Winchester and a Winchester Model 70 Featherweight 300 WSM. Both were taken on industry-sponsored hunts in Wyoming. Neither rifles nor loads used were ever chronographed, which didn't make a bit of difference.

Now let's talk about some shooters who might need chronographs. As odd as it might sound I think the cowboy action shooter might need one. I can hear someone saying, "What are you talking about? All they do is dress up and then fling bullets at big steel targets placed really close." That may be true but consider this; cowboy action competition is one of the few games where the rules dictate that certain velocity levels must be adhered to. SASS (Single Action Shooting Society) rules say that competitors' single-action revolver loads cannot exceed 1000 fps and their rifle loads cannot exceed 1400 fps. That's precisely because their targets are steel and heavy loads might damage them, but more importantly high-velocity bullet fragments might rebound and damage somebody.

It's not hard to keep 44-40 or 45 Colt smokeless handloads under the 1000 fps or 1400 fps velocity levels from revolvers and lever guns. Surprisingly, however, blackpowder or Pyrodex powered loads can break that 1000 fps mark from long-barreled revolvers. I've clocked more than one 7 1/2-inch single-action handgun breaking 1000 fps with FFFg blackpowder. Also, some cowboy shooters are going to smaller calibers in an effort to escape recoil. An example would be the 32-20 with, say, 80- to 90-grain bullets, and it's not too hard to get those little slugs moving in excess of 1000 fps.

Also I hear it's being considered in cowboy action circles to institute a minimum velocity. This is because some competitors are using loads so light that the bullets can almost be seen in flight. If this comes about it would be smart for competitors to *know exactly* just how fast or how slow their bullets are traveling before spending the bucks to go to distant events only to find out that one's ammunition won't qualify.

And one last reason why I think cowboy action shooters might benefit from chronographs is related to this habit of using very light loads. That is the problem of ballistic inconsistency. Cowboy calibers mostly use huge cartridge cases that were intended for large charges of blackpowder. Those are 45 Colt, 44-40, 38-40 and even the later vintage 38 and 44 Special rounds that were developed with blackpowder in mind. Loading meager charges of smokeless powders in those huge cases can be problematic, especially if the shooter is aiming for velocities in the sub-700 fps range.

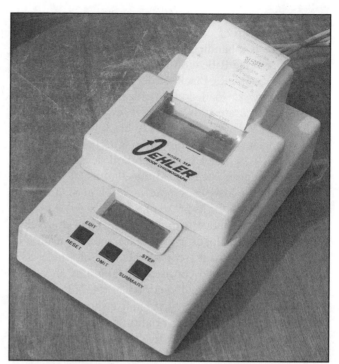

An Oehler Model 35P.

The author doesn't often rely on the paper feeds of some models of chronograph but he likes ones that give averages and other data.

A chronograph will indicate such ballistic inconsistency in the handloads by the velocity variation of a string of rounds. Personally I feel that a proper performing charge in a case like a 44-40 or 45 Colt will give no more than approximately 50 fps variation in a 5- or 10-shot string. If you test such a load and it varies more than 100 fps, then my recommendation would be to stop shooting it. With such variation at very low velocities it might be possible to stick a bullet in a barrel. In speed events like cowboy action competition that can be dangerous because it's virtually impossible to stop your hands from shooting, even if you hear a light report. Firing another round with a bullet stuck in the barrel at best ruins the barrel; at worst it may take the handgun apart.

Another group of competitors who will greatly benefit from testing their handloads over chronographs is the Black Powder Cartridge Rifle crowd – both silhouette and other long-range disciplines. Blackpowder tends to be very consistent when *properly* loaded in cartridges. That is one reason it can be so accurate at distance. For instance, my personal limit velocity variation in regards to blackpowder cartridge rifle loads to be used in competition is 15 fps for a 10-shot string. Or if you prefer to use standard deviation (SD) if your machine gives such a read-out, that usually amounts to about 4.0. If a load gives more variation or SD than that then I start to look for its problem.

Often a mere change in primers will tame down high variations in BPCR loads. For instance, once I ran a test of primers using a 6X RHO scope-sighted Shiloh Model 1874 Sharps 45-70. The load consisted of 60 grains of Swiss 1 ½ Fg blackpowder under Lyman bullet #457125 weighing 520 grains. Ten primers were tried in five-shot strings at 100 yards. The tightest velocity variation came with CCI-200 Large Rifle primers with only five fps change from shot to shot. Average velocity was 1125 fps. The highest velocity variation was 43 fps with an average of 1144 fps, and that came with Federal 155 Large Pistol Magnum primers. Now get this; the group with the CCI primers was 1-1/2 inches, which isn't bad but not astoundingly good either. The group with the Federal pistol primers was a mere ragged hole of three quarters inch.

On the surface that would indicate that velocity variation was not so important. But remember, that little test was done with the target only at 100 yards. Move it back to 500 or more yards and you would begin to see more vertical dispersion with the higher velocity variation loads.

Once when testing a new rifle, a Shiloh Model 1874 45-90 I could have saved myself considerable powder and lead if I hadn't been so lazy as to not set my chronograph up. I shot that rifle for several days without getting a decent group and couldn't figure out the problem. I tried different bullets, powders, and primers with no luck. Then I finally fired a few of the loads over my chronograph screens and the problem was immediately evident. All loads were varying 40 or more feet per second in five- and 10-shot strings. I started thinking then and like a light bulb coming on it dawned on me that I was using brand new Starline 45-90 brass. Starline brass comes from the manufacturer fairly hard, which works fine for most smokeless powder loading. However, for good results with lower blackpowder pressures it needs to be annealed. That was done, and the next loads fired in the 45-90 gave those 15 fps or less velocity variations to which I was accustomed.

Although I don't compete in any other rifle disciplines than the BPCR ones, I would imagine most serious high-power competitors see chronographing their handloads as important. These last few years I've been reloading for and shooting a wide variety of World War II military rifles,

The author feels that competitive shooters, such as this fellow involved in BPCR Silhouette, benefit from test-firing their handloads over a chronograph.

A chronograph is needed by cowboy shooters firing at these distances and because their sports have definite velocity limitations.

The author standing in the door of his shooting house. Note the PACT two-foot screen bar and the author's setup for adjusting the screens to different heights.

and I always use a chronograph when test-firing their loads. That might sound odd to some since I said above I don't think hunters need chronographs. They're using the same basic type bottleneck, high velocity cartridges. Here's the difference. Those military rifles mostly have sights graduated in yards or meters to considerable distance. If handloads duplicate the ballistics of original military loads, then there is a very good chance the rifles' sights will be on at various distances with those loads. So far I've been tinkering with calibers ranging from the 6.5mm Japanese to the 8mm Mauser and settling on good duplicates of their military loads is pretty easy – with the aid of a chronograph.

There are so many different types of chronograph on the market today that in all honesty I don't even try to keep apprised of them. I have three down in my shooting house, plus that Cadillac of all chronographs, the Oehler Model 43 Personal Ballistics Lab. It is capable of determining bullet speeds at the muzzle and at distances, calculating the ballistic coefficients of each bullet fired, plotting the groups on a computer screen *and* if a strain gauge is applied to the rifle, it will read pressures for you. That machine is definitely for the serious experimenter and would require an in-depth article just to describe it. My chronographs kept on hand for everyday use are an Oehler Model 35P, which I understand are not being sold anymore, a PACT Professional Model, and a PACT Mark IV Timer.

The author doesn't chronograph hunting loads but since becoming interested in World War II military rifles he chronographs all of his test loads. From top; German Mauser K98k 8mm, British No. 4 Mk1 303, and Russian Mosin-Nagant Model 91/30 7.62x54mm.

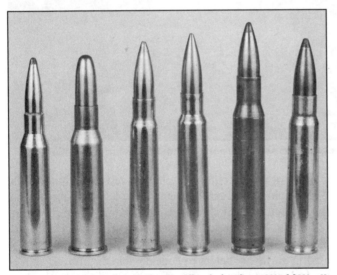

The author has been developing handloads for these World War II military cartridges that duplicate original military service load ballistics. From left: 6.5mm Japanese, 7.62x54mm Russian, 303 British, 7.7 Japanese, 30-06, and 8mm Mauser.

All have given good service for thousands of rounds fired over their screens, but I actually have a soft spot for that Mark IV Timer because of its versatility. You see, its primary function is as a timer for speed shooting. Back when my wife and I were regularly shooting cowboy action matches, we would practice using the Timer. It can be set to give a slight delay and then a loud *buzz* as the 'go' signal. Then it clocks however long was required for any number of shots to be fired. When used as a chronograph it is simply switched over and then the photoelectric screen plugged in. It doesn't give a paper read-out, but it does do the math for a string of shots and present the user with average of the string, total velocity variation and SD numbers. The PACT Professional Model chronograph does the same thing but can deliver all that to the user on paper. For some reason I have never developed the habit of taking advantage of the paper read outs, preferring to just jot down the totals after each string is fired. Perhaps, I've had batteries go dead in the middle of a project too often with the stored data being lost. Like I said, chronographs remind me of mules.

The Oehler Model 35P actually takes two readings of a bullet's travel. In a four-foot screen bar there are three photoelectric skyscreens. The machine reads the bullet's speed twice, which "proves" it valid, hence the P in 35P. If the two readings given are within a couple fps of one another then the reading is proved. If they vary wildly, then that shot should be discounted.

Many shooters who must use public ranges have to transport their chronographs and screens to the range and set the screens up on camera tripods or photography light stands. When doing this many like to set them up as far as 10 to 20 yards downrange. That does keep them from being effected by heavy rifle muzzle blast. Here at home I have target frames at 100, 200 and 300 yards, but they are elevated slightly as the distances increase. Therefore I have a piece of angle iron with moveable brackets and put both my PACT and Oehler screen bars on spotting scope window mounts so they clamp on easily to the angle iron. Then I can raise or lower my piece of angle iron so it lines up with 100-, 200-, or 300-yard targets as desired. However, to have this convenience, I must have the screens fairly close to the shooting house. Once in a while a rifle's heavy muzzle blast will blow off one of the plastic skyscreen light defusing shields, but that isn't a great problem. And since I do fire considerable blackpowder over the skyscreens occasionally it's necessary to wipe the fouling off of their little photo-electric eyes.

If I were not a full-time gunwriter, would I still have a chronograph? All joking about blowing them up along with cameras aside – yes, I would. As long as I'm a competitor in a shooting sport I would want a chronograph. If I someday become a plinker and once-in-a-while hunter then, no, I wouldn't need a chronograph. I doubt if that ever happens.

It took 400 years
to develop the
modern case, so
treat it with respect
when you reload.

Cartridge Cases

By Todd Spotti

GO TO ANY large public shooting range, and you'll very likely to see that the ground is heavily littered with used brass cartridge cases. This seems to be especially true during the late Summer and Fall seasons when the great majority of the nation's deer hunting fraternity makes their annual pilgrimage to the range with a couple of boxes of store bought ammo to either zero in a new scope on their hunting rifle, or to ensure that the zero on their old scope hasn't shifted since the previous year. Inevitably, the brass cases from that brand new factory ammo ends up on the ground when the hunter is satisfied that their gun is shooting properly and leaves.

This is a great time of year for reloaders like myself to pick up (literally) all kinds of once-fired brass in prime condition. Whether it's fairly common 30-30 or 44 Magnum brass from those who like to hunt with lever guns, or exotic magnums, it's all there. Interestingly, a lot of this discarded brass, like some from the Weatherby magnums and many others, can cost a dollar and more each. Yet, here it is, lying on the ground, free for the taking. The story of the how the modern cartridge case evolved to the point that it is considered to be little more than trash after being

Once-fired cases free for the taking at the range were reformed into the 338 Whisper wildcat and produced this great group.

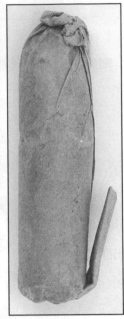

A 54 Harpers Ferry Model 1841 paper cartridge; this rifle was also referred to as the Mississippi Rifle.

used only once is extremely interesting. Let's take a very brief look at just a few of the highlights in this long and complicated history.

First all, the general concept behind the rifle cartridge of today has a history that probably goes back roughly 400 years or so. Think of it. What other invention that was in widespread use back then, is still in common use today – only in a more advanced form. Not many.

Four hundred years of research, refinement, and manufacturing advancements bring us this technological marvel which is used only once by the overwhelming majority of shooters, and then thrown away without a thought.

Whoever was the very first person to come up with the concept of the firearms cartridge has been lost to history. However, the idea that you could combine a pre-measured amount of powder, the lead projectile and the container to hold them in a single package was absolute genius.

That very first cartridge was nothing more than a piece of paper rolled into a loose, fairly crude tube that contained the powder and a round ball. The paper tube was twisted at the ends and then tied with string somewhat like an old-fashioned sausage. The end of the tube could be simply torn off with hands or teeth, and poured down into the barrel, with the paper forming a convenient funnel. The paper could also then be used to make a wad for the powder, and/or a patch for the bullet that is then rammed down on the charge. A bit of the pre-measured powder was saved to be poured into the rifle's flash pan to ignite the main charge. Having pre-prepared cartridges was a huge advantage to both hunters for their convenience and to especially the military, as the rate of fire could be increased significantly.

There's no doubt that paper cartridges of this sort had been around for some time, but it was in the early 1600s that King Gustavus Aldolphus of Sweden ordered that his army should be supplied with them. The fact that one of the dominant European armies of the period had standardized on the paper cartridge was quickly noticed by the other powers and the practice became universal.

However, the cartridge was still missing a means of igniting the powder, a vital component to make it completely self-contained. Ignition was being provided by an external source – usually a spark from a flint attached to the rifle's hammer striking the frizzen (a portion of the firearm's iron flash pan). This was pretty much how things were done for around two hundred years before the Rev. Alexander Forsythe, a Scot, patented his idea in 1807 of using fulminate of mercury in a percussion cap made of copper and later of brass. Flintlocks were easily modified to use the new percussion cap and while ignition was still being provided by an external source to the cartridge, an important advancement in its evolution had taken place. Now the goal was to marry the cartridge and the new means of ignition into the same package.

Firearms design was also evolving. The various militaries of Europe and America were very interested in the concept of breech-loading. There were several advantages. However, the most important of these was a dramatic increase in the rate of fire. However the fairly loose and flimsy nature of early paper cartridges was totally incompatible with breech loading. Consequently, there was a lot of experimentation during the next 30-40 years to strengthen the paper cartridge case so that it could stand up to being rapidly inserted into a breech-loading mechanism and which also, when fired, ensured the chamber would be fully sealed and not blow gases and unburned powder back into the face of the shooter. There were all kinds of materials being experimented with such as cardboard, linen, varnished paper, silk, etc. The zenith of the non-metal cartridge in a breechloader was probably reached in 1842 when Dreyse, a Prussian, patented his infamous "needle gun." The needle gun cartridge had a

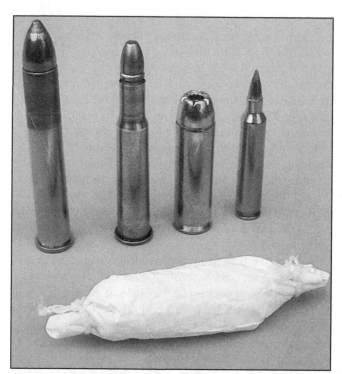

The paper cartridge tied with string was the stroke of genius that led to the modern brass cartridge of today.

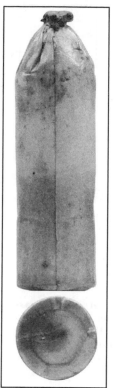

The Prussian Needle Gun cartridge was ignited by a very long firing pin that actually traveled through the powder charge to ignite the primer, which was located just behind the bullet.

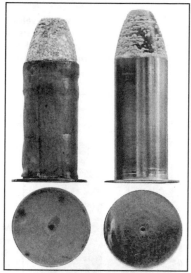

The 50 Maynard, which was used extensively during the Civil War, was ignited by a paper tape containing the primer material.

thick, heavy paper body with a 61-caliber acorn-shaped bullet sitting on the powder charge. Two things made the Dreyse gun the very first of the modern military firearms. The first was that the cartridge finally contained and integrated all the components of modern ammunition i.e. a case, a bullet, powder, and very importantly, the primer. The second was that the Dreyse rifle was the first mass-produced bolt-action rifle adopted by a major military power.

The primer material was located at the base of the bullet way up at the top of the cartridge. Consequently, in order to ignite the primer, a very long needle-like firing pin had to pierce the base of the paper cartridge and travel through the length of the case filled with powder in order to strike the primer material. By igniting the powder column at the front end of the case, combustion was said to be more efficient and complete. Indeed, this idea keeps popping up from time to time even into the 20th century. The Prussians quickly embraced the needle gun for their army and used it in 1866 to slaughter the Austrian army.

The fact that the Prussians had a bolt-action rifle using a fully self-contained cartridge gave them a huge advantage over any enemy using a traditional black powder type rifled musket. First of all, in a test during that period, it was demonstrated that the needle gun could fire five shots for every one fired from a standard military black powder musket. Second, the bolt-action needle gun could be reloaded from the prone position. This was a huge advantage. On the other hand, an opponent using a regular musket had to stand up in order to pour the powder down the barrel when reloading, thus exposing themselves to Prussian fire. Consequently solders facing the Prussian army were sitting ducks (make

that standing ducks) to needle gun firepower. The needle gun's rate of fire was so devastating, that it was considered by many to be a terrorist weapon and highly immoral to boot.

However it did have a weakness, which is of interest to our brief look at cartridge history. The paper cartridge didn't burn completely in the chamber, and after a number of shots, enough debris accumulated there to prevent a good seal when the bolt was closed. Subsequent shots would then blow gas and unburned powder granules into the face and eyes of the shooter. When this happened, it's said that the Prussian solders would hold their rifles away from their faces and often fire their guns from the hip in the general direction of the enemy. Obviously, aimed fire went out the window at this point. Nevertheless, the sustained massive rate of fire was still more than enough to overwhelm an enemy, even if it was less accurate after the first half-dozen shots or so.

With the advancement of breech-loading technology, the middle 1800's saw the development of several types of cartridges using metal in their construction as well as the development of various priming schemes. In most cases the metal of choice was copper. Copper seemed to be a reasonable choice since it was readily available, lots of people had experience working with it, and it could be worked into thin sheets to form cases. When subjected to pressure it also readily expanded to seal the chamber so none of the expanding gases leaked out of the breech. There was a problem with copper, however. Having no inherent ability to spring back to near its original diameter after being fired, a copper cartridge would often be difficult to extract. Brass, on the other hand, can both expand readily to seal the chamber and just

The 22 Short was developed by Smith & Wesson for its Model 1 revolver and is still used in Olympic competition today.

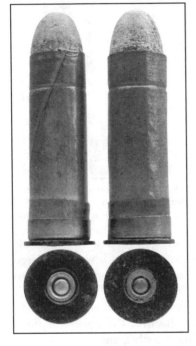

Made of coiled brass wrapped around a mandrel, the 577 Snider cartridge became the mainstay of the British Empire.

as readily springs back, thus allowing for easy extraction.

The Maynard Rifle Company was certainly an innovator in its day and took advantage of the ability of brass to expand and spring back. In 1851 it patented an all-brass case. This was a simple tube with a round base soldered on the end. In the center of the base was a flash hole. A lock mechanism advanced a paper roll of "caps" (similar to those once used in children's toy pistols) in front of the flash hole when the hammer was cocked. When stuck by the hammer, the cap would explode sending an igniting flame through the flash hole into the powder. The Maynard rifle and cartridge still used an external ignition source but it was getting close to the ideal of having the primer integral to an all-metal case.

Probably the first to reach that ideal was the Smith and Wesson 22 Short. S&W brought out this cartridge for a small, self-defense pocket pistol in 1858. It was the first successful rimfire cartridge produced in this country. The rimfire successfully packaged together all of the elements of a fully integrated metal cartridge i.e. powder, primer, bullet, and case. It was also easy to make.

A copper disk was drawn into a tube shape and the end was bumped into a hollow rim. Fulminate of mercury was placed into the rim and 4 grains of blackpowder and 29-grain bullet came on top. Here we now had a totally self-contained package that was robust, easy to carry, very resistant to the elements, and was very reliable. The rimfire worked so well that it wasn't long before others were making larger and larger versions of it even up to 56 caliber, which was used in the Spencer carbine. 41-caliber rimfires were very popular in the derringer pistols of the middle 1800s as well. However, one problem with the large rimfires was the fact that pres-

This American-designed Snider breech-loading action was retrofitted into existing Enfield muskets, which then became the first long arm to use a brass cartridge in the British army.

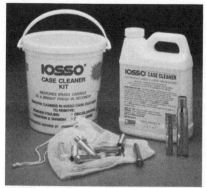

This case spinner from Sinclair International is a handy tool to rapidly clean and polish small numbers of cartridge cases.

Wet case cleaning with the Iosso system only takes a few minutes.

Rotary rock tumblers like this one from Thumler clean brass just as fast as vibe types and are extremely durable.

sures/velocities had to be kept low because the early copper – and even brass – cases weren't very strong in the head area. If loaded too hot the case could burst. Consequently, the low velocities typical of most large rimfires made their effectiveness fairly marginal. Cases sticking in the chambers were also common.

Certainly one of the very first successful centerfire cartridges was the 577 Snider. Adopted by the British Army in 1867, it had a long distinguished history and saw extensive service thoughout the Empire, including the Zulu wars. Believe it or not, there are Snider rifles still being used in the hinterlands of places like India and Nepal. Even today, American GIs are bringing back Snider rifles from Afghanistan as souvenirs.

The Snider cartridge had a metal base and originally a cardboard body and so vaguely resembled a shotgun cartridge in that respect. Then Col. Edward Boxer of the royal arsenal (who invented the Boxer primer) reworked the cartridge so that it was now made of "coiled" brass. Very thin (.005") brass strips with a paper backing were wrapped twice around a mandrel with a quarter-inch overlap and glued together. Additionally, the interior of the case was varnished and lined with paper to prevent corrosion from the blackpowder. Obviously, the Snider case wasn't very strong, but it did the job very well with the low pressures that the cartridge operated at. Eventually modern, drawn brass cases were produced for the 577. However, it's interesting to note that because of the widespread use of the Snider rifle throughout the British colonies, ammo using coiled brass cases was still being manufactured in England as late as the 1930s. Evidently this ammunition was reserved for sale exclusively to the civilian colonial market.

The thing that made the Snider cartridge stand out was the fact that it had an integrated primer in the base of an all-metal cartridge - an unusual all metal case, but all metal never the less. Additionally, it was not a short-lived oddity like so many others, but a full-fledged, standardized military cartridge for the most powerful nation on the earth at that time.

The totally integrated, self contained, all metal rifle cartridge finally arrived. Even though case heads on those early all metal cartridges were relatively weak, slowly and surely the design became thicker and stronger. In turn, this allowed higher and higher pressures to be used which resulted in faster velocities, flatter trajectories, and greater effectiveness on the target.

Even though modern brass cartridge cases are strong, extremely durable, and manufactured to precise dimensions, once they've been used, they require a certain amount of care if they're going to be reloaded again. The first thing every shooter needs to do before starting the reloading process is to inspect the cases for splits and cracks. This is especially true if the cases have been used a number of times, are from military surplus sources, or have been in uncontrolled storage for very long periods of time.

Splits and cracks can occur for a number of reasons. The most common is that previous loads in the case were too hot. Overcharging a case can stress it way beyond what it was designed to accommodate. Sooner or later that abused case will develop a crack just above the head. Often these cracks will be very small and difficult to see. Some times, in really severe cases, the head of the case will be totally severed. Obviously, safety becomes a major issue when this happens. Case cracking and head separations can also occur

Annealing by hand with a torch is awkward and slow.

when a gun has an overly long chamber and the headspace is subsequently excessive.

Splitting usually occurs in the neck of bottleneck cases or at the mouth of straight wall cases. This happens when a case has been fired too many times. While case necks are very resilient, they become work-hardened somewhat every time they are expanded and contracted during the reloading process and when the gun is fired and the bullet released. This hardening becomes cumulative over time. When a case neck is work hardened excessively, it becomes brittle. The same is especially true of straight-wall pistol brass, which is usually belled outward to accept the bullet and then crimped solidly against the cannelure. Here, the work-hardening is severe and splits around the mouth of the case can rapidly appear, depending on the "hardness" or severity of the crimp. Splitting is far more common than case cracking. At any rate, if a case develops a split, accuracy will be adversely affected at a minimum.

Being that splitting and cracking are conditions that can occur when cases are used hard, we need to be on the lookout for these conditions before we can proceed into the handloading process. Trying to visually detect these conditions when the cases are dirty, covered with powder residue, and dull with surface oxide is difficult. If the cases are clean and bright, the job is much easier. Consequently, the first thing we want to do is to properly clean our cases so that we can do a proper job of inspection.

The handloader has two general types of cleaning methods to consider i.e. wet or dry. Wet cleaning has the advantage of being much faster, and large numbers of cases can be cleaned as easily as small numbers. It cleans out the inside of the case as well as the outside. This is no small matter as I've seen some cases where a hard crusty residue had built up in the interior, reducing powder capacity. If the same amount of powder is put in a crusty case as in a clean case, over-pressure will be the sure result, with its nasty consequences.

When wet cleaning, dirty cases are simply immersed into a plastic bucket containing a weak acid and soap solution, such as is available from the Iosso Company. The cases can be shaken from time to time to increase the efficiency of the process. After 5-8 minutes or so, the solution is strained out and put back into the original container; it can be reused many times. The cases are then rinsed with water and then dried in a 200-degree oven on an old pizza pan or such. The cases will be clean and bright but not shiny. Quite often wet cleaning will even clean out primer pocket residue. Once the cases are cleaned up, detecting cracks and splits becomes much easier.

If you want that factory-new brilliant shine, polishing in addition to cleaning is required. For a small number of cases (50 or less), I like the case holder/spinner from Sinclair International. This is a little gizmo that holds the case and is chucked into an electric drill or power screwdriver. The brass is rapidly spun and a wad of 0000 steel wool is held against the case. The steel wool rapidly removes dirt, carbon residue, and tarnish and leaves the case clean and shiny. For an even more brilliant shine, "Never Dull" polishing wool, found at auto supply stores, can be used instead.

To process large numbers of cases to a brilliant shine, tumbling is the way to go. It typically takes 8-12 hours, and tumblers can be loaded up and left unattended during that period. Tumblers come in two types: vibratory and rotary. There are many claims that vibrator types are faster, but in a side-by-side experiment some years ago I could see no difference between the two in speed or efficiency. I personally prefer the rotary tumbler with a rubber liner made by Thumler. It was originally designed for rock polishing, and so is very tough and durable. It's also very quiet and has a super heavy-duty motor that will last decades.

Tumbling media falls into two categories as well: ground walnut and fine ground corncob. Ground walnut is a good cleaning material and will put a basic polish on cases. Large 20 lb. bags that will last a long, long time are often available at very modest prices at pet supply houses where it is sold as litter for rabbits, hamsters, etc. Small bags of walnut are available from shooting supply sources. When augmented with rouge abrasive, ground walnut becomes an even better cleaning material that puts a very nice polish on brass. Corncob provides the best polish of all but it's too fine and soft to be a very good cleaner. Consequently, you'll have to first clean with walnut and then polish with cob. However, when cob is combined with aluminum oxide as is sold by RCBS, it becomes an excellent cleaner/polisher combo.

Tumbling will often leave fine dust from the media on your case that has to be wiped off with an old T-shirt or such. Throwing a sheet of laundry anti-static material in the tumbler will usually take care of the problem. After you've tumbled your brass, make sure the primer pockets don't have any tumbling media packed inside and that the flash holes are clear.

Once our newly-cleaned cases have been thoroughly inspected for defects, we want to insure that they don't develop any neck splits after the next time they're used. After all, we want to get as many reloadings out of our expensive brass as we can. The best way to do that is to anneal the necks. It's not necessary to do this preventive procedure after every firing, but more like after every five firings.

As mentioned previously, firing a cartridge case puts a lot of stress on the neck area. Running the case through our various reloading dies also works and stresses the case. Even when the bullet is inserted into the case, the neck is under great tension and stress. All this squeezing and expanding of the thin neck makes it hard and brittle, and liable to split. Annealing is a heat process to restore the neck's flexibility.

For small numbers, cases can be simply stood in a small pan of water and the necks manually heated with a propane torch to relieve the stressed metal. The water protects the base of the case from the heat and insures that it will retain its strength. Some advocate that the necks should be heated cherry red and the case then tipped over into the water.

The Ken Light auto-case annealer puts just the right amount of heat on case necks to restore their flexibility.

However this is taking things to an extreme degree. We need only to ensure that our clean necks develop a light blue patina with pink overtones when heated. So go lightly with the torch. Once the necks take on these colors, the proper degree of anneal has taken place. It's not even necessary to tip the cases over into the water afterwards.

An even better way to anneal brass is to use a Ken Light case annealer. Whether you have a small number of cases or a large amount, this is the way you want to go. The Ken Light machine is a small motorized carousel in which the cases are placed in holes around the diameter of a cast aluminum plate measuring about a foot across. The interior of the plate is dished out and filled with water. The water ensures that the temperature of the plate and the brass never exceeds the boiling point of the water, and therefore keeps the body and head of the case from being overheated. A small electric motor rotates the plate containing the brass in front of a couple of propane torches. As the plate rotates, the cases rotate 360 degrees in their holes as well, guaranteeing that all sides of the neck will receive the same amount of heat. The speed of the plate's rotation also insures that the case necks are exposed to the torch's flame for just the proper amount of time to properly anneal them. This little machine really makes this job fast and easy, especially if you have a large number of cases to process.

The long history of the cartridge case is extremely complex, but through the strenuous efforts of many dedicated individuals, this product of amazing simplicity and functionality ended up literally changing the events of the world on many occasions. Even though the modern brass cartridge case is commonplace today, the handloader would be well advised to treat it with respect. Failure to do so can invite disaster. However, when the case is cleaned, inspected and reloaded in a common-sense manner, it will provide the shooter many enjoyable experiences both at the shooting range and in the field. It doesn't get any better than that.

Moose may be the biggest deer in North America, but elk are the toughest.

Loading The Medium Bores For Elk

By Steve Gash

THE ADULT BULL tips the scales at about 560-700 pounds. Cows are a bit smaller, but still top out at around 450-525 pounds. Elk inhabit some of the roughest country around, and have the strength and stamina to negotiate it. Plus, elk bones are considerably heavier than those of deer, and their hides are thicker. All this adds up to a large, tough animal that is no pushover. To be adequate for elk, a rifle needs long-range horsepower, and plenty of it.

This inextricably leads us to a definition of the minimum requirements for the task, and indeed to decide what is a "medium bore." About forty years ago, Jack O'Connor stated that the medium bores started at 32 and went to 40 caliber, and considered the 338 and 375 "big bores."

New cartridges and high-tech bullets developed over the past few years offer increased range and capabilities of elk rifles, and allow us to lower the caliber bracket to 30 without hindering our ability to take elk cleanly at longer ranges. At the other end of the spectrum is what may be the most useful cartridge ever spawned, the queen of the "mediums," the 375 H&H Magnum.

I can already hear the anguished howls from lovers of the 270 Winchester, 7mm Remington Magnum, and other similar cartridges. But if we're going to go after what is arguably the toughest of the deer clan, we

Our survey of great elk cartridges includes *(from left)*: the 30-06, 300 H&H Magnum, 300 Winchester Magnum, 300 WSM, and 300 Weatherby Magnum.

The hits keep coming with *(from left)*: the 8mm-06, 325 WSM, 8mm Remington Magnum, the new 338 Federal, the 338 Winchester Magnum, and the ponderous 340 Weatherby Magnum.

Medium bores in the 35+ crowd feature *(from left)*: the 358 Winchester, 35 Whelen, 358 Norma Magnum, 9.3x62 Mauser, 9.3x74R, 375 H&H Magnum, and the new 375 Ruger.

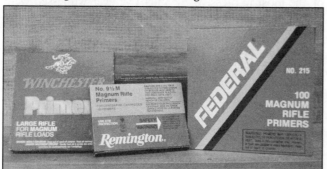

Magnum primers in the larger cases used for most elk loads usually result in more uniform velocities, an aid to long-range hitting.

might as well concentrate on optimum calibers, and the bullets that make them cook. Power is of little use if you can't apply it properly, but as with all hunting, shot placement is still paramount.

Bullets For Elk

Before we delve into the case-by-case loading recommendations, let's quickly look at a variety of new developments in bullet technology that widen the elk cartridge window considerably.

We have had a bevy of excellent "traditional big game" bullets for decades. These include the Hornady InterLock and SST, the Ballistic Tip and Partition from Nosler, Remington's CorkLokt, the Sierra GameKing, and the Speer Hot-Cor. These are all variations of the "cup-and-core" bullet, and offer various degrees of penetration and expansion. All are fine bullets, but the high velocity of a large magnum on a close shot or a low impact velocity of a very long shot may limit their performance.

We have recently seen a flurry of new bullet designs, and they almost universally offer dramatic improvements in the expansion-penetration-accuracy continuum, and we can now select a designer bullet for almost any anticipated field condition. The introduction of new cartridges and new (mostly slower) powders has aided this situation, too. The new bullets utilize a variety of approaches to the perpetual problem of controlled expansion: bonded cores, dual cores, no cores, or a combination of these technologies.

The Hornady InterBond and Nosler Accubond are the best examples of the bonded core bullets in which the lead alloy core is permanently affixed to the gilding metal jacket, thereby preventing core-jacket separation. Both are very accurate, and offer extended range at both ends of the spectrum. Remington's new Premier CoreLokt Ultra Bonded and the Swift Sirocco II fit in here, too. Speer's Grand Slam is essentially bonded, too, as the core is molten as it's poured into the jacket.

Nosler separates the two cores of its famous Partition bullet with a wall of jacket material. The front part of the bullet expands rapidly, but the rear part keeps on penetrating. Swift's A-Frame also has a "cross member" and the front core is bonded to the jacket.

Then there are the "no lead" bullets. Barnes' Triple Shock-X bullet and the brand new E-Tip from Nosler are examples. Both offer good expansion and deep penetration. And if some Peoples' Republics outlaw lead bullets, these effective alternatives are already in place.

Caliber-Specific Loads For Elk

We cannot, of course, discuss *every* potential cartridge and bullet combination suitable for elk. But we can structure our choices by bullet and caliber groups. The load table includes loads that I have either hunted with or range-tested extensively, and which the elk hunter can use with confidence. (Just because a specific cartridge or bullet is not mentioned does not detract from its potential usefulness.)

I consider the loads listed as working maxima in my rifles, so as with all load data, reduce the charges about 6 percent or so, and work up, watching for signs of high pressure. Note that case and primer types are provided. If you change one or the other, or switch bullets, invoke the "reduce by 6%" rule. If you don't have a chronograph, get one. Otherwise, the only thing you'll know about your loads is accuracy. Follow the usual safety rules, test carefully, and you'll have fun.

The 30 Calibers

We must start with probably the most popular hunting round in history, the 30-06 Springfield. For elk, the traditional bullet has been the 180-grain, and there is little reason to change. The Nosler Partition or AccuBond, and Hornady's InterBond are perfect matches for the '06's velocity. With near-maximum loads, most 180-grain bullets can be pushed at least 2700 fps, and the high ballistic coefficients of the pointy ones will deliver a lot of "*umph*" at long range. A charge of 58.0 grains of Reloder 22 in my 20-inch skinny-barreled Ruger M-77 Lightweight gives the 180-grain Speer Grand Slam a velocity of 2459 fps, and is delightfully accurate. The Hornady InterBond works well with this load, too. Fans of the Nosler Partition can rejoice with a load of 57.0 grains of Ramshot's Hunter at 2487 fps. As with many (relatively) smaller cartridges, trajectory is the limiting factor here. The folks at Barnes will protest that with the deep penetration of their TS-X Bullet, you can drop down to a 165-grain, and still get results, and there is ample field evidence for this.

With the 30-caliber magnums, we really get into "elk territory," and there are several good choices. They offer extra velocity that translates into a flatter trajectory and more down-range power.

My all-time favorite big 30 is an old-timer, the 300 H&H Magnum. From its inception in 1925 to this day, it has provided riflemen with just about the optimum combination of power and accuracy. In 1983, Remington graced us with its M-700 Limited Edition Classic in "Holland's Super 30," as it's called across the pond, and I had to have one. In the intervening years, I have taken more elk (and mule deer) with it than any other cartridge. Other rifles come and go, but my 300 H&H has a permanent home. Launch a good 30-caliber bullet out of a 300 H&H (or similar-sized) case at ramming speed, and you're soon up to your elbows in elk innards.

Back when I started loading the 300 H&H, I'd had good success with Speer bullets in other calibers, so I bought a box of their 180-gr. soft points (they weren't "Hot-Cors" in those days). With 69.0 gr. of IMR-4831, I got a velocity of 2970 fps, and 1-inch groups. I sighted in two inches high at 100 yards, and confidently went after elk, and took several with it. That doesn't mean that I haven't dallied with other loads over the years. Two I can recommend also use IMR-4831 powder. The 180-grain Partition over 68.0 grains gives a velocity of 2846 fps. Accuracy is top notch, and the penetration is legendary. For the heavy-bullet crowd, try the 200-grain Speer Hot-Cor, with 65.5 grains at 2708 fps.

Since 1963, the 300 Winchester Magnum has pretty much ruled the roost in the elk fields, and with good reason. It imparts excellent velocities to tough bullets with good sectional densities, and has plenty of power, and great accuracy. I have seen a couple of 300 WMs in use. Mine is an ancient Parker-Hale Mauser that looks a bit rough, but which shoots very well. Velocities with this particular 300 WM are somewhat lower than most 300s, however. I settled on two powders: IMR-7828 and Norma's MRP. With 75.0 grains of the former under the 180-grain Hornady Inter-Bond, velocity is a modest 2826 fps, but it is uniform and very accurate. With 74.0 grains of MRP, the 180-grain Partition is propelled at 2821 fps, and is also a good load. The excellent Swift A-Frame or Barnes Triple Shock-X bullets also shoot well and dump elk.

The 300 WM's prowess on game is well known, and some of the most impressive elk kills I've ever witnessed were accomplished with a 300 Winchester Magnum, but not with me behind it. My elk-hunting partner, Jan Larson, uses his Ruger M-77 in 300 WM with deadly precision. Three years in a row Jan clobbered three elk with his 300 WM – a 5x5 bull and two fat cows. The bull had the temerity to wobble for about 50 yards on rubber legs before collapsing. The cows hit the ground so hard they bounced. Jan stuffs 180-grain Grand Slams over 76.0 grains of Reloder 22. This is a smidgen under maximum, and you can't argue with the results. Velocity is 3140 fps, and with him so armed, any elk within 350 yards is in big trouble.

I briefly had a fling with the 300 Weatherby Magnum,

and it was impressive. Given its power and velocity, the 300 Weatherby may just be the best 30-caliber overall cartridge for elk. Mine was also a Remington M-700 Classic. It was light, accurate, and deadly. It also kicked considerably. While I use 180-grain bullets over 74.0 grains of IMR-4831, the round is probably at its best with heavier bullets. My favorite load was the 200-grain Speer Hot-Cor at a velocity of 2948 fps produced by 81.0 grains of IMR-7828. I have taken only one elk with this load, and it was DRT (dead right there). I have also shot Barnes TS-X bullets with great results and their brand-new MRX bullets look even better on paper.

The 32 Calibers

If there is a Rodney Dangerfield of bore diameters, it has to be the 8 millimeters, and the very mention of the caliber gives most shooters a case of the vapors. But there are three old-timers, and one newcomer, that warrant our attention as elk getters.

The old 8x57mm Mauser may not be flashy, but enough game has been taken with it to establish its credibility. With the great bullets of today, and modern rifles, it is certainty adequate. My 8x57 is yet another Remington M-700 Classic, and is a first-rate big game rifle. For great loads within its range, one need look no further than the 195-grain Hornady InterLock over 49.0 grains of Ball-C(2) for 2506 fps, or the 200-grain Accubond with 53.0 grains of H-414 at 2544 fps. While I have not taken an elk with these loads, I did harvest a nice whitetail buck with the latter, and he dropped in his tracks. The Swift 200-grain A-Frames, Barnes 180-grain TS-X, and the 200-grain Nosler Partitions also shoot well and lend utility to this fine old round.

The 8mm-06 has a checkered past. After WWII, a lot of returning GIs had their liberated 8mm Mausers re-chambered to 8mm-06. This made a fine rifle even better, and many continue to see use to this day. My shooting chum Jens Barclay graciously loaned me his custom V24 Mauser for load testing. A load of 51.7 grains of IMR-4064 under the 200-grain Speer Hot-Cor zips along at 2547 fps. Speer states that this bullet is of "tough construction" and was designed for the 8mm Remington Magnum, so it is certainly suitable for elk. Another great 8mm-06 load is 55.5 grains of W-760 and 195-grain Hornady InterLock at 2510 fps. This bullet is also of stout construction.

Not much happened in the 8mm world until 1978 when Remington unveiled the 8mm Remington Magnum in the M-700 BDL series. A real masher, the 8mm RM has the power and range, but not the sales, and the BDL was discontinued in 1985. My M-700 BDL was made in March of 1978, and is one of 3600 shipped that inaugural year. While not as accurate as other rifles detailed here, it definitely shoots within MOE (minute of elk). Two tough 200-grain bullets that make the 8mm RM cook are the Partition and AccuBond. With 85.0 grains of H-1000, the former blasts along at 2928 fps. The latter propelled by 81.0 grains of IMR-7828 at 2889 is not only powerful but also accurate.

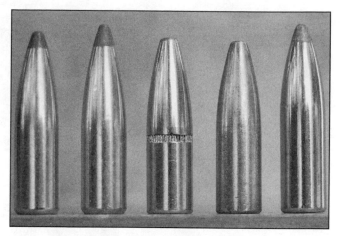

The sleek profiles of these 30-caliber bullets help flatten their trajectories *(from left)*: 180-gr. 30-caliber bullets, and here are five: the Sierra Spitzer, Nosler Partition, Speer Grand Slam, and Remington CoreLokt Ultra. On the right is the Speer's 200-gr. Hot-Cor.

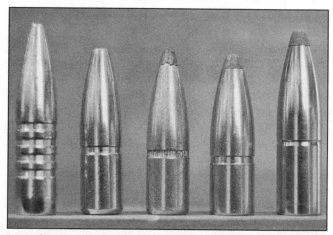

New in the "no lead" bullet race is Nosler's E-Tip, shown here in its 180-gr. 30-cal. persuasion.

Long, heavy, and tough, these bullets will plough through elk *(from left)*: 8mms: the 200-gr. Barnes TS-X and Swift A-Frame, and Hornady's 195-gr. SP. The 338s are represented by Nosler's 210- and 250-gr. Partitions.

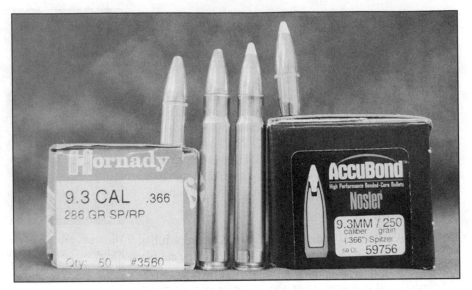

Think the 9.3x62 Mauser is dead? It was number 49 on RCBS's list of die sales in 2006. These two new, high-tech bullet help explain why.

The best overall load (of 47 tested) is the 195-grain Hornady InterLock and 84.0 grains of Reloder 25 at 2936 fps, which consistently groups into an inch.

The 8mm RM's larger case capacity also allows us to use heavier bullets at good velocities. The super-tough and extra sleek Sierra 220-grain SBT shines over 83.0 grains of H-1000. Velocity is within a whisker of 3000 fps, and its ballistic coefficient of .512 gives a very flat trajectory, and allows it to deliver a tremendous punch down range. If you think that I like this load, you're right.

I've saved the 325 WSM for last because, like a spoiled child, it has wormed its way into my heart. Introduced in 2005, the 325 WSM is actually an 8mm. Note that it's not called the "8mm SM." They didn't even call it the "323 WSM." Winchester carefully disguised it as something else. That 8mm stigma again. Prior to its introduction, there was speculation that the next larger SM would be a 338, but extensive testing by Winchester showed that the .323-inch bore produced better ballistics. While the 325 can't best the larger 8mm RM, it comes pretty close, and does so with a lot less powder, and the rifles are shorter and lighter. My M-700 BDL in 8mm RM checks in at 9-1/2 pounds. My Browning A-bolt 325 weighs less than 8 pounds.

I literally just finished testing the 325. The day before I penned these lines, I was on the range, testing the final 22 loads in my 325 WSM. Velocities of over 2800 fps are easy with 200-grain bullets, and the 220s come close to 2600. I tested six powders, but one could get by with just IMR-4831. A charge of 68.5 grains works great with 200-grain bullets. With the Swift A-Frame, it delivers a bone-crunching 2844 fps, and averaged 0.98-inch groups, and with the AccuBond; velocity is 2853 fps. The 220-grain Sierra SBT achieves 2548 fps with 64.5 grains of Hunter. Any of these three loads would be almost perfect elk medicine.

The 33s

My first medium bore rifle was a 338 Winchester Magnum. With it I took several elk and mulies before its recoil and weight took their toll. The 338 is extremely popular in the West as an elk rifle, and with good reason. With bullets of 225 or 250 gr., it will do the job.

With all the great loads for this cartridge, I'll pass on just two proven ones. The .338-inch 210-gr. Nosler Partition is one of the all time great game bullets, and in the 338 WM, it can be driven to over 2700 fps. Seventy-six grains of Reloder 19 is my favorite with this bullet. The velocity is 2887 fps, and I can personally attest that this load is absolute dynamite on elk.

With 250-grain bullets, either the Partition or the Grand Slam is also terrific. I once nailed a large cow at 374 yards with a GS, and as I brought the Ruger down from recoil, all I could see of the elk were four hooves, pointed skyward. The load was 69.0 grains of IMR-4831 for a speed of 2676 fps. The 250-grain Partition over the same powder charge is also a great load.

The biggest 33 with which I have taken elk is the 340 Weatherby. It kicks like a mule, but the 340 delivers more power, farther, than almost any cartridge in existence. With either 210- or 250-grain bullets, it will lay low an elk and its flat trajectory make hits at extended ranges not only possible, but probable. I narrowed my loads down to two. The 210-grain Partition over 89.0 grains of MRP gives 3089 fps, and a charge of 89.0 grains of Reloder 25 pushes the 250 Grand Slam to 2745 fps.

A real sleeper for elk hunting is the fine old 9.3x62mm Mauser. Since 1905, it has earned an enviable reputation in game fields worldwide. My CZ M-550 is a bit heavy, but is very accurate, and delivers its 0.366-inch bullets with authority. The 250-grain Ballistic Tip or AccuBond have the toughness and high ballistic coefficients to make them potent elk medicine. A charge of 56.0 grains of IMR-3031 gives either of these bullets a velocity of 2523 fps. A less efficient but still fine load is the 270-grain Speer SS over 53.0 grains of Benchmark for 2305 fps. The 286-grain Barnes TS-X or Partitions or the 250-grain Swift A-Frame make up into good elk loads, too.

Last in our survey is the 375 H&H Magnum. What more can be said about the great cartridge? If you like heavy bullets and lots of power, and don't mind a little recoil, this is the cartridge for you. The cadre of .375-inch bullets these days is fantastic. For the most in long-range capabilities, stick with the 250- and 270-grain pointed bullets, preferably with boattails. The jacket on the 250-grain Sierra SBT is the same thickness as that for their 300-grain SBT, so it is plenty stout. The 270-grain Speer SBT over 66.0 grains of H-4895 produces 2523 fps, and a reasonably flat trajectory. For fans of heavyweight bullets, try the 300-grain Hornady IL and 75.0 grains of IMR-4350. At over 2500 fps, this bullet will ruin an elk's day.

Load Evaluation

Three things make – or break – an elk load. First, it has to be accurate. Second, it must have a suitably flat trajectory. And third, it must have the raw horsepower to drop an elk at our maximum range.

The trajectory of the load is key. For elk, we should probably limit the rise above LOS to no more than 3 inches, and impact below the LOS to a maximum of a foot – without applying "hold-over." For long shots, one of the new trajectory-compensating reticles, like the Zeiss Rapid-Z, Leupold's Boone and Crockett Big Game, and Burris' Ballistic Plex are great aids. If you don't have a ballistic program for your computer, get one and use it. Shoot at long range to confirm the trajectory of your chosen load. Laser range finders are available, inexpensive, and accurate, and should be considered required equipment for the elk hunter.

The rifleman must know his, and his cartridge's, limitations. Here's my test for elk hunters: Put up a 9-inch paper plate, at whatever range you want, and blaze away from various shooting positions. The maximum range from which you can *reliably* hit the plate – from whatever distance or position – is the maximum range from which you are justified in shooting at an elk, period. Practice and make perfect. A grand game animal like an elk deserves no less.

Medium Bore Loads For Elk

CASE	PRIMER	POWDER	CHARGE (GR.)	BULLET WT., MAKE & TYPE	VELOCITY (FPS)	COMMENTS
Caliber: 30-06 Springfield, Test Gun: Ruger M-77RL, Barrel Length: 20 inches						
Win.	Fed-210	Re-22	58.0	180 Speer GS	2459	Very accurate
Win.	Fed-210M	Hunter	57.0	180 Nosler Partition	2487	Great penetration and accuracy
Caliber: 300 H&H Magnum, Test Gun: Rem. M-700, Barrel Length: 24 inches						
Win.	Fed-215	IMR-4831	69.0	180 Speer HC	2970	My standard elk load for years
Win.	Fed-215	IMR-4831	68.0	180 Nosler Partition	2846	Even better than above load
Win.	Fed-215	IMR-4831	65.5	200 Speer HC	2708	Powerful and accurate
Caliber: 300 Win. Mag., Test Gun: Parker-Hale M-1200, Barrel Length: 24 inches						
Win.	Fed-215	IMR-7828	75.0	180 Hornady IB	2846	
Win.	Fed-215	MRP	74.0	180 Nosler Partition	2821	
Caliber: 300 Win. Mag., Test Gun: Ruger M-77R, Barrel Length: 24 inches						
Win.	Fed-215	Re-22	76.0	Speer GS	3140	Absolutely devastating on elk
Caliber: 300 Weatherby Mag., Test Gun: Rem. M-700, Barrel Length: 24 inches						
Wby.	Fed-215	IMR-4831	74.0	180 Hornady IB	3100	Powerful and flat shooting
Wby.	Fed-215	IMR-7828	81.0	200 Nosler Partition	2948	A classic elk load
Caliber: 8x57mm Mauser, Test Gun: Rem. M-700, Barrel Length: 24 inches						
Rem.	R-P 9 ½	Ball-C(2)	49.0	195 Hornady IL	2506	Excellent for both deer and elk
Rem.	R-P 9 ½	H-414	53.0	200 Nosler AB	2544	A great all around load

Medium Bore Loads For Elk

CASE	PRIMER	POWDER	CHARGE (GR.)	BULLET WT., MAKE & TYPE	VELOCITY (FPS)	COMMENTS
Caliber: 8mm-06, Test Gun: Mauser M98, Barrel Length: 24 inches						
Win.	CCI-200	IMR-4064	51.7	200 Speer HC	2547	Accurate and deadly
Win.	WLR	W-760	55.5	195 Hornady IL	2510	Very uniform load
Caliber: 325 WSM, Test Gun: Browning A-Bolt II, Barrel Length: 23 inches						
Win.	WLRM	IMR-4831	68.5	200 A-Frame	2844	A great load
Win.	WLRM	IMR-4831	68.5	200 Accubond	2853	Good accuracy and penetration
Win.	WLRM	Hunter	64.5	220 Sierra SBT	2548	Flat trajectory
Caliber: 8mm Rem. Mag., Test Gun: Rem. M-700, Barrel Length: 24 inches						
Rem.	Fed-215	H-1000	85.0	200 Nosler AB	2928	A masher
Rem.	Fed-215	IMR-7828	81.0	200 Nosler Partition	2889	Terrific load
Rem.	Fed-215	H-1000	83.0	220 Sierra SBT	2894	Great power
Caliber: 338 Win. Mag., Test Gun: Ruger M-77R, Barrel Length: 24 inches						
Win.	Fed-215	Reloder 19	76.0	210 Nosler Partition	2887	Very accurate and drops elk like a rock
Win.	Fed-215	IMR-4831	69.0	250 Speer SG	2676	Good, powerful load
Caliber: 340 Weatherby Mag., Test Gun: Wby. Mark V, Barrel Length: 26 inches						
Wby.	Fed-215	Norma MRP	89.0	210 Nosler Partition	3086	Devastating and flat shooting
Wby.	Fed-215	Reloder 25	89.0	250 Speer GS	2745	A quintessential elk load
Caliber: 358 Winchester, Test Gun: Ruger M-77R, Barrel Length: 22 inches						
Rem.	R-P 9½	H-322	44.0	200 Hornady SP	2542	High velocity for the caliber
PMC 308	R-P 9½	Benchmark	46.0	225 Nosler Partition	2467	Good velocity and great accuracy
Win.	R-P 9½	XMR-2495	45.0	250 Speer SP	2302	Great all-around load
Caliber: 35 Whelen, Test Gun: Rem. M-700, Barrel Length: 22 inches						
Rem.	R-P 9½	H-4895	54.0	225 Sierra SBT	2447	Good load
Rem.	R-P 9½	IMR-4320	55.0	250 Speer HC	2344	Not fast but deadly
Caliber: 9.3x62mm Mauser, Test Gun: CZ-550, Barrel Length: 23.6 inches						
Rem.	R-P 9½	IMR-3031	56.0	250 Nosler AB	2533	Excellent load
Rem.	R-P 9½	Benchmark	53.0	270 Speer SS	2305	Not fast, but very accurate
Caliber: 375 H&H Mag., Test Gun: Rem. M-700, Barrel Length: 24 inches						
Win.	R-P 9½M	H-4895	66.0	270 Speer SBT	2523	A good, tough jacketed bullet
Rem.	Fed-215	IMR-4350	75.0	300 Hornady IL	2503	Power and range a plenty

Abbreviations: HC, Hot-Cor; GS, Grand Slam; IB, InterBond; SBT, Spitzer Boat Tail; SS, Semi Spitzer.

Here's one
of the few
shooting events
that mandate that
the competitors
use handloaded
ammunition.

Match Loading Black Powder Rifle Cartridges

By Mike Venturino
Photos by Yvonne Venturino

BENCHREST SHOOTERS RELOAD by the nature of their game, and by the same token such is true of my own favorite sport – NRA Black Powder Cartridge Rifle Silhouette. Be certain, the rules don't specifically state that BPCR Silhouette competitors must shoot handloads. Instead the only ammunition allowed must contain straight black powder (with Pyrodex being the only substitute permitted) and only lead alloy bullets sans any sort of metallic jackets or gas checks. You can't just go out and buy such ammunition, especially of match quality.

Furthermore, it should be stressed that BPCR Silhouette is far from some sort of "bullet flinging" contest, wherein the smoke and noise generated or the competitor's attire are as important as actually hitting a steel target. It is a game dedicated to precision shooting, requiring a finely accurate rifle, a darn good shooter/spotter team, and perhaps most importantly, extremely good quality handloaded ammunition. We can carry that statement even further—the extremely good quality handloaded ammunition must also carry cast bullets able to deliver near-minute-of-angle accuracy all the way to 500 meters.

That's a tall order and the prime reason why I say that the top shooters

These are metallic silhouette targets, each shown with the distance at which they are shot: ram, turkey, pig and chicken.

in BPCR Silhouette competition are the "sharp end" of the spear in regards to handloaders in general.

Before getting into the details that I think important in handloading match-quality BPCR Silhouette ammunition, let's cover some specifics and history of the sport.

BPCR Silhouette's inaugural match was held in September of 1985 at the NRA's Whittington Center near Raton, New Mexico. Along with about 33 other shooters interested in BPCRs and obsolete cartridges, I attended to see what the NRA might have up their sleeves. The course of fire was the same as with High Power silhouette. That is metallic cutouts of chickens, pigs, turkeys and rams at 200, 300, 385, and 500 meters respectively. The main difference between BPCR Silhouette and High Power is that the competitors must shoot all rounds offhand in the latter discipline but only offhand at chickens in the former. The more distant targets can be fired at from a crossed stick rest – either sitting or prone.

That was the difference in the course of fire. The rifles permitted were vastly different from High Power. They could only be single shots with and exposed hammer and of original American design introduced prior to 1896. Also there are restrictions on stock dimensions and a weight cap of 12 pounds, two ounces. Sights also could only be "tradi-

tional" types without click adjustments. The cartridges these rifles were chambered for also had to have been of original American design introduced prior to 1896 and, as said in the beginning, they could only contain straight blackpowder or Pyrodex and either cast or swaged lead alloy bullets. Typical of the rifles used are Sharps Model 1874, Remington Rolling Blocks and Hepburns, Winchester High Walls, etc. Cartridges at that first match ranged from 40-65s to 45-100s.

That first event was a hoot. Many of us even wondered if a 45-70 would knock down those 50-pound rams at 500 meters. Therefore I took along a 45-100 Shiloh Sharps Model 1874, and on the drive home had to stop and buy some pain pills for my aching shoulder. We need not have worried. Even 40 calibers with 380-grain bullets were taking the rams over despite the fact that such a bullet starts out at only about 1200 fps.

In 1986 the NRA again hosted such a match at Raton; this time with over 50 competitors. That was enough to convince them they had a viable idea so in 1987 the match became an official NRA National Championship. That started the ball rolling. Soon there were local clubs holding NRA sanctioned monthly matches. (Denver was the first such place. Livingston, Montana, was the second and I was match director there.) Now there are scores of locations holding BPCR Silhouette matches all over the country, from New York to Florida and from California to Virginia. The National Championships topped out at about 400 shooters one year but high gasoline prices have dropped that down to 220 to 240 in the last couple of years. That said, the sport itself is not in a decline as new locations and new state and regional championships are being added every season.

By the size of the targets in silhouette, a rifle producing two minutes of angle grouping out to 500 meters should be competitive. Personally, I won't compete with a rifle unless it will group 10 shots into 1½ minutes of angle. Also, since I have my own private range here in Montana with the furthest berm being at 300 yards, that's the distance at which I test loads. If I could shoot conveniently at 500 meters, that's what I would do. Occasionally, and especially on the Internet you'll hear someone brag that their BPCR always shoots minute of angle 10-shot groups. I won't say that's nonsense, but I will say no one has ever been able to demonstrate it to me on demand. We all get the occasional astounding group, usually of five shots, that's minute of angle or less, but that seldom happens with 10-shot groups, and I've never seen anyone be able to reproduce a spectacularly small group on call. It's also interesting that the Internet braggers never seem to show up at a BPCR Silhouette match and clean everybody's clocks with their "super accurate rifles." Heck, they almost never show up at all.

Also, before going on, one other new facet of this sport should be mentioned. Because a great many of the avid BPCR Silhouette competitors were aging normally, many started to lose the eyesight needed for good scores with ordinary peep sights. Therefore the NRA inaugurated a "scoped class" to BPCR Silhouette, and even has a separate two-day National Championship for scoped shooters following the regular National Championship. Rifle and course of fire rules are the same, with the scopes being restricted to 3/4-inch tubes with maximum 7/8-inch objective bells. Mounts cannot be click adjustable and rifle weight with scope can be up to 15 pounds. Contacting the NRA's Silhouette Department and ordering one of their rulebooks for a few bucks can get exact details of all these rules.

Finally let's take a look at handloading match-quality BPCR ammunition, and at this point I want to give the readers a warning. This is merely my method for assembling such. It's not carved in stone and other equally good or better-scoring shooters than me do things differently. That said, I would say that I'm a master class shooter in the game and usually (not always) manage to stay in the top 10 to 15 percent of shooters at a match.

The place to start in producing match quality BPCR loads is the bullet. Ask anyone who wins any sizeable BPCR state, regional or national championship what alloy he or she cast their bullets from and I'll bet it is between 1:20 and 1:30 tin-to-lead alloy. It won't be wheelweights and it won't be Linotype, and it won't be salvaged lead from hospital X-ray rooms. Some competitors haunt metal salvage yards looking for scrap sheet lead and then mix it with tin, but a great many of the top competitors bite the bullet and buy certified foundry alloy. It's expensive but the reason they go that route is that the alloy is then always repeatable.

Next, ask one of those same winning shooters what bullet moulds they use and about 99 percent will say it's a custom mould from makers like Steve Brooks, Paul Jones, Hoch Moulds, or Pioneer Products moulds. Once in a while a champ reports using an off-the-shelf Lyman, RCBS, or Redding/SAECO mould. Why the emphasis on relatively expensive custom moulds? One reason is that the buyer can order a bullet of the dimensions and weight he specifies. Another reason is cast-ability. The custom moulds are on larger blocks that make casting the large 40- and 45-caliber bullets mostly used in this game easier in that they don't heat up as quickly as smaller blocks.

Twenty-five percent of the targets in a BPCR Silhouette match, the chickens at 200 meters, must be fired at from the offhand position.

The overwhelmingly most popular bore sizes in BPCR Silhouette are .40 and .45. Back in the original days of blackpowder cartridges a very heavy bullet for any 40-caliber was 370 grains and for 45 it was about 500 grains. (1000-yard competitors often used 550-grain 45-caliber bullets.) For BPCR Silhouette a 400-grain 40-caliber bullet is considered on the "light side" and such is true also for 500-grain 45-caliber bullets. Most competitors are using 520- to 560-grain 45-caliber bullets and 410- to 430-grain 40-calibers. Depending on their exact configuration such bullets will measure between 1.20 to 1.50 inches in length. Speaking of configuration, most bullets used are of Postell, Creedmoor, or simple roundnose shape (see photos for examples). However, some pointed bullets have done well, although they actually don't offer flatter downrange trajectories when started at the low velocities given by BPCRs. In fact, I actually won the 2000 Montana State Championship using a Steve Brooks 425-grain pointed bullet in my Lone Star Rolling Block 40-65.

Except for the offhand chickens, all other targets in BPCR are fired from crossed stick rest with about 99 percent of the shooters going prone.

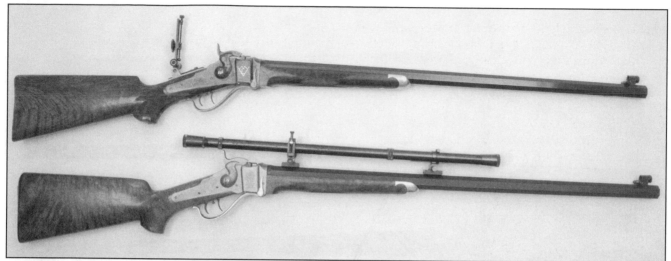

NRA BPCR Silhouette now has two separate divisions with each having their own National Championship. One is fired only with iron sights as with the Shiloh Model 1874 Sharps 45-70 (top) and the other is fired with scopes as with the Shiloh Model 1874 45-70 below. Scope is 6X and 28 inches long, by Montana Vintage Arms.

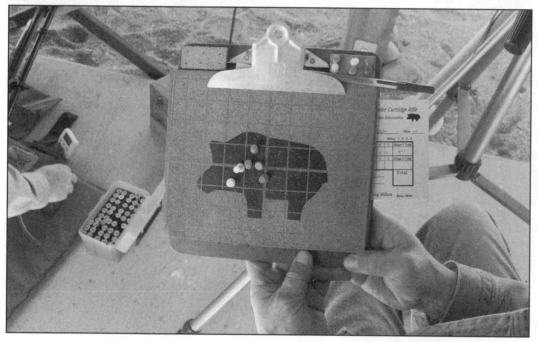

As this group plotted on a spotting board indicates these BPCR rifles must deliver fine accuracy to be competitive.

Here's one other item that is almost universal among the top shooters. They cast their bullets by the ladle method instead of using a bottom-pour lead pot. Why? Because dipped bullets weigh more consistently than those poured by a bottom-dump pot. Personally, my criterion for match-grade cast bullets is plus/minus three-tenths of a grain, or six-tenths total variation. That is miniscule variation in such bullets as the 560-grain ones I favor for 45-70 but that's what I do. I also cast my bullets in lots of 115 at a sitting. After weighing, anywhere from 100 to 110 will fall in my arbitrary weight range.

There's an old cast bullet myth that goes "No sizing of cast bullets is the best sizing." And to be honest I accepted that at face value for most of my life. For most of my BPCR Silhouette career I would have bullets fall from the mould at say .408-inch and then run them through a .409- or .410-inch lube/sizing die. It just applied the bullet lube but didn't actually size the bullets. Then custom mould maker Steve Brooks said to me one day, "I always size. I want my bullets to be perfectly round." So I gave that a try and along with some other things I think its one of the reasons why my scores have improved in the last few years despite worsening eyesight. Now I run my 40-calibers through a .408-inch die and my 45s through a .458-inch die.

While on the subject of lube/sizers, there are now a plethora of BPCR bullet lubes on the market, but the first introduced was SPG brand back in 1987. I remember exactly because SPG stands for Steven Paul Garbe, and I was his partner in the SPG business from 1987 until I sold my half to him in 1995. It is the only lube I use, and interestingly at the 2007 BPCR National Championships the top three placing competitors all listed SPG as their lube. (PO Box 1625,

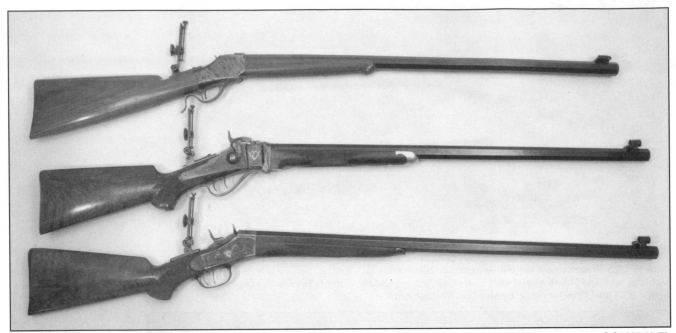

The three most popular rifle types in the BPCR Silhouette sport are (top) High Walls, this one being a C. Sharps Arms Model 1885 40-70 Straight. (Middle) Sharps Model 1874, this one being a Shiloh 45-70. And (bottom) Rolling Block, this one being a Lone Star 40-65.

The three most popular BPCR calibers in use in the silhouette game are (left) 45-90 (3rd Place), 45-70 (1st Place) and 40-65 (2nd place).

most cases are barely touched by doing them every time, but it is noteworthy that occasionally one takes a significant trim and sometimes one is trimmed on one side but not the other.

Most competitors, I would opine, only neck-size their brass but personally mine are all full length-sized because I have more than one rifle for each caliber. Some shooters, again especially on the Internet, say they don't use neck tension at all but instead just thumb-seat their bullets without any case sizing. I don't recall seeing any of those guys in the winner's circle at large matches. However, some top competitors do have special case mouth expanding dies made up that are larger than factory issue ones. For example, most 45-70 case mouth expanding dies have .454-inch plugs, but custom makers offer .456-, .457- and even .458-inch die plugs. Personally, I've stayed with the .454-inch ones with perfect satisfaction.

A one-time-only step in prepping the cases is to uniform the primer pocket depth and the flash holes. Some competitors even drill out their flash holes, but I don't. I did ream some out and try loads in those cases along side loads in cases left alone. There were no significant differences in the groups shot with them.

Once the cases are prepped then its time to seat primers, and this is one area that is wide open. The primers in use by the top BPCR Silhouette shooters range from Remington 2 ½ pistol primers to Federal 215 Large Rifle Magnum primers. What's best? That's anyone's guess, but your rifle will tell you what it shoots best. Avoid anyone who tries to tell you exactly what primer to use. It means they don't know much. Listen to those who tell you to try an assortment of primers and then make up your own mind. Personally I have always started my load development for a new rifle with Federal

Cody, WY 82414). What's different about a BPCR lube and a smokeless powder lube? The blackpowder ones mix with blackpowder fouling and help keep it soft. Smokeless powder lubes, especially the hard crayon types, don't do that.

Now let's move from bullets to brass prepping. My eyes have been opened on this factor in the last few years also. For many years I avoided case trimming and especially annealing as obnoxious chores and not important anyway. Then a fellow shooter told me he trimmed and annealed his brass for every loading. I thought he was crazy, but there was nothing shabby about his scores. So I gave that a try and my scores, on the average, are up. For annealing speed I bought one of the Ken Light Machines (PO Box 2745, Lake Havasu City, AZ 86405) and run all my brass through it for a light annealing before every loading. As for trimming,

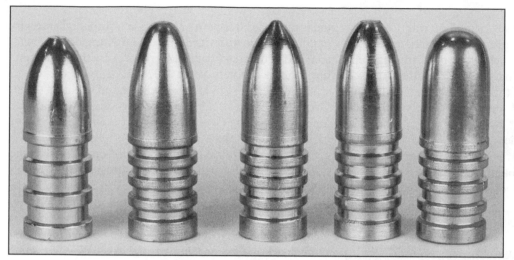

These 45-caliber cast bullets show some of the variety being used in the BPCR Silhouette game. From left, Paul Jones 500-grain semi-pointed, Pioneer Products 525-grain Postell, Brooks 525-grain pointed, Hoch 550-grain Creedmoor, and Brooks 555-grain "Government" roundnose.

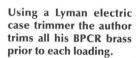

Using a Lyman electric case trimmer the author trims all his BPCR brass prior to each loading.

Using a Ken Light annealing machine the author anneals each BPCR case prior to each loading.

Match Loading Black Powder Rifle Cartridges 265

215s, and then vary from there, usually trying CCI Benchrest next. For three of my current BPCR Silhouette rifles, the Federal 215s and CCI Benchrest primers shoot groups approximately equal in size, but it seems that the "core" of the groups are tighter with the CCIs and that's what are loaded for those three rifles. I still won't swear that's the only way to go.

Now we get to blackpowder and note I said "blackpowder?" Pryodex is allowed but just about no one uses it. In fact, at the 2007 National Championships not a single contestant listed it on his tabulation form. In the United States

To put the blackpowder in the cartridge case the author trickles it through the drop tube, taking about three to four seconds to pour a 60- to 70-grain charge.

These are the blackpowders in common distribution in the United States at this writing. From left Schuetzen (made in Germany) Swiss (made in Switzerland) and Goex (made in USA).

today the three blackpowder brands in distribution are Swiss (naturally made in Switzerland), GOEX (made in Louisiana) and Schuetzen (made in Germany). By the tabulations turned in by shooters at the 2007 Nationals, of the top 15 scoring shooters 14 used Swiss powder and one used Goex. Overall there were roughly five shooters using Swiss powder for every one using Goex. It seems sort of un-American but it's the way things were.

Once a type of blackpowder is settled upon, there is the question of whether it should be powder measured by volume or weighed exactly. There many of the top competitors differ, but I'll go out on a limb and say that probably more weigh each and every charge than just simply powder-measuring it. Then, overwhelmingly, the powder is trickled through a drop tube into the cartridge cases. Why? For some reason it makes the powder burn more efficiently and thus with less residue and with far better accuracy.

A frustrating question often asked by newcomers to blackpowder cartridge loading is, "How much powder should I use." That's an impossible question to answer. The correct amount is how much fits into your choice of cartridge case, whether it's full-length-sized, neck-sized, or not sized at all, and whatever your bullet seating depth is. And also, what thickness of wad you choose to put between powder and bullet. As said, metallic gas checks are forbidden by the rules of this game but plastic, vegetable fiber or even cardboard disks or wads are permitted. They protect the base of the bullet from damage by the powder's gases. I hand-punched many thousands of wads out of .020- to .030-inch cardboard before an Oklahoman named John Walters (500 N. Avery Drive, Moore, OK 73160) began selling vegetable fiber wads. His are .030- or .060-inch in thickness and I use only the latter, and furthermore I never intend to take wad punch in hand again as long as that man is in business.

Anyway, back to powder charges. The correct amount of blackpowder to load in any case is however much fills up the case so that the bullet's base comes at least in contact with the wad when seated. Also some compression of the powder might not hurt, but if more than about .010-inch of compression is needed it shouldn't be done by seating the bullet. Special compression dies will be needed, and I've heard of guys actually compressing powder charges up to a half-inch. However, I've never heard of those guys winning anything, either. Again, the rifle will tell the shooter how much compression, if any at all, is best by how closely it puts bullets through the target papers at any given distance.

Personally speaking, my 40-65 and 45-90 match loads compress the powder not at all. A bullet can be pulled from a loaded round, the vege-wad fished out, and the cartridge's powder will pour out freely. My 45-70 loads are compressed about .010-inch. So again I would like to stress this: *The Exact Amount Of Black Powder Used In A Cartridge Is Not Important. The Idea Is To Fill The Case Up, Leaving Just Enough Room For The Wad And Bullet.*

Many BPCR Silhouette competitors rely on special in-line

bullet seating devices because for these cast bullets to deliver a requisite degree of precision all the way to 500 meters, they must be in the cases straight. In fact most of the master-class shooters I am familiar with use concentricity gauges to check bullet run-out. A general rule of thumb is that .002-inch of runout is adequate. Covering all the different in-line bullet seating systems on the market just for BPCRs would be too lengthy to discuss here. Besides, I have no experience with most of them. Mine for 40-65 and 45-70 are sold by Shiloh Rifle Manufacturing, and are cut with the same chambering reamers used on their Model 1874 Sharps rifles. I use them for much of my bullet-seating chores. Also, however, I use Redding's Competition seaters when using bullets with nose configurations different from what my Shiloh stems are custom-fitted to. Also I would like to mention that my 45-90 bullets are seated with an ordinary off-the-shelf Lyman seating die. Those 45-90s give a run-out of a mere .0015- to .002-inch and I've shot some of my highest scores with that rifle with ammo loaded with standard, no-frills dies.

Here I want to put in a little personal information as examples. I've refined my silhouette handloads down to the following ones. For 40-65, a Brooks 425-grain pointed bullet is used over 57.0 grains of Swiss 1 ½ Fg in Winchester brass with CCI Benchrest primers. Velocity is about 1210 fps from the 32-inch barrel of my Lone Star Rolling Block.

For 45-70 the load is a 560-grain Brooks Creedmoor-shaped bullet over 64 grains of Swiss 1 ½ Fg, again in Winchester brass and again with CCI Benchrest primers. Velocity of that load from the 30-inch barrel of my Shiloh Model 1874 Sharps is about 1130 fps.

For 45-90 the load is a 555-grain Brooks Government-shaped roundnose bullet over 70 grains of Swiss 1 ½ Fg with Starline brass and CCI Benchrest primers. Velocity from the 32-inch barrel of my rebarreled original Remington Creedmoor Rolling Block is about 1155 fps.

There are the basics; now I have to add this. The 40-65 load can be used for all targets. It is mild enough. However, despite the low velocities of the 45-70 and 45-90 loads, I feel their recoil is too heavy to use in offhand shooting. To be brutally honest, those loads leave my shoulder black-and-blue after a match if a shoulder pad is not worn. And the shoulder pad adds too much length to the rifle for offhand shooting.

Therefore, I have been experimenting with lighter bullets of from 450 to 500 grains for chicken shooting with both 45-caliber cartridges. So far my best results have come with the RCBS .45-500SIL bullet over 57 and 70 grains respectively for 45-70 and 45-90. Still the jury is out and I hope to settle upon an even milder load during this winter's test shooting.

Assembling match-quality BPCR Silhouette ammunition is definitely time-consuming, and one reason I do so much bullet casting and case prepping during Montana's long winter evenings. Also putting together all the specialized tools from custom moulds to concentricity gauges can get expensive. Both of those factors are probably why we don't

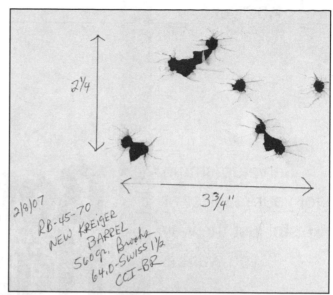

When the author gets one of his BPCRs firing groups like this at 300 yards, then he feels ready to compete with it.

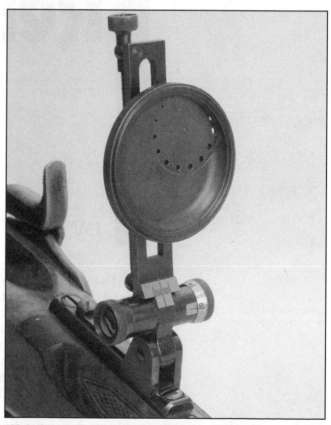

This is the most common peep sight in use in the BPCR Silhouette game, a Soule style by Montana Vintage Arms. Note the Super Size Hadley eyecup with a variety of apertures.

see too many young bachelors in the shooting circuit. But if you like to handload, not just to save money but because you honestly like using all the precision gadgets available, and then you like launching a bullet at a tiny, distant steel target with an excellent chance of knocking it down, then BPCR Silhouette might just be your game.

Serve up ammo
for your revolver or
pistol just the way
you want it.

Better Handgun Reloads

By Brian Pearce

WITH BASIC RELOADING equipment, combined with proper instruction and components, handgunners can assemble reloaded ammunition that duplicates and even exceeds the performance and accuracy level of factory ammunition. Specialized loads can be assembled that produce a performance level not available in factory ammunition, making a given handgun more versatile. For example, there are no "reduced" or "mid-range" loads currently offered for the 44 Magnum, but handloaders can develop loads that are accurate, perform on small game with minimal meat destruction, and offer much lighter recoil. Others may want a low-recoiling target load for their favorite 45 ACP pistol, or 38 Special revolver. And for those just wanting to duplicate the power and performance of factory ammunition, that too is easily accomplished. Developing loads for a favorite handgun is fun and challenging and can offer savings that typically range from 60 to 70 percent, and for those interested in casting their own bullets (highly recommended by this writer) savings can go as high as 90 percent. As a result, most handloaders substantially increase their shooting skills and enjoyment of firearms. Let's look at basic reloading steps, procedures, safety tips and how to assemble top-notch handloads from the onset.

Author used handloads, containing bullets he cast and handloaded, to take this mule deer.

Choosing the Correct Die Set

Most handgun die sets will consist of three and occasionally four dies that feature a 7/8"x14 (tpi) body thread. As a result, modern presses and dies from RCBS, Lyman, Hornady, Redding, Lee and others can be interchanged. In other words Lyman dies can be used in an RCBS press, etc. Dies are used to size fired cases (sizer die), prepare them to receive the bullet (expander die), then seat and crimp the bullet in place (seat/crimp die). Choosing the correct set is important to success. For example most straight-wall (and semi-straight wall) revolver cartridges, such as 38 Special, 357 Magnum, 44 Magnum, 45 Colt and etc., are best served with a roll-crimp die set. These dies are so named because they produce a rather abrupt crimp that will help hold bullets firmly in place and obtain proper ignition (especially important when dealing with magnum cartridges and slower burning pistol powders). "Standard" die sets feature a steel sizing die, which requires case lube be applied to the case prior to sizing; after sizing the lube should be removed. To increase the speed and convenience of sizing cases, a carbide (commonly known as "carbo" or "tungsten carbide") sizing die is suggested, which only costs a few dollars more and is money well spent. When using a carbide-sizing die no case lube is required for the sizing process.

For popular autoloading cartridges such as the 9mm Luger, 40 S&W, 45 ACP and others of similar design, a taper crimp die set is suggested. These work essentially the same as the above dies; however, the seat/crimp die is designed to give a more gradual taper to allow cases to headspace correctly on the case mouth. The crimp applied to autoloading pistol cartridges also serves to "hold" the bullet in

Pearce often hunts using handloads. This rockchuck was taken using a USFA SAA Flattop 44 Special at around 100 yards.

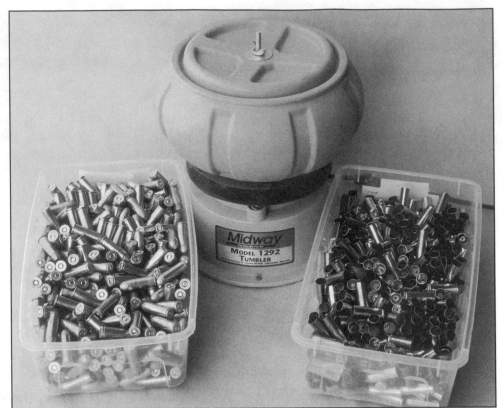

Cases should be cleaned prior to reloading. As a bonus, the finished product will look better.

place while the cartridge is slammed into the feed ramp and chamber, and provide enough "pull" to assist in igniting the powder properly.

Another feature to look for, preferably before purchasing dies, is a set that has the correct seater plug to match the type of bullet (or bullets) that you plan to handload. For instance, the seater plug is shaped to fit a specific bullet nose shape or profile. If a semi-wadcutter (SWC) style bullet is seated using a Round Nose seater plug, the nose will likely be deformed while being seated. And there may be excess bullet run-out if it is seated crooked in the case and may not chamber or be accurate. Seater plug options include Round Nose, SWC and wadcutter profiles. Die sets can be purchased with all three styles, or seater plugs can be purchased separately for a minimal cost.

Just a word of caution for those that may have found a "good deal" on some used reloading equipment. Some older die sets manufactured from the 1940s and as late as 1980, had issues with correct dimensions. In some instances the sizer die failed to reduce cases enough to reliably hold bullets firmly. Other dies featured an expander ball that was too large and resulted in a poor bullet-to-case fit. On the other hand, many older dies feature correct dimensions and will load perfectly good ammunition.

Basic Handloading Steps (Revolver)

Before starting the handloading process, cases should be inspected for defects and checked for the same at each stage of the handloading process. Defects usually include a split case body or mouth. Many cases will feature a can-

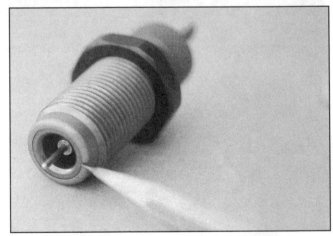

This RCBS sizer die features a carbide insert, which does not require cases to be lubed prior to sizing. Note the adjusted position of the decapping pin.

nelure (circumferential groove around the case body) that can become the source of a rupture or leaking gas and is best spotted before tumbling or cleaning cases. Other defects may be a manufacturing flaw, or were crushed or damaged at some point after firing. Regardless, such cases should be rejected.

Cases should be cleaned prior to handloading, with dirt, bullet lubricant and other undesirables removed. Several manufacturers offer vibratory case tumblers that make this job quick and easy, with cases coming out looking almost like new in just an hour or two. A clean case not only looks better, but also chambers, extracts and ejects easier.

When a cartridge is fired, the case holds the gases (and

pressure with the support of the firearms chamber) generated by a given cartridge. As a result it expands to conform to the gun's chamber, or increases in diameter. The case should be re-sized (using the sizing die) back to its original dimensions. Full-length sizing is generally recommended, as this not only allows the reloaded cartridge to drop easily back into the chamber, but also plays an important role in obtaining the crucial bullet-to-case fit. (More on that in a moment.)

Most modern sizing dies, produced in approximately the last 30 years, are designed to size the case and decap, or remove, the old primer in one step. It is suggested to carefully read the die manufacturer suggestions on adjusting this die. However, the basics include inserting a shell holder (cartridge-specific) into the top of the ram, then placing the die into the top of the press. To adjust the die, the decapping unit body should be about 3/16" above the bottom of the die. If the decapping unit is set too close to the bottom of the die, it may contact and bind with the inside of the case, or web, possibly damaging both. The decapping pin (not to be confused with decapping unit) should extend below the bottom of the die just enough to reliably decap the spent primer. If it is adjusted out more than necessary, the pin may break. Decapping pins are inexpensive to replace, and having on hand is a good idea.

A "Standard" steel sizing die should be turned into the press until it contacts the shellholder when it is raised to its highest position. If using a carbide sizing die, the die body should be set about .011-inch (or about the thickness of matchbook cover or three sheets of common paper) from the shellholder. This is especially important as carbide is hard and brittle and, if contacted by the shellholder, may break.

We are now ready to size cases and decap old primers. Insert a case into the shell holder and raise the ram inserting the case into the die. Go slow at first until a "feel" is learned to prevent snagging the case mouth on the sizer die, which will ruin the case. Make certain that cases are fully inserted into the shellholder before being inserted into the sizing die. As previously stated, after cases are sized, they should be inspected again. If a case suddenly sizes easier than the others do, it should be scrutinized as it may be defective. Occasionally cases will fail or split while being sized, and should be discarded.

After cases are sized is the correct time to trim cases, however, if the brass is new, or once-fired, they probably won't need trimming. The Small Arms and Ammunition Manufacturers Institute (SAAMI) has established a "maximum" and "minimum" case length for each cartridge. Cases that exceed these figures will need trimming to the minimum length, or they may not correctly release the bullet when fired, which can drive pressures up. In other instances an excessively long case may not chamber correctly. Cases that are of uniform length will provide a more consistent crimp and therefore lower extreme spreads and better accuracy. Virtually all major companies that offer presses and reloading dies, offer excellent case trimmers that range from fundamental to power versions. After trimming, a case will need to be deburred (using a deburring tool) inside and outside the case mouth. Again, there are hand-held versions that cost less than $20, or there are power-assisted versions at a somewhat greater cost. Once cases are cut to the correct length they can often be reloaded 10 and even 20 times without additional trimming (depending on cartridge, load and pressures).

The next step includes the use of the expanding die. Fol-

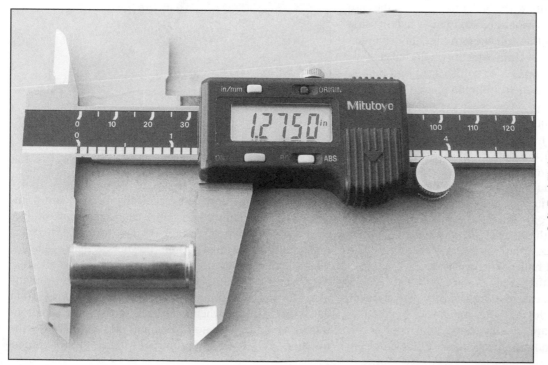

Cases should be trimmed to correspond with industry specifications. This 44 Magnum case measures 1.275 inches and is minimal for this cartridge.

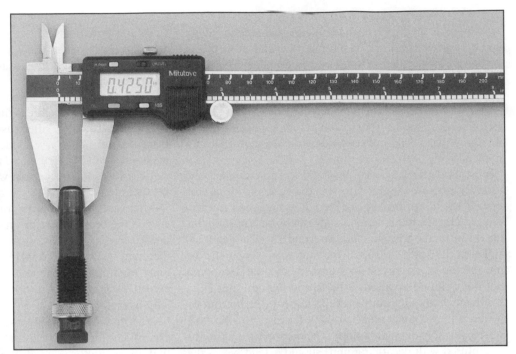

This expander ball should measure .003- to .005-inch smaller than bullet diameter. This 44 Magnum die measures .425" while .44 Magnum bullets measure .429" to .430".

low the die manufacturer's directions on adjustment. The purpose of the neck expander is to prepare the way for the bullet and bring the inside of the case to correct dimensions for bullet-to-case fit. Generally the expander ball should measure .003- to .005-inch smaller than the bullet diameter. For example, if loading the 44 Magnum, the expander ball will typically measure .425" while bullets run .429 to .430". This helps (along with the crimp) to keep the bullet in place while being subject to recoil (in a revolver). It also plays an important role in helping the powder ignite properly and results in more accurate ammo. The expander ball features two steps, with the second (or upper part) expanding the case mouth slightly to allow the bullet to start into the case about 1/16-inch. The die should be adjusted so that the case is not over-worked, as this will shorten life, but expanded enough to prevent the case from catching on the bullet while it is being seated. If using cast or soft swaged lead bullets, this bell also prevents lead from being shaved off during the bullet seat/crimp step. As cases are expanded, watch for small cracks at the mouth and discard.

The next step is priming. The previously fired primers will leave a residue in the bottom of the primer pocket. It is optional to remove it (using a primer pocket brush), however, with repeated firings this residue can build up and cause misfires. This writer generally recommends removing the residue, a job that only takes a few moments (or about 30 cases per minute with practice).

Before priming cases, it is imperative to select the load including powder and bullet. The primer is an often over-looked component of the cartridge and they are not all created for the same application, however, they play a crucial role in how a load performs. Often the novice handloader assumes because they are reloading a magnum revolver cartridge they need Magnum primers. It is not that simple, as

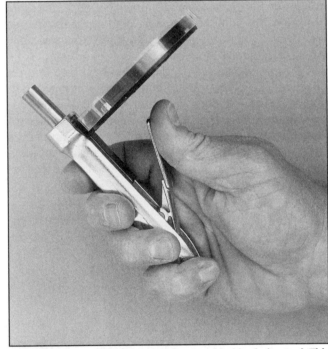

Author suggests a bench-mounted or hand-held priming tool. This Lee Auto Prime is inexpensive, fast and convenient.

many powders are designed specifically for Standard primers and not Magnum, even when used in a magnum revolver cartridge. For example, Alliant Powder (formerly Hercules) offers some of the most popular powders available to handgun reloaders. They do not recommend the use of Magnum primers with any of their handgun powders. In many instances Magnum primers cause pressures to increase from 9,000 to 13,000 psi when compared to the same load containing a Standard (or non-Magnum) primer. This raises the question "Why Magnum primers?" Magnum pistol primers

For those desiring to cast their own bullets, savings are great, and the end product can give excellent performance.

Author often uses handguns to hunt; naturally, with handloads. This Ruger Blackhawk 44 Magnum "Flattop" has accounted for considerable game and is generally stoked with Keith-style cast bullets driven with an appropriate charge of Alliant #2400 powder.

Powder charges should be carefully viewed before seating bullets. Make certain all cases received a charge and that no cases inadvertently received a double charge.

are best when matched to ball powders such as Hodgdon H110, Lil' Gun, Winchester 296 and others that require significant ignition to burn properly. In fact, these powders can give erratic pressures and velocities if they are not ignited properly with a Magnum primer. To help determine the correct primer for a given load, consult a reputable reloading manual, or contact the powder manufacturer.

There are a number of methods for seating primers. Most presses come with a fundamental press-mounted priming method; however, most are not particularly sensitive and slow to use. This writer suggests a faster and more accurate tool that is usually sold separately and is relatively inexpensive. For example, there are a number of hand-held and even bench-mounted tools that allow fast priming and prevent touching primers. *(Please note, primers are highly sensitive to oil and if exposed they can misfire. Hands should be completely clean of such contaminants if primers are touched.)* Primers should be seated to .003 to .005" below flush. The anvil should just contact the bottom of the primer pocket, but never forced or crushed, as such damage may result in a misfire. If the primer is not seated deep enough, it may also misfire as the firing pin uses up some of its "energy" to drive it home (seating it deeper). As a result there may not be enough energy left to properly ignite the primer. A primer seated "high" may also drag on the recoil shield of revolvers and prevent the cylinder from turning freely and can even prove dangerous. With some practice, just the right "feel" will be mastered so that primers are seated correctly. A caliper (capable of measuring 0.001") can be used to determine primer-seating depth.

We are now ready to charge cases with powder. Cases

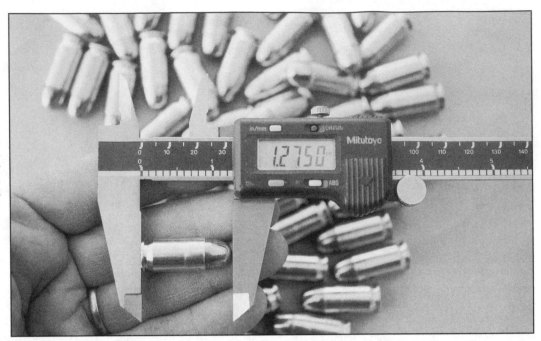

The overall cartridge length should be carefully regarded, especially when dealing with autoloading pistol cartridges such as the 45 ACP.

should first be set up in a case-loading block. Most powder measures are capable of throwing powder charges to near perfect uniformity, so there is no reason to consider weighing each. It is imperative to make certain the charge being thrown is correct and conforms to published data from a reputable source. (Data provided on the Internet from unknown sources should be avoided!) Double check and triple check on an accurate powder scale (capable of measuring at least 1/10th of a grain) and make certain that the scale is read correctly. (Many mishaps occur due to mis-read powder scales.) Practice throwing charges on the scale until you know you are doing it correctly. As a tip, make a complete and uniform "throw" of the powder measure handle.

After all the cases in the loading block are charged with powder, they should be visibly checked for two items. First, that they all have powder. Second, the powder charges are even with each other. Watch carefully for a case that somehow received a double powder charge! Holding the loading block below good light will help spot potential problems. This is a crucial step in assembling safe loads, so distractions should not be allowed.

Once all cases are correctly charged with powder, place bullets in the case mouth, where they will stay on their own if the case mouth was expanded correctly. The base of the bullet should start into the case about 1/16-inch.

We are now ready to seat bullets and apply the crimp. The seat/crimp operation is usually the most confusing to the novice handloader and can be the source of frustration. The method this writer recommends for adjustment is very simple, but perhaps more difficult to explain in just a few words. First, understand that the die body provides the crimp, while the seater plug seats the bullet into the case, and controls how deep it is seated. To begin, let's seat the bullet to its recommended depth. (Most commercial jacketed bullets for

revolvers will have a crimp cannelure at the proper depth, while most cast bullets will feature a crimp groove. Nonetheless, use calipers to measure the overall cartridge length to match that of the load data provided by a reputable reloading manual.) The die should be placed in the press, but not screwed in deep enough for the crimp to be applied to the case. Place a case (with bullet in the mouth) in the shell holder and raise the ram to its highest point. Now begin turning the seater plug down (but not the die body) until it contacts the bullet. At this point, lower the ram and note how much further the bullet needs seated into the case, then turn the seater plug down accordingly, but don't turn it too far as that will result in a bullet seated too deep. Insert the cartridge into the die multiple times, making small adjustments to the seater plug each time, until the bullet is seated to exactly the correct depth. At this point turn the seater plug up (or remove it), so that it cannot touch the bullet. Again, with the cartridge in the shellholder and the ram fully raised, turn the die body down until the crimp begins to apply. The cartridge can be inserted (raise and lower the ram) into the die several times while making small die body adjustments each time until the perfect crimp is obtained. Now set the die's lock ring and (with ram raised and cartridge in the die) and turn the seater plug down until it contacts the bullet, then set the locking nut. Once this method has been practiced a few times it takes only seconds to adjust the seat/crimp die for a given load. We are now ready to seat bullets and apply the crimp with a single step.

A problem that occasionally surfaces when dealing with a seat/crimp die featuring minimal dimensions and a cartridge that has a rather thick case includes shaving of the bullet while seating. While this is primarily a problem with cast bullets, when it occurs using jacketed bullets, the case often buckles during the seat/crimp operation. This does not happen often and usually the die manufacturer will modify the die (at no charge) or send a new one. Another option includes seating the bullet and applying the crimp as separate steps. For example the bullets would be seated without applying any crimp, then the die adjusted and the cartridge crimped as a separate step.

Additional Tips for Handloading Autoloading Pistol Cartridges

The same steps described above for common rimmed revolver cartridges also apply to autoloading pistol cartridges, however, the taper crimp will require some additional attention. For example, rimless cartridges such as the 9mm Luger, 40 S&W and 45 ACP headspace on the case mouth. Therefore it is imperative to make certain the crimp is sufficient to hold the bullet, but not excessive wherein the case mouth is too small to correctly contact the end of the chamber. There are industry specifications to obtain the correct crimp, however, the beginning handloader will do well to purchase calipers (blade) capable of measuring accurately to 0.001" and measuring the crimp diameter (at the case mouth) of factory loads for a given caliber, then duplicate it using a taper crimp die. Generally the seating and the crimp should be accomplished in separate steps (as outlined above) when dealing with most auto-loading cartridges.

Most autoloading pistols are rather sensitive to overall cartridge length. For the most reliable feeding and function, those lengths should be held to industry specifications.

Tips and Conclusion

The final inspection of loaded cartridges will prove beneficial. Since cases will likely be reloaded many times, most handloaders prefer to purchase plastic ammo boxes for storage and use. It is advised to carefully record details of the load in the form of a label. Include bullet manufacturer and weight, powder type and charge, primer, date of assembly and any other information that is pertinent. This serves as a safety factor, but can also be referred to when wanting to duplicate a favorite handload. Never try to remember a load, but write it down and keep records of accuracy and performance. And one last tip for the accuracy-minded shooter, avoid mixing cases of different manufacture – and even lot numbers from the same maker. Instead, use a "batch" of cases that are of the same make and lot number. Doing so will improve the consistency of your reloads.

If all of the above steps are carefully followed, a beginning reloader can produce safe, reliable and accurate ammunition from the start. Have a great day at the range.

Handloads should be checked for accuracy. This Freedom Arms .454 Casull placed five shots into a single ragged hole at 25 yards.

Both clay target shooters and hunters can tailor their shotshells for specific purposes.

Building Light Specialty Shotgun Loads

By Steve Gash

SPECIAL LIGHT SHOTGUN loads can fill the bill for a variety of shotgun pursuits. The clay target competitor who shoots a lot will find loads to start off the season, and get his shoulder toughened up before switching to full-charge loads as the match season wears on. The hunter will also note the application of ammo especially tailored for a particular furred or feathered game. The back-yard clay pigeon buster will likewise appreciate the comfort and economy of such loads. Here's how to build 'em.

I came to appreciate light loads quite honestly. Years ago, I shot competitive Skeet almost every weekend Colorado weather allowed, and usually tallied over 5000 registered targets a year, plus the occasional practice. At the start of the match season in the spring, I used to shoot my normal, full-charge loads of 1 1/8-ounce 12-gauge and 7/8-ounce 20-gauge. This is all well and good, but after a winter off, my shoulder was not used to the pounding, even with the smaller bore. Eventually, I saw the light, and scoured sources of loading data for reduced loads with which to start off the season.

Skeet shooters shoot four guns: 12-, 20- and 28-gauges, and the .410-bore, and it is an article of faith that the velocities of all loads, regardless of

The proof in the pudding – all five bores lined up with a sample shell, ready to hit the range or fields. The versatility of all five of these bore sizes can be increased by carefully tailoring loads to a specific purpose.

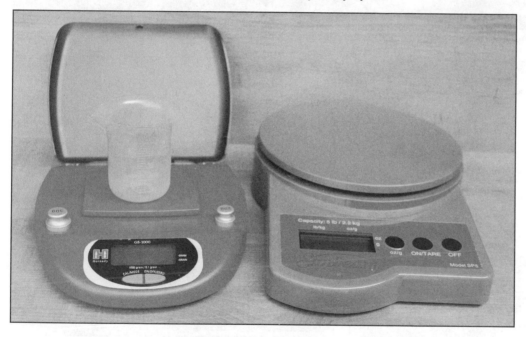

For weighing shot, use either your powder scale or an electronic postal scale, like this Sunbeam SP5.

bore size, *have* to be the same so that the leads would also be the same. The velocity of all four sizes of skeet loads is standardized at 1200 fps. So, my search for lighter loads centered on lighter shot charges, but at 1200 fps. The philosopher and mathematician Bertrand Russell once observed that faith is a firm belief in something for which there is no evidence. I had the faith, but not the evidence. Lower velocity loads, I would later learn, shot just fine at skeet, thank you.

Shotgun loading manuals in the 1970s had only meager data for reduced loads. Since I, like everyone else on the planet, loaded Red Dot in 12-gauge loads, it seemed like a logical powder to examine first.

The Hercules (now Alliant) powder outfit actually had some data for Red Dot and 7/8-ounce of shot in the 12 gauge. I loaded up a few boxes, and tried them. Wow! Not only did they pulverize a clay bird just as well as with the hard-kicking 1 1/8-oz. loads, the recoil in my 7 1/4-pound Browning Superposed Skeet was less – a *lot* less! And if there was any difference in the leads, it escaped my notice. I then had no idea what the velocity was, but I was sure it was 1200 fps. (It was actually about 1145 fps.)

My success with the 12-gauge led me to investigate a similar load for the 20-gauge. Soon I found that ¾ ounce of 9s also did quite well. And why shouldn't it? The lovely little 28-gauge was everyone's favorite, and it busted birds like its larger siblings. And here I was using essentially a 28-gauge load in the 20. It worked like a charm.

The utility of these loads is not lost in the hunting fields, either. About that same time period, my wife and I regularly engaged in the serious pursuit of blue grouse and ptarmigan. These critters aren't collectively called "fool hens" for nothing. The trick was to find them. Actually shooting them

A Universal Charge bar from Multi-Scale will speed will make volume loading of exact powder and shot charges easy.

Powders in the "medium" burning rate category, like Alliant's new 20/28 and Hodgdon's International Clays, are best suited for light loads.

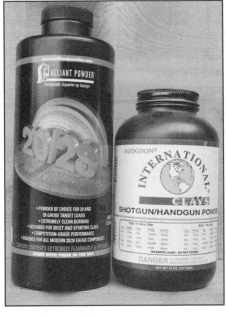

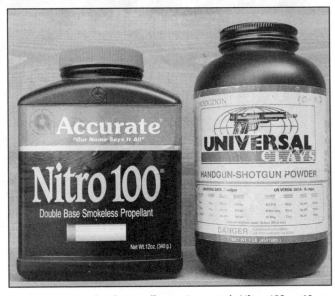

Another great pair of propellants: Accurate's Nitro 100, a 16-ga. standout, and Hodgdon's Universal, terrific in almost any gauge.

was no problem at all. As you approached a blue grouse, it frequently hopped up on a downed tree to better view the proceedings. Ranges were short, and the birds were pansies. Ptarmigan are lovely little grouse, but are dumber than the proverbial bag of rocks. Their protection is perfect camouflage, not flight, so a range of a few feet is not uncommon. Plus, the rest of the bunch of ptarmigan usually stands around obligingly while the hunter fills out his limit. Ptarmigan live above the timberline, so every ounce you carry up a mountain weighs a pound after you get there. Plus there's water, grub, binocs, etc. So, the lightest shotgun available is just the ticket. I frequently used a .410 single-shot that weighed less than 5 pounds, and it was perfect.

The Mechanics of Fit

The major consideration in building reduced shotgun loads is fit. There is a finite volume in any shotshell, and it has to be filled just right so that a proper crimp can be made. For reduced shot charges, there are basically three solutions to this volume dilemma. First, just use a different wad. Nowadays, there are one-piece plastic wads especially made for lighter charges in the 12-gauge, like the Winchester AA 12L and 12SL columns, designed for 1- and 7/8-ounce 12-gauge loads, respectively. (In my experience, these two wads work perfectly with 7/8- and ¾-ounce loads.) The second approach is to stuff smaller diameter card or fiber filler wads of varying thickness in the shot cup of a plas-

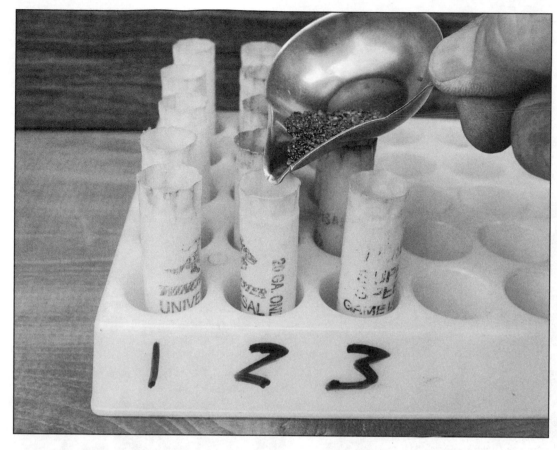

Assemble your experimental shotshell loads with the same care you would use on your pet elk rifle, and keep good records.

tic wad under the shot to take up space. Additionally, one can use an old-fashioned nitro card over the powder, then place a one-piece plastic unit on top of it. Lastly, you can combine variations of the latter two methods. It varies by gauge, depending on what wads are available. Fortunately, there are lots of components available. One-piece plastic units abound, and several sources offer card and fiber filler wads of various gauges and thickness to obtain the perfect fit. Don't hesitate to experiment with volume changes to achieve a perfect crimp.

These reduced loads are just for fixed-breech arms. Don't use them in your semi-auto, unless you like a very heavy single-shot. The recoil impulse and pressure are just too low to cycle a semi-auto.

Chronographing Shotshells

Rifle and pistol reloaders would just as soon be without their favorite sizing die as to be without their chronograph, and for good reason. Data in the loading manuals and ammo catalogues is fine and dandy, but when the rubber meets the road, there usually is considerable variation in the results. The same is true for shotshells. The only way the reloader can know what his loads are doing is to measure them. This is a science project in itself. Chronographing shotshells is much different than for single projectiles, and there are two very different ways to do it: the way the ammo companies do it, and the way reloaders do it.

All modern chronographs have a "start" and a "stop" device to measure the time it takes an object to travel a known distance. For a single projectile, this is (relatively) easy, but for a mass of shot, it's a problem. The ammo companies' chronographs have start and stop "coils" that sense the entire mass or "clump" of shot as it travels over them. A computer examines a complete record of the movement of the shot cloud over the screens, determines the time the "center" of the mass crosses the start and stop coils, and then calculates the velocity. This system is available in the Oehler System 84, but is beyond the needs (and usually the means) of the home reloader.

Almost all rifle and handgun reloaders have a counter chronograph with sky-screens these days, and they can be used for shotshells, as well. But the measurement system is quite different from the "coil" system described above, and the results can be misleading, unless you know how to interpret them.

When we chronograph shotshells, our sky-screens actually measure the very first pellet that zooms across the start and stop screens. These pellets are obviously the fastest, usually about 2 to 5 percent faster than the "average" pellet, but it's quite variable. Another problem is shot stringing. A Full choke actually squirts the shot mass forward a bit after it leaves the muzzle, imparting a little extra velocity to that first pellet; this also increases the observed velocity. Using the most open choke you have minimizes this problem.

When setting up your chronograph for use with shotshells, use a close screen spacing; 2 feet is ideal. Some people use the diffusers, but I have had excellent results without them. When shooting, keep the gun's muzzle only about 10

Proper positioning of the gun, shooter, and the chronograph screens is critical for good results. Note that the line of shot is only about 3-4 inches above the screens, and that the gun's muzzle is less than a foot in front of the baffle. A sturdy wooden baffle protects the screens from muzzle blast and hunks of wads. The 2x4-inch rectangle in the baffle through which to shoot works perfectly. Note muzzle blast soot around the opening. Be careful not to nick the baffle!

Chronographing is the only way to actually know the velocity of your shotshell reloads, and to assess their uniformity with the standard deviation.

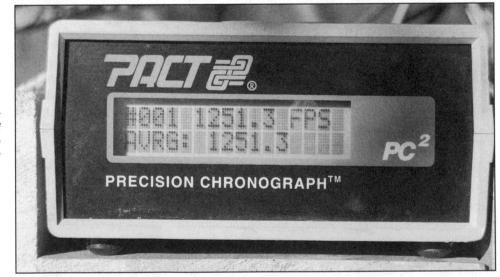

inches in front of the start screen. This ensures that the shot cloud is still pretty small in diameter as it goes over the screens.

This, however, introduces yet another quirk of shotshell velocity measurement. The expanding powder gases are going faster than the shot, so the muzzle blast can trigger the start screen before the first pellet gets there. This pro-duces short count times and incorrectly high velocity read-ings. The easy way to solve this problem is to construct a baffle out of a 3/4-inch plywood. Mine is 13x21 inches, but the size isn't critical. Cut a 2x4-inch rectangular opening in the middle of the baffle. Mount the baffle on a couple of 1x2s, and stick them into a target stand. Mount the baffle on the 1x2s high enough so that you don't have to hunker

Two Winchester 12-ga. wads with light loads of #8 shot (from left): WAAL with 2, .125" 20-ga. Card wads under 1/2 oz.; WAAL with ¾ oz.; a WAASL with 1, .135" 20-ga. Card under 3/4 oz.; and a WAASL holding 7/8 oz. These light shot charges with the proper fit make highly functional ammo with nice, firm crimps.

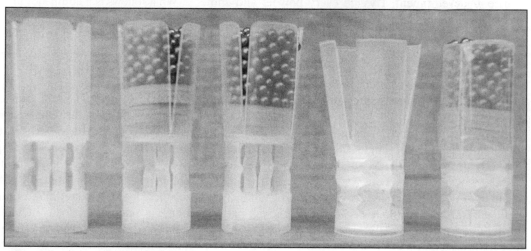

The mainstay wads for 20-ga. light loads are the WAA20 and the RXP-20. Here (from left) the WAA20 holds ½- and 5/8-oz. of shot over .125" 28-ga. cards as under-shot fillers. The RXP (right) has ¾-oz. over 2, .125" 28-ga. card wads.

Everybody's favorite gauge – the 28. The WAA28 wad will fit in almost all case brands. The one on the right has 5/8-oz. of shot over a .125" .410-bore card wad. The crimp on the shell at left is almost too pretty to shoot.

down to shoot through the opening. Keep the gun's bore parallel to the screens, keep the line of shot only 3-4 inches above the screens, and carefully shoot through the opening in the baffle. The baffle also helps protects the screens from extraneous objects. Be sure to wear eye and ear protection while testing.

The usual statistics on a string are available, just as for rifles and handguns. Strive for uniformity, just as you would for your favorite deer rifle. Low standard deviations (SD)

and a coefficient of variation (CV) of less than 2 percent are good yardsticks of uniformity. (CV is the SD expressed as a percentage of the average, and allows "apples-to-apples" comparisons of loads.) Test at least 5 rounds of a particular combination; a 10 round sample is better.

Make up a data sheet, and record your results. Write down everything; you never know when an obscure factoid will come in handy later. Sometimes very light loads produce "bloopers" or wide velocity variations due to inadequate pressure or a poor powder burn. You'll want to discover and weed out these combinations before the first match or opening day of the dove season.

The results we get for a given load will be different from those listed in the ammo companies' catalogs. As noted above, our velocities are usually a bit faster than the factory data, but this is really not a problem. We all have fired lots of factory fodder – where else to get empties to reload? And, for sure, we have favorite ammo for each gauge or game. So the task becomes just chronographing the factory load we like best, and tailoring our reloads to produce similar results *on our measurement* system. Here's an example. One of my pet 20-gauge factory loads is Fiocchi's No. 20LITE75, with 3/4-ounce of 7-1/2s. Catalogued at 1075 fps, on my chronograph system, used as described above, it averages 1039 fps, with a SD of 3.8 fps. For a duplicate load, these are my velocity and uniformity goals, and my reload with 20/28 powder clocks 1057 fps; close enough.

Load Assembly

Assembly of your experimental loads is quite different from the volume loading you'll do after you've selected a load. Select a case and wad that you have loaded successfully in the past, or that you happen to have a lot of. Several brands are shown in the load tables, but I really don't think it makes a lot of difference, as long as everything fits in the shell, you stick with the same component set, and you get uniform ballistics that you want. Note from the tables that just changing the case or wad type can drastically alter the results.

In load development, I weigh every powder and shot charge. Balance beam powder scales are ubiquitous, and they can be used for shot, but they're a pain because even one pellet off pegs it over or under. An electronic powder scale used in the "gram" mode works well. Also good is an inexpensive postal scale that registers in tenths of an ounce or in grams. Check to make sure you've converted ounces to grains or grams correctly.

After a load is selected, volume loading is a snap. If it's not already, equip your single-stage or progressive loader with an adjustable charge bar, and carefully set it to throw the exact powder and shot charges for your load.

The light charges of these specialty loads call for fairly small shot. Otherwise, there just won't be enough pattern density to do their job. For clay targets, stick with #9s. For light hunting loads, I rarely use anything larger than #6s. After chronographing, set up the pattern board, and see if there are holes a well-fed quail could walk through. Since these are essentially close-range loads, pattern assessment can be done close, too.

By the Numbers

It should by now be obvious that the key to specialty light loads is the careful assembly of selected components for a good fit, and keeping the pressure high enough to produce uniform ballistics, as measured with a chronograph. The load tables show this or that card or fiber filler wad in the wad columns. These are just "spacers." Remember, the weight of a dinky card or filler wad is miniscule compared to the shot charge, so if you need to vary the thickness of wad to make the load fit, do it. This will ensure a firm crimp to hold everything in place.

What follows is a compendium of several specialty loads by gauge culled from years of experimentation. The loads described are just examples, but have been "field tested" and have busted many a clay or feathered bird. In addition, a few "normal" loads and even the occasional factory load are shown for comparison.

The 12 Gauge. One-half ounce of shot in a 12-gauge doesn't sound like much, and it's not, but this is simply the lightest-recoiling load you're likely to shoot. While most 12s are too heavy to carry for close range hunting, this load will powder a skeet target – if you center it. The short, fat shot column patterns very well. Old SR-7625 is just the ticket for these loads. A better all-around light starter load is 3/4-ounce at a nominal velocity of 1150 fps. Guaranteed to cure a flinch or bust a grouse. American Select is my pick for 3/4-ounce loads.

Another fine target or game load is 7/8 ounce at about 1150 fps. Hodgdon's CLAYS and Alliant's standby Red Dot do all that's needed. With just a bit more weight, it surpasses the 3/4-ounce load, but with only a hint more recoil. It is,

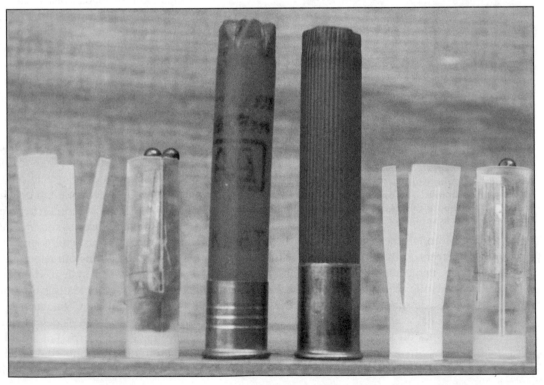

Yes, Virginia, you can download a .410. Shown here are a couple of WA410 wads stuffed with #3s – a key ingredient for blue grouse over a campfire, or fricasseed ptarmigan.

of course, just a 20-gauge load in disguise. Many four-gun shooters never shoot a 12-gauge, but simply use their 20-gauge in the 12-gauge event. My buddy, the late Joe Davis, used his 20 thus, and I've seen him shoot a 96 with it more than once – from the hip. The one-ounce load lumbering along at 1084 fps is also dynamite on clays. CLAYS is king for 1 ounce. Just forget the "low" velocity, lead 'em, and crush 'em.

The 16 Gauge. Here we come into our own with super loads that are light, and just right. The 16 is one of my favorites, and of all the loads listed in this report, I use 7/8-ounce of 8s over 16.0 grains of Nitro 100 more than any other. It is just that good. Recoil is minimal, and it is a terrific dove load. A bit lighter but just as useful is 3/4-ounce over either 18.0 gr. of PB or 17.8 gr. of Unique. Note that these loads utilize a card wad under the plastic wad. Some may question this, but it's either that or stuff the shot cup full of wads to make it fit. This leaves almost the entire shot column exposed to the ravages of bore contact. This does nothing for patterns. The dual-wad arrangement works just fine. (Check the Ballistic Products 16 gauge manual for more info.)

Another 16-gauge load that approaches perfection is one ounce of shot. With 7 1/2s or 8s, it does just dandy on doves, quail, or targets. At a modest velocity of around 1100 to 1150 fps, it's a winner. Again, it's CLAYS and Red Dot to the rescue.

The 20 Gauge. As with the 12, 1/2-ounce of shot in the 20 also works well, as long as you are close, as does its ballistic isomer, 5/8 ounce. Loads with both weights register about 1100 fps with similar charges of SR-7625. Better all around is 3/4-ounce. With 13.5 grains of Universal, this is my early season Skeet load. Over 13.0 grains of Alliant's new 20/28 powder, 3/4-ounce of 9s patterns well and is very uniform.

The 28 Gauge. Loads with 5/8 ounce of shot make the 28-gauge into even more of a marvel. As with the 7/8-ounce 16-gauge, I can't think of a better performing light load for this gauge. Alliant's new 20/28 powder gets the nod here. The standard 28-gauge load of 3/4-ounce at a velocity of 1188 fps with 17.0 gr. of W-540 (or Hodgdon's HS-6) is deadly on targets or game.

Okay, so 13/16-ounce of shot isn't a "light" load, but it shoots so well, I had to pass it along. I'd like to take credit for it, but the truth is I gleefully pilfered it out of the Hodgdon Manual. With 7 1/2s or even 6s at 1223 fps, it will dust a rooster.

The .410-Bore. Okay, I know what you're thinking: How can you load a .410 "down?" It's easy. Remember those ptarmigan at 10 feet? Here 1/2-ounce of shot is more than adequate, but with small shot, you tend to pulverize a lot of succulent bird bites. The solution? Load larger shot.

I simply use my bar adjusted for my standard .410 Skeet loads, but substitute #5 or 4 shot. The pellet count varies from about 60-75, but even a couple of these relatively large missiles will flatten a blue grouse or a ptarmigan. We used such loads with complete success for years. The velocity is a bit higher than I'd like, but this load has worked so well for so long, who cares?

So, if your favorite scattergun is languishing in the safe, pining to be set free, load up a couple of boxes of light loads, and head for the range or game fields. Your shoulder and pocketbook will be glad you did.

Alliant's New 20/28 Powder

Those clever fellows at Alliant Powder are always on the prowl for ways to improve the lot of shotgun reloaders, and they've scored a hit with their new 20/28 powder. As the name implies, it is designed for 20- and 28-gauge target and light field loads with 7/8- and 3/4-oz. shot charges, respectively. 20/28 is a flake powder that looks like Bullseye, and has (for shotgun loads) a "medium-burning" rate. It is very clean burning, and has provided uniform velocities in my tests. (I can't wait to try it in the 16-gauge.) Representative loads for popular cases and wads at the standard target-load velocity of 1200 fps are shown below, courtesy of Alliant Powder. More load data for 20/28 are available from Alliant at www.alliantpowder.com.

Alliant 20/28 Powder 28 Gauge Load Data, ¾-Oz. Shot

CASE	PRIMER	WAD	CHARGE (GR.)	VELOCITY (FPS)
Federal	Fed. 209A	28S1	12.5	1200
Federal	Fed. 209A	CB-5034-8HS	13.0	1200
Rem. STS	Rem. 209P	PT-28	12.8	1200
Rem. STS	Rem. 209P	DW-2834	12.4	1200
Win. AA-HS	Win. 209	PT-28	13.2	1200
Win. AA-HS	Win. 209	WAA-28HS	13.0	1200

Alliant 20/28 Powder 20 Gauge Load Data, 7/8-Oz. Shot

CASE	PRIMER	WAD	CHARGE (GR.)	VELOCITY (FPS)
Federal	Fed. 209A	20S1	16.5	1200
Federal	Fed. 209A	Windjammer	16.5	1200
Rem. STS	Rem. 209P	RXP-20	15.5	1200
Rem. STS	Rem. 209P	Clay Duster	15.5	1200
Win. AA-HS	Win. 209	WAA-20	15.5	1200
Win. AA-HS	Win. 209	Versalite	16.0	1200

Load Table 1

12-GAUGE:

Test Gun: Browning Citori Sporting Clays, 28-in. barrel, skeet choke

CASE	PRIMER	POWDER	CHARGE (GR.)	PLASTIC WAD	20-GA. CARD WAD(S) UNDER SHOT*	SHOT CHARGE (OZ.)	SHOT SIZE	AVE. VELOCITY (FPS)	SD (FPS)	CV (%)	COMMENTS
Win. AA	Win. 209	SR-7625	20.0	WAA-12SL	2, .125"	1/2	9	1107	15	1.36	excellent light load
Win. AA	Win. 209	SR-7625	19.7	WAA-12L	2, .125"	3/4	8	1154	12	1.04	good early skeet load
Win. AA	Win. 209	Titewad	17.0	WAA-12L		3/4	8	1229	18	1.46	
R-P Black	Win. 209	Am. Select	17.5	WAA-12L	1, .135"	3/4	9	1226	16	1.31	perfect fit
Fed. GM	Fed. 209A	700-X	16	Fed 12S0	1, .135"	24 g	8	1149	20	1.74	3% lighter than 7/8-oz.
Fed. GM	Fed. 209A	PB	20	WAA-12SL		24 g	8	1152	19	1.65	good load, great crimp
Win. AA	Win. 209	CLAYS	18.3	WAA-12SL		7/8	8	1247	19	1.52	
Rem. STS	Rem. 209P	Red Dot	16.5	WAA-12SL		7/8	9	1197	21	1.75	terrific skeet load
R-P Black	Win. 209	CLAYS	15.5	CB-1100		1	7 1/2	1084	13	1.20	nice, light load
R-P Black	Win. 209	CLAYS	15.5	WAA-12		1	7 1/2	1124	17	1.51	
Rem. RXP	Win. 209	CLAYS	15.5	RXP-12		1	7 1/2	1154	16	1.39	
Win. AA	Win. 209	Red Dot	16.5	WAA-12SL		1	8	1151	23	2.00	classic skeet load

* vary under shot wads as necessary for good crimp
abbreviation: GM, Gold Medal; CB, Clay Buster

Load Table 2

16-GAUGE:

Test Gun: Remington Model 870, 28-in. barrel, modified choke

CASE	PRIMER	POWDER	CHARGE (GR.)	16-GA. .135-INCH CARD WAD(S) OVER POWDER*	PLASTIC WAD COLUMN	28-GA. .070-INCH CARD WADS UNDER SHOT*	SHOT CHARGE (OZ.)	SHOT SIZE	AVE. VELOCITY (FPS)	SD (FPS)	CV (%)	COMMENTS
Federal	Win. 209	Unique	17.8	1	Rem. SP-16	1	3/4	8	1180	12.2	1.03	
Federal	Win. 209	Unique	18.3	1	Rem. SP-16	1	3/4	8	1207	14.4	1.19	
Federal	Win. 209	Nitro 100	16.0	1	Rem. SP-16	1	3/4	8	1200	11.5	0.96	very uniform
Federal	Win. 209	Int. Clays	18.0	1	Rem. SP-16	2	3/4	8	1214	14.1	1.16	good fit
Federal	Win. 209	PB	18.0	1	TC-16		3/4	8	1122	15.0	1.34	
Cheddite	Win. 209	PB	18.7	1	TC-16		3/4	8	1156	20.1	1.74	
Federal	Win. 209	Unique	18.0	1	SP-16	1	7/8	8	1198	16.0	1.34	excellent load
Federal	Win. 209	Nitro 100	16.0	1	SP-16	1	7/8	8	1164	15.1	1.30	
Federal	Win. 209	Nitro 100	16.5	1	SP-16	1	7/8	8	1236	17.5	1.42	
Cheddite	Win. 209	PB	18.0	1	TC-16		7/8	8	1154	21.1	1.83	good target load
Cheddite	Win. 209	PB	19.0	1	TC-16		7/8	8	1183	26.0	2.20	
Cheddite	Win. 209	WSF	19.0	1	SP-16	1	7/8	8	1044	19.0	1.82	light recoil, perfect fit
Federal	Win. 209	PB	18.7	1/2**	TC-16		7/8	8	1168	14.1	1.21	
Federal	Win. 209	WSF	19.0	1	SP-16	1	7/8	8	1135	22.2	1.96	good fit
Federal	Win. 209	Universal	19.0	1	SP-16	1	7/8	8	1027	26.7	2.60	very uniform
Cheddite	Win. 209	Unique	19.5		SP-16	1	1	8	1198	5.6	0.47	
Federal	Win. 209	Universal	20.0		SP-16		1	8	1160	25.9	2.23	perfect fit
Federal	Fio. 616	HS-7	26.0		SP-16		1	8	1023	18.0	1.76	very light recoil
Federal	Win. 209	Herco	21.0		SP-16		1	7 1/2	1212	29.4	2.43	
Federal	Win. 209	Unique	19.0		SP-16		1	8	1141	11.5	1.01	
Federal	Win. 209	Unique	20.0		SP-16		1	8	1221	14.0	1.15	
Federal	Win. 209	PB	18.0		SP-16		1	8	1113	16.0	1.44	
Federal	Win. 209	PB	19.0		SP-16		1	8	1199	15.0	1.25	

R-P	Win. 209	Unique	19.0		SP-16		1 1/8	7	1128	15.9	1.41	factory load duplication
Federal	Fio. 616	HS-7	26.5		SP-16		1 1/8	8	1031	19.8	1.92	mild recoil, good patterns

FACTORY LOADS:

Winchester No. XU168 (2-1/2, 1, 8)							1	8	1137	9.7	0.85	
Federal No. F162 (2-3/4, 1-1/8, 6)							1 1/8	6	1091	23.9	2.19	
Federal No. HF16 7.5 (2-3/4, 1-1/8, 7 1/2)							1 1/8	7 1/2	1119	56.9	5.08	
Remington No. SP16 (3-1/4, 1-1/8, 4)							1 1/8	4	1207	47.8	3.96	

R-P, Remington-Peters; TC, Trap Commander

* vary over powder or under shot wads as necessary for good crimp
** split wad in half for use

Load Table 3
20 GAUGE:

Test Gun: Winchester Model 101, 28-in. barrel, skeet choke

CASE	PRIMER	POWDER	CHARGE (GR.)	PLASTIC WAD COLUMN	.125 INCH 28-GA. CARD CARD WADS UNDER SHOT*	SHOT CHARGE (OZ.)	SHOT SIZE	AVE. VELOCITY (FPS)	S SD	CV (%)	COMMENTS
Win. Univ.	Win. 209	SR-7625	14.5	WAA-20	2	1/2	9	1057	4.3	0.41	very uniform
Win. Univ.	Win. 209	SR-7625	16.5	WAA-20	2	1/2	9	1150	14.1	1.23	
Federal	Win. 209	SR-7625	16.8	WAA-20	1	5/8	9	1068	11.5	1.08	µice, light load
Win. Univ.	Win. 209	Int. Clays	12.7	WAA-20	1	5/8	9	1098	12.8	1.17	
Win. Univ.	Win. 209	SR-7625	15.2	WAA-20	1	5/8	9	1031	28.9	2.80	great grouse load
Win. Univ.	Win. 209	Universal	16.6	WAA-20	1	5/8	9	1108	34.7	3.13	
Win. Univ.	Win. 210	20/28	15.0	WAA-21	1	5/8	8	1185	20.0	1.69	
Win. AA	Win. 209	Int. Clays	12.7	RXP20	2	3/4	8	1091	22.8	2.09	
Win. Univ.	Win. 209	Int. Clays	13.5	WAA-20	1	3/4	8	1149	10.0	0.87	
Win. Univ.	Win. 209	Universal	16.0	WAA-20	1	3/4	9	1152	18.9	1.64	6-point crimp
Win. Univ.	Win. 210	20/28	13.0	WAA-20	1	3/4	8	1057	7.0	0.66	light, uniform
Win. Univ.	Win. 211	20/28	15.0	WAA-20	1	3/4	8	1169	16.0	1.37	good quail load
Federal	Win. 209	Universal	17.0	RXP20		7/8	7 1/2	1067	36.9	3.46	good dove load

FACTORY LOADS:

Fiocchi No. 20LITE75 Trainer						3/4	7 1/2	1039	3.8		good light loads,
Fiocchi No. 20VPI8						7/8	8	1152	5.4		both very uniform

* vary under shot wads as necessary for a good crimp

Load Table 4
28 GAUGE:

Test Gun: Winchester Model 101, 28-in. barrel, skeet choke

CASE	PRIMER	POWDER	CHARGE (GR.)	PLASTIC WAD COLUMN	.125 INCH .410-BORE CARD WADS UNDER SHOT*	SHOT CHARGE (OZ.)	SHOT SIZE	AVE. VELOCITY (FPS)	SD (FPS)	CV (%)	COMMENTS
Federal	Win. 209	20/28	12.5	WAA-28	1	5/8	8	1171	14	1.20	great load
Federal	Win. 209	20/28	13.0	WAA-28	1	5/8	8	1227	3	0.24	perfect fit
Noble Spt.	Win. 209	800-X	14.0	WAA-28HS		3/4	8	1153	12.1	1.05	good fit
Noble Spt.	Win. 209	Blue Dot	18.0	WAA-28HS		3/4	8	1205	34.9	2.90	fast, good fit
Rem. STS	Win. 209	Universal	13.5	Rem. PP		3/4	8	1194	21.5	1.80	
Rem. STS	Win. 209	Win. 540	17.0	Rem. PP		3/4	8	1188	20.1	1.69	perfect fit
Rem. STS	Win. 209	Win. 571	19.0	Rem. PP		3/4	8	1227	15.3	1.25	
Rem. STS	Win. 209	800-X	13.1	WAA-28		3/4	8	1149	8.3	0.72	great load
Rem. STS	Win. 209	Universal	14.1	WAA-28		3/4	8	1222	9.5	0.78	a bit fast

Load Table 4, continued

Test Gun: CZ-USA Ringneck, 26-in. barrel, cylinder choke tube

Case	Primer	Powder	Charge	Wad	*	Shot	Size	Vel	SD	CV	Comments
Federal	Win. 209	Unique	14.0	WAA-28		5/8	5	1224	19.4	1.58	grouse load
Federal	Win. 209	SR-7625	13.8	WAA-28	1	5/8	8	1187	8.0	0.67	
Federal	Win. 209	SR-7625	14.0	CB-28		3/4	8	1174	20.8	1.77	
Federal	Win. 209	Unique	13.0	WAA-28		3/4	8	1169	2.1	0.18	super load
Federal	Win. 209	Universal	14.5	WAA-28		3/4	8	1152	16.2	1.41	
Federal	Win. 209	Win. 540	17.5	WAA-28		3/4	9	1172	11.4	0.97	good dove load
Rem. STS	Win. 209	Win. 540	17.0	WAA-28		3/4	9	1178	6.9	0.59	perfect fit
Win. AA	Win. 209	Win. 540	16.4	CB-28		3/4	9	1185	10.6	0.89	good crimp
Federal	Win. 209	Longshot	15.5	CB-28		13/16	7 1/2	1223	5.0	0.41	terrific field load

* vary under shot wads as necessary for good crimp
abbreviations: PP, Power Piston; CB, Clay Buster;

Load Table 5

.410-BORE, 2 1/2-INCH

Test Gun: Winchester Model 101, 28-in. barrel, skeet choke

CASE	PRIMER	POWDER	CHARGE (GR.)	PLASTIC WAD COLUMN	SHOT CHARGE (OZ.)	SHOT SIZE	AVE. VELOCITY (FPS)	SD (FPS)	CV (%)	COMMENTS
Win. AA	Win. 209	W-296	13.7	WAA-410	0.43	5	1251	28.0	2.24	great ptarmigan
Federal	Win. 209	2400	14.5	PP	0.44	6	1262	25.1	1.99	and blue grouse loads

abbreviation: PP, Power Piston

Table 6. Shot Weight Conversion

OUNCES	DECIMAL FRACTION	GRAINS	GRAMS
1/2	0.50	218.8	14.2
5/8	0.63	273.4	17.7
3/4	0.75	328.1	21.3
13/16	0.81	355.5	23.0
-	0.85	370.4	24.0
7/8	0.88	382.8	24.8
1	1.00	437.5	28.4

Table 7. Powders Used In Specialty Light Loads

(In order of approximate burning rate—fastest at top of list)

POWDER	12 GAUGE	16 GAUGE	20 GAUGE	28 GAUGE	.410-BORE
Nitro 100		X			
Red Dot	X				
CLAYS	X				
Titewad	X				
American Select	X				
700-X	X				
International Clays		X	X		
PB	X	X			
Universal Clays		X	X	X	
20/28			X	X	
Unique		X		X	
SR-7625	X		X	X	
WSF		X			
W-540				X	
Herco		X			
Longshot				X	
800-X				X	
HS-7		X			
W-571				X	
Blue Dot				X	
2400					X
W-296					X

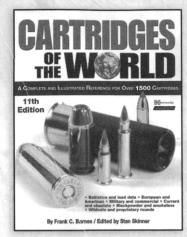
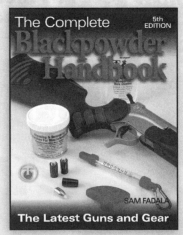
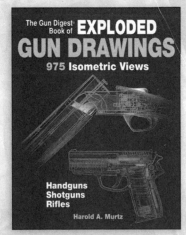

Charlotte Zolotow

The WHITE MARBLE

ILLUSTRATED BY

Deborah Kogan Ray

THOMAS Y. CROWELL   NEW YORK

Library of Congress Cataloging in Publication Data

Zolotow, Charlotte, 1915–
The white marble.
Originally published: London; New York:
Abelard-Schuman, 1963.
Summary: Two children find beauty and wonder
in the park on a hot night.
[1. Night–Fiction] I. Ray, Deborah. II. Title.
PZ7.Z77Wh 1981   [E]   81-43131
ISBN 0-690-04152-7   AACR2   ISBN 0-690-04151-9 (lib. bdg.)

1   2   3   4   5   6   7   8   9   10
FIRST EDITION

To Augusta and William Prince
−Charlotte

For my daughters, Karen and Nicole, with love
−D.K.R.

Oh, it was a hot night. The heat sat like a feathered bird over the city as the sun went down. It folded its wings, and the pink and orange plumage of the sunset was covered by the fleecy gray and purple sky.

Not a breath stirred. John Henry's thin white bedroom curtain hung lifeless, dropped in limp folds down the side of his window. It had hung so in the sunlight all afternoon. Even John Henry had found it too hot to do anything but sleep.

Now that supper was finished, and the heat still hovering over everything, his mother and father decided they would all go out to the park.

He was wide awake. His mother looked tired. His father looked tired. But the hot city night seemed beautiful to John Henry as he skipped along between them.

There wasn't a star in the darkening sky.

A pink zigzag of lightning cut across the park ahead of them.

"Perhaps it will rain," said John Henry's father.

"I'm afraid that's the heat," his mother said.

Their voices seemed far away to John Henry.

They crossed the street and as they reached the dusky park, John Henry stopped. He stooped down to pick up something in the grass. He stared at it for a minute with clear brown eyes and then slipped it quickly into his pocket.

"What'd you find, John?" his father asked.

"Nothing," said John Henry.

When they found a bench John Henry sat between his mother and father.

Two old men had a checkerboard open between them on a bench in the lamplight. The smoke from their pipes coiled slowly upward, cloudy and blue, and the scent of tobacco mingled with the nighttime smell of park grass. The branches of the trees, close to the lamplight, seemed to be rustling with golden leaves.

John Henry was the only child in the park.

He listened to the hot nighttime hum of grown-up voices. Even sitting here, between his mother and father, John Henry felt alone.

He knew it was special to be allowed out now and he sat like them, pretending to be grown-up like them, but all the time his eyes searched in the distance where the golden light of the lamps shone down on the park paths.

Then, far down the path, there came something white. He leaned forward–it was true–a white dress gleamed in the darkness and moved toward them slowly like a white moth until just across from their own bench, a mother and little girl sat down.

It was Pamela from school. He watched her spread out her dress on either side like white wings, just as she did at school when Miss Dawson had them bring their chairs around for story time. But tonight Pamela was different.

As he watched her, his hand stole up to his pocket and he smiled.

She saw him and smiled too, and to him it was as though she had said, "I understand. They are grown-up, but we *know,* we see, what tonight is really like."

Suddenly he stood up.

"Let's run," he called, and without waiting to see if she was following, he cut over behind the benches, across the darkening park. He could hear the soft echo of her footsteps skimming over the grass behind him.

They kicked off their shoes and were off, bare legs flashing. Like two wild things, intoxicated with the soft, cool smell of rain about to come, they ran together. Never, never had the air smelled so fresh and sweet; never, never had the night seemed so lovely.

It belonged to them. Even when they flung
themselves down panting on the soft grass, with the
heavy purple sky folding into night above them, and
the unceasing grown-up murmur of laughter and

voices around them, they were alone.

They lay there kicking their legs up and down
behind them, saying nothing.

Suddenly John Henry touched her hand.

"Look," he said, and pulled a small white marble out of his pocket.

She reached out to touch it but he closed his fingers around it quickly.

"It's beautiful!" she said.

No grown-up would have known.

They lay there, again kicking their legs up and down behind them in silence while the little rain wind ruffled their hair.

"Are you thirsty?" she asked.

They picked up their shoes and started off to the water fountain. They passed a clump of lilac bushes, immense in the gathering darkness. Pamela put her hand on John Henry's arm until they turned the corner, to where the water fountain sprinkled up white and foamy in the night.

They bent their heads together, and they could feel each other's hair against their cheeks as the water bubbled up cold and sweet straight into their faces, wetting their skin, running down their necks, so that with the iciness of it they began to laugh.

"John Henry..." called his father.
"Pamela..." called her mother.
But neither of them heard.

"JOHN HENRY..."

"PAMELA..."

The grown-up voices trailed off, swept up in the rustling of the cool storm wind that started the whole park moving and sighing with the flutter of hot, dusty lamplit leaves.

"JOHN HENRY," his father called, "ice sticks..."

Without wiping the water from their faces, they ran back to the bench where their parents were waiting.

Sure enough, there, with the tinkling of little bells and merry lights gleaming like a miniature carnival, was the ice-cream man's cart transformed from the everyday yellow wagon they knew. They sat side by side, their legs swinging as they ate the icy pineapple sticks.

Across from them now, John Henry's father stretched his arm along the bench and his mother rested her head against it while they talked to Pamela's mother.

"Time to go..." the grown-ups finally said.

Pamela slipped off the bench and took her mother's hand. They started down the lamplit path. Streak! streak! streak! went the lightning now.

Suddenly Pamela broke loose and ran back.

"John Henry," she called.

He turned.

Her eyes were green and gold as she looked at him.

"Good-night," she said.

A streak of starlight jetted across the dark sky.

John Henry stared at her. He put his hand in his pocket and pulled out the white marble. For a moment it lay there on his palm like a small white moon gleaming in the half darkness. Then he pressed it into Pamela's hand.

"Keep it," he said.

From far away came the rumble of summer
thunder and there was already the patter of raindrops
in the dusty leaves of the city trees.